ANTI-B

A Cultural Critique Book

Cesare Casarino, John Mowitt,
and Simona Sawhney, Editors

ANTI-BOOK

ON THE ART AND POLITICS OF RADICAL PUBLISHING

Nicholas Thoburn

A Cultural Critique Book

UNIVERSITY OF MINNESOTA PRESS
Minneapolis · London

Portions of chapter 2 were published as "Communist Objects and the Values of Printed Matter," *Social Text* 28, no. 2 (2010): 1–31; copyright 2010 Duke University Press; all rights reserved; reprinted by permission of the publisher, Duke University Press, http://www.dukeupress.edu. Portions of chapter 3 were published as "The Strangest Cult: Material Forms of the Political Book through Deleuze and Guattari," *Deleuze Studies* 7, no. 1 (2013): 53–82. Portions of chapter 5 were published as "Ceci n'est pas un magazine: The Politics of Hybrid Media in *Mute* Magazine," *New Media and Society* 14, no. 5 (2012): 815–31. Portions of chapter 6 were published as "To Conquer the Anonymous: Authorship and Myth in the Wu Ming Foundation," *Cultural Critique* 78 (2011): 119–50.

Published by the University of Minnesota Press
111 Third Avenue South, Suite 290
Minneapolis, MN 55401-2520
http://www.upress.umn.edu

Printed in the United States of America on acid-free paper

The University of Minnesota is an equal-opportunity educator and employer.

22 21 20 19 18 17 16   10 9 8 7 6 5 4 3 2 1

Library of Congress Cataloging-in-Publication Data
Names: Thoburn, Nicholas, author.
Title: Anti-book : on the art and politics of radical publishing / Nicholas Thoburn.
Description: Minneapolis : University of Minnesota Press [2016] |
Series: A cultural critique book | Includes bibliographical references and index.
Identifiers: LCCN 2016003058 (print) | ISBN 978-0-8166-9999-5 (hc) |
ISBN 978-0-8166-2196-5 (pb)
Subjects: LCSH: Publishers and publishing—Political aspects. | Electronic publishing—Political aspects. | Self-publishing—Political aspects. | Authorship—Political aspects. | Pamphlets—Publishing. | Communist literature—Publishing. | Periodicals—Publishing. | Politics and literature. | Digital media. | Alternative mass media. | BISAC: LITERARY CRITICISM / Books & Reading. | LITERARY CRITICISM / Semiotics & Theory. | SOCIAL SCIENCE / Media Studies.
Classification: LCC Z278 .T48 2016 (print) | DDC 070.5—dc23
LC record available at https://lccn.loc.gov/2016003058

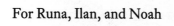

For Runa, Ilan, and Noah

Contents

Preface ix

Acknowledgments xv

1. One Manifesto Less: Material Text and the Anti-Book 1

2. Communist Objects and Small Press Pamphlets 61

3. Root, Fascicle, Rhizome: Forms and Passions of the Political Book 109

4. What Matter Who's Speaking? The Politics of Anonymous Authorship 168

5. Proud to Be Flesh: Diagrammatic Publishing in *Mute* Magazine 224

6. Unidentified Narrative Objects: Wu Ming's Political Mythopoesis 272

Notes 301

Index 361

Preface

Books about books commonly introduce their content by reference to the object that readers hold in their hands, be it comprising bound printed paper or networked code and touchscreen interface. This is a useful conceit, for it brings textual content and media form into a momentary resonance, soliciting an embodied and reflexive appreciation of that which tends otherwise to be lost to the immersive flow of a book's words. I would not break with this practice, because interference between textual content and media form is the stuff of *Anti-Book*. But I will unsettle it a little, for such introductions can be too comforting, nestling the object in its reader's hands and habits when our time calls for a more troubling materiality.

Let me start with the title. A book's title serves a dual function. It introduces readers to the text's theme, prefatory reference to which would normally assist in carrying readers into the book's flow of text, but it also helps place the book in a market, an observation that orients attention to more medial and structural features. As Franco Moretti writes of literary titles, "Half sign, half ad, the title is where the novel as language meets the novel as commodity."[1] The title of *Anti-Book* is no different, its brevity further serving the commodity function of market visibility even as the book seeks to contribute to the undoing of the commodity form of books. There is communist intent to *Anti-Book,* then, but it is a communism that would draw attention to such contradictions and not make as though its intent can lift it from the world of capital.

Moving to the book's wider commodity features, there are numerous ways to possess a book but, file-share scans notwithstanding, I venture that many of you will have purchased the commodity you hold in your hands from Amazon, a retailer and technology company whose profit margins from the sale of print and digital books, among other things, are dependent on pioneering industrial techniques in such arenas as logistics, digital rights management, consumer profiling, and the electronic surveillance and intensification of labor. Such economics of distribution and marketing in which *Anti-Book* is a participant by no means exhaust its implication in capitalist social relations. These include the book's structure of authorship, which binds it to bourgeois models of individual creativity and proprietary rights, and the class, gendered, and racialized dimensions of the partition between work and leisure, the latter providing some readers with an environment of more or less leisurely consumption wherein the medium of the book finds its natural home, while leaving others a fit between book and daily life that is rather less clean. Yet we tend not to think of the capitalist form of books. We imagine books to be transcendent intellectual, moral, and aesthetic goods unsullied by commerce, just as we perceive our own individual encounters with these quintessential objects of culture to confirm and augment only our intellect, taste, or political commitments, the textual object greeting and flattering its reading subject as if the two meet outside social determination.

This terrain of the commodity book was the substance of *Amazon Noir*, a collaborative artwork centered on the unauthorized appropriation from Amazon, and peer-to-peer distribution, of some three thousand e-books.[2] Amazon entices its customers' attention through the marketing tool "Search Inside This Book," which enables word search through whole books while preventing access to their whole. Exploiting this function, *Amazon Noir* comprised a software script that would obtain a book's entire text via repeated searches, substituting the last words of one search for the first words of the next. Each complete book was automatically saved as a PDF and introduced into file-sharing networks, and, for the exhibition of the artwork, one of the "stolen" books—Abbie Hoffman's *Steal This Book*, naturally—was printed, bound, and displayed in an incubator. *Amazon Noir* served to articulate the inequity of the privatization of the nonscarce resource of digital text, while taking advantage of the means by which the technological affordances of digital text are mobilized to excite consumer desire. It was an art project, but it was also an intervention into the field of publishing, in which context it prompts the guiding question or problem of *Anti-Book*. What is a communism of writing and publishing that is concerned not only with the *content and meaning* of text but also with the *media forms and social relations* by which text is produced, circulated, and consumed? More simply, what is a communism of textual matter?

It is a problem encountered in radical politics only rarely, which, in line with the general trend, more usually pursues writing and publishing for ideational effects alone, for the enlightening and organizing impact of ideas. That said, the problem is not new. The focus of this book is on publishing experiments in the twentieth and twenty-first centuries, but we can take an earlier example, William Blake's self-published "illuminated books" of the 1790s, works that move us from the practical critique of copyright into the broader materiality of the book commodity and that assist in indicating that in the field of the anti-book, communism finds a certain medial instantiation.

In these prefatory sketches of Blake and *Amazon Noir,* I am seeking to convey an impression of the communism of textual matter, before this problematic is developed through specific concrete platforms, publishing paradigms, literary forms, and concepts in the chapters that follow. As poet, painter, and printer, impressions were Blake's stock in trade. In his illuminated books, play between image and text, complex systems of allegory, textual ambiguity, and the confrontation of opposites were intricately woven components of the struggle to attain "the infinite." Here the "horizon of our being," in Saree Makdisi's presentation of Blake's politics, "is not a narrow formal selfhood, a self as opposed to others, but rather our participation in the common body of God," a life of the infinite body and "infinite brain," as Blake puts it.[3] This infinite was posited against the sovereign individual of the bourgeois polity and the constrained everyday conditions of labor and oppression, but, and this is what is so enticing for my purposes, it was practiced immanently to the medium within which it was articulated. In other words, Blake's infinite was (along with much else) a *struggle in and against the book,* against its dominant effects of self-referential authority, textual devotion and submission, and dualism of mind and body. The illuminated books are at once the medium through which Blake's textual and visual images flourish and are *themselves* articulations of these images.

In *The Marriage of Heaven and Hell,* Blake describes a vision of an infernal printing house, and in so doing reveals his singular method of "illuminated printing." Using relief etching, he interlaced image and text on the same copper plates in etchings that no longer reproduced a prior original work but were integrated in the creative process. As Makdisi describes it, variation was now immanent to reproduction, in critical and practical opposition to the repetition of the same that characterized the Gutenberg book qua uniform and equivalent commodity. And Blake's vision simultaneously reveals the *sensory politics* of his printing technique, a production of the infinite against the "barr'd and petrify'd" reduction of perception in the finite sovereign subject:

> first the notion that man has a body distinct from his soul, is to be ex-punged; this I shall do, by printing in the infernal method, by corrosives, which in Hell are salutary and medicinal, melting apparent surfaces away, and displaying the infinite which was hid.
>
> If the doors of perception were cleansed every thing would appear to man as it is, infinite—
>
> For man has closed himself up, till he sees all things thro' narrow chinks in his cavern.[4]

The textual dimensions of Blake's anticapitalist condition of the infinite were to take shape, then, not only in words and images but also in their method of printing and their published form. It is a singular achievement in content and form, in their interplay, indubitably so. And yet this success may blind us to the nature of the relation. Neither in *Amazon Noir* and Blake nor in the writing and publishing projects that fill the pages of *Anti-Book* do textual content and media form achieve integrated identity. In what served as a germinal seed for this book, Gilles Deleuze and Félix Guattari provide a compelling slogan for the politics of textual matter: "There is no difference between what a book talks about and how it is made."[5] And yet as much as this sentence tips us into a politics of textual matter, it also confounds, for there are in fact *many* differences between textual content and the social processes and media forms by which a textual work comes into being, as Deleuze and Guattari well knew. Such are the differences that Leah Price has argued persuasively that we might best grasp the nature of relations between content and form, and the specifici-ties of each, by attending less to moments of apparent convergence and more to their *disjunctions,* moments when they "pull apart, when (for example) an anticolonial manifesto is printed on paper imported from the metropole, or when an oath of revenge is sworn upon the same bible whose text preaches forgiveness."[6] To do otherwise is to risk losing the specific qualities and effects of media form to a relation of identity with signifying content, as media form becomes merely content's confirmation, or, when conjunction does not occur, as is more common, an irrelevance.

Hence, if we *do* want to bring content and form together in a textual politics that is a weave of the two, as is the aim of the experimental works explored in *Anti-Book,* such a politics needs to be attentive to two aspects of this relation. First, it must reflexively attend to aspects of a work's material conditions that it is *not* able to critically refashion, where content comes into relation with media form as *critical opposition.* Second, in instances when content and form come into a generative and political relation of codetermination, we should attend to the *specificities* of a text's media forms, the ways that its conceptual registers and political aims are extended, interrogated, swallowed up, or exceeded in the specific sociomaterial relations and forms by which it is manifest in the world. From such critical and generative interplay arise the many materialities of political text. In their midst, the field of writing and publishing, which has been so central to the *transmission* of communist thought, can become also a vibrant arena of its *materialization*—a fleeting and fragmentary "literary communism."[7]

Acknowledgments

To thank the many people who contributed to this book is a true pleasure. I especially want to thank those who generously gave their time to talk to me about their publishing projects: Josephine Berry, Chris, Jakob Jakobsen, Pauline van Mourik Broekman, Fabian Tompsett, and Simon Worthington. Some of these meetings developed into conversations and friendships that accompanied the progress of the book, for me one of the joys of writing. Much of *Anti-Book* was first aired in seminars and conference talks, and I would like to thank the organizers of these, in particular Pablo Lafuente for Publications on Art: Cultural, Social, and Political Uses in Seville; Tim Stott and Aislinn O'Donnell for a talk at the Graduate School of Creative Arts and Media in Dublin; Audrone Zukauskaite and Kasparas Pocius for two conferences in Vilnius; Juan Pablo Macías for a convivial few days in late summer at the Histories of Publishing seminar at Villa Romana, Florence; and Branka Ćurčić, Zoran Gajić, Zoran Pantelić, Savo Romčević, and Borka Stojić of Kuda.org for hosting a most enjoyable time discussing the anti-book and other matters in Novi Sad, Belgrade, and Zagreb.

Stephen Zepke generously lent his critical eye to the material in this book at different stages of its formation; for this and his friendship I am most grateful. Many of the ideas in *Anti-Book* were formed during my time affiliated to the Centre for Research on Socio-Cultural Change (CRESC) at the University of Manchester and the Open University, where I benefited greatly from discussions across the disciplines, especially with Eleanor Casella, Jeanette Edwards, Gillian Evans, Penny Harvey, Hannah Knox, Chris McLean, Damian O'Doherty, Madeleine Reeves, and Kath Woodward. CRESC also provided me with two periods of much-needed research leave. Friends and colleagues in Manchester, London, and elsewhere contributed in different ways to the writing of this book: Koyes Ahmed,

Jeremy Anderson, Selina Asombang, Wendy Bottero, Bridget Byrne, John Cunningham, Mehdi El Hajoui, Leah Hargreaves, Brian Heaphy, Graeme Kirkpatrick, Saree Makdisi, Sas Mays, Martha Michailidou, Khalid Nadvi, Sara and Sami Nadvi-Byrne, Simon O'Sullivan, Bev Skeggs, and Sivamohan Valluvan. My parents, June and John, and my brother Alan have been, as ever, a great source of love and support.

It was in conversation with my good friend Cesare Casarino that my anti-book ideas were first nudged toward book form, and Cesare, John Mowitt, and Simona Sawhney have been a pleasure to work with in bringing it to publication in the Cultural Critique series. I am most grateful to Doug Armato at the University of Minnesota Press for commissioning the book and guiding it to completion and to Erin Warholm-Wohlenhaus for all her help in the production stages. Many thanks to Holly Monteith for her fine copyediting. The manuscript benefited much from two anonymous readers, not that they or anyone else acknowledged here are responsible for the book's errors.

Runa Khalique has shared the joys and trials of writing this book from its earliest days, feeling out fledgling ideas, raising an eyebrow at strange tales of communist publishing—and at my obsessions with them—and leading us on many adventures outside the world of books. During the writing of this book, Runa and I became parents to beautiful twin boys, Ilan and Noah. They have made their father proud and happy beyond words. It is to Runa and our boys that I dedicate the book, with much love.

1

One Manifesto Less

MATERIAL TEXT AND THE ANTI-BOOK

> One can speak out only through the mouth, but the book's
> facilities for expression take many more forms.
> —EL LISSITZKY, "Our Book"

> The impossibility of thinking of an aesthetic medium as nothing
> more than an unworked physical support.
> —ROSALIND KRAUSS, *"A Voyage on the North Sea"*

The communism of writing and publishing that is developed in these pages
is against the book, it is "anti-book," but not, as you might imagine, as
some kind of manifesto tilted at a media form on the wane and packaged
with the hubris of the technological "new." For neither manifestos nor
technological functionalities are the most promising means to a communism of textual media. *Anti-Book,* rather, is a critique of the book that is
immanent to its medium or to the forms of textual media more broadly
conceived. Allow me to explain a little by presenting a first approximation
of the concept that orients this book in its encounters with experimental
political publishing.

　　An anti-book is a work of writing and publishing that critically interrogates its media form. That is to say, it is a self-reflexive textual work.
But reflexivity here is not confined to the domain of text and literary form.
Anti-books test, problematize, and push to the limits their *full materiality,*
or significant aspects thereof, where the materiality of a book comprises
the dynamic interplay of textual content and media form, a critical and
generative relation operative at scales both concrete and abstract. This
materiality includes physical properties and technological affordances, certainly, but also signifying strategies, graphical arrangements, and sensory

1

qualities, all of which are interlaced with publishing paradigms, linguistic structures, and economies and practices of production and consumption. And such materiality is *political*. Anti-books articulate the encounter between communist thought and experimental practices of writing and publishing, where these encounters are not contained within social movements but emerge—albeit in a fragmentary and occasional fashion—across the terrain of textual media, a terrain where the commodity form plays a role no less commanding than it does for the audiovisual. In foregrounding the formal and sensory qualities of textual media, the anti-book is also an *aesthetic* figure; this is the "art" of political publishing, one that occasionally takes leave of the textual dimensions of textual media altogether. As to the sociohistorical context of the concept, the anti-book might be said to have troubled textual media since the invention of the Gutenberg letterpress and the generalization of print, but it comes to the fore and takes on particular qualities in the digital media environment, as anxiety about the "future of the book" and the proliferation of communication platforms impress on collective consciousness the material specificities of text.

This is a minimum definition of the anti-book. Yes, it is somewhat stripped down, but that quality is inherent to its purpose. For with these lineaments of the anti-book, I seek not to clarify and contain the many and various features of works that might be identified as such, to establish a definite class of anti-books, but to provide an abstraction, a conceptual map, that can concentrate attention on concrete experiments in political writing and publishing, in all their rich materiality and multiform variety. While the concept of the anti-book is a guide to such works, a focalizer, it is not, hence, an ideal type; indeed, the abstraction is itself necessarily open to destabilization and modification by the publishing experiments it surveys. The chapters that follow this introductory chapter all concentrate on such concrete experiments in political publishing and writing, each of which is interlaced with one or more concepts of its own: communist objects, the rhizome-book, anonymous authorship, diagrammatic publishing, unidentified narrative objects, to name some of these. In its focalizing work, the concept of the anti-book is at once immanent to these other concepts, emerging from them and drawing alliances between them, and swallowed up by them, as they do their own work without such assistance.

Whereas the other chapters in this book explore the features of the anti-book through particular empirical projects, this introduction seeks to place the concept in relation to three domains or problematics in writing and publishing, domains that pertain to the concept of the anti-book as sites of its emergence and intervention. The domains in question are art experiments with the form of textual media that go by the name of "bookworks" or "artists' books"; communist writing and publishing, especially with regard to the passing of the workers' movement and the commodity forms of text; and the "post-digital" mutations and publishing potentials of contemporary textual media. To different degrees of emphasis, each of these comprises theoretical orientations, points of aesthetic and political problematization, and concrete practices. All three have in their margins produced a formulation of the "anti-book," but it is in the interplay of these domains that the concept as I use it arises—not exactly at their intersection but at various and discontinuous points of proximity and interference between them. Before considering these domains, let me first introduce the broad orientation toward writing and publishing that extends throughout this book, the notion of "material text."

MATERIAL TEXT

The material forms and qualities of writing and publishing have long remained marginal to the academic study and popular understanding of text. There have certainly been significant and persistent exceptions, but Andrew Murphie grasps well the situation in his remark that "publishing as a process (as opposed to the contents published) has tended to be seen, only occasionally, out of the corner of one's eye."[1] When material forms of text *are* present to conscious articulation, more often than not they feature as clichéd artifacts that are coextensive with or insufficiently distinguished from the textual genres that they typically carry, as Lisa Gitelman notes: "Say the word 'novel,' for instance, and your auditors will likely imagine a printed book, even if novels also exist serialized in nineteenth-century periodicals, published in triple-decker (multivolume) formats, and loaded onto—and reimagined by the designers of—Kindles, Nooks, and iPads."[2] This situation is, however, undergoing considerable change, change associated in large measure with transformations in technology as the dominant form of media has shifted from one organized by the affordances of print and paper—albeit that these have been highly various, comprising multiple forms and technologies of reproduction other than the codex and letterpress—to those of digital and online media. It may have been the very ubiquity of print media that kept its material forms away from critical attention, as if this had the normative effect of making the *particular* conventions of print appear to be *universal* features of textual expression, and unremarkable as such. Consequently, as N. Katherine Hayles argues, as print ceases to be the default medium of publication, "the assumptions, presuppositions, and practices associated with it are now becoming visible as media-specific practices rather than the largely invisible status quo."[3]

Or, if we approach this question from the perspective of digital and networked media, it may be the particular properties of the latter that have brought new attention to textual matter. With the media forms and commercial platforms of e-mail, blogs, Facebook, Twitter, Reddit, Tumblr, and so forth, made continuous and fully mobile by the smart phone, writing and publishing have not only become interlaced with social practice in myriad and mutable ways but features of media form persistently push into the frame of content—we are not "writing," so much as tweeting, messaging, commenting—making a felt appreciation of media form increasingly common, even necessary, while radically unsettling the distinction between form and content. Think, for example, of how the structural function of the Twitter hashtag—"inline metadata" that aggregates and organizes the multiplicity of Tweets in the expression of trend patterns and "ambient affiliations"—is an immanent feature, and consciously so, of the text that participants construct and consume.[4] Bucking trends toward thinking the *immateriality* of digital text, Kenneth Goldsmith draws the plausible conclusion from such developments that "never before has language had so much *materiality*—fluidity, plasticity, malleability—begging to be actively managed by the writer."[5]

Whatever the causes, it is now more commonly recognized that an exclusive focus on semantic content is an inadequate means of grasping the full meanings and effects of text. For, as Michele Moylan and Lane Stiles describe it, texts are not "disembodied mental constructs transcending materiality, culture, and history," "there is no such thing . . . as a text unmediated by its materiality."[6] Concern with the materiality of text has a foundation in the discipline of book history and is now central to more recent developments in digital humanities and speculative computing.[7] These intellectual fields are too large and various to review here, but I will draw from them a few themes that situate my approach to material text.

If there is a shared ground to these different disciplines and perspectives, it is that any written work is a product of the interplay between textual *content* (the words, concepts, rhetorical structures, literary forms, etc., that are read in the work) and *medium* (the affordances, qualities, and constraints of its physical materialization and structure as artifact, technology, and social and institutional form). Both content and medium are of course highly various in themselves and interlaced in complex and mutable relations of codetermination, making the broad distinction useful only as a heuristic for approaching the particular features of any given work of textual matter. Any particular material text is a multiform entity, with many different and divergent meanings, effects, and scales of operation. As Hayles argues, it is thus "impossible to specify precisely what a book—or any other text—is as a physical object" (where "physical" here denotes the material features or media forms of the work, including "the social, cultural, and technological processes that brought it into being").[8] Her solution to the potentially confounding effect of this field of difference is to attend to the ways that *particular works themselves* interrogate and mobilize their material forms and relations, a category of works she names with the term "technotext." A technotext emerges "when a literary work interrogates the inscription technology that produces it."[9] Insofar as the materiality of a work is in this way "bound up with the text's content," it "cannot be specified in advance" but is, rather, an "emergent" condition.[10] A technotext, in other words, at once interrogates and produces its material form. At this point we need to bring in a third determining element to the text's emergent materiality alongside content and medium, that of the *reader,* her "interactions with the work and the interpretive strategies she develops—strategies that include physical manipulations as well as conceptual frameworks."[11] Indeed, it may be the reader that makes a technotext, because a text that does not reflexively address its material forms can be made to do so by the act of reading and interpretation. So, while Hayles's concept of technotext foregrounds works that critically reflect on their material forms, she notes that ultimately *any* text can be understood in these terms, given that all texts are mediated and actively consumed, whether they reflexively embody this or not.[12]

Such interplay between content, medium, and reader generates a complex and open material text, but it is not of course without determination. If a technotext is an interrogation of the specific logics and constraints of its material conditions—its particular forms of textual inscription but also its broader social, economic, and technological relations—it is also a *product* of these. Needless to say, these logics, constraints, and conditions are no less complex than any individual material text and so cannot be easily mapped in the abstract, but a considerable body of research has done much to explore their broad parameters. For instance, if we follow Roger Chartier, the organizing structures of the medium of "the book" and its associated discursive formations can be understood as a conjunction of three interlaced innovations: the *codex,* which replaced the scroll in the early Christian era, establishing the book as the basic unit of written work and as a textual object distinct from all others; the *unitary work,* which arises in the fourteenth and fifteenth centuries and integrates book, work, and author; and the arrival of the moveable type *printing press* in the mid-fifteenth century, which generalizes print and the book as the dominant technology for the mass reproduction of the written word.[13] These are not only technical forms but are integrated with forms of property (notably, the "author" as means by which unitary works are established as units of property) and patterns of reason (the linear or deductive form encouraged by the movement of textual inscription onto a page) as well as with the different forms, functions, and hierarchies of media object (book, newspaper, magazine, pamphlet, poster, letter, bureaucratic document, etc.) and functions of the written word (legal, aesthetic, political, etc.).

Thus are some of the determinations of the media form of the book, which order the production and consumption of writing in particular ways. But the productive role of the *reader* is no less subject to determination. While various in each instance, the meanings of books, and the subjects of reading, occur within patterns that are established by the discursive and institutional forms of literature (and other textual genres) and the marketing mechanisms of the publishing industry, as the study of most best sellers, for example, will readily reveal.[14]

These social, economic, and technical logics and conditions all affect the *meaning* of a text, but this is not their only arena of social impact; we should equally attend to the *nontextual* impact of textual materials and their institutional forms. As the product of particular logics and conditions, a media object is also their bearer, at once consolidating and extending the social relations associated with its production, circulation, and consumption. Pursuing this line of reasoning, significant research has associated the material texts of print media with particular features of modernity: the role of print in the formation of nationalism, for instance, or in the French Revolution.[15] The most influential instance of this is Elizabeth L. Eisenstein's argument that the printing press and "print culture" were agents of standardization, dissemination, and fixity that had considerable impact on the progress and intellectual structure of the Protestant Reformation, the Renaissance, and the Scientific Revolution.[16] In the course of her argument, Eisenstein provides an intriguing possible explanation for the historical lack of critical attention to the material forms of print that I noted earlier, for here the specific material qualities of print culture served as it were to *dematerialize* the medium of the book, as effects of stabilization meant that, as Daniel Selcer presents Eisenstein's thesis, "texts were no longer defined by the particularity of their material form":

> Rather, their ubiquity, their (in principle) infinite reproducibility, and the stabilization of the conventions governing their format and appearance allowed for what we might call their *dematerialization,* whereby particular books and other printed matter became mere exemplars of a now inviolate authorial content that reappeared as an identical page each time another object with the same title and printing-house genealogy was examined or a new print run undertaken.[17]

Eisenstein's influential thesis has not gone uncontested. In response, Adrian Johns in *The Nature of the Book* makes a compelling case that far from simplifying the material forms and relations of text, the complexities of production and circulation associated with the expansion of print may rather have "*destabilized* texts," to quote Selcer again, by "opening a myriad of new avenues through which readers may approach texts and by rendering more complex the chain of sovereign authorial production that connects authors to their texts and texts to their readers."[18] Johns does not refute that there are strong tendencies to fixity, though he invites us to consider how this was not an intrinsic property of the technical forms of print but an emergent, contingent, and unstable product of the manifold labors and representations of the individual and institutional actors involved in printing, publishing, and reading over time and space.[19] Techniques of accreditation took a central role, as the practices of particular individuals, institutions, and readers generated and conferred veracity on works that were in fact prone to piracy and careless printing. Eisenstein's error slips in because such practices were subject by internal pressures to make it *appear* as though stability had a technological source, the labor of print publishing being necessarily dedicated to "effacing its own traces," because only in this could print "gain the air of intrinsic reliability on which its cultural and commercial success could be built."[20] Johns's suggestion, then, is that Eisenstein, taking the myth of technological standardization as fact, succumbed to this effacement. And so, while nominally recovering the materiality of print, she did so in a manner that abstracted its technological form from its material labors, uses, and contexts, whereas a full materialism would proceed on the basis of their codetermination.

Concordant with this thesis, Johns invites renewed critical attention to *piracy* and the "dangers" presented to fixity, in so doing proffering a highly variegated picture of the field of early modern print, one less governed by the interpretive paradigm of norm and exception.[21] The immanence of piracy to the early publishing industry was such that anomalous forms and activities were less exceptions to fixity and uniformity than constant sources of disruption to, and spurs to the development of, the epistemic structures of knowledge, authorship, and accreditation and to the economic and publishing paradigms of the book trade. I ask you to keep Johns's thesis in mind in what follows. The aims and practices of piracy do not map onto those of the anti-book, but Johns's thesis is a significant inspiration for my argument insofar as it shows that if standardization and fixity are a feature of publishing—as I spend some time arguing—

publishing, both digital and print, is also characterized by much material complexity, anomaly, and disruption, qualities central to its politicization.

BOOKWORK

Holding to Johns's injunction to attend to the situated, complex, and multiform materiality of publishing, I will turn now to the first of the three domains with which the concept of the anti-book is in critical exchange, the *artists' book* or *bookwork* (terms I use interchangeably). The artists' book is a mode of aesthetic production that takes as its object the physical, formal, and institutional qualities of the textual medium of which it is constituted. As Johanna Drucker defines it in her seminal book on the many manifestations of this art form, an artists' book is an original work that "integrates the formal means of its realization and production with its thematic or aesthetic issues."[22] Its field is playfully presented diagrammatically by Clive Phillpot, who has tracked this aesthetic form (and its changing nomenclature) since its inception (Figure 1).[23] The share of the field with which we are concerned is here labeled "book art" and "book objects."

Before developing the notion of the bookwork further, I want to place it in the broader camp of what Rosalind Krauss calls the "self-differing medium," for this helps further specify the materiality in question. A self-differing medium is constituted when the conventions and structures that determine the medium of a particular artwork are themselves taken up in the work in a fashion that alters those determinations, as the work comes to specify itself and hence becomes self-differing.[24] The medium, then, "is something made, rather than something given," or made as much as it is given.[25] There is no direct correspondence between a work's medium and its content, but more a *baggy fit,* allowing it a certain degree of latitude in the way it responds to its material forms, even as in doing so it becomes a successful work only insofar as it constitutes their necessity to itself. Moreover, and this is a feature of Krauss's argument that is especially pertinent for the concept of the anti-book, her understanding of the medium is not confined to its physical substance (as it is in Clement Greenberg's canonical definition of medium-specificity) but can also take

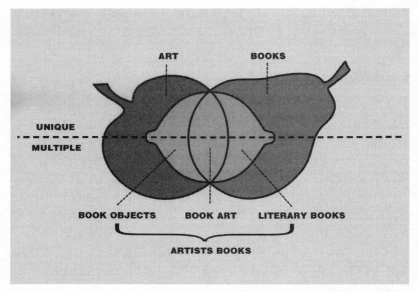

Figure 1. Clive Phillpot, "Artist Books Diagram," 1982. Courtesy of Clive Phillpot.

an epistemic form, including rules, logics, and paradigms, and tends not toward a progressively more refined adequacy to a medium's singularity (again, in contrast to Greenberg) but to an open and recursive emergence through successive loops of self-interrogation.[26]

There is clearly some comparability between the bookwork qua self-differing medium and Hayles's concept of technotext that I introduced previously. But constituted in the field of plastic arts rather than literature, the concept of the self-differing medium is sometimes more useful for my purposes, because it explicitly sets its sights on the full breadth of the material and formal qualities of a book, without any necessary priority given to its *text*. Ulises Carrión conveys this aspect in describing the bookwork as an "autonomous space-time sequence," a "self-sufficient form" that "consists of various elements, *one of which might be a text*. . . . In a book of the new art words don't transmit any intention; they're used to form a text which is an element of a book, and it is this book, as a totality, that transmits the author's intention."[27] Although text will usually play a central role in bringing into expression the material forms of a particular bookwork, *often it will not,* being at most a catalyst to the bookwork's array of expressive features and effects. Guattari helps clarify this point. He suggests that to place such attention on the expressivity of materials is not to undermine the importance of text, or to "minimiz[e] the role of the text and of the writing machine in the putting to work of these mute redundancies," but is rather to allow for the autonomy and polyvocality of different expressive materials, against the linguistic "overcoding" of text.[28]

Drawing this discussion into explicit alignment with this book's guiding term, if not yet its concept fully formed, it was these kinds of recursive and open-ended relations among the breadth of a book's materiality, along with the associated experimental impulse, that led Richard Kostelanetz in the 1970s to designate artists' books as "anti-books."[29] Rather than "succumb[ing] to the conventions of the medium," Kostelanetz argued that the artists' book confounds received reading practices and "envisions what else 'the book' might become." As such, it "is likely to strike the common reviewer as a 'non-book' or 'antibook.'"[30]

This emphasis on experimental engagement with forms and material qualities may appear paradoxical, because the emergence of the artists' book as a named phenomenon is closely associated with 1960s and 1970s conceptual art and the move *away* from the art object into dematerialized practice.[31] Certainly the artists' book traveled along with the tendency for art to become concept and theory, as paradigmatically exemplified by the journal *Art-Language,* but it held on to the material terrain of the production and consumption of such art/theory and other linguistic/aesthetic operations. In this, artists' books can be distinguished from conceptual art, and also in their often critical relation to the commercial instrumentalization of art, as part of what Lucy Lippard calls "a broad, if naïve, quasi-political resistance to the extreme commodification of artworks and artists."[32] For while conceptual art claimed its dematerialization to serve critique of the art commodity—as Krauss puts it in her polemic against conceptual art, postminimalism, and relational aesthetics, conceptual art "abjures" the aesthetic object as "mere commodity"—in fact, as Alexander Alberro has shown, it tended to reproduce the values and perceptual frames of an increasingly dematerialized capitalism that was taking off through marketing and advertising.[33]

This is not to say that artists' books took textual matter to be in and of itself external to relations of authority and capital. As Gwen Allen argues, for many practitioners and theorists of this art form, "the page is not a neutral or universal space—a 'museum without walls'—but is shot through with various institutional and ideological forces," operating to codify and consolidate hierarchies of authorship and structures of aesthetic value.[34] Handling the practical critique of such forces while cleaving to the materialities and social relations of text entailed a range of practices and orientations. The artists' book emerged as a mode of art practice that was relatively inexpensive to produce and consume, multiple and hence potentially nonauratic, reasonably accessible, at least insofar as it was encountered in everyday life and at readers' own rhythms, and peripheral to the gallery system and conventions of the art establishment, with the latter's integration of critical and commercial structures of value.[35] It has also been constituted in relation to networks of politics and sociality, where the mobility that is intrinsic to the form of the book, as well as the participatory nature of small-scale book production and of exchange, has been associated with particular events, alternative institutions, or political currents. For these kinds of reasons, artists' books have sometimes been understood as "democratic multiples," but these books, at their best, have tended not to construct or partake in the universal field of some generalized democratic "public" but have functioned as media specific to particular problems, themes, or minorities and have often been acutely aware that the democratic polity operates through the *exclusion* of their terms. The adoption of the artists' book by feminist and queer political scenes is particularly notable in this regard.[36]

Naturally, the bookwork has not escaped the circuits of commercial value and the star system and has come to be a relatively established art practice. But in the qualities I have been describing, it also contains a considerable impulse to *nonidentity*, breaching the bounds of the media forms and practices that it designates. That quality is apparent in Lippard's grappling with an adequate definition, where she comments that "artists' books are best defined as whatever isn't anything else. They aren't quite photo-books, comic books, coffee-table books, fiction, illustration."[37] And yet they are not distinct either; as Phillpot argues, artists' books lose something essential about their form and intervention if they are treated "as separate from other books" or hived off into an institutional, art-oriented collection separated from books more generally conceived.[38] I would run with this and suggest that the promise of the artists' book is that it loses distinction as a circumscribed genre to emerge within and across *all* textual media as a condition or quality of formal experimentation. The point has been made recently in Michael Hampton's *THEARTISTSBOOKANEWHISTORY* (an edition by the artists' book project Banner Repeater, run by Ami Clarke, whose project space has the uncanny appeal of being located on the platform of a working train station, Hackney Downs platform 1). Hampton's expanded and decentered history of the artists' book, whose narrative order is fragmented by its published form as a folded A2 sheet, opens to such a diverse range of works, materials, and methods that it performs his speculation that, as the medium of the book cedes the data management function to the computer and so frees up its experimental capacities, the borders of the artists' book will become indistinct, "no longer circumscribed by art world protocols, and steganographically indistinguishable from the book itself."[39] I will pick up this point later under the theme of "post-digital publishing," but what I draw from it now is that on the terrain of *political* textual media, *Anti-Book* shares this boundary-breaking orientation. The anti-book is not a distinct body of practices and works but the experimental condition of communist publishing, where communist publishing is not a circumscribed field of social movement media but designates a potential—a potential charged with conflict and politics, certainly—of all textual production.

Having sketched the principal features of the bookwork qua self-differing medium, I would like to provide an illustration with Kostelanetz's irregular serial publication *Assembling* (1970–87), which he founded with Henry James Korn as something of a hybrid of magazine and book (they use both terms to describe it). Given that it was established by writers interested in the literary avant-garde, *Assembling* was never going to be held to established genres of textual expression, but the magazine's challenge to constraints of form was manifest as much in its physical and design characteristics as in its texts. It was anomalous indeed; in Allen's evocative description, *Assembling* was "a chaotic and uneven (in every sense of the word) mix of art, poetry, and other kinds of texts and documents with inconsistent margins, fonts, and layouts, printed on a heterogeneous range of papers, from colored construction paper to college-ruled notebook paper."[40]

Assembling entered the field of the bookwork as a problematization of the "editorial/industrial complex" of commercial publishing, whose economic and aesthetic paradigms functioned as a bar to the publication of experimental writing.[41] It did so as a "counter-editorial" experiment whereby the "restrictive, self-serving nature of traditional editorial processes" were surrendered in a commitment to publish all and any submissions the editors received, following each issue's invitation to writers and artists to submit, ready for publication, "otherwise unpublishable" works on paper (for the first issue: up to four sheets of 8.5" × 11" in multiples of one thousand for an edition of the same number, one of which was Ed Ruscha's "Chocolate," a thousand sheets of paper marked with a smudge of that confection).[42] In this way the contributors were compelled to take on many of the practical and design functions previously the preserve of the publisher, so becoming their own self-publishers as they learned the reproduction methods most conducive to their work. *Assembling* also surrendered its property rights, returning copyright to the contributors. With these characteristics in mind, we might understand *Assembling* as a work that held together simultaneously the processes of assembly *and* disassembly. Contributions were pulled into each bound issue, while the concentrating functions of editorial, publishing infrastructure, and copyright were pushed out or distributed to contributors and the unity of form and content was found in the magazine's very disunity, as it "gain[ed] its cohering definition (which is approximately repeatable) from its unprecedented diversity."[43] Not that *Assembling* was wholly without consistency, for each issue's call for contributions invited works along a theme (as an example, "our place in nature and nature's place in us" for number 12). But even these thematic concerns were handled in the assembling manner, where, given that there was no editorial evaluation, each issue theme was expected to "appear sporadically through the magazine—a flexible motif recurring through the collage, appearing in widely different forms."[44]

If that was the coherence of the magazine—a disassembling assembly, if you will—the conventional relationship between published work and reader was caught up in a similar dynamic, in a printed entity that was more to be "enjoyed" than "evaluated," that could "be read backwards, as well as forwards, or from the middle outwards," where "the leaps from one chapter to the next are so great" that it might best be read in a fragmented fashion, "in circumstances that encourage discrete pauses."[45] And just as centralized editorial judgment was surrendered, the function of evaluation was devolved to the reader in what may have been a disconcerting experience:

> Many readers feel the need to be reassured by an authority figure; feel that a work must be consecrated by some sort of expert; feel the need to be told what is good and what is not. *Assembling* makes no such assurance; publication in *Assembling* does not consecrate or validate anything. Instead, it returns the responsibility of judgment to the reader, where it belongs.[46]

One might have expected this unedited heterogeneity to result in the devaluation of art practice in an unregulated banality, but if the remit of *Assembling* for the "unpublished and unpublishable" was a negation of editorial evaluation, it was less a refusal of quality than an injunction to unconstrained experiment. As the call for the ninth issue put it, "*Assembling* offers every contributor an unparalleled opportunity not only to transcend editorial restrictions but also to surpass his or her previous work with a singular contribution that will stand out from the surrounding pack."[47]

Assembling was constituted as an anti-book, then, across its textual, editorial, commercial, formal, and physical properties. Indeed, it expressed the anti-book's recursive and anti-identitarian sensibility not only in these aspects of textual and media form but in its self-understanding as a publishing project; as Kostelanetz wrote in the first issue, "in the end, ... we should like to find the dissemination of experimental writing changed so radically that *Assembling* would have no further need to exist."[48]

COMMUNISM, WRITING, PUBLISHING

The second domain of intervention of the anti-book is the material culture of communist writing and publishing, especially with regard to developments in communist thought after the passing of the historical workers' movement and to the capitalist conditions of textual media. It is here that *Anti-Book* is most directly located. If I seek to fashion an anti-book orientation and sensibility from the domain of the bookwork, it is to draw out and develop the *bookwork of communism*—though I make this point with the strong proviso that the conjunction contains an impulse toward nonidentity.[49] The conjunction of communism and bookwork does not designate a specific body of works, nor a depoliticized aestheticization of communist publishing, but interference between the two domains toward an expanded understanding of the materiality of communist textual expression.

The term *anti-book* has arisen in the domain of communist publishing too, as a description Guy Debord applied to *Mémoires*, the communist bookwork he constructed with Asger Jorn in the late 1950s, which famously embodied its critical valence in its covers of heavy sandpaper. I will save consideration of that work until chapter 3 and instead set out the broader features of the anti-book intervention in relation to the domain of communist writing and publishing. It is useful to this end to work with an essay by Régis Debray, "Socialism: A Life-Cycle," published in translation in *New Left Review* in 2007.[50] Though ultimately unsatisfactory, Debray's piece is striking for its account of the imbricated or "ecological" relation between "socialism" (his inclusive term for the ideological spectrum of the historical workers' movement) and its media forms, helping to orient our attention to the materials and forms of political text.

Debray's essay is grounded in his broad thesis that we cannot grasp the nature of conscious collective life without understanding "the material forms and processes through which its ideas are transmitted," its "mediological" "ecosystem."[51] His articulation of this thesis here is that the media ecology of the nineteenth- and twentieth-century workers' movement was wholly integrated with, and patterned by, the material and intellectual culture of print, of which a guiding image is the alignment of the inauguration of the First International (1864) and the invention of the rotary press (1867), which multiplied the speed of impressions tenfold. All the components are here for a rich materialist ecology of socialist media: printers, typographers, print runs, distribution circuits, text durations, books, newspapers, parties, intellectuals, reading habits, and pedagogic styles. The printer is something of a nexus, the "pivot" of socialism as "a worker intellectual or an intellectual worker"—the very word *socialism,* as if to confirm the point, coined by a typographer, Pierre Leroux. And the newspaper is the privileged media form.[52] Here Debray's thesis dovetails with Lenin's account of the preeminent organizational power of the party newspaper (a point I return to in chapter 5), but Debray's analysis of the immanent relation between print and socialism has considerably more ontological and epistemological reach.[53] Not only newspapers, Debray assesses the place of letters, fliers, illicit newssheets, pamphlets, journals, books, archives, libraries—the historical workers' movement was a veritable weave of text and textual forms. And for Debray, this was intrinsic to the social production of revolutionary politics, a culture of reading and writing through which the abstraction of thought could break with the sense impressions of the immediate present and open the possibilities for thinking revolution: "Writing collectivizes individual memory; reading individualizes collective memory. The back-and-forth between them fosters the sense for history by unearthing potentials within the present, creating backdrops and foregrounds; it is fundamental for the idea of socialism."[54] Let me step from this to reflect a little on the place and value of writing to communism.

Statements like Debray's here are not uncommon. Vilém Flusser argues, for instance, that movement between the production and consumption of writing is not only key to the capacity of writing to carry collective meaning but, in so doing, and in its capacity to form a linear movement through time, writing is also the *essence* of politics: "the truly political gesture is to write and publish texts. All other political engagement follows from and submits to texts."[55] Naturally, I consider the production and consumption of writing and publishing to have a significant role in political composition, though my enthusiasm is more tempered, and I would frame it rather more critically. As the title of Flusser's book *Does Writing Have a Future?* suggests, his affirmation is framed as a defense, or at least a specification, of writing in the face of ascendant screen media. The context of Debray's argument, as we will see shortly, is not dissimilar. My argument differs somewhat. In affirming the political value of material text, *Anti-Book* in no way approaches writing as a residual technology under threat from the ascendant image; with the ubiquity of text–screen interfaces and the social media platforms of Twitter, Facebook, and so on, we may not be "deeper in words than we've ever been," but text is hardly on the wane.[56] If writing is not under threat, neither is it to be wholeheartedly affirmed or placed in as pivotal a place as it is in Debray and Flusser. Writing and publishing are in fact rather *ineffectual* political means. The ever-expanding volume of revolutionary text should confront communist writers with a degree of introspection as to the value of our endeavor. Gilles Dauvé and Karl Nesic memorably put it like this:

> There's little chance that a person who's never once felt the urge to blow anything up will write meaningful subversive stuff. But the same is true of a person who has never felt some derision when looking at bookshelves full of revolutionary books and archives, or at the infinite availability of similar books and archives on the Internet. There's no relevant theory without an awareness of the limits of words in general and theory in particular.[57]

Moreover, while revolutionary politics would seem to be inextricably entwined with writing and publishing, at times "indistinguishable from its expression in print," as Kevin Gilmartin notes of radical protest in early-nineteenth-century Britain, this is an overdetermined historical outcome, not an inevitability.[58] It comprises different causes, for example, the elevation of publishing as a political practice in its own right that was attendant on its state repression in the early years of the workers' movement, or the possibility that writing and publishing afford of practicing politics, or feeling that one is doing so, in times when the horizon of collective action is limited. And the prominence of publishing in radical history should not blind us to the latter's strong and significant oral and audiovisual forms or to the fact that text will likely be ever more interlaced with such forms in the future.

It is important to register also that the relation between revolutionary politics and writing has by no means always had progressive outcomes. For all that the cultures of publishing opened new dimensions and possibilities in radical politics, they also had significant class and gender effects of closure and exclusion. James Vernon makes a convincing case that as the balance of radical expressive culture in Britain tipped toward print media during the nineteenth century, print, championed as "the universal tool of reason," was in fact "far from universal."[59] Print and its cultures did not herald the arrival of mass politics, as is the received account, but tended "to reconstitute the public political sphere in an ever-more restrictive fashion, excluding groups believed to be 'irrational' like women and the illiterate poor from public political debate."[60] A significant role was played by legislation, which sought to shift the locus of political subjectivity onto the possessive individual of the bourgeois polity, with measures that "privileged the uses of print in order to erode the public and collective character of oral and visual politics with a conception of politics as the private affair of (male) individuals."[61] Even in the more radical currents, it seems that the cultures of writing and print were overburdened by Enlightenment rationalism, which served to generate a field that was somewhat desiccated in comparison to the "pungent oratory" and radical themes of the oral culture from the same quarter, as Iain McCalman describes his disappointing experience of reading this press from the 1819–21 period.[62] Returning to the twentieth century, radical print also contains a troubling pedagogical orientation, in the ascendant model of socialism as the "raising of consciousness," a model accompanied by an often hallowed respect for the intellectual and the corresponding division between leaders and led. This is a division central to Lenin's model of the party and its textual plane of composition, the newspaper, with its one-way communication between writer/party and reader/masses.[63] It is a division, as I consider in chapters 3 and 6, that was found as extreme in the grotesque compound of intellectual and tyrant that characterized state communist regimes, where "the most philistine despot found himself wreathed in the laurels of knowledge."[64]

Returning to Debray, the *temporality* of print has a significant place in the further specification of his socialist media ecology. It took a full twenty-five years for the first French edition of *Capital* to sell out, and yet the slow take-up of Marx did not unduly affect the global impact of his work. Marx was saved from oblivion, Debray asserts, by "the backwardness of cultural circuits in relation to those of market production."[65] If this notion of retarded cultural production is suspect—I will argue shortly that market relations were intrinsic to modern publishing from the start—comparison between nineteenth-century publishing and now lends support to his thesis. For the speed of turnover today is such that books have little time with which to establish themselves in the market before they are lost in the Niagara flow of publication, and beyond the bounds of the book, the rapid cycle of obsolescence of online media is of course intrinsic to its corporate and subjective forms.

With this comparison, we move into Debray's explanation for the demise of the socialism–print ecology. It is the *ubiquity* of media that is decisive—in the form of television, though the inclusion of social media (which postdates Debray's text) would not upset his thesis. Socialism, Debray suggests, survives in its ability to carve out an independent milieu against a hostile environment; newspaper, party, clandestine cell, counterculture are all constituted in relation to forces that besiege them from the outside. But the ubiquitous media of television collapses that separation: "The homogenization of symbolic flows tends to dissolve non-conformist nuclei into a common hegemonic gas. Television, now the principal interface of all social groups, erodes the boundaries between inside and out, and levels access to information."[66] Without such boundaries, socialism is lost in the ubiquity of information, as, it seems for Debray, is *all* emancipatory politics, left behind in the predigital age: "Behind the 're' of reformation, republic, or revolution . . . there is a hand flicking through the pages of a book, from the end to the beginning. Whereas the finger that presses a button, fast-forwarding a tape or disc, will never pose a danger to the establishment."[67]

Appealing as Debray's thesis is for its close attention to the material forms and social lives of political textual media, it is considerably flawed. Not least of its problems lies in interpreting the rise and fall of the workers' movement in this way exclusively through the lens of media form, for it was a complex, overdetermined entity, fully interlaced with mutations in capitalist social relations as a whole, and should be analyzed as such. But if it is reductive to explain the collapse of the workers' movement by the rise of television, Debray is correct that the substantial social subject that was the workers' movement has met its end. There is a melancholic quality to his assessment of the passing of this "great fallen oak," but that is not the way I understand it.[68] The demise of the workers' movement would seem to be the end of the possibility of socialism understood as a substantial subject, an independent or autonomous movement that in its bounded sociopolitical forms, its identity, offers a living, breathing alternative to capitalism. But for the political perspective of *Anti-Book,* on the contrary, the end of the workers' movement (and the forms of Taylorist and Fordist industrial capitalism of which it was the special product and antagonist) is the condition for an *invigorated* communism. I will take a moment to develop this point, to flesh out a little the references I make in subsequent chapters to a communism without identity.

The temporal arc of Debray's media ecology broadly pertains to the period and form of working-class struggles that the French communist journal *Théorie Communiste* has called "programmatism," where communist futures were to be founded on social relations formed in present modes of struggle, such that communism was the affirmation of an existent proletarian subjectivity. In their words,

> programmatism is ... a theory and practice of class struggle in which the proletariat finds, in its drive toward liberation, the fundamental elements of a future social organisation which become the *programme to be realised.* This revolution is thus the affirmation of the proletariat, whether as a dictatorship of the proletariat, workers' councils, the liberation of work, a period of transition, the withering of the state, generalised self-management, or a "society of associated producers."[69]

Marx in his more visionary moments pointed beyond the framework of programmatism, positing the proletariat as the class not of self-affirmation but of *self-abolition.* It is a formulation, as in this example from *The Holy Family,* that crackles against his time and ours: "The proletariat ... is compelled as proletariat to abolish itself and thereby its opposite, private property, which determines its existence, and which makes it proletariat. It is the *negative* side of the antithesis, its restlessness within its very self, dissolved and self-dissolving private property."[70] But up until the 1970s, the nature of the class relation, or the capitalist organization of production and reproduction, was such that the working class was socially determined to recognize itself as a positive identity, amassed and concentrated in factories and industrial cities, and affirmed as such first through its independent institutions, by which it gained organizational power and social respectability, and later through its political and legal recognition within the social democratic state. Under these conditions, the program of revolution was carried within the working class on the basis of its role as provider of labor. This is the transhistorical understanding of labor that was intrinsic to the workers' movement, labor "that constitutes the social world and is the source of all social wealth," as Moishe Postone's critique characterizes it.[71] In so taking a historically specific feature of capitalism alone to be a universal human condition, the resultant politics necessarily took its field of contestation to be *distribution of the products of labor* and not *critique and abolition of labor and its subject,* a "new mode of politically administering and economically regulating the *same* industrial mode of production to which capitalism gave rise."[72]

Hence the apparent autonomy of the working class from capital, as established in the institutions of the labor movement, turns out to have been the specific form of its *integration with capital,* as its institutions and motivations fashioned an affirmative subject out of that which was imposed by capital and so all too easily came to merge with the motivations of capitalist development. As such, the workers' movement "loses its way" not so much in being insufficiently revolutionary but in having a content that was insufficiently differentiated from that of capitalist revolution.[73] Of this tendency, the state-led and totalitarian industrialization of the Soviet Union, which far exceeded in rapidity what market capitalism could have achieved, is the most acute moment, Bolshevik "counterrevolution" as "the accomplishment *against* [*proletarians*] of *their* revolution."[74] This, then, is the structural impasse of the workers' movement, whereby "the proletariat seeks to liberate against capital its social strength which exists *in* capital" and exists there only.[75] Even in its more radical variants that come after 1917 as a challenge to the counterrevolution of Bolshevism, communism was still formulated as a question of *organizational form*— most emblematically, the "workers' council" versus the Leninist party— rather than as practical critique of the *content of work* and capitalist social relations, or, it is the same thing, of itself as subject of labor.[76]

For *Théorie Communiste* and others in the "communization" current, it is only now that this horizon of the affirmation of labor and the positivity of working-class identity can be overcome, after the cycle of struggles of the late 1960s and early 1970s (where the "refusal of work" within the sphere of labor, and struggles over social reproduction among women, racialized groups, and others structurally marginalized by that sphere, signaled the crisis of the programmatic affirmation of workers' identity) and the subsequent restructuring through globalization and neoliberalism. This is in large measure because what Marx called the "real subsumption" of labor in capital has reached a stage where capital no longer needs an affirmative subject of labor—having found the rigidities of national labor markets, the welfare state, collective wage bargaining, and so forth, to be obstacles to valorization—and is instead increasingly self-positing. There is simply no ground on which to found a positive and enduring workers' identity or to project its coming into being as a revolutionary subject. The global fragmentation of labor; the long-term decline in real wages; the move to the heart of the wage relation of flexibility, precarity, and under-unemployment; the extension of super-exploitation and informal work attendant on the tendential rise in "surplus population"— from all this comes "the impossibility of the proletariat to relate to itself positively against capital: the impossibility of proletarian autonomy."[77] In other words, class—the condition of needing to sell one's labor, whether achieved or not, and of being dependent on those whose labor power is enabled by the unpaid work of social reproduction—is evacuated of positive identity and becomes increasingly experienced as an external imposition, and apparent as such.

This is of course experienced as a resounding defeat, that which is registered in Debray's essay, but for *Théorie Communiste*, it is also a considerable opportunity, for now the class relation has itself removed the obstacle of the self-affirmation of workers' identity. Grounding communism in a defeat of this magnitude might sound like a parody of the forced and deluded optimism of Trotskyist sects or of the progressive logic of traditional Marxism, but communization theory is fully cognizant that the prospects look brighter for barbarism than for communism. The point, rather, is that if struggles amid our crisis of social reproduction tip in anticapitalist directions—and the structural impasses presented to any other route out of the crisis suggest that they just may—they will no longer be caught by the self-defeating limit of workers' identity, that communism now cannot but be the immanent rupture of capitalist social relations.

But where, then, is communism located? If a program founded on the affirmation of workers' identity is now lost, communism turns instead on encounters with the *limits* to identity, on the structural impasses, complicities, and exclusions that condition sectoral identities, social movements, racialized and gendered groups. Here the limit is less a boundary that solicits transgression than the immanent horizon of self-overcoming. It is the challenge to and dissolution of the subjectivities that populate capitalist society as its integral product and necessary anchor, *including* the identities of struggle. "The theory of communization alerts us to the limits inherent in . . . struggles, and indeed is attentive to the possibilities of a real revolutionary rupture opening up because of, rather than in spite of, those limits."[78] And again, emphasizing now the seemingly paradoxical presence of communization *within* struggles, "communization occurs only at the limit of a struggle, in the rift that opens as this struggle meets its limit and is pushed beyond it."[79] It may appear a surprising association, but as a politics of limits, communization can thus be understood as a sociohistorical specification of Maurice Blanchot's characterization of the wrenching nonidentity of communism: "Communism is what excludes (and excludes itself from) every already constituted community."[80]

Returning to our theme, how can we conceptualize the place of *textual media* in such a communism without identity? Clearly it cannot take the shape of an integrated ecology of political subjects, institutions, and autonomous media forms, for this is lost with the loss of the workers' movement. A communization media theory—to imagine such a thing for a moment—might be expected to turn to the determinate conditions and limits of the ideas, textual expressions, and media forms arising in contemporary struggles and movements. But *Anti-Book* takes a different approach, pivoting from the terrain of struggles to the terrain of textual media, indexed as it is to experimental practices in media form. In this, *Anti-Book* both shares features with and departs from communization theory. It shares the insistence on the nonidentity of communism, communism as the self-abolition of the proletariat that is immanent to the social relations of capitalism. As such, the anti-book experiments explored here emerge immanently to particular encounters between communist thought and media form, as they draw into focus, trouble, and undo the subjectivating and commodifying forms of textual media in capitalist societies. As a communist critique of writing and publishing, the anti-book is situated, various, discontinuous, and resistant to effects of integration and identity, even as, or because, it is caught up in the media relations and forms of capitalism.

As to this book's difference to communization theory, in being grounded in experimental political publishing and not in struggles as such, the nonidentity of communism is freed up to develop across diverse modalities of sociomaterial being—sometimes developing in close proximity to common themes in communist politics (when I take up the question of the textual and authorial dimensions of the party, for example), other times moving in less common arenas (regarding sensory relations to objects, diagrammatic modeling, the passional dimensions of signs, the indirect voice of myth and media editorial). And while I associate these with a communism against and beyond workers' identity, they are not indexed to it as the outcome of a determining structural limit of the present moment. Indeed, taking advantage of the discontinuities and experimental pockets of the history of writing and publishing, I mostly draw examples of anti-book practice from periods that were broadly conditioned by the programmatic form of workers' identity. Some of these projects arose in critical scenes that intimated the critique of this identity, in others the challenge was more direct, while some had no direct relation to communist thought at all but have much to offer an expanded communism of textual matter all the same.

In none of this does *Anti-Book* suggest a *prefigurative* theory of communist media; I contend only that communist writing and publishing, in its immanent critique of the forms of capitalist media, can be developed beyond the domains and powers of ideas and concepts alone to become a more fully materialist site of experimental practice. In their small way, these practices articulate a wrenching pull toward postcapitalist modes of being but are only this insofar as they operate amid the conditions of life—or of writing and publishing—determined by the capitalist mode of production. To enumerate the features of such practices and group them here under the abstraction of the anti-book would contradict the aim of this concept to push in the other direction, to encourage attention to the specificities of particular projects. Instead I want to move now to situate the broad argument of this book in opposition to two aspects of textual media: the textual form of the "manifesto," which could plausibly be described as the primary textual correlate of programmatism, of the workers' movement as historical subject; and the capitalist structures of mediated communication, in social media and in the history of the book.

ANTI-MANIFESTO

My casual opening remark that *Anti-Book* is not a manifesto could have taken a more systematic form, and with some cause. For the anti-book breaks with this mode of political writing that has for so long, and all too easily, been adopted by leftists that it is as if it is the *natural* form for self-consciously political writing to take. What, then, is this textual form, and what is wrong with it? In its revolutionary or avant-garde mode, the manifesto is a purloined textual form, appropriated from the institutions of state and church where it served as a means to disseminate injunctions backed by force. As with its form in such institutions, the revolutionary manifesto articulates authority, and yet this authority is of a peculiar kind, for it is wholly fabricated, having no basis in existent institutional power. This feature is patently clear in Marx and Engels's *Communist Manifesto,* arguably the founding text of this modern genre of radical writing. One need simply to juxtapose its claims to meet the "nursery tale of the Spectre of Communism with a Manifesto of the party itself," a manifesto that proclaims no less than the inevitable triumph of world communist revolution, with the actuality of its birth, initial impact, and institutional setting, as a work commissioned by a few dozen émigré radicals in the back room of a London pub and which, after some influence in the 1848 German revolutions, went largely unnoticed for some twenty years.[81] This gap between claim and reality must be overcome if the manifesto's proclamations are to hold any plausibility, and it is this overcoming that is key to the manifesto's specific textual procedures, hitched, as Martin Puchner has argued, to a particular subjective form.[82]

The modern manifesto works by constructing a political subject through the diagnosis and presentation of the subject's historical emergence and future actualization. In turn, in a performative loop, this projected future flourishing of the subject lends authority to the text in the present where the subject is lacking. The manifesto works, in other words, in the future perfect; its claim to authority in the present *will have been* sanctioned by the actualization of its subject in the future. It is a performance for which a certain theatricality—the staging of the authority that it lacks—is at once necessary and necessarily ever excised.

Yet the manifesto is a decidedly twentieth-century textual form, one made redundant not so much by the waning of its performative power caused by overrepetition (though boredom with the manifesto form must surely set in eventually) but by the historical loss of any referent that might plausibly serve as its subject.[83] For a communism, and a state of global struggles, that operates through the immanent rupture of identity rather than the programmatic coming to presence of a collective subject, the manifesto form is politically ineffectual, without purchase on the conditions of social being. And yet, perhaps in concentrating on the classical form established by Marx and Engels, I have taken the manifesto's structure too literally and missed the particular qualities it has taken in other contexts. It is worth considering the arguments of some of the manifesto's advocates, pertaining to the twentieth-century avant-garde and feminist writing. Shifting our attention to the avant-garde, Alain Badiou makes the case that a manifesto is a "rhetorical envelope" that protects and nurtures "*something other than what it overtly names or announces.*"[84] Its function is not to realize its promise per se but to "devote every energy" to the otherwise "precarious and almost indistinct" nature of real action in the present, action that has the evental or convulsive quality of the coincidence of its instantiation with its undoing.[85] For Badiou, then, "we should not be surprised by the correlation between vanishing works and staggering programmes," for it is precisely the ephemeral quality of real action, and not a coming substantial subject as such, that the manifesto envelopes and offers to the future.[86]

It is an appealing formulation, though one that should be treated with some circumspection. On shifting scale from the rhetorical structure of the manifesto's emerging subject to the more micro and intimate level of the "vanishing works" it nurtures, it is not at all clear that the manifesto's claim is in fact so radically altered. For the avant-garde manifesto is historically indexed less to "precarious and almost indistinct" evental action than the identitarian tendencies of vanguard organizations, where the group functions like a microcosm of the announced subject that, in the latter's absence, it must stand in for as substitute. As often as not, these "staggering programmes" have been alloyed with subjectivities that are as equally staggering in their pompous self-regard. Here the manifesto form has been more a means of establishing the ideology, subjectivity, and boundaries of vanguard groups than of confirming their evental undoing, with the concomitant tendency to degenerate, as Debord has it, into "party patriotism," "theoretical paralysis," and "wooden language" as the group calcifies against the exterior world that it must of necessity appraise as distinct and hostile or as having fallen short of its idea.[87]

However appealing is Badiou's formulation of the manifesto as a textual agent of the convulsive event, partisans of the latter would do better, then, not to seek a new manifesto but to subtract this integrating and self-bolstering textual form from the field of political writing—to create "one manifesto less," in Deleuze's framing—so as to reflect and confirm the demise of the unitary political subject and, with it, the politics of the avant-garde.[88] That said, something of a subtractive procedure can be conducted within the manifesto form itself, through a deconstruction or ironizing of its formal techniques and subjective patterns, now shifting us to a third mode of manifesto production. Janet Lyon and Kathi Weeks have argued compellingly that this has been a route often pursued in feminist manifestos, with Donna Haraway's "Cyborg Manifesto," for example, standing out as an indubitable success.[89] Attention to such ironizing textual procedures in particular manifestos would work against the weight of my discussion of the manifesto thus far, which has presented only a conceptual formalization. To correct this in line with the method of *Anti-Book* would necessitate engaging not only with the textual procedures and qualities of particular manifestos but also with their *extratextual* dimensions, their many materialities. As an indication of what this might entail, we can consider the singular example of Valerie Solanas's *SCUM Manifesto*.

As all self-respecting manifestos, Solanas's text launches against its object with a vertiginous clarion call: "'Life' in this 'society' being, at best, an utter bore and no aspect of 'society' being at all relevant to women, there remains to civic-minded, responsible, thrill-seeking females only to over-throw the government, eliminate the money system, institute complete automation and eliminate the male sex."[90] Yet the subject that is indicated here, and unfurls riotously through the text's pages, functions as much to undercut the standard revolutionary agent of the manifesto form as it does to establish any kind of proto-separatist constituency. The apparent universality of the political subject of the generic manifesto is achieved in no small part by hiding its gender particularity, a task performed in the abstraction of gender neutrality. In this it shares the gendered structure of the bourgeois public sphere, as Melissa D. Deem describes it, whose "logics of invisibility and abstraction render the male body invisible while simultaneously condemning the female to hyperembodiment."[91] In *SCUM Manifesto,* that abstract universality is overturned by Solanas's vicious particularization of the male body as a decrepit and debased biosocial form. Conversely, freewheeling SCUM women—"funky, dirty, low-down SCUM gets around"—who have "seen the whole show" of embodied sexuality, take on, in Deem's words, the "frictionless" role previously reserved for men.[92] Yet the chance of establishing an alternative subject on these grounds is simultaneously undercut by the excision of all but a handful of women who would meet the exacting standards of the text's "Society for Cutting Up Men." For the effect of this is less to establish a privileged point of aggregation, a SCUM groupuscule, than to undo the subject of woman, to remove the possibility that this subject might act as a living alterna-tive to patriarchal society, because that would be a brake on the situated unfurling of feminist politics. As Lyon acutely frames it, and in a manner resonant with my preceding discussion of the nonidentity of communism,

> Solanas's "we" is strategically singular: anything more inclusive would preclude the possibility for random action in the name of feminist anar-chism; anything more inclusive would fix identity, thwart performativity, register a sexed normativity. Anything more inclusive would, in short, reify a category called "women" whose political history would most certainly outstrip its utopian possibilities.[93]

That is the textual effect of *SCUM Manifesto,* or a part of it, but what of its broader sociomaterial forms? Commercially published by Maurice Girodias's Olympia Press in August 1968, shortly after Solanas's near-fatal shooting of Andy Warhol, this book did a considerable job of refashioning and reduction of Solanas's material text. At least, Solanas objected to it. In 1977, she committed the most unusual act of defacing the copy (Olympia Press's second edition) held by New York Public Library, in effect disowning her published work by striking out the author's name on the covers and replacing it with that of Girodias, a move that is all the more arresting for the extent to which the looming face on the cover binds the book to Solanas as author (Plate 1). But this was a commercial publisher's construction of the author. Girodias was guilty, Solanas wrote here, with an intensive script that in places punctures the page, of inflicting "sabotaging typos" on the text (the addition of punctuation in the *S.C.U.M.* of the title for one, and as Breanne Fahs describes it, the removal of her playful and erratic use of punctuation, grammatically distorted sentences, and marginalia).[94] And Solanas's defacement of the book moves also against the marketing of dissent: against the book's market-oriented form as a work of scandal, as secured in the first Olympia Press edition's salacious and opportunistic paratextual framing through the Warhol shooting, and against its positioning in relation to an existent subjectivity of "Women's Liberation militants," as the aim of Vivian Gornick's introduction is described on the back cover, with this collectivity and Gornick's name receiving at Solanas's hand the appellation "flea."[95]

By contrast, the first edition of *SCUM Manifesto,* published in fall 1967, is a considerably more awkward entity, a "luminously scummy creation," as Sara Warner and Mary Jo Watts have it.[96] It has qualities that were neither "captured nor preserved" by the Olympia edition, the latter functioning more as an act of substitution and erasure than of publication, or as publication *as* "manipulation and sabotage," to adopt the terms of Solanas's defacement.[97] Her first edition was a self-published mimeograph of 21 A4 pages, stapled once at the top left. In contrast to Olympia Press's perfect-bound book, it carries something of the ephemeral and viscerally noncommercial quality intrinsic to much radical and fringe publishing of the time, with its covers adorned not with the consumer-seducing visage but a rather more estranging typed-text comprising the author's name, the work's title, a brief abstract, the publication date, and (I will comment on this anomaly shortly) a copyright notice.[98] Reading across the critical and popular works devoted to Solanas, it is apparent that the ephemeral quality of this edition holds considerable attraction, and in ways that are not always progressive. Dana Heller shows that in Mary Harron's Solanas biopic, *I Shot Andy Warhol* (1996), the ephemerality of the manifesto ("blurry mimeographed pages lost in the gutters of the 1960s," as Harron imagined it) is commandeered to figure the decline and eclipse of print media and radical writing at the expense of the ascending order of the image.[99] Here Solanas and her encounter with Warhol are not taken up within the complexities of her situation but are simply made to personify the losing party in a confrontation of technologies of cultural reproduction, the "poverty of print [that] cannot possibly stand up to the opulence of the silkscreen," the "originality and impermanence of print" that fails against the "enduring order of Factory-reproduced images."[100] As Heller points out, that Solanas would likely not have apprehended her story and that of radical print media in this way is starkly apparent from the considerable emphasis *SCUM Manifesto* places on new technology, its "vision of a world in which mechanization and systems of mass (re)production would render work, sexual intercourse, and the money system obsolete."[101]

I develop a more critical account of print ephemerality in chapter 2, but to continue the discussion of Solanas's manifesto, let us agree that ephemerality is not in itself enough to constitute the self-published edition as a "SCUMMY thing," to use a phrase that Warner has unearthed from Solanas's archive, an extratextual articulation of her politics.[102] For that, other aspects of her manifesto must come into play, of which I will consider only the relation of writing to money and work—or "unwork," as the manifesto describes the sabotage of labor.[103]

Solanas's material text was interlaced with money, but in embodied, gendered, and proletarian ways somewhat different from the articulation of money in the Olympia Press edition. She sold it by mail order and on the streets of Greenwich Village priced at $2 for men and $1 for women, thus performing a reversal of the gender inequality that is intrinsic to the universal equivalent of money.[104] This performance gains traction because money had an inescapable hold on Solanas's life and writing, the street-corner and mail order sales of her texts serving, albeit rather unsuccessfully, to finance her precarious and often homeless existence, along with panhandling, prostitution, and the occasional writer's fee.[105] We see this hold and its contradictions poetically displayed if we contrast Solanas's efforts to *repel a political constituency* of sympathetic readers— following the hitherto discussed logic of the manifesto's text—with her mocking invitation to her enemies to *sell* a 1977 self-published edition as quasi-commodity. The following is taken from two different advertisements that she placed in *Village Voice* and the feminist newsletter *Majority Report*:

> Olympia Press went bankrupt and the publishing rights to *SCUM Manifesto* reverted to me, Valerie Solanas, so I'm issuing the *CORRECT* edition, *MY* edition of *SCUM Manifesto*....
> I'll let anybody who wants to hawk it—women, men, Hare Krishna, Daughters of the American Revolution, the American Legion. Maurice Girodias, you're always in financial straits. Here's your big chance—Hawk *SCUM Manifesto*. You can peddle it around the massage parlor district. Anita Bryant, finance your anti-fag campaign selling the only book worth selling—*SCUM Manifesto*. Andy Warhol, peddle it at all those hot shit parties you go to....
> Everybody, make big money selling the anti-money system *SCUM Manifesto*. Don't defend it, don't interpret it, don't even like it. Just SELL IT! SELL IT! SELL IT![106]

Solanas's steadfast commitment to copyrighting her text can also be seen in this context.[107] It is a contradictory and depoliticizing move to copyright a manifesto, claiming individual proprietary rights over a text that purports to speak from a position of universality, but as Solanas's proprietorial claim departs from the politics of the manifesto form, it finds a place in the proletarian condition of her writing, her effort against all odds to be a writer and to earn a living as such. Solanas wrote to survive, while seeking means of survival that freed her up to write. Writing *as* work, writing as an *escape* from work—these pull in different directions, certainly, but both carry Solanas's political reversal of her abject existence that is the fulcrum of "SCUM" in its nonacronym mode, a politics apparent for example in her text "A Young Girl's Primer on How to Attain the Leisure Class." It was published initially in the *Playboy*-esque magazine *Cavalier* in 1966 (under a different title) and then compiled with her play *Up Your Ass* in a self-published "SCUM Book," as is the handwritten imprimatur.[108] This "primer" poses the "typically feminine dilemma of carving out . . . in a male world a way of life appropriate to a young girl of taste, cultivation, and sensitivity," to which it offers the somewhat less orthodox solutions of panhandling, charging for conversation, shoplifting, and prostitution: "There must be nothing crass—like work. However, a girl must survive."[109] Hawking her textual product on the streets was not so different from panhandling—a reversal of abjection that is here mediated by self-published print. And yet it was clearly no solution to her condition. The abject reality of Solanas's life displays the gendered and classed nature of writing, or the impasse that the cruel amalgam of gender and class can present to writing, an impasse that was no doubt confirmed for Solanas in the occasional moments of interest in her writing from those who could provide access to a market—from Girodias, Warhol, the *Village Voice*—as she fell back into abjection from encounters that could not, in any case, have had outcomes adequate to the impossible subject of her manifesto. Shooting Warhol may have been as much a product of the limits to women's proletarian writing, a magical solution, as it was of Solanas's critique of men, of a propensity to violence, or of mental instability (not that these dimensions of her life were unrelated). It was a magical solution she put into words in a subsequent phone call to Warhol: "I want you to drop all criminal charges, pay twenty thousand dollars for my manuscripts, put me in more movies and get me booked on Johnny Carson. If you don't, I can always do it again."[110]

It is apparent, then, that the modern political subject of the manifesto can be successfully unworked and that shifting from the terrain of a manifesto's text to its sociomaterial relations allows other qualities and effects of writing and publishing to come into view and open to political intervention. And yet even in such ironizing achievements, the manifesto's subject remains, negatively, as the object of critique, acting as a constraining attractor, a situation that leaves ironizing manifestos ever more without purchase the more the subject they undo is itself undone by the social relations that remove the grounds of its existence. Unlike the subjects of the classical and avant-garde manifesto, feminist problematization of subjectivity and the conditions of collectivity is of course sociopolitically salient, but its passage and intervention in textual form is, I would argue, no longer best taken by the manifesto. Describing Haraway's adoption of the manifesto form as "perhaps an obvious choice," given the socialist feminist intent of the text, Weeks quotes Lyon thus: "To write a manifesto is to announce one's participation, however discursive, in a history of struggle against oppressive forces."[111] But what happens when the obvious choice is *not* taken, when the political dimensions of writing and publishing are developed in altogether different directions? One might respond that the solution to the limits of the manifesto is to turn attention from the textual content of manifestos to their material qualities and effects — the direction I have taken regarding Solanas, or that I take in chapter 4, regarding the anonymous authorship of the *Communist Manifesto* — but that begs the question, why, then, write manifestos at all, and not develop textual procedures of more critically inventive and pertinent kinds? This book concerns these other kinds of experiments with text and media form, though for now, I will continue a little more with a critique of the manifesto, so as to situate it more firmly in the contemporary conjuncture, specifically in the media dimensions of recent struggles.

A certain dissatisfaction with manifestos plays out in *Declaration,* a recent e-pub pamphlet by Michael Hardt and Antonio Negri on the global uprisings of 2011. The media form of *Declaration* exhibits political qualities. Written and published amid upheaval and crisis, of which it seeks to diagnose dominant features, it was self-published, priced cheaply at 99¢, and initially available only digitally, as if to match the urgency of the text with speed of distribution — though, as others have noted, unlike much of the online critical material associated with the crisis, *Declaration* still requires monetary exchange, is subject to a copyright license, and is bound to the proprietary format of Kindle.[112] There is a certain urgency also in its graphic design, with the stripped-back cover based on the first page of text — in Courier font with the title picked out, as if on the hoof, in yellow highlight — pulling in the reader without delay.[113]

Given our habits, these are design qualities that might well indicate to readers that they are encountering a manifesto, but Hardt and Negri are quick to disabuse that assumption, opening *Declaration* with the words "This is not a manifesto."[114] "Manifestos," they continue, "provide a glimpse of a world to come and also call into being the subject" of that world. They "work like the ancient prophets, who by the power of their vision create their own people." But this form has reached its terminus, Hardt and Negri suggest, because contemporary social struggles "have reversed the order, making manifestos and prophets obsolete. Agents of change have already descended into the streets and occupied city squares, not only threatening and toppling rulers but also conjuring visions of a new world."[115]

For all that this resonates with my argument, Hardt and Negri's explanation of the manifesto's obsolescence is not wholly adequate. It is itself too consonant with the formal structure of the manifesto: the projected people *have now arrived,* can create their own visions, and hence no longer have need of the manifesto's projections. It is not that Hardt and Negri are incorrect in observing a more immanent relation between the textual output of recent struggles—the Arab Spring, the Spanish Indignados, Occupy, and others in the "movement of the squares"—and their grassroots actors, a more *tactical* than representational orientation to this media. Prominent exemplars are the Egyptian pamphlet *How to Revolt Intelligently*—which seemed to strike a chord for its use of diagrams to circulate tactics rather than text to describe ideological goals—Occupy's refusal to make representational "demands," and the significant place of social media in recent political organization. The U.S. movement against the murderous structural racism of police and state, known for a time through the Twitter hashtag #BlackLivesMatter, is a crucial example of the latter, as was the use of social media in reporting the Israeli state's maiming and murder of Palestinians in Gaza in July–August 2014, a partial outmaneuvering of the formidable Israeli propaganda machine.[116] But while this more immanent mode of textual political mediation does indeed seem to have navigated past the manifesto mode of political representation, it hardly describes the arrival of a self-representing subject, a conclusion all the more confirmed as the Arab Spring became contained and overrun by highly repressive regimes. Rather than declare the realization of the manifesto form, we would do better to move outside of its explanatory and rhetorical structures altogether.

AGAINST COMMUNICATION

Hardt and Negri do in fact make tracks in this direction, for there is a second dimension to their assessment of contemporary media politics, a call to intervene immanently in the media forms of contemporary communication. Elsewhere in *Declaration,* they pick up on the critique of communication that Deleuze develops in his analysis of "control society."[117] "Speech and communication have been corrupted," Deleuze remarks in a 1990 interview with Negri. "They're thoroughly permeated by money— and not by accident but by their very nature."[118] And, in another text: "If there is no debasement of information, it is because information itself is a debasement."[119] In part, this describes communication as *command,* the reduction of expression to the linear exchange of unambiguous signals, whereby the signifying field is flooded with clichés and order-words, a "psychomechanics" of automatic response.[120] But it also entails a popular compulsion *to communicate*: "Repressive forces don't stop people expressing themselves, but rather force them to express themselves."[121] A dozen years before the rise to dominance of the compulsive communication of social media, this is an impressionistic yet prescient observation. Drawing on it, Hardt and Negri argue that the diffusion of social media and its integration with socioeconomic life have created a dominant subjective form of the "mediatized," a fragmented and distracted capitalist subjectivity absorbed in a perpetual present of communication, participation, feedback, and attention.

Here they are in the company of a significant body of research that has addressed the capitalist dimensions of social media, the co-implication of mediated sociality and subjectivization with new forms of commercial capture and control. Jodi Dean's cogent critique in *Blog Theory* and elsewhere of the subjective forms of what she calls "communicative capitalism," for example, attends to something like a preconscious compulsion encoded in the sociotechnical infrastructures of social media, with the real time immediacy of attention, connection, and user production that is inscribed in each platform's mundane functionality, front-loaded as they are with "status" and "timeline" functions that incite users' interaction.[122] In the ever additive pursuit of links, likes, comments, followers, friends, shares, page views, and so on, the *act* and *quantitative volume* of communication come to displace *what* is communicated, a kind of general equivalence of indiscriminate communication: "unlike a message, which needs to be understood, a contribution is just an addition," "a fundamental communicative equivalence" where "each message is communicatively equal to any other."[123] And this comes with its own affective bind, as users are captured in compulsive repetition, fueled by "tiny affective nuggets," "a smidgen of attention" from each communicative act, momentarily relieving the ambient anxiety that is part and parcel of curating a successful personal profile, a profile that is in turn at once a training ground for the entrepreneurial self and a weak compensation for otherwise precarious lives.[124] True, the point can be overstated; meaning remains, though now in a slippery and ephemeral form, and biographical narrative is key to the self-disclosure intrinsic to Facebook, for example, as Beverley Skeggs and Simon Yuill stress.[125] But these serve social media's infrastructural imperative of quantitative expansion, not the other way around.

A book such as mine on the many materialities of text would not proceed far if it opposed mediatized subjectivity and extralinguistic association per se; the problem is that this is an *incapacitated* subjectivity, which is reciprocally constituted with a particular business model, one integral to its software architecture. As Robert W. Gehl and others have shown, users produce, supply, and rank online media content for free, at once generating the content that attracts user attention and granular marketing data about the tastes, preferences, trends, and values associated with that attention, to be sold and mined as differentiated audience to advertisers, now in real time.[126] Hence, on one side of the interface, social media compels compulsive individuation and self-disclosure, while on the other side, it generates revenue by "simultaneously 'dividuating' that data into multiple aggregate representations to be monetized as targeted ad space," as Skeggs and Yuill put it.[127] And, in the case of Facebook, this economic model is integrated with financialization through stock trading based on monopoly control of its data, tax avoidance, and diversification and expansion well beyond the firm's original structure, including into mobile communications infrastructure, financial services, and drone technology.[128] Social media, then, is "*class* media," as Dean stymies the cozy associations of this collective noun.[129]

All this incitement to communicate on the technical and affective plane of the interface dovetails with the heralded values of our time, as discourses of participation, communicative democracy, and freedom of expression offer no line of opposition but serve to further arouse and sanctify our communicative subjection.[130] That the multi-billion-dollar information firms such as Google, Apple, and Facebook emblazon themselves with such values (while of course resolutely guarding their proprietorial rights to data) should be indication enough of the need for circumspection. Granted, one might respond with good reason that social media nonetheless offers ample possibility for political use by those with different values, namely, that it enables greater and broader access to the production, dissemination, and consumption of critical news and ideas; speedy and networked modes of organization at local and transnational scales; rerouting around corporate news agendas; and rapid circulation and intensification of political passions. The examples given earlier of Occupy, the Arab Spring, and #BlackLivesMatter illustrate these points. Yet too often in celebrating activist and political *use* of social media, analysis fails to attend to the way that nominally critical use can leave untroubled, or even extend, social media's incapacitating subjective and economic forms.[131]

I register here this critique of the subjective forms and business models of social media communication, forms and models to which *Anti-Book* is opposed, but this book does not add to this burgeoning research field. My focus, rather, is on critical alternatives, and those that are often located, as I argue toward the end of this chapter, in "post-digital" domains adjacent to digital media. On this terrain of experimental textual matter, the critics of social media tend to make less headway—though see the important research associated with Amsterdam's Institute of Network Cultures, especially the Unlike Us network, and Coventry University's Centre for Disruptive Media.

I will continue with Dean here, because as well as providing a cogent critique of communicative capitalism, she is a prominent figure in the recent return to "communism" in political theory that has been associated with Badiou and Žižek, and so we might reasonably look here for a communist media practice.[132] Yet while Dean is herself a keen blogger of radical content, her formulation of communism is organized around a stark dichotomy between media activity and direct action, where the former disperses in amorphous circuits of compulsive communication and the latter concentrates a collective subject in physical space that institutes a "division" or "cut" in the status quo, a cut that is necessarily also enacted with the circuits of social media.[133] In response to what must be a nagging question of whether there are *any* possibilities for "a media politics that does not merely circulate contributions," Dean evokes an apparent range of options, but they are hardly convincing, even I think to her: "from the cultivation of critical media competencies and local, face-to-face, street-level activism to the organization of covert cells of communist hackers."[134]

One more possible means of a counter media practice is noted in *Blog Theory,* that of the medium of the book, which Dean comes to while marking the apparent perversity of using a book, with its slow writing and publishing schedules, to develop a critique of social media, with its rapid technological transformations and revelry in the ever new. But herein lies its political value. The book's very slowness, she argues, enacts the cut in circuits of compulsive communication that enables thought to emerge, a structure of intervention that she intriguingly associates with the "slow-down," from the classical repertoire of workplace struggle: "As an object whose form installs delays in sampling and syndication and whose content demands postponed gratification, the book mobilizes the gap of mediacy so as to stimulate thought."[135]

Appealing though this point is for shifting attention to media forms adjacent to social media, it has two significant problems. First, as a move into media politics, it is woefully dematerialized. Whereas capital requires intricate and complex technoaffective mediations to arouse, interpolate, and nullify human biosociality in communicative patterns conducive to its perpetuation, here the book's politics lies only in the possibility of better "thought," whose ground is a subject refounded on signification (the return to "symbolic identity" against the rootless "imaginary identity" of social media, in Dean's Lacanian formulation).[136] If unconvincing, it has a certain logic in her argument. Having made the strongest of cases for the critique of media form, where critical content is rendered irrelevant, or worse (because it fuels the subjective compulsions and market paradigms of communicative capitalism no less than any other content), Dean seeks to found a media politics on content now *shorn* of media form. But how, then, is content to be generated and carried, beyond immediate "face-to-face activism"? Here the book steps in as a medium that facilitates thought and meaning without getting in the way—a medium perfectly married to the signifying forms and capacities that it apparently carries. This leads to the second problem, for if the book is hence a medium without any medium-effects, as it were, it is implicitly a medium outside of capitalist social relations, relations that would be grasped in and through an appreciation of its media form. But in fact the medium of the book has the strongest of capitalist pedigrees, as I consider in what follows. This is not to say that there is no mileage in investigating the comparative speed and slowness of different media forms—indeed, it is a feature of my argument in subsequent chapters—but to appeal to the slowness of books as facilitator of thought, while leaving their capitalist forms untouched, is clearly inadequate for a communist media politics.

In any case, is the medium of the book today really so slow? The intermediation of textual media and the broader communicative patterns of contemporary capitalism are such that books cannot be understood as actually so separate from the compulsions and anxieties of the social media field, the "temporal take-over of theory [which] displaces sustained critical thought, replacing it with the sense that there isn't time for thinking."[137] Insofar as books, particularly those by writers with high social media profiles, are reviewed and promoted in social media and marketed through the promotional algorithms of Amazon, Facebook, and the like, the book demands to be understood less as a *cut* from communicative capitalism than as a particularly effective vehicle for extending it, multiplying connectivity, feeding communicative compulsions, and exhausting readers (and authors too, no doubt) in equal measure.

BOOK AS COMMODITY

Notwithstanding the intensity and extent of the capitalization of communicative capacities and mediums today, it is not a new phenomenon. I want to take a little time to sketch how the commodity form has accompanied the medium of the book since the inception of modern capitalism, for, as I indicated earlier, the point is often missed. The pages of *Anti-Book* explore many and various formal and material features of writing and publishing against the commodity forms of textual media, but an understanding of the more generic condition of the book qua commodity can stand as a background to this study of anti-book publishing, a condition that later chapters gesture toward as they make their particular arguments or that they refine and extend in specific contexts.

There is a strong tendency in the popular imaginary to see books and the culture of text as forms and practices that transcend the realms of capital; it is, Ted Striphas suggests, "one of the most entrenched myths of contemporary book culture."[138] If the spiritual quality of the book plays a part here, as I discuss in chapter 3, it is also a function of the broad tendency of capitalist societies to accord works of "culture" a transcendent value beyond that of economic utility (a value that in reality is far from extraeconomic, being interlaced with class distinction and functioning as rationale and resource in any number of state and corporate schemes of governance, plunder, and profit).[139] Of this tendency, books are perhaps the privileged instance, so much identified as repository and receptacle of culture—of the intellectual, moral, and aesthetic good and true—that they become indistinct from it.[140] This transcendence of books does not happen all by itself, of course, but is a discourse that has played a central part in institutions of the book and learning, not least the publishing business. As Trish Travis argues, publishing has couched its advanced *industry* in a discourse that presents books as objects immune to commodification, "goods which pretend not to be goods at all."[141]

It is not a uniform picture, however. Laura J. Miller makes a nuanced case for considering the supposedly extraeconomic, elevated culture of books to have been historically achieved by drawing distinctions against certain classes of books, those books associated with the young, the working class, and women (dime novels, romances), whose commercial nature was this time *foregrounded,* proffered as index of their appeal to base and popular desires, as books that "reduc[ed] culture to a profane commodity while emphasizing whatever would appeal to the largest audiences."[142] It is an important reminder that critique of the commodity form of the book needs to be careful so as not to replicate the tropes of bourgeois distinction.

Yet this observation does nothing to challenge the fact that print, popular *and* elite, existed from its earliest days as an industry, "governed by the same rules as any other industry," where the book was first and foremost "a piece of merchandise," as Febvre and Martin decisively put it in their canonical study of the emergence of the printed book.[143] And in this, books have by no means been reluctant players; books have not only kept up the pace, as any good commodity, but have often been quite the innovators across numerous fields. Indeed, the printed book was the first uniform and repeatable mass industrial commodity—not comprising measured quantities of indeterminate volumes, as Benedict Anderson clarifies the point with regard to other early industrial commodities such as textiles or sugar, but a volume in its own right, a distinct and self-contained object.[144] In combining moveable alphabetic type (a repurposing of metal-processing techniques employed since antiquity for minting coins) with a mechanical press (as adapted from that used in pressing wine), the Gutenberg letterpress shifted the manufacture of books from the self-directed movements of the scribe to mechanical process, subject to the rhythm of the machine, and so marked "the line of division between medieval and modern technology."[145]

We see in this also the proximity of printing to the move during the late eighteenth century to constitute and divide intellectual and manual labor, as was integral to the emergence of the capitalist form of "abstract labor," toward the creation and generalization of which mechanical process was oriented. As such, the mechanical press enabled a transformation in the organization of labor as work tasks took on the quality of the assembly line, subdivided according to roles and parts in the production chain, and subject to the dictates of productivity that the conjunction of mechanism and time enforced. For example, at the close of the sixteenth century, it has been estimated that a pressman, one role in the print workshop, had to take off on average twenty-five hundred sheets in a fourteen-hour day, a rate of one sheet every twenty seconds.[146] This is probably a consider-able overestimation; we should avoid projecting the extent, uniformity, and intensity of today's division of labor into the past, as D. F. McKenzie counsels.[147] But the theoretical principle of the transformation of labor associated with mechanical print is not in doubt, and by the 1830s, this was established to the extent that it was the copperplate engraving of the printing trade (and not, say, the textile mill) to which Charles Babbage turned to illustrate the logic of modern industrial production (in his theories of mechanical process and the division of labor that informed Marx's analysis of the same in the *Grundrisse*).[148] Tending toward unifor-mity and equivalence, books could now be manufactured in considerable quantities, as is what happened; it appears that between 12 million and 20 million books were printed before 1500 alone, a mere half-century after the invention of the Gutenberg press.[149]

This movement toward abstract labor in the print house was inter-laced with developments in the labor of writing, which took a different direction. As Tim Ingold has argued, efforts to decompose skill into the creative intelligence and imagination of *art,* on the one hand, and the habitual bodily technique of artisanal *labor,* on the other, revolved in large measure around the status of engraving, "whose natural affiliations [were henceforth seen to] lay with the printing trade," with labor and technological reproduction.[150] From the late eighteenth century, the writer thus came to be seen "as an author rather than as a scribe," divorced from the multisensory production of "lines" to instead become a composer of intellectual "texts," an "author engaged in verbal composition."[151] In contrast, the job of the printer became merely "to run off innumerable copies of the author's work." The author became "a literary artist," the printer "a typographic artisan."[152]

If we move from the *production* of books to the complementary pole, we find, as part of the nexus of capitalist social relations of which the mechanical press was both product and bearer, that the mass production of print is contiguous with the first signs of mass *consumption.* Indeed, the rise of the bourgeois class, with its expanding demand for technical and literary text, was a significant social push for the invention of the

Gutenberg press, the latter a technical solution to a social problem that was taxing inventive minds all across Europe.[153] Once established, early print media were associated with a host of mechanisms for the maintenance and cultivation of reading publics, from the simultaneous production of different books so as to avoid heavy losses if one failed to concentration on best sellers, of which Martin Luther's texts were perhaps the first, binding together Protestantism and the early print industry (a conjunction I return to in chapter 4 through Luther Blissett's novel *Q*).[154] The publication of heretical texts, for which publishers could be put to death, was also as much a question of meeting demand and cultivating markets—especially necessary at times of economic downturn, when demand for books would rapidly fall off—as it was an expression of political aims or any other of the desires and values that were amalgamated in the decision to publish. The printed book was closely associated also with the development of copyright, for which the author-function—with its associated cultural values of individual "creativity" and "originality"—emerges as product and guarantor, as I discuss in chapter 4.

All the same, my emphasis on the print–capitalism nexus should not indicate indistinction between the two, blinding us to the variations and contradictions of this nexus or its relative density as compared with other industrial sectors. Although the book industry has played a pioneering role in the development of capitalist production and consumption, it has not always been at the leading edge. Indeed, its socioeconomic structure remained wedded to petty-commodity production for some time after generalized commodity exchange had taken hold elsewhere. In the development of its specifically modern form, a pivotal role is played by copyright. The Statute of Anne (1709) and the series of legal decisions culminating in the judgment of *Donaldson v. Becket* (1774) shifted copyright from a right of the publisher to make physical copies to the right of the author over the text as "incorporeal property."[155] Henceforth, text—the labor and product of writing—was an alienable commodity like any other, a development that N. N. Feltes shows to have been integral to the nineteenth-century shift from the petty-commodity production of books as luxury goods to generalized commodity exchange, with the arrival of what he calls the "commodity-text."[156] Here, mass-produced books and mass bourgeois readership were constituted in "simultaneous and reciprocal" relation, with both, moreover, emerging as expressions of the social relations of capital, as it extended and intensified the production of surplus value through the publishing industry.[157] The outcome was of course neither inevitable nor unilinear; in Feltes's Althusserian conceptualization, the commodity-text is an overdetermined, differential network. As such, it invites consideration of the interplay between literary content and commodity form. Serial production was the dominant formal feature, as the nineteenth-century book moved from the luxury three-volume novel to book serials, periodicals, and part-issue novels—a development that maximized sales volume and integrated readers through the punctual consumption of discrete parts of a whole, building up effects of interpellation through the unfurling of the rich and varied detail of setting, character, and action that seriality allows.

Innovation on this front continues throughout the life-span of the book industry, as Miller, Squires, and Striphas have shown.[158] In the development of consumer credit, for instance, books pioneered debt-driven purchasing, where their esteemed cultural value eased consumers to overcome the negative moral connotations of debt. More recently, books have had a pronounced presence in just-in-time, warehouse-based online retail, for it was the rationalized capitalist structure of books and the book industry, exemplified by the sophisticated logistical mechanism of the International Standard Book Number (ISBN), that encouraged Jeff Bezos to found Amazon.com on the sale of books and not another commodity.[159] And in the realm of the e-book, the book industry is currently at the forefront of technical and legal developments in rent and control, where systems of digital rights management stymie the reproducibility of digital text by locking ownership to individual consumers and time-limited contracts.[160]

We should inquire further of the "people of the book," the book and its *class*. I have noted already the reciprocal relation between mass-produced books and bourgeois audiences in the emergence of the modern book commodity. Looking more closely at that class of readers, it is apparent that the culture of books and of reading has been intimately associated with and patterned by a complex of cultural values that designate and solicit class distinction and separation. George Steiner grasps well a number of the dimensions of this complex. After noting that the book, in its "classic phase," is a "privately owned object," he writes,

> A man sitting alone in his personal library reading is at once the product and begetter of a particular social and moral order. It is a *bourgeois* order founded on certain hierarchies of literacy, of purchasing power, of leisure, and of caste. . . . The classic act of reading . . . is the focus of a number of implicit power relations between the educated and the menial, between the leisured and the exhausted, between space and crowding, between silence and noise, between the sexes and the generations.[161]

As we have seen, it is often lamented today that digital and online media, and the distracted and fragmented forms of attention with which it is correlated, are eroding the autonomous practice of concentrated, deep reading and, as research on neural plasticity appears to indicate, the very cognitive capacity for such.[162] It is a development compounded by the loss of leisure time associated with the extension and intensification of work across the span of the waking day (including the extension of pseudo-work for those formerly designated as "unemployed," now subject through workfare and punitive welfare regimes to the discipline of work, if not quite its content). But Steiner's comments should remind us how much the norm of deep reading has always been a classed capacity and resource. That is not to deny the significance and value of practices and institutions that countered this condition—we should recall here the centrality of cultures of text to the political associations of the historical workers' movement, for example, and that reading was considered enough of a threat to the class power of the Southern slave regime that slaves who were caught teaching others how to spell were commonly hanged—but to register that the historical norm of book culture has a strong bourgeois hue and a considerable role in the maintenance of class distinction.[163] To extend this point with regard to the particular media form of the novel, James Thompson has shown how it facilitated the bourgeois construction-in-separation of the economic and domestic spheres and hence of the social as cleaved by gender.[164] The eighteenth-century novel encapsulates, imagines, and projects an apparently noneconomic sphere of the domestic, where totality is grasped, but only as marriage, and literary form, such as the perceived objectivity of "free indirect discourse," presents a picture of closure and authority. More generally, the novel enabled "a nascent, heterogeneous, and fragmentary middle class to envision itself as coherent, unitary, and stable before such coherence and stability came into being."[165]

This appreciation of the class and gendered distinctions of book culture invites consideration of its other stratifications, not least of which concerns the role of the medium of the book in colonialism. Relativizing our notion of the book, Walter Mignolo assesses its place in the history of colonial conquest in Latin America. Like Deleuze and Guattari, as I show in chapter 3, he considers the integration of religious authority with the book to have been less a particular manifestation of this media form than an *integral feature* of its historical emergence, the book as stand-in for God:

> One could surmise that "the idea of the book" may have entered into the system of representation of graphic semiotic interaction at the point when "writing" gained its autonomy from orality and the "book" replaced the "person" as a receptacle and a source of knowledge. It is quite comprehensible that when the word was detached from its oral source (the body), it became attached to the invisible body and to the silent voice of God, which cannot be heard but can be read in the Holy Book.[166]

Once established in this form, and no doubt derived from these features of autonomy and spiritual truth, the book was subsequently projected as a universal standard across time and space. Mignolo shows how, starting in the European Renaissance, books became entwined with an evolutionary model of thought that understood the codex to be an achieved form that had existed *in potentia* since the inception of writing and hence the standard against which other forms of writing and technologies of inscription should be assessed. A series of equivalences were drawn, whereby "true writing" is alphabetic writing, writing is indistinguishable from the idea of "the book," and this identified with the medieval and Renaissance codex. As with time, so with space: this is the model that accompanied the colonial and missionary encounter with non-Europeans, whose writing systems and signifying practices were viewed through the European lens to be inadequate "books" and thus to be burned as works of the devil and/or substituted with the material and ideological forms of the Western codex. As Mignolo insists, then, it is not in the *content* per se but rather in the *form* of the book that colonial power was manifest—albeit, as we will see in chapter 3, that this was a form that downplayed the significance of its material instantiation in favor of a fixation on the spiritual unity of its content.[167]

A more recent instance of the colonial impact of the form of the book is provided by its place in the deligitimization and destruction of the distributed textuality of Australian Aboriginal peoples. Like Mignolo, McKenzie invites us to appreciate the "nonbook" textual forms of non-European cultures, in this case where landscape is dotted with organic and geological features that are embedded in narrative structures and symbolic forms. Here the "real absurdity" lies not in treating rocks as textual forms but in the importation into such symbolic systems "of a single-minded obsession with book-forms."[168]

POST-DIGITAL PUBLISHING

A contemporary account of the many materialities of political publishing needs a way of handling the relationship between print and digital media; this is where *Anti-Book* finds its third broad domain of intervention. If colonialism provides an opportunity to relativize the normative standard of the book, digital networked media institute a more direct and pervasive decentering, suggesting, as Jay David Bolter puts it in *Writing Space,* that "like the specializations on outer branches of an evolutionary tree, the printed book is an extreme form of writing, not the norm."[169] In the early enthusiasm for digital media, Bolter and others foresaw that new network functionalities—notably, the branching and nonlinear structure of hypertext—might serve to realize the potential of avant-garde and experimental writing and publishing, to realize the "antibook," as he describes it, where "antibooks . . . disrupt our notion of how a book should look and behave before our eyes."[170] For Bolter, this realization would simultaneously remove the critical ground from predigital experimentation, as the (now digital) medium shifts from resistant object of critique to one of facilitation. Take Derrida's work of textual and graphic experimentation,

Glas (which reads Hegel in relation with autobiographical writing by Jean Genet), as Bolter describes it:

> In the printed *Glas* the network of relationships that normally remains hidden beneath the printed page has emerged and overwhelmed the orderly presentation we expect of a printed book. In the World Wide Web, on the other hand, the many relationships among textual elements simply float to the surface. An antibook like *Glas* would no longer be an antibook in an electronic edition, because it would work with rather than against the grain of its medium.[171]

It is of course true that digital and online media dramatically alter the field of writing and publishing, but, twenty-five years after *Writing Space,* it is apparent that our situation is less one of the realization and suppression of the anti-book in digital hypertext than one where the anti-book finds new conditions within which to gain far-reaching traction, to move beyond hitherto established confines. Contrary to the picture of a rhizomatic release of digital hypertext, core aspects of the object of the anti-book's critique have come to proliferate, innovate, and intensify at quite some pace. Established mechanisms of the author-function and the capitalist forms of publishing have a renewed vigor in contemporary textual media, and these are interlaced with born-digital instruments of capture and accumulation, not least of which, ironically, is the linking function of digital hypertext, as we have seen in the case of social media. Concurrently, the effect of digital media to decenter the printed book, loosening much textual media from the hold of the data management function, has freed up its other capacities, which serve as the terrain for a renewal of the critical sensibility of the anti-book, now less bound to specialist fields and potentially released across the broad terrain of writing and publishing. This terrain, then, is at once transformed by digital media and includes print media as an integral part.

It is this last point that I focus on here, for it is key to understanding how this book approaches the contemporary relation between print and digital media. To do so, I will push against another figure that Bolter employs to characterize the changed status of the book: "the late age of print."[172] It is an expression more recently taken up by Striphas to characterize the condition I have been describing where the preeminence of the book has waned, relative to the wealth and diversity of digital audiovisual and textual media ("it seems difficult to imagine books shouldering much world-historical responsibility any more"), at the same time as it has been transformed by digital technology and the broader changes in production and consumption associated with post-Fordism.[173] Striphas has a keen sense of the intermediation of communicative media, but the characterization of this condition as "the late age of print" is unhelpful. It conveys a strong impression that we are living through a period of epochal change from one media form to another, a "period of transition," as Striphas has it, the "passing" of the "Age of Print" for Hayles.[174] No doubt there is considerable truth in this naming of the contemporary as a particularly transformative period in the movement from paper to pixel; as I write, e-books, only a credible mass phenomenon since 2007, have overtaken print books in sales volume.[175] And yet such temporal framing does a disservice to the content of this body of research, for it channels the complexity of contemporary media forms into a linear narrative of change, and one that downplays the significance in the present of the medium that is deemed to be passing.

Anti-Book parts with this linear characterization of the passing of the printed book and proceeds instead on the understanding that *the digital future of the book has already arrived,* wherein print media has a fully contemporary place. We live in a time of "post-digital" publishing, as Alessandro Ludovico and Florian Cramer have characterized the situation, where digital technology has transformed all aspects of media such that, in Kim Cascone's words, its "revolutionary period . . . has surely passed."[176] The post-digital "describes the messy state of media, arts and design *after* their digitization (or at least the digitization of crucial aspects of the channels through which they are communicated)."[177] Not only have smart phones, tablet computers, e-books, e-mail, and social media become ubiquitous and thoroughly enmeshed with social life but online digital media have also colonized their prehistory, as *print itself has become digital,* paper publishing now traversed and articulated by the most advanced technologies, infrastructures, and compositional paradigms. Cramer offers an illuminating image, if a little tongue in cheek, to convey the character of this transformation: "Paper publishing has largely become a form of Digital Rights Management for delivering PDF files in a file sharing–resistant format (but also, a more stable form of long-term storage of digital content than electronic storage)."[178] To make the more general case, today's printed books are composed, manufactured, marketed, distributed, reviewed, and debated through media that are thoroughly digital in their structure. And so printed books are not the last vestiges of predigital publishing but are forms of "post-digital print," where the relationship between print and digital media is no longer characterized by linear succession but is one of *hybridization,* a complex and variegated set of publishing relations and forms, at once interlaced and specific. With this hybridization comes a loosening of the boundaries and authority of the book, which is now only one form among an interlaced and variable set of media forms, where publishing has come to infuse social life and is increasingly indistinct from writing and mediated communication more generally conceived. Murphie is right, then, to describe *mutability* rather than postprint as the essence of publishing today: "Publishing is now a generative, recursive network of events, with multiple forms of feedback into the ongoing mutation of forms of publishing themselves."[179]

One of the benefits that accrue from approaching the field of publishing in this way, rather than as a linear succession of mediums, is that it encourages attention to the potential contemporaneity of *any* medium, "old" and "new" alike. Such is apparent in a recent Banner Repeater pamphlet by Nina Power, *A Pamphlet about a Book about a Blog,* which discusses her experience of publishing a printed book, *One Dimensional Woman,* from writings that had first appeared on her blog, *Infinite Thought.* The title and published form of this work reverse the linear order of the "new," so serving to bring blog, book, and pamphlet into contemporaneous juxtaposition. Power's text has the same post-digital effect in considering the difference *and* interplay of these mediums while addressing the changes that digital media has introduced into writing and the difficulties and experimental possibilities that arise when writing migrates across them: "if making the transition from blogs to books was problematic, making it from Twitter will be even more interesting."[180]

Older media can in these ways, hence, be fully part of the present, but they can also have a structuring effect on the *future.* As Simon Worthington puts it, "there is already a lot of 'book' in the digital—the vector of incursion moving as much from print to digital as it does from the digital into our notionally stable, 'enshrined' cultural form of the book."[181] Certainly the book has been decentered from its dominant cultural position in the realm of textual media (though newspapers, job printing, documents, and so forth assured that it was never *quantitatively* dominant), and yet, as Derrida has it, in the new media environment, the "figures" of the book continue to impact the digital field. He makes a good deal of the inherently figural quality of the book, where a series of metonymies shift *biblion,* the Ancient Greek root of "book," meaning a *support* for writing (itself derived from *biblos,* the internal bark of the papyrus), toward *writing* in general, and only then to *book,* whose artifactual form was originally not the codex but the scroll. I have counseled already, following Mignolo, against seeing the book as a linear progression of forms of textual inscription; the modern codex *is* a distinct and particular entity, compared, say, to the scroll. But the history of the figures of the book suggests, all the same, that there is slippage and mutation in the physical forms that count as books. And so there is nothing fundamentally ersatz about an electronic reading device being called a "book." Electronic readers may well come to shrug off the book as a means of self-classification, but they may not, given all the features of books and book cultures with which they are interlaced; the book as unit of discourse, pagination, bodily habits of reading, page turning, bookmarking, the prescribed rhythm of reading, modes of legitimation, the author-function, proprietary regimes—all these are prolonged into the terrain of the e-book and digital publishing.

I do not mean to suggest that such interplay between print and digital media is an inherent good. In the face of the digital restructuring of textual media, Derrida seems to take comfort from the living on of the book (where "we can trust in the conservative, even fetishistic impulse" to "sanctify—sanctify once again—the book, the aura of culture or cult of the book"), whereas an anti-book orientation would be more critical, for which Johanna Drucker's research is instructive.[182] By contrast to Bolter's notion that digital hypertext is the *realization* of the aesthetic promise of experimental print, Drucker argues compellingly that the aesthetic potential of digital text has in fact been *hidebound* to the clichéd and reductive iconography of the book that abounds in culture, with "too much emphasis on formal replication of layout, graphic, and physical features and too little analysis of how those features affect the book's function."[183] It results in aesthetic forms and design applications that are often *less* complex and dynamic than the three-dimensional object of the codex, the branching structure of hypertext contrasting less than favorably to the "n-dimensional" reading of the printed page, as Jerome McGann has described the "multivariate" potential of the page for multiple, layered, and discontinuous meanings and semiotic interactions.[184] Drucker calls instead for a "diagrammatic writing" of new textual mediums and semantic effects that is truly responsive to the spatial and graphic potential of fungible electronic environments, a move that would break the conservative hold of book iconology on digital media while allowing books to continue their work of experimentation, apart and, no doubt, in interplay with digital diagrammatic writing.[185] Again, we see here the post-digital difference and interplay of mediums in their specificity, which Drucker embodies in her own practice as researcher and practitioner in both the digital realms of speculative computing and printed artists' books. Other compelling experiments in this post-digital terrain include work on "hybrid publishing" and the "unbound book" at centers like Leuphana University's Hybrid Publishing Lab, Amsterdam's Institute of Network Cultures, and Coventry University's Centre for Disruptive Media, where the unbound book, as Gary Hall describes it, develops "the book as something that is not fixed, stable and unified, with definite limits and clear material edges, but as liquid and living, open to being continually and collaboratively written, edited, annotated, critiqued, updated, shared, supplemented, revised, re-ordered, reiterated and reimagined."[186] I should mention also the astonishing resource of experimental post-digital publishing curated by Silvio Lorusso, the Post-Digital Publishing Archive.[187]

I take up some of these themes of hybrid and unbound publishing with regard to magazine form in chapter 5, but this book is more strongly informed by a different aspect of the post-digital. Here the post-digital signifies a critical distance to digital media and its commercially induced pull of the "new," what Lorusso calls "an obsessive quest for future models," where the space that experimentation and innovation is sought "frequently corresponds to the narrow ecosystem of the newest device or platform."[188] In this sense, with Cramer again, "the term 'post-digital' can be used to describe either a contemporary disenchantment with digital information systems and media gadgets, or a period in which our fascination with these systems and gadgets has become historical."[189] Regarding the presence of print in post-digital publishing, it is not, for example, a revival of mimeographed zines but "zines that become anti-blogs," even as zines are at the same time transformed by the ethical and organizational conventions of online and open source cultures.[190] This is a feature of the considerable interest in print publications that has accompanied the expansion of digital media, where the post-digital is characterized by an experimental focus on the materialities, aesthetics, and properties of printed media. There is a historical dimension to it, apparent in high-profile exhibitions in London, for example, on the dissident Surrealist journal *Documents* at the Hayward Gallery in 2006 (where the *journal* took center stage rather than the movement), Futurist and avant-garde books at the British Library in 2007–8, and bookworks at the Victoria and Albert Museum in 2008. This historical focus might have suggested a last gasp of interest in print publishing, its specific qualities becoming visible at the moment of its demise, had it not been accompanied by a burgeoning practitioner field of small-scale print publishing—in art and critical theory circles but also in more overtly political scenes. Examples of the latter include *STRIKE! Magazine* (2012–), which has the rare distinction of being the last paper newspaper in Fleet Street, London's traditional home of the print industry; *LIES: A Journal of Materialist Feminism,* a queer and antiracist project framed compellingly as "a communist journal against communists"; *Letters: An Anti-Political Communist Journal* (2007–), experimental in both content and form; *Chto Delat?* (2003–), newspaper of the Russian art and activism group of the same name; and *Tiempo Muerto* (2012–), an anarchist arts and letters newspaper from Mexico City. This realm of print publishing is also sustained by a wealth of small press and self-publishers' fairs and centers. To name a handful of these with which I am familiar, London's Publish and Be Damned, DIY Cultures, Small Publishers Fair, London Art Book Fair, the London Anarchist Bookfair, New York's NY Art Book Fair, and bookwork centers like Minnesota's Open Book; New

York's Printed Matter and Franklin Furnace; and London's bookartbook-shop, Book Works, London Centre for Book Arts, and Banner Repeater.[191]

In the post-digital manner that I have been describing, such contemporary print projects tend to be highly attentive to the particular aesthetics and social relations of printed matter, holding a critical and reflexive distance from digital and online media, while also utilizing digital capacities. For instance, while the Chto Delat? group publish online, they see the organizational, social, and sensory qualities and effects of the printed newspaper—a Russian and English bilingual publication in print runs of one thousand to nine thousand, distributed for free at exhibitions and political events—as a key dimension of their practice. Or take the small press AND Publishing (2009–), which focuses on the aesthetic and political capacities of the print technology of print on demand (a publishing process I discuss in chapter 5), whose digital capacities enable the publication of printed artists' books "without having to compromise and conform [to] the conventions of a mass market."[192] And a number of small press publishers employ open source business models where books are simultaneously available as purchasable hard copy and free downloadable e-pubs, as is the case with Open Humanities Press, Punctum Books, re.press, Minor Compositions, and Open Book Publishers.

No doubt there are reactionary elements at play in contemporary print scenes, of a future-canceling "retro" culture, and class dynamics also, what Jess Baines describes as a striving for social distinction through technical specialism and aesthetic rarity, as posited against the perceived plebian accessibility of digital and online media.[193] But my thesis is that burgeoning cultures of print also carry a post-digital sensibility, where paper, pixel, and critique of media form open out into a complex field of publishing potential unconstrained by the depoliticized fixation of the technological "new." Let me stress that in no sense do I aim to map this field, which is developing in numerous exciting directions that I have not addressed here. The contribution made by *Anti-Book* to the contemporary field of post-digital publishing is to introduce and extend specifically communist problematics as they pertain to the many materialities of text.

Anti-Book carries a post-digital sensibility, then, with explorations of paper and print publishing taking a dominant place in many of the chapters that follow. Some of these, notably the works I consider in chapter 3, come from a time before digital publishing. My point in approaching these with a post-digital eye is not to say that differences of media history and sociopolitical conjuncture are now collapsed by the post-digital condition, as if these works have been made wholly contemporary. Rather, their salience is as historical instances of experimental material text that indicate alternative trajectories through the largely text-bound history of political textual media. These trajectories in part become visible because of the perceptivities that are opened by digital media, which, as Derrida put it, might "liberate our reading for a retrospective exploration of the past resources of paper, for its *previously* multimedia vectors," but this is only insofar as they are also grasped by contemporary problems in the politics of material text.[194]

In the chapters that engage with digital media, I refrain from discussing the dominant social media platforms of Twitter, Facebook, and their ilk. It is not that I see no possibility here for the articulation of critical content or for political network effects, but their technical forms, subjective patterns, and business models have something of a black hole effect with regard to media alternatives, sucking too much textual production into their distributed core. And so I have chosen to look elsewhere for experimental media form, to small press and self-published writing projects. This is not to say that I subscribe to the common notion of media "independence" or "autonomy," as if a writing and publishing project could exist outside of capitalist relations (a point I develop in chapter 5). Rather, I am developing a view from the margins with the aim not of staying marginal, or marginal for the sake of it, but of unsettling the center, even if only marginally.

CONTENT

It remains for me to outline the content of the following chapters. Each chapter explores the politics of a particular media form, where these are sometimes media platforms—pamphlet, book, and magazine (chapters 2, 3, and 5)—and other times media forms of a more structural or literary nature, such as the author, or rather the author's undoing through anonymity (chapter 4), and mythopoesis (chapter 6). I count all of these as "media forms," as instances of "material text" (a field that of course includes many forms not encountered here, or only marginally so: poem, slogan, communiqué, newspaper, leaflet, letter, autobiography, blog). The focus of the book is European, with a few examples drawn from China, Russia, and the United States. Clearly the book makes no claim to universal coverage; at most it is a critical sampling of an open field.

Chapter 2 is an exploration of the media form of the self-published pamphlet. As with all the chapters, and in keeping with Hayles's call for "media-specific analysis," I seek to hold together two aims: to develop an understanding of the specificity of this media form and to approach this specificity as only ever situated—enmeshed in, emergent from, and expressive of specific social contexts and political problematics.[195] We find the specific media form of the pamphlet, then, only in the many, various, and open-ended specificities of its instantiation and problematization. This chapter approaches and contributes to this form-in-variation through a specific problematic that was introduced into art and material culture by the Russian Constructivists in the early years of the Soviet Revolution, a problematic that Christina Kiaer has called the "socialist object," where revolutionary politics was to entail the liberation not only of the human but also of the *object*—the object as "comrade," to employ Alexsandr Rodchenko's formulation.[196] Here, however, with the aid of Walter Benjamin's affirmation of the "useless" and anthropological work on fetishism, I draw the object away from the productivist orbit of Constructivism to develop a concept of the "communist object," a concept that I then bring into relation with three publishing and archiving projects: Unpopular Books, 56a Archive, and Infopool. Although I concentrate on the pamphlet as object, I do not leave the textual content of these projects entirely behind; rather, following Adorno, I seek to find points of "mimesis" between the pamphlet objects and their political orientations, paratextual elements, and, occasionally, specific arguments. Here my choice to refrain from close engagement with the specific textual content of the pamphlets is a deliberate product of the chapter's formulation of the communist object. In other chapters, readers may find themselves wanting more detailed discussion of the textual content of the works considered, for detailed engagement with content is sometimes a casualty of this book's aim to engage with the broader materialities of text which are more usually left aside and unnoticed. I hope you think it a price worth paying.

Chapter 3 explores the problematic of the political book, situated at the point where the book as a political medium intersects with books that are expressly political. I focus on the properties of four works: Mao Zedong's Little Red Book, Russian Futurist books, Antonin Artaud's paper "spells" or *gris-gris,* and Guy Debord and Asger Jorn's *Mémoires.* The analysis draws strongly on Deleuze and Guattari's typology of the form of the book, which grasps the intersection of signifying and subjective processes, sensory forms, expressive qualities, and politics. The field of modern books, as Deleuze and Guattari approach it, is inherently political, patterned by three competing structural forms or "abstract machines": the "root-book," the "fascicular root-book," and the "rhizome-book." Though their concepts of root and rhizome have become widely influential, very little research has sought to explore the specific relation of these concepts to the media form of the book, and even less has deployed them in empirical investigation of actual books, a deficit that this chapter seeks to address. The critique of Mao in this chapter contributes to what amounts to a minor theme of *Anti-Book.* While communism features in this book in the specific context of the politics of writing and publishing, I occasionally approach it more broadly, and in critical relation to that which has often gone by the name—in this instance, in relation to Mao and the Cultural Revolution, a politico-philosophical system and a historical sequence that has had not inconsiderable presence in contemporary efforts to revive a so-called communism for our times.

Chapter 4 shifts from a focus on media platforms to consider the literary forms of anonymous and pseudonymous collective authorship, approached as a political challenge to the author-function. The chapter begins with a critique of the author-function through Marx and Foucault and teases out their respective accounts of the politics of anonymity, where anonymity is not a case of dropping one's name but is a complex and situated production. I pursue this through a number of writing projects and problematics: the collective pseudonym of Luther Blissett and his novel of the Radical Reformation, *Q*; Bernadette Corporation's pseudonymous novel *Reena Spaulings,* through its interplay with Michèle Bernstein's *All the King's Horses,* her breezy fictionalization of life with her comrade and husband Guy Debord; and, taking a prompt from the radical journal *Tiqqun,* the theme of anonymity in Marx's formulation of the "party," where certain practices in communist writing and publishing are drawn out through consideration of the May 1968 journal *Comité,* within which Blanchot had a pivotal role, and the communization journal *Endnotes.*

Chapter 5 returns to consider a particular publishing platform, in this case the magazine. But here the focus is exclusively on a single publishing project, the London-based art and politics magazine *Mute.* What makes *Mute* such an enticing project for my purposes here, and justifies dedicating to it a full chapter, is the extent to which it established a critical and practical self-differing orientation at the heart of the magazine. In this chapter, I take as my entry point one of *Mute*'s more enigmatic strap lines, "Proud to Be Flesh," to develop a model of *Mute*'s publishing practice that I call "diagrammatic publishing." This model attends to the complex of publishing platforms, participatory mechanisms, aesthetic styles, editorial and commissioning paradigms, temporal modes, and commercial structures that compose the magazine, understood not as an integrated and centralized medium but as a distributed and open entity that is immanent to neoliberal social relations. *Mute* is not "autonomous," then, or "independent"—those oft trumpeted and rather tired designators of political publishing—but a publishing project that revels in its critical immersion in the technosocial flesh of the world, with all its complicities and contradictions.

Chapter 6 takes up the specific literary form of political myth as it is constructed in the writing practice of Wu Ming, collective author of five novels and a large body of political texts published in print and online mediums. Myth is a terribly compromised political phenomenon, one that political theorists and practitioners might reasonably avoid like the proverbial plague—all the more so if they are interested in communism, given the brutality associated with the political myths and personality cults of orthodoxy. I begin with this structure of the cult of personality in Mao and its interpretation by Badiou. If the Chinese and Soviet authorities invested in and propelled the cult of personality, it was always a touchy subject, given that Marx coined the expression to help *excise* this formation from the communist movement. I follow Marx's lead here, but that does not mean we should drop myth from the repertoire of political writing and publishing. This chapter shows how alternative models of communist myth might be developed, paying attention to a fragmented and decentered form of mythopoesis—the power of "the false," as Deleuze has it, the "story-telling function of the poor."[197] This chapter explores the particular textual and media procedures by which such myth is constructed, focusing especially on Wu Ming's epic fiction and their method of the "unidentified narrative object."

2

Communist Objects and Small Press Pamphlets

Our things in our hands must be equals, comrades.
—ALEKSANDR RODCHENKO, "Letter to
Varvara Stepanova, May 4 1925"

If the invention of the printing press inaugurated the bourgeois
era, the time is at hand for its repeal by the mimeograph, the
only fitting, the unobtrusive means of dissemination.
—THEODOR W. ADORNO, *Minima Moralia*

Print media has had an integral place in modern movements of art and politics, of which the "journal" or "revue" is perhaps the preeminent instance. *La Révolution surréaliste, Internationale situationniste,* and *Quaderni rossi,* to take three iconic examples of radical periodicals, are something like the mobile ground upon which Surrealism, the Situationists, and Italian Operaismo came into being through time—key sites and means by which these currents and movements honed their ideas and aesthetic styles, established group coherence, and gained purchase on the social imaginary. The point is aptly made by Guy Debord, and with a droll tone that strikes an appealing contrast to the hallowed respect that more usually accompanies talk of *Internationale situationniste*: "Even the fact of publishing a slightly 'regular' journal is very tiresome; and, at the same time, one of our only weapons to define and hold on to a base."[1]

In plain terms, then, journals are significant sites of political writing and publishing. And yet in their correlation between movement and medium, they reveal themselves to be just that little bit too obedient, "tiresome" even—ordered and contained by the requirements of a movement. In this respect journals tend more to the form of "media ecology," in Debray's terms discussed in chapter 1, than to the anti-book, because to warrant the latter designation would require a self-critical and disruptive relation with the organizations and audiences with which media are associated—an "inoperative" quality to their communism, to borrow from Jean-Luc Nancy—that is inimical to the consolidating tendencies of movement media.[2] Advocates for periodical publications will have numerous examples with which to challenge this assessment—indeed, in chapters 4 and 5, I consider some myself, and even this chapter turns to a journal at one point—but I make it as a helpful means of contrast to the media form that is the focus here: the "pamphlet."

Small press pamphlets tend to be much less correlated with social movements, allowing them a more indeterminate, exploratory, and critical character, in relation both to their sites of publication and circulation and to their sociomaterial forms and contexts more broadly conceived. Therefore, consideration of the medium of the pamphlet allows more atypical and anomalous instances and qualities of political media to come into view, even encouraging us to find the seeds of media communism in these atypical instances, over and against the more movement-oriented forms of political publishing.

A first elaboration of this point can be found in Jacques Rancière's early book *The Nights of Labor*. Here Rancière attends to the strange literary and aesthetic artifacts created by nineteenth-century worker-poets, -painters, and -writers as they struggled at night, in the precious moments between work, to breach their separation from intellectual practice and a life condemned to labor. Rancière at one point describes these artifacts, in a most evocative phrase, as "hieroglyphs of the anticommodity."[3] The use of the term *hieroglyph* here is anachronistic, certainly, but I will hold on to it for a little while, because Rancière's formulation moves us some considerable distance. In distinction from Marx's famous characterization of the "social hieroglyphic" of the commodity, which is surely a deliberate point of reference, Rancière does not employ the term principally to signal a strategy of demystification, where specialized interpretation of the object and its relations would reveal a truth obscured by its mysterious form. Rather, he seeks to put into service precisely the mysterious, indecipherable quality connoted by the popular usage of the word, to *champion* the anomalous and paradoxical expressive features of these works. The point is clear in his gloss on the words of one bemused observer of said works:

> Our "friend of the workers," Ledreuille, was on target: "woods that aren't there, letters you would not know how to read, pictures for which the models have never existed." They would be so many hieroglyphs of the anticommodity, products of a worker know-how that retains the creative and destructive dream of those proletarian children who seek to exorcise their inexorable future as useful workers.[4]

If this indecipherable quality is, in concrete terms, a product of the amateur hands and heads of workers unschooled in bourgeois aesthetics, it is the social relations that the works index—or, better, *refuse* to index—wherein lies their anti-commodity valence. These artifacts created at night by "a few dozen 'nonrepresentative' individuals" are not the typical, popular productions of the working class (should such things exist); quite the contrary, they *confound* class identity, in a way that is manifest not only against the immediate capitalist imperatives of work but also, more significantly, against the role assigned to these workers by the workers' movement, whose mobilizing images, organizational forms, hierarchies of value, and visions of the future served, however unwittingly, to confirm the capitalist subject of "man-the-producer."[5] In Rancière's cutting assessment—and we should recall here the critique of programmatism in chapter 1—the discourse of the workers' movement "never functioned so well as when it was doing so in the logic of others or for their profit."[6] I say confound rather than escape, for these hieroglyphs of the anti-commodity have no autonomous existence; they articulate flight from the "dictatorships . . . of king work" that, paradoxically, reveal the impossibility of such flight under the social conditions of capitalism.[7] The mysterious, hieroglyphic qualities of these works lie, then, in this impossibility—at most they exist as a "gap" in the distribution of the sensible, calling forth worlds that are wholly unrepresentable within the social and aesthetic regimes whence they arose.

Significantly for my argument in this chapter, Rancière's formulation also carries associations of physical materiality, of the media *object,* because the hieroglyph is in origin a sign carved into material, a "sacred carving" (from the Greek roots *hieros* and *glyphe*). Indeed, if we draw a little on a later book, *Mute Speech,* in which the hieroglyph is a recurring trope, it is clear that Rancière invests a great deal in the political potential of physical form (albeit that I would not want to substitute the class dimension of the anti-commodity in his earlier book with the false universals of "people" and "nations" as he does here).[8] More than words, bound as they are to the rules of signification within dominant discursive regimes, it is in the material forms of such anomalous aesthetic works that the anti-commodity finds its most adequate articulation. For here we have a "mute" expressivity that is elevated to the status of poetry, the "poeticity of the world," where the *medium* of signification becomes more decisive than the signification that it ostensibly carries: "mute-speaking works, works that speak as images, as stones, as matter that resists the signification whose vehicle it is."[9]

A poem, a painting, a piece of printed matter can, then, be an anti-commodity, or a paradoxical invocation of such, as it reveals the impasses of the social and discursive regimes of work and its identities. Moreover, this quality may be most apparent in the "mute" material form of such artifacts. It is a rare construction indeed. And yet this formulation of the anti-commodity remains somewhat undeveloped and difficult to grasp, especially in its material instantiation, its mute speech (no doubt, for Rancière, this is necessarily so, given its "hieroglyphic" resistance to meaning). While adhering to Rancière's feeling for the paradoxical quality of such entities, in this chapter I seek a more precise concept of the anti-commodity, what I call the "communist object." I form this concept out of three problematic fields: Russian Constructivist approaches to the object as "comrade" and the "intensive expressiveness" of matter; Walter Benjamin's analysis of the "collector," with particular attention to his critique of "use value"; and the confounding dynamics of the "fetish." After setting out the communist object, the chapter then mobilizes this concept in exploration of self-published or small press pamphlets, drawing on interviews I conducted with producers and an archivist of contemporary projects of nondoctrinal communist persuasion: Chris of South London's 56a Archive; Jakob Jakobsen, founder of Infopool; and Fabian Tompsett, publisher and printer of Unpopular Books.

THE OBJECT AS COMRADE

In formulating the concept of the communist object, one has to work against a dominant image of the place of things or objects in Marxism, that of communism as an ascetic order, hostile to or distrustful of objects. This image is associated with an at best simplified reading of Marx's diagnosis in *Capital* of the fetish nature of commodities, where, in a dichotomous relation between humans and objects, social relations between objects determine objectlike relations between people. Marxism in this image would seek to revalue people against the capitalist fixation on objects, in the process stripping objects of their seductive, diverting capacities and subjecting them to rational order and the plan. Bolshevik philosophy and official Soviet culture stand as the prime intellectual and empirical referents for this image of ascetic socialism. However, it is also in the midst of early Soviet art and culture, in the Constructivist movement, that an especially innovative formulation of communism and the object can be found, one that lays the groundwork for a concept of the communist object.

As Christina Kiaer has argued, the problematic of the object and its transformative relation with human thought and sensory experience had a pivotal place in Russian Constructivism, whose materialism she characterizes as having an "obsessive, even unseemly emphasis on . . . things themselves."[10] Indeed, writing home from the 1925 Paris International Exposition of Modern Industrial and Decorative Arts, Aleksandr Rodchenko quite astonishingly presents capitalism as the exploitation of the human *and* the object and projects their possible relation as one of equality, elevating the object to the status of *comrade*: "The light from the East is not only the liberation of workers, . . . the light from the East is in the new relation to the person, to woman, to things. Our things in our hands must be equals, comrades, and not these black and mournful slaves, as they are here."[11]

This "socialist object," as Kiaer names the Constructivist problematic, is an unstable entity emergent from numerous themes and contexts: the extension of art into industrial production toward the transformation of everyday life (the "expedient," utilitarian object) with all the associated issues concerning the place of the artist in industry; an achieved socialist revolution that projected beyond property ("not . . . the elimination of material objects, but . . . the elimination of a possessive relation to them"); and the persistence of the commodity form (under the New Economic Policy's reintroduction of private capital and the global context of the endurance of capitalist commodity culture).[12] One of the many strengths of Kiaer's argument is that she understands the Constructivist object to be operative not in pristine autonomy but in the midst of the affective field of the commodity, where desiring relations to objects in capitalism are less to be negated than explored, teased out, deployed, and transcended in socialist material culture. All this leaves Constructivism as a highly complex and precarious project traversed by many points of tension, but the importance for my argument is the way the object features here as a sensuous entity in material equality with the human, the object as comrade. These features of the Constructivist object are at the forefront of Boris Arvatov's highly original essay "Everyday Life and the Culture of the Thing" (1925), a text that warrants extended discussion.

Against idealist tendencies in Marxist philosophies of culture that foreground social consciousness at the expense of the material everyday, Arvatov places the "universal system of Things"—the field of "production and consumption of material values"—firmly at the center of social life.[13] This is of considerable historical significance, taking aim as it does at Trotsky's position in *Literature and Revolution,* but for the reader of Marx today, it is hardly contentious. Where Arvatov is still truly striking is in his communist alternative, the possibility of a proletarian material culture "imbued with the deepest sense of Things," even of the "becoming . . . thinglike" of communist politics.[14] Let us follow his argument, first through his critique of the commodity form, then into his vertiginous politics of the object.

COMMODITY FETISHISM: THE A-MATERIAL FORM OF THE OBJECT

Arvatov makes his move initially from the perspective of consumption. As he sees it, the structure of consumption in capitalist culture as a private, individual arena separated from machine-rich collective production creates an object that is experienced as severed from its genesis, its manifold material relations, and that is as a result constituted as an isolated, "finished," and repeatable unit of private property.[15] In this manifestation, style and form become "clichéd," subject to "imitative conservatism" in a world where the potentially dynamic object is reduced to a token in the affectations of bourgeois individualism.[16] This has effects too on the object's sensory form. A property relation to the object, for all its affective power in the composition of bourgeois identity, is a reduction of the human sensorium. As Marx puts it, "*all* the physical and intellectual senses have been replaced by the simple estrangement of *all* these senses—the sense of *having*."[17] For Arvatov, then, the object consumed as a commodity is a dead and solitary object:

> The Thing as an a-material category, as a category of pure consumption, the Thing outside its creative genesis, outside its material dynamics, outside its social process of production, the Thing as something completed, fixed, static, and, consequently, dead—this is what characterizes bourgeois material culture.[18]

This "a-material" manifestation of the object in consumption is a structural complement to its mode of existence in production, where exchange value, not utility or material quality, is the object's determining aspect. It is a point best pursued through Marx directly. In a dozen or so dazzling pages of *Capital,* Marx famously argues that the capitalist commodity has a strange kind of agency, a mystical power that appears to emanate, fetishlike, from the object itself, as if "endowed with a life of [its] own."[19] Marx is explicit, however, that this mystical agency is not a product of the material qualities of the object—it has "absolutely no connection with the physical nature of the commodity and the material [*dinglich*] relations arising out of this"—but of its specific existence in capitalism, its *commodity form.*[20]

The explanation lies in the structure of labor. To précis Marx's account of commodity fetishism, the source of value in capitalism is social or "abstract" labor, the uniform quality of labor in general that arises in the production and circulation of commodities. Abstract labor is a product of the myriad different instances of "concrete labor" undertaken by the multiplicity of producers. However, abstract labor is not manifest in the labor process itself, where concrete labor is undertaken in relative isolation, but in the circulation of commodities after they have been produced. For it is only through the manifold practices of exchange that the uniform quality of labor in general (abstract labor) can emerge from all the different kinds of private, concrete labor. Since this occurs in the sphere of commodity circulation, apart from and outside the sphere of their production, the social character of capitalist *labor* appears to be a property of *commodities*—whence comes their fetish quality, as value appears to emanate from the commodities themselves, with their circulation in a very real sense determining the form of their production, that is, the concrete labor so expended.

Much more can be said about commodity fetishism, but to stay focused on the aims of this chapter, there are two points to underscore. First, the concept of commodity fetishism does not posit that capitalist cultures are overly enamored with objects, as it is commonly understood. Marx's principal point, rather, is that the production and circulation of commodities *structure the form of labor*—or, better, constitute social activity *as* labor—isolating people qua producers from a fully social relation with each other *and* with objects. Workers' experience becomes one of "pure subjectivity," as the communist journal *Endnotes* describes Marx's position, "all objectivity existing against [them] in the form of capital."[21] To be clear, this is not somehow the fault of the object; the perverse aspect of the commodity form, the fetishlike inversion, is that it is the very characteristics of social labor that perform and entrench workers' a-social subjection. Second, insofar as commodity fetishism does also describe a broader condition of social veneration of commodities, it is quite the opposite of the common understanding. Commodity fetishism is veneration not of the commodity *object* but of *private property,* whose value lies not in its material specificity but in its universal exchangeability; put otherwise, commodity fetishism is the social veneration of value as an end in itself, of self-expanding value. Thus, in commodity fetishism, the object is *emptied* of materiality; commodity fetishism is a fixation on the *a-material.* The point is well made by Peter Stallybrass: "To fetishize commodities is, in one of Marx's least understood jokes, to inverse the whole history of fetishism. For it is to fetishize the invisible, the immaterial, the supra-sensible. The fetishism of the commodity inscribes *im*materiality as the defining feature of capitalism."[22]

THE INTENSIVE EXPRESSIVENESS OF MATTER

From Arvatov and Marx we have learned that the realms of consumption and production entail the production of both object *and* subject, which are sundered from each other as such. By contrast, Arvatov's communist material culture is oriented toward an elimination of the "rupture between Things and people" at the level of their dynamic interaction, where the object has an agential power—it is retrieved from "immobility," "inactivity," and the "absence . . . of any element of instrumentality"—in the practical, psychological, and sensual reconfiguration of the human.[23] Devoid of the constraining "*egoistic* nature" of the property relation, as Marx has it, here inorganic nature "has lost its mere *utility*" in a world of "*social* organs" in mutual and transformative exchange with "*social* object[s]."[24] And so, by contrast to the foreclosed sensorial scope of the commodity object, communism, in Marx's ecstatic expression, is "the complete *emancipation* of all human senses and attributes" as humanity comes to "suffer" the object: "To be *sensuous,* i.e. to be real, is to be an object of sense, a *sensuous* object, and thus to have sensuous objects outside oneself, object's of one's sense perception. To be sensuous is to *suffer* (to be subjected to the actions of another)."[25]

The question remains as to how to advance such a communism— of where it may come, how it might be glimpsed. For Arvatov, it is the movement away from individual property in the *sharing of complex technical objects* that enables this opening of the isolated and clichéd commodity to a social collectivity of objects and sensations, of which he attends to two aspects. First, the material qualities of things come to the fore, something the human acts upon as form cedes to function:

> Glass, steel, concrete, artificial materials and so on were no longer covered over with a "decorative" casing, but spoke for themselves. . . . The thing was dynamized. Collapsible furniture, moving sidewalks, revolving doors, escalators, automat restaurants, reversible outfits, and so on

constituted a new stage in the evolution of material culture. The Thing
became something functional and active, connected like a co-worker
with human practice.[26]

I will return to the utilitarian theme in this passage shortly; for the moment, let me underscore the strong presence here of a culture of materials, what Arvatov elsewhere describes as an engagement with matter at
an "elemental" level, at its "intensive expressiveness."[27] To push that
formulation a little further, materials here overtake the artist or producer,
who comes to interpret and respond to the forces and qualities of matter;
Tatlin, for instance, is described by Maria Gough as having sought to
"foster the volition of the material," displacing his role as creative subject
and "reconfiguring himself as the material's assistant."[28] This approach is
enhanced by a second aspect, Arvatov's concern with the "natural" life
of things, their expression of the "powerful and indefinitely expanding
energies of the material sphere."[29] While Arvatov looks to the institutional
research and production cultures of the American technical intelligentsia
for tendencies to communist material culture, the technical object here
still remains "self-sufficient" and "retired within itself" to the extent that
in capitalist culture it is severed from its relation to nature. As such, the
"dynamic-laboring structure" of the object "and its living force are never
simultaneously present; thus both become 'soulless.'"[30]

Yet for all Arvatov's appreciation of the "intensive expressiveness" of
matter, it vies with a dominant imperative in his work, and Constructivism more widely, toward the utilitarian or "expedient" object. The proper
environment of the Constructivist object in mass production and its part in
the transformation of everyday life through the rational reorganization of
Soviet society is the profound promise of Constructivism, but also its most
troubling feature. For having foregrounded the expressive and disruptive
forces of matter, now even the most abstract and experimental material
values—the "qualities of pure color, line," for instance—become subject to
the plan and the imperatives of social utility against any "unorganized ar-
bitrariness."[31] There is a logical basis for this apparent contradiction. Constructivism, in keeping with Leninist orthodoxy, conceived of the transformation of capitalist industry to socialism as a process of collectivization,

the transfer of ownership of the forces of production from the capitalist class to the State. Industrial production so transferred was the condition for the socialist object to flourish. But this approach fails to appreciate the immanence of capitalist structures and imperatives to the production process itself; socialist factories are still factories. And so the socialist object reaches its limit, being too comfortable in a social regime that leaves the capitalist relations of production—the domination of the worker by the technical machine, the social affirmation of the subject of work, and the separation of production from consumption—largely untroubled.[32]

OBJECTS AGAINST USE

What, then, might be a communist object, a material comrade, that is not traversed by the imperatives of utility and production? Benjamin's speculations on the socioaesthetic phenomena of collecting and collections help answer this question. It is a testament to Benjamin's great originality that he discerns that to undo the commodity it is not enough to ward off exchange value; if an object's intensive expressiveness is to come forth, then its *use* must also remain in suspension. I will explain how.

Faced with the situation of commodity fetishism outlined earlier, it is not uncommon for critics (Marxists included) to reach for "use value" as the reassuring ground for a politics of the object—use value grasped as an extracapitalist and needs-based relation to the object that is only secondarily caught up in commodity relations and from which it can hence be disinterred. But this is a position that Marx refutes. I have already quoted Marx on the sensory movement of communism beyond "mere *utility*." We can now develop this point. As he writes in a passage that has considerable impact on Benjamin's theory of collecting, our estranged relations to objects are a product and experience not only of "property" and "capital" but of "*use*" also: "Private property has made us so stupid and one-sided that an object is only *ours* when we have it, when it exists for us as capital or when we directly possess, eat, drink, wear, inhabit it, etc., in short, when we *use* it."[33]

Use, in this formulation, is what patterns and regularizes the object for iteration in the commodity mode. It is not an exteriority to exchange value but the foreclosed metabolic and sensory experience of the object formed within and functional to the atomized, everyday life of capitalism, where the uses of objects are a "*means of life*; and the life they serve is the *life* of *private property*, labour and capitalization."[34] This is implicit in the Constructivist critique of the reduced sensorial scope of bourgeois things, but for Benjamin the communist alternative must be no less removed from utility. As he puts it, the proper materialist approach to the object "entails *the liberation of things from the drudgery of being useful*," a thesis that Adorno considered to be Benjamin's "brilliant turning-point in the dialectical redemption of the commodity."[35]

It is to this end that Benjamin makes his move into the politics of collecting, for him a mode of experiment in the "Sisyphean task of divesting things of their commodity character" (Sisyphean because uselessness is a momentary breach in capitalist relations rather than an achieved escape).[36] In a fashion that is initially not so different from Arvatov, Benjamin's collector has a "tactile instinct," an immersive relation to the object that complements the optical sense with touch, handling, smell, contemplation, love, and imagination, where the object is experienced as an affective "strike" on the sensorium, a destabilizing sensory event.[37] Marx's point about "suffering" the object becomes clearer. As Esther Leslie argues, this is "an intensified perception, bound up with shock, impact and curiosity," one that at the level of everyday material culture complements the enhanced technological perception Benjamin famously detects in photography and cinema: "everything—even the seemingly most neutral—comes to strike us."[38] But in contrast to Arvatov, the functional, useful properties of objects do not elicit this experience, they *get in its way* and hence need to be evaded or excised. Collectors, these "physiognomists of the world of objects," appear to value everything *but* the object's usefulness, for collecting is

> a relationship to objects which does not emphasize their functional, utilitarian value—that is, their usefulness—but studies and loves them as the scene, the stage, of their fate. . . . The period, the region, the craftsmanship, the former ownership—for a true collector the whole background of an item adds up to a magic encyclopedia whose quintessence is the fate of his object.[39]

This formulation of the object requires, hence, an environment that suspends use, if only momentarily. Against the social relations of work within which the useful socialist object fits comfortably—that is, Arvatov's object qua "co-worker"—the collected object is a co-*zero*-worker. Its environment is not an advanced plane of industrial production but a resolutely nonproductive, unstable, and momentary arrangement of pure consumption, a "collection."[40] The object is not here produced but encountered. And it is encountered as a fragment or, to use Leibniz's term that I develop later on, a "monad," a selection of the world that is simultaneously a world unto itself. In the "circumscribed area" of a collection, objects are "extracted" from their determining social relations of use and exchange, so allowing the collector to encounter the *shock* of their undetermined material specificity, as a sensorial field is opened that overtakes the collector: "for a . . . real collector . . . ownership is the most intimate relationship that one can have to objects. Not that [objects] come alive in him; *it is he who lives in them.*"[41] As Cesare Casarino remarks, this most intimate relation is thus also the "most extimate."[42] It is an intimacy that *opens out* and *unsettles* the subject of consumption, against the usual logic of possession whereby objects come alive in the consumer, reflecting back the image of the successful buyer who "bestows life on inert matter through the demiurgic power of money, and whose love of objects, therefore, can only be a narcissistic gesture of self-congratulation."[43]

Given the common image of collecting as a somewhat fusty practice, it is perhaps difficult to appreciate the collection as a *dynamic* mode of association, until one recognizes that, for Benjamin, it is a "balancing act of extreme precariousness" and psychological intensity, created of chance encounters, protracted searches, intensive strategies of acquisition, and, as the fictional and factual cases explored by N. A. Basbanes attest, even criminal activity.[44] A collection is a permeable contour, maintained at the edge of disorder. And the tactile appreciation of the object here contains a destructive aspect that aligns the collector with the noncontinuous mode of historical perception Benjamin conjures in "Theses on the Philosophy of History," as the intensive constellations of the collected object, in their little way, "blast open the continuum of history," the reified linear progression of "empty time" produced by the rhythm of commodity production.[45] There is a development here too of Arvatov's concern with the destabilizing forces of nature, for in the appreciation of the singular "fate" of the object—its orbits, its streams of past and future—the collector is attuned to the dissipative properties of matter. The collector's mode of relation thus opens to the many and singular durations of things, so displaying an "anarchistic, destructive" passion, a "wilfully subversive protest against the typical, classifiable."[46]

It is a little disconcerting that Benjamin makes acquisition and ownership constituent features of the collected object, given Marx's critique of property as the a-material experience of the object; even more so that he posits private collections against public collections, where, in the latter, the "phenomenon of collecting loses its meaning as it loses its personal owner" and "objects get their due only" in the former.[47] But the point about the collector, her passion at once "domesticated" and "dangerous," is that property is the starting point for its undoing.[48] Benjamin is seeking a mode of relation to objects that is situated in the everyday field of commodity consumption, while seeking to undo its structures of use and value and the identity forms these impart and confirm. (In any case, while the public collection may superficially appear to be "less objectionable," in Benjamin's words, he sees it as complicit with capitalist property, with its correlated bourgeois myth of the generic public and its practice of wresting objects from their contexts "to create the illusion of universal knowledge," as Douglas Crimp presents it, "displaying the products of particular histories in a reified historical continuum.")[49] As to the obvious objection that collecting has an intimate association with class distinction and speculation, Benjamin retorts that the "passion" of the true collector is sparked not principally by objects of commercial value but by the anomalous, kitsch, popular, mysterious, and discarded items of mass production. It is a practice within reach of all.

FETISHISM OF THE ANTI-COMMODITY

The qualities of the communist object discussed thus far can be brought into greater focus through a little comparison with the Surrealist *objet trouvé,* or "found object," perhaps the most influential formulation of the object as a politico-aesthetic entity. Benjamin places great stress on the revolutionary transformation of things—"enslaved and enslaving objects"—in Surrealism, a movement that "bring[s] the immense forces of 'atmosphere' concealed in . . . things to the point of explosion."[50] These are objects that slip out of and rise up against the circuits of commodity exchange; indeed, André Breton characterizes such objects of "prolonged sensual contact" in precisely our terms as "useless."[51] Yet Breton's found object is ordered by chains of psychosexual association that impose a second-order use upon that which had initially escaped the determining relations of utility. This is no more apparent than in his account in *Mad Love* of flea market finds with Alberto Giacometti, where the narrative moves from an initial flux of undetermined objects—"between the lassitude of some and the desire of others," as Breton describes the object constituted in a field of chance encounter—to the imposition of a most determined psychoanalytic pattern of meaning, as the secret of the wooden spoon that attracts Breton's attention is found, in that tired refrain, to be "a symbolic figuration of the male sexual apparatus."[52]

When pushed, the Surrealist formulation of the found object may reveal further compromised patterns of association. In bracketing off the avant-garde pedigree of the Surrealist approach to objects and mapping instead its emergence in relation to its wider social milieu, Romy Golan detects a strong correspondence between the structure of the Surrealist object and the colonial fantasies, art markets, and commodity tastes of 1930s France.[53] This adds a socioeconomic dimension to Deleuze and Guattari's polemical assertion that "Surrealism was a vast enterprise of oedipalization."[54] But that points away from our concept of the communist object, which I will continue to develop by drawing now from the margins of Parisian Surrealism.

Georges Bataille's dissident Surrealist journal *Documents* (1929–30) indicates a more fruitful resonance with Benjamin's collected object, through the tropes of the "document" and the "fetish." The journal's title announces its obsessions, its pages filled with what it understood to be "documents"—such things as Hollywood film stills, images of abattoirs, prayer scrolls, coins, flies, flowers, and works by Giacometti, Pablo Picasso, André Masson, and the latter's young daughter Lili. This list indicates the ethnographic leveling at work in the trope of the document, breaching divisions between artifact and art, while heightening appreciation of the heterogeneity and material specificity of each documented entity. As Denis Hollier describes it, the document signifies less a *sur*-real experience than a realist "condemnation of the imagination": in its alien heterogeneity, the document presents a material and antimetaphorical "shock-value."[55] This formulation recalls my discussion of the destabilizing shock of the object in Marx and Benjamin. But to this Hollier adds an additional aspect, irreverently presenting these qualities through the category of the *fetish*, a point he seeks to convey with this quotation of Bataille, from an essay in *Documents* 8: "I challenge . . . any art lover to love a canvas as much as a fetishist loves a shoe."[56]

If one keeps in mind that the fetishism being developed here is not the psychosexual kind (despite the choice of Bataille's Freudian example), then Hollier's formulation is most helpful. I touched on this earlier, with Stallybrass's astute observation that commodity fetishism is an inversion of the history of fetishism, in that it is a fetishism not of objects but of suprasensible value. Now we can go further, beyond Marx's playful inversion, and claim the fetish for communism, the communist object as *anti*-commodity fetish. As Peter Pels elucidates in his reckoning with "the spirit of matter" (working with William Pietz's exemplary three-part work on fetishism in the journal *Res*), a fetish is a destabilizing object, an anomalous singularity whose "lack of everyday use and exchange values makes its materiality stand out" and "threatens to overpower its subject."[57] In this sense, the notion of the fetish is proximate in structure and effect to Benjamin's collected artifact. But there is an aspect of the fetish that sheds light on a feature of the communist object that is less overt in Benjamin, its persistent interaction with the commodity form. As Pietz shows, the fetish, as both object and idea, is a "cross-cultural" entity, one "arisen in the encounter of radically heterogeneous social systems" and having no proper existence in a prior discrete society.[58] The concept originated in the efforts of seventeenth-century Dutch merchants to account for what they perceived to be the irrational attribution of value in West Africa to arbitrary objects; what was valued was not the universally exchangeable object of money but any "'trifle' that 'took' an African's 'fancy.'"[59]

The fetish only existed, then, in the encounter of noncapitalist and capitalist value systems. And if we can deploy it today—giving a positive valence to this category born of mercantile plunder and misrepresentation, and no longer using it to name a relation in need of demystification—then it is this feature that lends itself especially well to thinking the communist object. Characterizing the communist object as a fetish helps hold together, as necessary complements, both its excessive materiality *and* its disruptive interaction with the commodity form. It is a compound apparent in this description from Pels:

> The fetish is an object that has the quality to singularize itself and disrupt the circulation and commensurability of a system of values.... Its singularity is not the result of sentimental, historical or otherwise personalized value: The fetish presents a *generic* singularity, a unique or anomalous quality that sets it apart from *both* the everyday use and exchange *and* the individualization or personalization of objects.[60]

With the fetish, we have come full circle: from the commodity fetishism that is challenged and unmasked as the atomizing subjection to a-material value to a fetishism of unbound and disruptive materiality that operates *against* the commodity, troubling its values of exchange and use and their structures of production, consumption, and subjectivity. At risk of being overly schematic, this invites a statement of the principal lineaments of the concept of the communist object drawn from the discussion so far. As "comrade," the communist object exists on a plane of equality with the human, so amplifying the sensory exchange between organic and inorganic matter and unsettling the affective organization of the capitalist subject. It is an object of neither utility nor commercial exchange— closed and dead as these commodity values are—but one open toward undetermined circulation and destruction. This is a circulation that is not found in laboring practice and market exchange but in fleeting and permeable arrangements or "collections" that call forth the object's singularity, its intensive expressiveness. Yet the communist object is not a rarefied other to the commodity; the passional and destabilizing bond it produces emerges in the midst of the everyday objects and desires of commodity culture. And here it has something of a fetish character;

it is not a discrete or fully achieved entity but an excessive materiality that emerges only in its disruptive intersection with commodity values. This is an abstract presentation of the concept of the communist object, but the intensive expressiveness of matter that it champions necessitates that it be approached as always already enmeshed with, and shaped by, the singular properties of particular objects. While displaying these generic features, the communist object is existent, then, only in its manifold concrete expressions. It is one of these, the small press pamphlet, to which I turn shortly.

PRINTED MATTER

Before considering the pamphlet, I want to address the broader question of how the concept of the communist object might assay the particular features of *printed* matter, where objects combine with text. The book and its margins may seem an all too obvious place to find communist objects, given the relatively free rein that textual media has given to the expression of communist ideas. But that would be to focus on textual media only in terms of its content, not its artifactual forms and broader sociomaterial relations. Editions of Marx's *Capital,* for instance, are not wholly, or even principally, communist objects; as Conrad Bakker has explored in his hand-carved and -painted mail-order replicas of *Capital,* a dominant modality of Marx's book is the *commodity* (Plate 2).[61] Bakker's replica draws attention to the social relations of labor, industry, marketing, and desire of the book qua commodity, and does so all the more effectively for barring access to the means, the book's textual content, by which such observations can be interrogated and unfurled. Such interrogation seems to need estranging interventions like this to overcome the strong tendency in the economies and cultures of books and publishing to obscure the capitalist forms of printed matter, a point I made in chapter 1. Granted, this obscured condition has an ironic benefit in the impetus it gives books as sites of projection beyond capital, as, in the realms of imagination, it loosens their tethering to the determining parameters of the commodity form: "By the specific ways in which they participate in and shape the world of goods, books allow us to believe that there is an escape from or an alternative to that world."[62] Nevertheless, what Trish Travis describes as this "transcendent identity" rather discourages a politics of the rich materiality of printed media, and it is this that I pursue here.

The media form of the book can have a strong affective allure that recalls the unsettling powers of the collected object; for some, "the archetype of the book is so powerful that it has a way of reaching out and grabbing you and taking you into a dimension of itself."[63] Benjamin would surely not disagree with the tenor of this statement, because much of his formulation of the destabilizing powers of the collection arises from reflection on his own practice of book collecting, where the collection takes the specific bibliographic form of the *library*. And yet, if he had some attraction to the "archetype" of the book, some kind of generic book form, what really grabbed him were the *individual copies* of books, books in their material particularity. Moreover, Benjamin's texts display a specific attraction to forms of textual media that exist at the limits or outside of the book form proper. In "Unpacking My Library," an essay that explores the collection's dialectical interplay between order and disorder in discussion of book collecting, Benjamin draws attention to the "fringe areas" of libraries, "booklike creations" that "strictly speaking do not belong in a book case at all."[64] These "prismatic fringes"—he lists stick-in albums, autograph books, leaflets, prospectuses, handwritten facsimiles, typewritten copies of unobtainable books, religious tracts, and pamphlets—appear to articulate in their anomalous and fragile forms the generative chaos that is the true dynamic of a collection. One might say that in not having a proper place in a library, they mark its *essence,* the library qua collection. And in *One Way Street,* he goes further, positing such fringe areas *against* the book, with its "universal" form, this time conjoining the fragmentary material quality of such media with the situated vitality of interventionist writing: "Significant literary work can only come into being in a strict alternation between action and writing; it must nurture the inconspicuous forms that better fit its influence in active communities than does the pretentious, universal gesture of the book—in leaflets, brochures, articles, and placards."[65]

Benjamin's library has moved us from the material politics of collecting to our specific object of discussion, the "prismatic fringe" of the pamphlet. But we still need to consider the place of signifying *content* in the materiality of print media. After all, books are objects with the capacity to be highly expressive through their content. Indeed, given the soaring achievements of text, it may well appear a perverse or tasteless move to seek the expressivity of books anywhere else, to concentrate on books as objects. Such an assessment is memorably dramatized in Mike Leigh's television play *Abigail's Party* (1977), when the petty bourgeois man of the house talks animatedly about the physical form of his volumes of Shakespeare, their bindings, gold emboss, only to remark—it is the comic effect that illustrates my point—that these are not items one can actually *read*. But the joke should be soured when the subject to which it appeals comes into clearer focus. For disdain toward those who would treat books as objects has been a central constitutive feature of the bourgeois subject constructed in the institution of literature and the culture of books. It is a culture entwined with the entrenched hierarchy of the senses that descends, as Agnes Blaha describes, from vision and hearing to touch and taste, with the European "eye man" at the top and the African "skin man" at the bottom, to take an example of this dismal tradition from the nineteenth-century naturalist and biologist Lorenz Oken.[66] Hence, as Leah Price has shown, in the content and cultures of the Victorian novel, and tied to the threat that the spread of literacy presented to class distinction, it was poor illiterates, effete gentry, women, and racialized others who were commonly portrayed as taking the wrong pole of a book–text dichotomy. These groups at the margins of the bourgeois public sphere, or upon whose exclusion it was structurally constituted, were deemed to value the material of the book, while lofty abstraction in the aesthetic work characterized the pole of value and its true subject: "the proper relation between a man of sense and his books," as the Fourth Earl of Chesterfield had it, speaking for his class, is "due attention to the inside of books, and due contempt for the outside."[67]

It is cheering, then, and in keeping with our focus here, that Benjamin's critical appreciation for the value of books comes through a critique of their socially valorized use as repositories of text: the "inveterate collector of books," he writes, proves himself by his "failure to read these books."[68] That orientation plays a part in what follows, in accord with Rancière's

feeling that the medium of signification may sometimes be more politically decisive than the content it carries, and perhaps this precisely in its
resistance to signification. And yet textual content *is* part of the material
form of the book, and so we need also to have a way of working with it in
a manner that is conducive to thinking the materiality of textual media.
Here Adorno's late essay "Bibliographic Musings" is illuminating, a work
considerably influenced by Benjamin's approach to books and collecting. I
will spend some time with it, because it is a singular philosophical excursus
on the content–form relation, a relation that is central to *Anti-Book* and
returns in various different ways throughout.

There are limits to Adorno's essay. It is too much a lament to a lost
archetype of the book unsullied by commerce; as I argued in chapter 1 and
will return to in chapter 3, there was never an Eden of the book before a
fall into the clutches of the commodity, the condition where, according
to Adorno, alternate formats, images, and loud colors (God forbid) force
us to "acknowledge that books are ashamed of still being books and not
cartoons or neon-lighted display windows."[69] And here Adorno holds
out little hope for the "fringe areas" that attract Benjamin's eye; those
who would seize on a new form, such as "the leaflet or the manifesto," to
express the true nature of the book in new times are "only acting as secret
worshipers of power, parading their own impotence."[70] Nonetheless, if we
can bypass Adorno's faith in the archetype of the book and hold on a little
more before considering the fringe area of the pamphlet, the essay offers
an enticing construction of the place of content in the book's materiality.

Adorno's case for printed matter is made through critique of the commodity book. As a commodity, the book "sidles up to the reader," existing
not "in itself" in expressive autonomy but "for something other," a generic
unit of exchange "ready to serve the customer."[71] Along with the general
design features noted earlier, Adorno presents a particular example, a trend
to omit the paratextual detail of place and date of publication from books'
title pages, so taking away "the *principium individuationis* of books . . . along
with time and space," as they become "mere exemplars of a species,
already as interchangeable as best-sellers," "drug[s] on the market."[72]
This has impact on content, for intellectual engagement, which requires
"detachment, concentration, continuity," is undone by the commodity

transformation of books "into momentary presentations of stimuli" (as ever, our contemporary fears surrounding the decay of reading echo those of earlier times).[73] But it is Adorno's work on the possibility of *opposition* to the seductive drug of the book commodity that is salient to this chapter.

Adorno locates the politics of books in their capacities to *resist* their owners, authors, and readers. He is well known for advocating the political value of difficult writing. As thought and language are invaded by capital—by clichéd patterns of meaning, by managed public opinion, by "the liberal fiction of . . . universal communicability"—writers must create a "vacuum" in language, the "suspension of all received opinions," if writing is to have any political effect. In this austere defense of modernism, those who would challenge "the word coined by commerce . . . must recognize the advocates of communicability as traitors to what they communicate."[74] But in "Bibliographical Musings," Adorno takes a different route, attending to the disruptive capacities not only of language but also of the form and materiality of the book itself. Books lose their owners, he writes, they fall apart, they reveal their errors to authors only after having taken the solidity of print. They mock attempts to recall their content or to find quotation, "as though they were seeking revenge for the lexical gaze that paws through them looking for individual passages and thereby doing violence to their own autonomous course, which does not want to adjust to anyone's wishes."[75] With this last point, Adorno moves from concern with the physical form of books to consideration of its interplay with *content,* which is what concerns us here. I will appraise this with regard to his comments on Marx.

If a limited number of Marx's statements are "spouted like quotations from the Bible," the form of Marx's writing otherwise defends itself by "hiding anything that does not fall into that stock of quotations."[76] Adorno traces this through the feeling Marx's work often conveys of having been written, as it often was, as commentary and marginalia, a condition that in the volumes of *Theories of Surplus Value* "becomes almost a literary art form," a "conspiratorial technique," perhaps unwittingly so, that expresses an "antisystematic tendency in an author whose whole system is a critique of the existing one."[77] In such instances are revealed the singular politics of the book as media form. For the commodity book is not challenged by the *meaning* of Marx's antisystematic critique of the capitalist system, or his resistance to quotation as such; the significant feature is the exchange between the two, a "mimetic" relation between meaning and form as the two heterogeneous domains are momentarily held together in an expressive unity that operates somewhere between language and object, what Jameson, in his essay on form in Adorno, calls a "poetic object."[78]

The nature of this mimetic quality of books becomes clearer in Adorno's detour through musical notation, whose graphical elements—notes' lines, heads, the arcs of their phrases—"are not only signs but also images of what is sounded."[79] We should expect the same of language, Adorno argues, but here the primacy of meaning, of the "conceptual-significative aspect," leaves the mimetic moment "much more extensively suppressed" than it does in music.[80] Indeed, it survives only "in the eccentric features of what is to be read."[81] We have seen this in his comment on resistance to quotation in Marx, though Adorno's interpretation of Proust's "stubborn and abyssal passion" for writing without paragraphs is perhaps more instructive.[82] Again, the reader is resisted, but in a way that foregrounds the *visual* and *spatial* qualities of writing and printing: "[Proust] was irritated by the demand for comfortable reading, which forces the graphic image to serve up small crumbs that the greedy customer can swallow more easily, at the cost of the continuity of the material itself."[83] Against this, Proust's sentences, in their "polemic with the reader," come to *resemble* the written content, in a mimetic mode of writing that "transforms Proust's books into the notes of the interior monologue that his prose simultaneously plays and accompanies."[84] Significantly, this mimetic exchange between content and form is not limited to elusive quotation and the graphic arrangement of the page but can be woven out of the range of a book's material and paratextual features:

> The eye, following the path of the lines of print, looks for such resemblances everywhere. While no one of them is conclusive, every graphic element, every characteristic of binding, paper, and print—anything, in other words, in which the reader stimulates the mimetic impulses in the book itself—can become the bearer of resemblance. At the same time, such resemblances are not mere subjective projections but find their objective legitimation in the irregularities, rips, holes, and footholds

that history has made in the smooth walls of the graphic sign system, the book's material components, and its peripheral features.[85]

Such mimetic resonance is of course difficult to fathom: "What books say from the outside, as a promise, is vague" (though, "in that lies their similarity with their contents").[86] And so the role of the engaged reader is central. If some mimetic resemblances come forward, have a certain objectivity in a work (Proust's antiparagraphs, for example), the reader "stimulates the mimetic impulses" in poring over the breadth of the work's semiotic and material components for resemblance. Chance too is decisive, the poetic object of mimesis being a "contingency temporarily transmuted into necessity," in Jameson's characterization.[87] Nothing, hence, is conclusive, but it is possible to refine this sensibility, and to the degree that the closest, most intimate relationship to books is one that *needs not read them.* And so we return to the collector's relation to books, only now, paradoxically, in not reading books we achieve the most profound relationship not only to their material form but also to their *content*: "the ideal reader, whom books do not tolerate, would know something of what is inside when he felt the cover in his hand and saw the layout of the title page and the overall quality of the pages, and would sense the book's value without needing to read it first."[88]

With Adorno's account of the mimetic experience of books, we have a particular rendering of the self-differing exchange between content and form that I proposed in chapter 1 to be a central feature of the anti-book. In this context Adorno does a considerable service in emphasizing that we are not necessarily in a specialist field of book production, for even great works of literature and philosophy can only be fully experienced in such relationship to their form. And yet it is at the same time a politics of the book that appears *limited* to such works—aside from Marx and Proust, Adorno mentions in these terms Kafka, Kant, Schiller, Baudelaire—and one that is both rare and dying. It also seems to be contained by a limited number of features of the book (bindings, paratext, paragraphs) and its circulation (being damaged, lost); should the author or publisher seek a more experimental trajectory—that is, head off more overtly on the path that will become the bookwork—he receives short shrift: "Books that refuse to play by the rules of mass communication suffer the curse of becoming arts and crafts."[89]

Having learned from Adorno's reading of the content–form relation in books by the great authors, it is time to turn to the pamphlet, a printed medium of considerably more minor provenance that has, nonetheless, had a persistent presence in radical scenes for some four hundred years.[90] To introduce what follows, the discussion moves from the fragmented circulation and compact folds of the pamphlet, through its self-institutional properties, its base and outmoded physical composition, and its ephemeral duration, before ending with a discussion of its "unpopular" interventions on the terrain of the public and the book commodity. Each of these dimensions of the pamphlet is pursued as it is appears in concrete publishing projects, and each draws out one or more of the features of the concept of the communist object. I do so in a fashion that seeks an exchange between particular pamphlets and the concept of communist object, expanding understanding of each while maintaining a sense of the processual openness inherent to that concept, a concept that sheds light on but does not determine the concrete field it surveys. In parts, I discuss the textual content of these printed objects, though the overriding tendency here is to approach content only insofar as it finds mimetic or self-differing relation to pamphlet form, such that it is more the political and conceptual orientation of a pamphlet's content that comes into view than its specific arguments. In other parts, I make no mention of textual content, in keeping with the thesis of the communist object, that "mute" materials and the nontextual dimensions of textual media are means of political expression in their own right.

FRAGMENTED CIRCULATION AND COMPACT FOLDS

In its resistance to conventional circuits of exchange and use, the pamphlet qua communist object necessarily circulates with a degree of autonomy and contingency. It is a feature that can be discerned through some comparison with the medium of the journal. In contrast with the cumulative thematic concerns and sedimented intellectual habits of a journal—the homogenizing tendencies of this periodical form—one of the defining experiences of reading a pamphlet is encountering a particular and focused discourse that is unmoored from a familiar and prestructured critical environment. Pamphlets are discursive fragments, isolated units that tend to be disseminated without the intellectual and institutional authority of an established and sanctioned discourse. This observation on the discursive form of pamphlets is simultaneously an observation on their circulation as objects. Lacking the institutional infrastructure, distribution, and temporal pacing that order and distribute periodical publications through time and across space, pamphlets tend instead to be circulated by varied and discontinuous informal flows and associations—friendships, chance encounters, political events, and the bookfair margins of the book trade. Johanna Drucker presents this as an aspect of printed matter that bookworks make their own, an "independent life," "a potent autonomy," an "animate quality." "Books, because they have the capacity to circulate freely, are independent of any specific institutional restraints (one finds them in friends' houses, motel rooms, railroad cars, school desks). They are low maintenance, relatively long-lived, free-floating objects."[91]

We need to be a little careful here, for this is in part the *ideology* of the book commodity, the autonomy of the bourgeois subject finding a complement to his freedom—apparently determined only by his personal will and intellect—in the vaunted autonomy of the book, equally undetermined by base social relations. As Price puts it of Victorian ideologies of the book, the "self-made reader . . . implies a self-propelling text."[92] Nonetheless, Drucker is surely correct that books have the capacity for a relatively high degree of autonomy and contingency in their circulation, and this capacity is something that the pamphlet form makes its own, with its self-published, unmarketed, and often extracommercial properties. It is a characteristic foregrounded in Iain Sinclair's remark about the newsletter published by the London Psychogeographical Association (LPA), established by Fabian Tompsett of Unpopular Books: "This anonymous, unsponsored, irregular, single-sheet squib is probably the most useful of all London's neighbourhood tabloids. And certainly the most entertaining. It has no fixed cover price and no distribution. If you need it, it finds you."[93] We do not need to follow Sinclair in attributing intention to the pamphlet to see in this an appreciation of the intensive quality of the chance encounter and a feeling that such encounters arise from and confirm an open and unknowable field, that which Jason Skeet and Mark Pawson indicate when writing of self-publishing that "it will always remain impossible to see the whole picture. A random sampling at a single point in time is the best you're going to get."[94]

If this haphazard mode of circulation gives to the pamphlet a quality of contingency and surprise, it also leaves it as a necessarily self-sufficient form. Rather than sidling up to the reader, unfurling across social space through an established infrastructure of production and consumption (as does the periodical journal, the work by a renowned author, or the best-seller book), the pamphlet as fragment holds back from the social world, circulating instead as a closed and compact object. This has an aesthetic quality, as the small press Guestroom conveys when it describes its core interest as constituted on "the love of books, . . . the compactness of the space they create."[95] It is a quality central to Mallarmé's understanding of the book. I refer not to his often cited spiritual formulation of the total book—"all earthly existence must ultimately be contained in a book"—but to a rarer feature of his conception, his appreciation of the *dense* and *compact* nature of books, their "folding" of time and matter: "their thickness when they are piled together; for then they form a tomb in miniature for our souls."[96] How are we to understand this folded compactness? Deleuze provides an answer in the gloss he gives to Mallarmé's somewhat esoteric construction. This is the book as "monad" with "multiple leaves," a particular selection or contraction of the world that is at once "a specific world absolutely different from the others" and "that which constitutes and reconstitutes the beginning of the world," a self-enclosed vessel "ready to burst open."[97] We encounter the book as monad, then, as the "extraordinary energy" of a compact fold of pages at the limit of unfolding.[98]

Yet surely Mallarmé's book qua folded monad conjures images of hefty leather-bound tomes—even of the book as total work, total *world,* to anticipate a theme from chapter 3—quite the opposite of the negligible volume of the pamphlet? Adorno would seem to be thinking in such terms when he describes the book, in Mallarméan fashion, as "self-contained, lasting, hermetic—something that absorbs the reader and closes the lid over him, as it were, the way the cover of the book closes on the text."[99] For these are sturdy books that can "stand solidly on their feet," they have spines broad enough to support their "face" of crosswise titles.[100] But what if the pamphlet, which has no proper spine for titles of *any* kind, were also a monad? What if its fragmentary character made it *especially* so? Deleuze argues that a fragment is less an extraction from a whole, as we might usually consider it, than a condition where there *is* no whole, "no totality into which it can enter, no unity from which it is torn and to which it can be restored."[101] The fragment displays "the extraordinary energy of unmatched parts," "parts of different sizes and shapes, which cannot be adapted, which do not develop at the same rhythm."[102] If the sturdy volume of the book, standing on its feet, produces and bears a feeling that the book is a world and the world a book, the self-evident incompleteness of the pamphlet produces the world as fragmentary, incomplete, and open, qualities held in its slim, compact closure. It is the textual fragment, then, and not the total book that is the true textual monad:

> It is well known that the total book is as much Leibniz's dream as Mallarmé's, even though they never stop working in fragments. Our error is in believing that they did not succeed in their wishes: they make this unique Book perfectly, the book of monads, in letters and little circumstantial pieces that could sustain as many dispersions as combinations.[103]

This feature of the pamphlet as compact and fragmented fold has an additional valence in the common tendency of pamphlets to comprise previously published text. Pamphlets often consist of original textual works, but equally often they are a selection or folding of works that have appeared elsewhere in different forms and contexts. This is a feature of editions by Unpopular Books, one that is often highlighted by the publisher in a manner that encourages the reader to appreciate its pamphlets as momentary concrescences, as publication takes up a text and presses it with new prefaces and other paratextual reframing, sending it off on a different course. But the most curious instance I have encountered of such reflexive refolding is a small press edition of Jacques Camatte and Gianni Collu's text "On Organization," copublished in North America by New Space and Beni Memorial Library. The text is itself a fragment, being an open letter that led to the dissolution of the group that was emerging around the French communist journal *Invariance* in the wake of May 1968, a result of the letter's critique of the "racket" function of political organization (that is, the furtherance of capitalist forms of identity and self-marketing in nominally anticapitalist milieus). But what interests me here is another letter, written by Beni Memorial Library and included with the posted copies of the pamphlet, a document enticingly titled "The 'On Organization' Pamphlet—A Bibliographic Dissection."

In a sense, this letter undermines the contingency and surprise of the pamphlet qua monad by locating the pamphlet's origin and the process of its production, but it does so in a way that unsettles the stability that such narrative placement might usually produce. The document informs the reader that the pamphlet comprises two texts that were sent to New Space (a Chicago book shop favorably inclined toward ultraleft currents) from Savona, Italy, most likely from the publisher of Camatte's Italian editions, Edizioni International, but that the package was sent anonymously, with no identification of the translator, publisher, or distributor, describing only the texts' original publication details in *Invariance.* The U.S. publisher goes to some length to highlight these details, even including in the document mock-ups of parts of the cover sheets that identify the original publication sources. But above all, the document makes apparent that here is a printed letter about a pamphlet that is a reprint of the text of a letter that had been published twice before, in the same journal, one time with a new preface. It is a textual fragment that has sustained many combinations indeed: "folds in folds, over folds, following folds."[104] The letter also describes in considerable detail the physical shape and format of the original documents and the subsequent processes of printing the pamphlet. *On Organization,* hence, is not only a textual folding but an artifactual one also, as it folds and unfolds from one concrescence to the next, from "mimeographed, black on white, 21 × 29.5 cm, corner-stapled, unillustrated," as the account commences, to "making plates, offset printing about 1500 copies, and collating, folding, binding," as it draws to an end.[105] And finally, just as the anonymity of the original package unsettled conventional paradigms of distribution, which integrate parties and objects in networks of money and obligation, the "bibliographic dissection" seeks to ensure that the pamphlet endures as a contingent and unbound fragment: "as with everything I distribute, I do not wish to put anyone under any obligation to do anything. Also, though I am poor, donations of money are gratefully refused."[106]

VULNERABLE POWERS OF INSTITUTION

The compact nature of the pamphlet as folded monad generates something of an *intimate* quality in its encounters, in its "collections" or permeable associations, but where the intimate, to recall my earlier discussion, is also an *extimate* relation. It is an affective aspect of printed matter—what Drucker calls "the densely informative immediacy and intimacy of the experience provided by books"—that has a prominent place in the understanding of the pamphlet developed by Infopool.[107] Manifesting the fetish quality of a communist object, Infopool's formulation of the unsettling material qualities of the pamphlet emerges in part through its encounter with commodity values, as described in the Infopool text "Operation Reappropriation." As we will see shortly, the text addresses a violation of the pamphlet's communist form that occurred when some Infopool editions crossed the threshold between two very different kinds of collection to become part of a major exhibition at the Tate Modern museum.

Based at times in London and Copenhagen, Infopool (2000–2009) was a collaborative writing, print, and Internet project established by the visual artist Jakob Jakobsen. It intersected with the research, exhibition, and social spaces of the East London Info Centre (1998–99) and the Copenhagen Free University (2001–7). As Henriette Heise and Jakob Jakobsen describe it, Infopool was founded on a commitment to self-publishing as "a vector of activity and thought—usually fueled by pleasure/disgust/lack," and an investment in the wider processual and associational properties of media across the boundaries of art and politics.[108] In terms of the content of the pamphlets, some comprise single essays, notably Howard Slater's text on the Scandinavian Situationists, "Divided We Stand" (*Infopool* 4). But there is a decided "R&D" orientation to the pamphlets, apparent for example in *Infopool* 8, a self-reflexive text and interview by and with Emma Hedditch on the process of writing an essay on the conceptual artist Adrian Piper, and *Infopool* 6, a photo essay by Stewart Home concerned to discover America while journeying through Britain. Other instances pertain to Jakobsen's art practice. *Infopool* 1, for example, includes texts on his experiments with the use and disuse of modernist objects, on experiencing one site in another through transposing imagery of the 1976 Seveso chemical disaster to the streets of south London, and on the domestic synthesis of plastic and beer. I consider the physical properties of these pamphlets in a different part of this chapter, but suffice to say for now that they are A5-size with metallic-silver covers that are uniform except for the different number and date of each edition.

Commonsense views of media chronology would see online availability of the Infopool texts as invalidating the pamphlet as a pertinent form, but Infopool had a more post-digital sensibility and saw it quite differently. Online availability relieves the pamphlet of the function of content dissemination, allowing other qualities and dimensions to come forward into expression, not least of which is the pamphlet's self-positing character. These are "self-institutional" entities, as Infopool describes it—they establish contexts and incite affects and modes of association:

> Taking the form of pamphlets is not irrelevant. Using a small press, or post-media form, implies that they are documents that are circulated in extremely small numbers. They are, in a sense, intimate and specific and, crucially, the communication they aim for is one that is unmediated. In short the pamphlets, infopool projects, are concerned with developing their own contexts.[109]

We are in the domain of Benjamin's collected object, its intimate capacity to have unsettling, extimate effects, though here the "shock" of encounter takes a specific and nuanced form. The permeable contour of self-institution has an explicitly *collective* dimension and a "fledgling" quality, infused with "vulnerability."[110] As Infopool describes it, without formal institutional structures or copyright protection, the pamphlets extend only a "contract of 'trust'" concerning sensitivity toward content and aim in an "unprotected offer of communication."[111] That may sound like a weakness, but it is in fact a signal feature of the self-institutional object. Since, in contrast to instances of political expression that are the products and bearers of institutional norms and regularities, this vulnerability affirms precisely the pamphlet's *emergent* quality, its existence only in the open, exploratory, and intimate "institutions" that are articulated, or held, in its encounters. It is hence no contradiction to say, as Jakobsen has it, that "the vulnerability of the pamphlet is also its power."[112]

It was most likely something of this self-institutional quality that appealed to the curators of the Tate Modern's 2001 *Century City* exhibition, when it chose, without notification or consultation, to bind together three Infopool pamphlets in newly fortified covers, doctor the cover text, and display the artifact threaded on a presentation wire (Figure 2). As Infopool see it, the museum's interest in these pamphlets is exemplary of the "valorization of socialization"—the commodification of social relations that seek to escape the commodity—that is common to contemporary cultural institutions as they cast around for content and legitimacy. In this particular case, it shows the inability of the Tate to understand and handle the very qualities of form, intimacy, and association that had caught the curators' attention in the first place. For in its new guise, the pamphlet's values of tentative and emergent self-institution were converted, with proprietorial disregard, into exhibition value—the value, as Arvatov has it, of "murdered objects" "hidden under glass."[113] The only adequate response was for Infopool to liberate the artifact from exhibition, documenting their "Operation Re-appropriation" with a damning critique of the museum's blunt and clumsy action:

> On display in a new hardback cover and threaded through with wire (the new vitrine) the pamphlets take on an aura that undermines both their form and content. They are no longer able to be passed on, given as gifts, and circulated to friends and fellow travelers i.e. to be self-institutional. In short the pamphlets have been commodified beyond their informal and nominal £1.00 price. The generator of value that is the Tate Modern has allotted them an immaterial cultural value (prestige, distinction) in exchange for the appearance of the value of their autonomy.... We picked the pamphlets up on Friday February 9th. To negotiate their exit would have taken too long.[114]

BARBARIC ASCETICISM

Having moved from the pamphlet's fragmented circulation and compact folds to its self-institutional capacities, we can turn now to focus on the more immediately physical properties of this medium, starting with paper. Far from a mere substratum or support, paper is a complex and sensual entity—for Derrida, "paper ... gets hold of us bodily, and through every

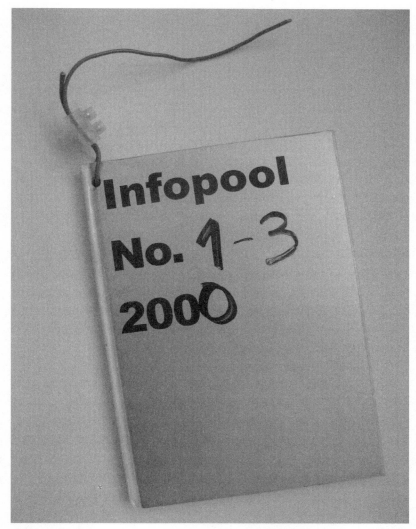

Figure 2. Reappropriated *Infopool*.

sense"—and is intrinsic to the pamphlet's peculiar physical and sensory form.[115] In his anatomy of the emergence and form of the pamphlet in early modern Britain, Joad Raymond shows that the properties and economies of paper had a central place.[116] The early modern pamphlet was a stitched rather than bound quarto, a size that allowed for the use of smaller, cheaper paper at a time when this material comprised up to three-quarters of printing costs. It would typically number between one and twelve sheets, giving between eight and ninety-six pages in total, and would normally be produced in editions of 250 to 1,500. Raymond places considerable emphasis on its physical attributes, arguing that "some of the most fundamental aspects of the pamphlet" were "its appearance, size, weight, texture," "readers knew what a pamphlet looked like, and how it felt in the hand."[117] The feel, ragged form, and relative lack of commercial value also played a role in the meaning and cultural associations of the early modern pamphlet, which, though it rose to some degree of recognition and influence in the seventeenth century, existed—unlike the manuscript, the book, and, later, the newspaper—as a somewhat disreputable entity. This is especially clear in Raymond's assessment of the common perception of this medium in the late sixteenth century: "Pamphlets were small, insignificant, ephemeral, disposable, untrustworthy, unruly, noisy, deceitful, poorly printed, addictive, a waste of time."[118]

Something of this base and ragged nature persists as a defining feature of pamphlets and associated inconspicuous media forms throughout the twentieth century. The Russian Futurist books and pamphlets of the 1910s were produced in very small editions using cheap paper and ephemeral materials, including burlap and wallpaper (as we will see in chapter 3). In the clandestine samizdat of the Soviet bloc, the functionality of carbon paper for illicit domestic reproduction made it a common material, and even today, with popular access to desktop publishing, strategies deployed in self-publishing often eschew the overly smooth and professional visual aesthetic (typified by *Wired* magazine) that such technologies enable. Tompsett, for instance, describes the contemporary possibilities of using an old Roneo mimeograph machine, with its poor register, to play with color and bleed—"entropy in print"—as a challenge to much contemporary design that he finds "so slick" that it induces one's "gaze to slide off the page."[119] Similarly, the physical attributes of pamphlets continue to be central to their material and sensory nature: their texture and feel, the variable smell of paper dependent on age and condition, the quality of the print, the physical act of turning the page. It is not necessary to pose a hard opposition between analogue and digital media to recognize the specific properties and pleasures of print:

> All books are visual.... All books are tactile and spatial as well—their physicality is fundamental to their meaning. Similarly, the elements of visual and physical materiality participate in a book's temporal effect—the weight of paper, covers, endpapers or inserts, fold-outs or enclosures all contribute to the experience of the book.[120]

An attention to such physical qualities of the pamphlet—with Arvatov, to the "deepest sense of things"—is an enduring theme in Infopool. Insistent on the coimplication of material, conceptual, and social aspects of this medium, Jakobsen talks of Infopool pamphlets as articulating an "everyday materiality," a "materiality of available means." Unlike the finished object of the mass-produced and perfect-bound book, the pamphlet "tells a story through its material," one that foregrounds the process of its production, or the "practical task" of developing a pamphlet "as an individual, as a little entity."[121] The vulnerable and emergent nature of Infopool's self-institutional gesture has a correspondence, then, with the story the pamphlets tell of their simple fabrication. These pamphlets were produced in relatively inexpensive fashion with photocopied paper and A5 covers assembled from metallic-silver card purchased from an east London remaindered-stationery shop. The cover text includes a combination of print and script numerals, playfully indicating the handwrought nature of the object while, in the contrast between the two graphic technologies, foregrounding the pamphlets' existence at the interface of different technologies of production.

There is also a revaluation of materials here, following a concern with the pamphlets' processes of emergence *and* dissipation. Jakobsen explicitly addresses this theme in a text that troubles the notion of the "new" through the construction of a table from discarded materials, a table connected to the self-institution (as site of display and discussion) of Infopool pamphlets.[122] Here Jakobsen comments on Baudelaire's ragpicker (a figure Benjamin closely associates with the collector) in terms of the creation of value from the gray zone between waste and utility, a practice that is disavowed in the Global North by the consumer object and its temporal pattern of novelty and obsolescence. Yet for Jakobsen, the revaluation of material is not simply extant in economy; rather, it seeks to tarry with the commodity form, unsettling the social and economic partitions of waste and value as the waste material is enlivened in its new social arrangements.

The destabilizing effects of waste have a further role to play in the pamphlet form. I noted earlier that digital media have freed up pamphlets from the function of content dissemination to take on other qualities and roles, but that post-digital assessment left something out. Is there not, all the same, an outmodedness to the pamphlet, as a form now eclipsed by the digital? We could still account for contemporary interest in the pamphlet form, considering it to be a product of the form's final illumination, a medium intensely appreciated at the moment of its extinction.[123] But I find that Benjaminian construction unsatisfying, preferring Adorno's variation on this theme. He shows interest in outmoded media, but less from the perspective of their imminent passing than from their *enduring relation to the newest forms,* to which they stand as a persistent negation, a "barbaric asceticism." As he argues, recently outmoded media present the opportunity to be "strategically nonsynchronous" with the "ostentatious" compound of new technology and capital, which commands social and affective adherence to the "united front" of the new: "Progress and barbarism are today so matted together in mass culture that only barbaric asceticism towards the latter, and towards progress in technical means, could restore an unbarbaric condition."[124] To this end, appeal to outmoded and "unobtrusive" media is not a celebration of the old but a "repudiation of false riches," for such media introduce a breach in the temporal structure of the new that, paradoxically, constitutes them as the most *contemporary* media: "older media, not designed for mass-production take on a new timeliness: that of exemption and of improvisation. They alone could outflank the united front of trusts and technology."[125] There is a *modernism,* then, to Adorno's advocacy of the outmoded, a barbaric asceticism of media form to complement, say, the violent linguistic asceticism of Samuel Beckett.[126]

Recalling the epigraph to this chapter, we can see now how it is that a somewhat clunky medium at the point of obsolescence—the mimeograph, a publishing technology that has had a pivotal place in modern pamphleteering—can be called on to repeal the book designed for commerce. It is an object lesson that, enticingly, Adorno put into play himself, in a first version of his canonical work with Horkheimer, *Dialectic of Enlightenment*—a version named by the subtitle of the later work, *Philosophical Fragments,* circulated among the associates of the Institute for Social Research—that took the form of a mimeographed typescript with decidedly unobtrusive covers comprising brown pasteboard.[127] The value of this work can be most appreciated when related to the *Dialectic of Enlightenment.* Apparently, Adorno's work of readying the text for its formal publication, as it morphed from self-published mimeograph to a book proper, entailed that he not only moderate its Marxian terminology, so as to ease the book and the Institute into a broad reading public, but also drop references to the work's incompleteness, so aiding its reception as a determinate entity, a movement confirmed in the change of title.[128] As such, the movement between the mimeograph and book presents an enticing instantiation, a mimesis of sorts, of Adorno's critique of the book qua commodity, which sidles up to the reader, only one that manifests his thesis to the extent that it undermines his book.

As for the pamphlet, to get back on track, if it is a post-digital form for its range of expressive qualities, Adorno's lesson in barbaric asceticism is that it is also this as a result of the fissure it opens with the fixation on the technologically new and the linear temporality of media "progress." That is not, however, the pamphlet's only temporal quality.

EPHEMERAL DURATION

Each pamphlet has a variable duration, dependent on its site and moment of political intervention, its mode and extent of circulation, popularity of theme, and so on; for Jakobsen, "the specificity of any of these self-publications is that they have their own time."[129] Such atypical specificity is accentuated by the *ephemerality* of pamphlets, their tendency to fall out of circulation, get lost, or accumulate undisturbed in a stack of documents. Indeed, the pamphlet has not only been rendered outmoded by digital and online media; it has ever been treated as a disposable object, a property clear in Thomas Bodley's interdiction against preserving pamphlets at (what was to become) Oxford's Bodleian as media "not worth the custody in suche a Librarie."[130]

Such singular existence courted by destruction can articulate a pertinent political value, what can be called, after the fetish, a value of the "untransposable." It is a value that pervades the 56a Archive (1991–). This open access archive and reading room based at a social center in London's Elephant and Castle holds ten thousand plus items of radical ephemeral media—media associated with direct action, anarchist, queer, squatting, antigentrification, feminist, and communist politics.[131] It was established in part as an *effect* of the ephemerality of self-published media, for as printed matter moved haphazardly through the networks of radical groups and individuals that used the center, some of it fell out of circulation to become the germ of the archive.[132]

Contrasting 56a's archival practice with tendencies in radical librarianship that would preserve a set of pamphlets in a perfect-bound book, Chris talks of ephemerality as a fundamental feature of these media objects: "the ephemerality of the zine or pamphlet, that's what it's about. Zines come to you because they will."[133] Pamphlets "make trails" through an open set of encounters, and these encounters are registered on their bodies.[134] An attention to these characteristics is clearly in tension with the conventional archival imperatives of completeness and preservation, but instead of resolving the tension, the 56a Archive holds it open through an articulation of the ephemeral qualities of the pamphlet in the archive itself. Material continues to arrive in a largely informal fashion, and the archive itself holds together at the edge of dissipation; the gentrification of inner London may well commit the collection to dispersal, should the social center be closed under pressure from property values and the class-cleansing effects of so-called urban regeneration. And within the archive, an emphasis is placed on a tactile relation to the media objects collected, a "sensuality," a "conscious relationship to stuff," and one that allows for decay. As Chris continues, "we just have the barest minimum, which is space full of things. And then time and climate does what it does, or weevils, or . . ."[135]

Far from suggesting that the pamphlet's temporality is only immediate, here ephemerality becomes, paradoxically, a quality that endures. It is a quality that permeates the printed object and colors its social encounters, providing a sense of the discontinuous and variegated nature of intellectual, political, and inorganic time. Benjamin's speculation that objects embody times and sensations associated with previous owners and contexts can manifest here in terms of their connection to, or expression of, particular political events, movements, or critical currents. It is a point picked up by Adorno. The strongest motif in "Bibliographic Musings" is the disfigured book as unity-in-disruption with the damaged life of emigration, where "damaged books, books that have been knocked about and have had to suffer, are the real books."[136] But he also makes a comment about ephemeral political media in these terms, now on board with Benjamin's taste for print's fringe: "Revolutionary leaflets and kindred things: they look as though they have been overtaken by catastrophes, even when they are no older than 1918. Looking at them, one can see that what they wanted did not come to pass. Hence their beauty."[137] Moreover, this catastrophic quality appears to be intrinsic to these media forms, for this is "the same beauty the defendants in Kafka's *Trial* take on, those whose execution has been settled since the very first day."[138]

Such an appreciation is apparent in Chris's remarks on archiving radical media, though the ephemeral revolutionary artifact is for him less beholden to the affect of mourning attendant upon Adorno's feeling for leaflets. This is how Chris frames the strong affective pull of original editions of political printed matter: "What is that impulse? We're not talking about collecting trophies. We're talking about a thing that has a desire for change, for revolutionary change."[139] From the perspective of Benjamin's collector, a trophy is the integrated object of linear, historical memory—the concern, as Leslie puts it, of the "souvenir-hunter."[140] In Chris's formulation, we can detect a political inflection of a more undetermined and future oriented charge, somewhat akin to the eventful shock of Benjamin's collected object, where memory is involuntary, "impromptu, bouncing off objects encountered randomly. It is lucid, pre-verbal, and coupled with euphoria."[141] What is most attractive here for a communism of objects is the meeting of matter and nonlinear time with revolutionary history, an unstable compound that Deleuze and Guattari seek to convey with their (somewhat counterintuitive) concept of the "monument":

> the monument is not something commemorating a past, it is a bloc of present sensations that owe their preservation only to themselves and that provide the event with the compound that celebrates it. The monument's action is not memory but fabulation. . . . [It] confides to the ear of the future the persistent sensations that embody the event: the constantly renewed suffering of men and women, their recreated protestations, their constantly resumed struggle.[142]

That said, the monuments of revolutionary printed matter have a more troubled relation to their own endurance than this concept implies. Indeed, the peculiar intensity of the ephemeral printed artifact can be destroyed, ironically, through efforts to preserve it. To explain this, we can return to Hollier's formulation of the fetish quality of printed matter. For Hollier, the materialist "document" has an intrinsic and affirmative relation to ephemeral instantiation, to "what does not last," an untransposable or evental quality that he detects in the journal *Documents* itself.[143] When subject to commercial reprinting—to preservation and iteration in the publication circuits of art history—the journal *loses* its value: "But it is for the kamikazes, for the most fleeting trackers of the avant-garde, those who have not even seen two winters, that the honor of the reprint is intended. He who wins loses."[144] It is a problem that surfaces too in the conceptualization of the political poster developed at Atelier Populaire, the occupied École des Beaux-Arts in the Paris events of May 1968, where it is said that some six hundred thousand silk-screen stencil posters were fabricated in 350 designs.[145] For Atelier Populaire, the integration of media with situated political practice was so tight that they not only opposed the sale of the posters, or a distracted appreciation of their aesthetic value, but deemed even archival preservation to be a violation of their singular, evental consistency:

> To use [the posters] for decorative purposes, to display them in bourgeois places of culture or to consider them as objects of aesthetic interest is to impair both their function and their effect. This is why the Atelier

Populaire has always refused to put them on sale.

Even to keep them as historical evidence of a certain stage in the struggle is a betrayal, for the struggle itself is of such primary importance that the position of an "outside" observer is a fiction which inevitably plays into the hands of the ruling class.[146]

I would not deny the importance of this move toward an immediate and irrevocable consumption of political art in the event. But the point to extract is that this antiarchival configuration is an expression of the *enduring vitality* of an object of 1968 today, a vitality that articulates that extrahistorical event precisely in the ephemeral object's untransposable resistance to preservation.

If, in such ways, the ephemerality and destruction of printed works are alloyed with the intensity of political events, the determination of these qualities is rarely independent of broader social forces. In 1970s Italy, to take one example, the possession of radical printed matter was regularly used as a pretext in the mass arrests and prosecutions of individuals involved with the Autonomia movement, such that it was common practice for militants to destroy their personal archives (a point registered on the 56a website with a quotation from Nanni Balestrini's account of one such episode from his novel *The Unseen*). And such destruction was not only an act performed by individuals. In Antonio Negri's case, following charges against him of "the publication and distribution of pamphlets and communiqués that incite armed insurrection," his pamphlets, such as *Domination and Sabotage* and *Workers Party against Work,* were pulped by the publisher, Feltrinelli.[147] Of course, the presence of the State in the practice of destruction in no way negates the notion that ephemeral media have their own time.

UNPOPULAR PAMPHLETS

For the properties I have been describing, the pamphlet can be a rather seductive object. Indeed, a certain seduction is present in its etymology, the word derived from the Greek *pamphilos,* meaning "loved by all," after the lead character of a popular twelfth-century love poem and publication, *Pamphilus seu de Amore.*[148] The concept of the communist object celebrates the seduction of the object, that should be clear by now, but not uncritically; generic love and popularity can be a problem, the nature of which is tested by Unpopular Books through experiments in pamphlet form, where the pamphlet is developed as an *unpopular* medium, manifest, as I consider here, in relation to the reading "public" and to the commodity.

Unpopular Books was established in the late 1970s by Fabian Tompsett, in part a product of his involvement in the cooperative print shop scene and the Rising Free book shop and press.[149] Rising Free published the first single-volume English edition of Raoul Vaneigem's *The Revolution of Everyday Life,* a book that suffered from poor knowledge of binding materials such that—in Tompsett's words, a foretaste of his rare feeling for mimesis in publishing form—it became an "autodestructive commodity," "the perfect Situationist book: it fell apart as you read it."[150] The first two editions from Unpopular Books are an indication of its somewhat unorthodox orientations: a Persian translation of Rod Jones's essay on factory committees in the Russian revolution, published in 1979 in a critical constellation with the Iranian Revolution, and an early text on "communization" by Jean Barrot, playfully titled by Tompsett like a beginner's guide: *What Is Communism.*[151] Though Unpopular Books has published books and leaflets, the pamphlet is Tompsett's preferred medium, a point he makes with reference to the pamphlet's textual and physical form and its processes of production: "It's not bulky, ideally you can put it in your pocket easily. It's not going to take you too long to read, but it's long enough to get somewhere. And you can make it in all these different ways."[152] We can consider some of the "different ways" Unpopular Books make and problematize pamphlets with regard, first, to the political problem of the public, once more starting with a contrast to the media form of the journal.

Journals and formal political organizations share the need to court and consolidate a sizeable public, in the mode of readership, market, or membership. For a journal, this requirement is determined in part by the financial demands of publication, whereas for an organization (and for movement journals), it is the dominant criterion for social validation as a pertinent political entity. By contrast, the low production cost and the fragmentary and occasional form of the pamphlet, along with its frequent remove from direct relation to organizations, frees it up from the journal's requirement of audience share. This makes it an ideal medium for a communist press that seeks, as does Unpopular Books, to challenge received political truths and the tendency of political groups and radical subjectivities toward self-flattery—a press that seeks to be, in other words, *unpopular*—while destabilizing any political community that the press itself may otherwise accrue from the prestige attendant upon such challenge. The appeal of intellectual autonomy in this regard is readily appreciable, notwithstanding the common attraction to dogma in political circles, but such a willfully unpopular approach to political community requires further elucidation.

Unpopular Books may seem a perverse name for a communist publishing project, and yet one of its sources is a remark from Marx: "Both of us scoff at being popular."[153] The remark is made against the emerging cult of personality attending to Marx and Engels in the 1870s and favors instead a formulation of communism as a *distributed* and *self-critical* process, a process that wards off any delimiting center of attraction. The remark is part of an epigraph to Camatte and Collu's "On Organization," a text we encountered earlier, though now as included in the Unpopular Books edition of Camatte's *Capital and Community*. And this is one of a dozen works published by Unpopular Books on communist theory that can be understood, inter alia, as reworking Marx's disdain for popularity through the critique of capital. If communism is a critical movement immanent to the mutating limits of capitalist social relations, and not a privileged political subject, organizational form, or repertoire of ideas, then the popularity of any of the latter is contrary to its imperatives, serving to close communism down to a delimited identity. Or, as Unpopular Books has it (if I can generalize from a comment made against the enduring appeal of the Situationist International), the "popularity" of a particular critical position is a manifestation "of the fact that the revolutionary movement has yet to overcome [its] weaknesses."[154]

If the communist critique of social relations turns against reified identities, organizations, and ideas, it turns also against the commodity object; this is the second dimension of this publisher's unpopularity. The Danish press release for Debord and Jorn's *Mémoires*, a book famously covered by sandpaper, establishes the work as an "unpopular book," doing so not on the terrain of its textual content but on that of the commodity: "in a time where all civilized nations battle to achieve the most popularity, using industrial design and mass-production of art objects and home appliances in the world market, a very unpopular book would be a much-needed rarity. . . . There is too much plastic, we prefer sandpaper."[155] While this is not a direct source of the name of Unpopular Books, it is neither an unwarranted association, for Tompsett has played a significant role in the critical appropriation of Situationist thought, not least as (re-)founder in the early 1990s of the LPA (an organization originally established and folded simultaneously as it fused with the Lettrist International and the International Movement for an Imaginist Bauhaus to found the Situationist International). Moreover, Tompsett's choice of name partook of the same critique of the popularity of the book commodity, playing as it did with the name and business model of the Popular Book Centre chain that was then common to the London high street, its prominent window banners succinctly articulating the economic dimension of the popular: "POPULAR BOOK CENTRE/EVERYTHING EXCHANGEABLE AT HALF PRICE/ HALF BACK CREDIT ON ALL BOOKS SOLD HERE."[156]

That is the communist terrain, then, of the unpopularity of Unpopular Books: against the identity of reified political communities and theories, and against the popularity of the commodity unit of exchange. Bearing this condition, Unpopular Books has developed a most enticing publishing practice. While Unpopular Books shares the critique of the commodity with *Mémoires,* the communist qualities of its publishing experiments are constituted more in relation to the ideas and practices of Jorn, who, in contrast to Debord after the 1962 split in the Situationist International, maintained an overt commitment to a communism of art and fabrication— to a "materialist's love for matter," as Jorn put it.[157] In the case of Unpopular Books, this materialism is manifest through engagement with the arts and conventions of printing and the means by which commercial and political value are articulated with printed matter. It is important to appreciate that aesthetic form and the critique of capital are here held close together, a point Tompsett directly addresses in an obscure unpublished text called "kArt Boo," which details some of the interventions by this press in publishing form. Enticingly, Tompsett does this in relation to a problematic that is foundational for the concept of the anti-book, namely, the relation between the artists' book and communist publishing.[158] If, as kArt Boo has it, publishing is a field of struggle—"publishing is war carried out by other means, or if you prefer war is publishing carried out by other means"—this is operative in the realm of printed form.[159] The artists' book intervenes in the latter, by definition, but kArt Boo suggests that it does so without a feeling for the conflictuality of the terrain, tending to reduce the book to an art object, a trajectory Tompsett disparages in this wry manner: "and now, hundreds of years later," after the invention of print and the book's entry into modern commodity production, "when the role of the book is being undermined by electronic media, the book is being abased to a level even below that of the simple commodity—the book is being turned into *Art*."[160] One might retort that labor—the conflictual form at the heart of communist thought—is a common theme in artists' books, but here it has tended to appear somewhat uncritically, with the artists' book "immersed in creating a parody of the old artisanal skills of the printer."[161] By contrast, Unpopular Books has "always prided itself on the shoddiness of the finished product," wearing its critique of labor on the printed surface of the page.[162]

Developing this theme, Tompsett comments thus on the labor and value of printing: "when you hear the term congealed labour you think of congealed ink. All the other printers do as well. . . . We would watch the printing press as the paper passed through it and imagine it squeezing value into these pieces of paper."[163] The matter that is "congealed" and "squeezed" here is complex, comprising dimensions that are *abstract* as much as concrete, dimensions that can only be grasped with the aid of thought—with critique of the commodity form. That is to say, Tompsett's reference is to the concrete dimensions of abstract labor, where the circulation of the print commodity determines the form and value of the congealed labor and ink invested in its production (an observation that has considerable historical purchase, given, as I noted in chapter 1, that print was central to the emergence of the social form of abstract labor, through its leading role in the mechanization of handicraft and the separation of aesthetic activity from technical work).[164] Not artisanal labor, then, it is the labor of industrial printing that Tompsett refers to, a point confirmed in kArt Boo, where the destruction of the print unions by News

International in the 1986–87 Wapping dispute indexes in time and place the more generic condition of the imposition of work.[165] But Tompsett's remark about congealed ink simultaneously gestures toward something else in the printing process, a value of inks and papers that, as it tarries with the commodity form of the printed object, can be understood as an anti-commodity fetishism. It is a point made in the material form of the Jorn pamphlet *Open Creation and Its Enemies* (Plate 3).

This Unpopular Books edition includes Tompsett's English translation of Jorn's "Open Creation and Its Enemies" and his "Originality and Magnitude (on the System of Isou)" with an introduction by Richard Essex (one of the numerous pseudonyms taken by Tompsett in his unpopular dissimulation of authorial property and prestige).[166] *Open Creation* was fabricated through reflexive attention to its material form in a fashion that repeats the bibliographic self-consciousness that Raymond shows was a common motif of early modern pamphlet culture.[167] Unusually for a pamphlet, Tompsett had it allocated an International Standard Book Number (ISBN) and logged a copy with the British Library. In this manner, it was placed and validated in the commercial field of the book as a uniform and determinate exchangeable commodity—and we should recall from chapter 1 that it was precisely the standardizing properties of print technology that enabled the Gutenberg book to set the example of the modern commodity, being the first uniform and repeatable mass-produced object.[168] But *Open Creation* enters this field in order to trouble it, playing with the mechanisms that constitute the pamphlet as a standardized and determinate entity. It was printed in contravention of the ISBN allocation regulations with two different covers (though for consistency across the pamphlets—"the particular mix of colours," "the same moisture going into the paper"—they were set out simultaneously on the same A2 plates).[169] A "Note to Librarians" on the back of each resolves this problem, but in a way that requires the antiarchival and devaluing act of physical destruction, for it advises that the cover, a highly designed and attractive lithographic print, is merely a protective for the text in transit and should be expunged to avoid confusion for future bibliographers. And the inside covers each announce different Unpopular Books editions—*A Trip to Edzell Castle* and *An English Hacienda*—that remain unpublished, so introducing doubt into the authority and reliability traditionally associated with the institution of the publisher and the act of print publication.

The *Open Creation* pamphlet is not, then, an autonomous entity wholly outside the structural patterns of the commercial book. Rather, as befits the fetishism of the communist object, it achieves its particular intensive expression of matter and value by operating immanently to them, as something of an *unreliable mimic* that opens a gap in the protocols and institutions that constitute the book as commodity. At the same time, this pamphlet cuts more directly against the commodity mode of the book. As with other pamphlets by Unpopular Books, it has a price, but it has no exchange value; no capital was invested to realize surplus value from its sale. That it was hence produced as something other than a commodity is not in itself so rare, but this fact was alloyed with other features. To take up again the problem of labor, Tompsett has often produced pamphlets in the downtime between commercial print runs. One might view this as a stolen moment of "unalienated" work, but it is better understood as a contemporary instance of the *unsettling* of work and its identities that Rancière, as I discussed earlier, calls the "nights of labor"—the flight from work that, paradoxically, reveals the impossibility of such flight under the social conditions of capitalism. And when this liminal labor is consumed, its utility can be further unsettled. For Tompsett also frames the production and consumption of the pamphlet as constitutive of a "potlatch"—the nonproductive expenditure of the extravagant gift—though in contrast to the mutual obligation of gift economies, the LPA would surreptitiously place such pamphlets in book and charity shops encountered on its excursions, a mode of noncontractual distribution Tompsett calls "negative shoplifting."[170]

With all these features, is *Open Creation* not a seductive object, just like a commodity? Yes and no. An object in its commodity mode is universally enticing, it has a most "empathetic soul," as Benjamin puts it: "If the soul of the commodity which Marx occasionally mentions in jest existed, it would be the most empathetic ever encountered in the realm of souls, for it would have to see in everyone the buyer in whose hand and house it wants to nestle."[171] By contrast, picking up again the theme of "unpopularity," *Open Creation,* as other small press pamphlets, has no need to be consumed simply for the sake of turnover because it does not valorize the labor of its production, and so it can elide such expansive appeal. Against the dominant mode of marketing commercial books today (even the most difficult works of theory and critique), it "does not demand the approach of a reader," to quote Mallarmé once more.[172] Relieved of this, its seductions—and they are indubitable—can be emergent to its assorted encounters, with all the gradations of affect and situated processes of negotiation and unsettling that such encounters produce.

In some of those encounters, the pamphlet will have an untransposable quality, a quality that is designed into an earlier version of *Open Creation.* The 1994 pamphlet is actually a revised edition; the preface notes a version published by the LPA the year earlier, in an issue of fifty to accompany a trip to the standing stones at Calanais in the Outer Hebrides, a Summer Solstice event associated with the commemoration of Jorn's death. There is a ritual dimension to the Calanais edition—it is something of a "talisman," in Tompsett's phrasing—that establishes the untransposable quality of this communist object. Unlike the revised edition, this pamphlet was not a mimic in the circuits of exchange of the book commodity but an artifact exclusive to its event, where an event can be described, in the topological terms of Jorn's text, as "the constancy of intensity and the unique feeling of the propagation of the process," "the transformative morphology of the unique."[173] This eventful existence is recorded in the preface of the Calanais edition with an account of its publication and exclusive distribution and is consolidated with a copy held by Tompsett in a sealed envelope, posted from Calanais on the date of its publication. A few other copies were sent (along with inserts of local plant matter) to copyright libraries, where the envelopes take their own part in the pamphlet's untransposable form. In contrast to the instruction in the later edition to destroy the finely crafted cover, here librarians were advised to consider the inconsequential envelope to be intrinsic to the publication—postmarked, as it was, and adorned with an LPA mock first day of issue stamp. A sticker on the seal deploys the topological trope of nonlinearity, a mimesis with the model of "open creation" developed in the enclosed text: "Open with caution as effects are irreversible."

3

Root, Fascicle, Rhizome

FORMS AND PASSIONS OF THE POLITICAL BOOK

> There is no difference between what a book talks about and
> how it is made.
> — GILLES DELEUZE AND FÉLIX GUATTARI,
> *A Thousand Plateaus*

> The book as an antiworld.
> — MICHEL FOUCAULT, "A Swimmer between
> Two Words"

The place of the medium of the book in the emergence of the political cultures and publics of the modern nation-state has been the subject of a considerable body of research.[1] Much less attention has been paid to its role in extraparliamentary politics, or—and this is where my interest lies in this chapter—to critique of the forms and functions of expressly political books. A rare exception can be found in Deleuze and Guattari's experimental work of philosophy *A Thousand Plateaus,* the second of their two-volume Capitalism and Schizophrenia collective writing project. In a singular philosophical appreciation for the politics of textual matter, here the common understanding of the book as a generic instrument of secular enlightenment is supplanted with an image of the book as a fraught and ambivalent material entity, one entwined with a rather troubling passion, a passion that is often most manifest in books that lay claim to a revolutionary cause. Highly critical of the dominant mode of the book and its associated semiotic and subjective patterns, what they call the "root-book," Deleuze and Guattari develop a set of concepts for a fully materialist understanding of this medium and its politics and point to the possibilities of a counterfigure, the "rhizome-book." It is one of the most persuasive and developed of modern philosophies of the book, and yet it has received scant critical attention. This chapter proceeds as an investigation of that philosophy through the concrete mediations of specific books, as the problematic of the anti-book is taken up through an analytics of the root and the rhizome.

As is apparent from my argument in preceding chapters, the materiality in question is complex and emergent. Materiality is not a fixed property of books but a mutable product of their physical, signifying, temporal, and affective materials and relations, including relations brought to them in acts of reading and other forms of productive consumption. It is well known that a concern with the full complexity of material relations is paramount in Deleuze and Guattari's work, and it is in bringing this materialism to bear on the politics of the book that their critique is most distinguished from that of other poststructuralist philosophers who have taken aim at the book. In Derrida and Blanchot, the most renowned of these, the "book to come" (as they frame the overcoming of the book qua total work) does address the formal properties of books, but it is *text* and *writing* that hold the singular power of transformation. In *Of Grammatology,* Derrida famously puts it thus: "If I distinguish the text from the book, I shall say that the destruction of the book, as it is now under way in all domains, denudes the surface of the text."[2] John Mowitt elaborates:

> By opening a space where not only the "totality" can be named and sum-
> moned forth, but where this naming takes place within precise and thus
> secure borders (i.e., the physical dimensions of the printed manuscript),
> the book necessarily reifies writing, understood by Derrida, as that which
> marks every border as precarious and ill-defined. In this context the text
> designates that which, in its denuding, both precipitates the decline of
> the book and emerges as the monstrous technology that survives it.[3]

True, in Derrida's later essays on the subject collected in *Paper Machine,* the physical and formal features of books and other mediums of textual inscription come into the purview of deconstruction, often in inspired ways that I make use of in *Anti-Book.*[4] And yet these are accompanied by a somewhat conservative attraction to books, as I noted in chapter 1, from which the politics of media form tends to fall away. As for Blanchot, he offers much for critique of textual media form, some of which I consider in chapter 4, and it is possible to detect an influence of his formulation of the book's "outside" on Deleuze and Guattari's rhizome-book, and yet, again, it is in *writing* that his media politics lies: "The book: a ruse by which writing goes toward *the absence of the book.*"[5]

Deleuze and Guattari's materialism, then, opens new and unexplored avenues in the politics and philosophy of the book. And yet it too presents some problems. Despite Deleuze and Guattari's materialist conceptual framing of the book—and, with *A Thousand Plateaus,* their own experiment in the rhizome-book—they in fact pay little attention to the concrete forms and materials of books and publishing, leaving their typology of the book too often in the domain of the concept alone.[6] This is in marked contrast to Deleuze's research on cinema and painting, where philosophical engagement proceeds through close attention the concrete specificities of the mediums of film and paint. It is not I think too bold a conjecture to find the cause for this lapse into abstraction in precisely the material and formal properties of the book that Deleuze and Guattari do so much to reveal. Against that tendency to abstraction, this chapter pursues these material and formal properties in ways that keep the rich materiality of books at the center of discussion, so contributing to an understanding of political books that is fully engaged with their concrete forms. As such, the chapter at once sets out the contours of Deleuze and Guattari's typology of the book and mobilizes it to assess the material properties of four specific works: Mao Zedong's Little Red Book, Russian Futurist books, Antonin Artaud's paper "spells," and Guy Debord and Asger Jorn's self-declared "anti-book" *Mémoires.*

You may already be questioning the wisdom of considering together such disparate works, of which only Mao's book fulfills the conventional criteria of a political book (the others sit more comfortably in the analytic framework of the cultural avant-garde). And one of these, Artaud's spells, are not books at all but single-sheet artifacts, closer to letters or artworks on paper. Why, then, have I brought this heterogeneous group together? Mao's book is included principally because it is a paradigmatic case of the political root-book, and yet a book about which very little has been written—curiously so, given its enormous sales and global impact. Investigation of the Little Red Book is also an opportunity for me to hone—by way of a negative image—the understanding of communism that inheres in *Anti-Book,* in this instance by presenting a critique of Maoism and the Cultural Revolution, a politico-philosophical system and a historical sequence that has had not inconsiderable presence in contemporary efforts to revive a so-called communism for our times. The other works that feature here are all selected because they are at once singular experiments in the form of the codex book and textual matter and particularly enticing examples for thinking with the concept of the rhizome-book. The heterogeneity of the set is part of the appeal, for I in no way wish to compose a unified group of rhizome-books; Deleuze and Guattari, it is well known, are not averse to finding value in the open-ended assemblage of disparate elements. As for Artaud's spells, they disrupt the classificatory schema of the bulk of the chapters in this book, a disruption that is awkward but not without some merit, because although I am keen to assert something of the specificity of the media forms of pamphlet, book, and magazine, I in no sense wish to impose strict borders between them. The specific reason for considering Artaud's spells here is that they are extraordinary examples of textual matter as a "body without organs," a concept that is central to Deleuze and Guattari's philosophy of the book, and yet they say nothing about the material forms of these spells, even when quoting from their text.[7] It is an enticing lacuna.

THE DELUSIONAL PASSION OF THE BOOK

In naming the three components of Franz Kafka's "writing machine"— the letters, short stories, and novels—Deleuze and Guattari exclude his diaries, for these they remark are "the rhizome itself," they "touch upon everything" as the energetic milieu of Kafka's work as a whole.[8] I would not make quite such a claim for the recently published entries from Guattari's diary, which cover the writing and publication of *Anti-Oedipus.* Nevertheless, *The Anti-Oedipus Papers* draws that book back into the psychological, social, and technical milieu of its composition and reception, providing insight not only into Deleuze and Guattari's own writing machine—which is revealed to have been dependent on a complex and libidinally charged "text flow" of letters, book notes, theoretical writings, and intimate journal entries that Guattari passed on to Deleuze, somewhat compulsively, via the mediation of Fanny Deleuze—but also into the career of *Anti-Oedipus* itself.[9] Amid reflection on such matters as the damaging effect of this book on Guattari's relations with Lacan ("He wanted to see the manuscript. I retreated behind Gilles who only wants to show him something completely finished. . . . Impossible to back out. Dinner invitation, next week, to lay the cards out on the table"), or his fears at becoming an established author subject to his written word ("The plane of consistency of writing doesn't let anything go, every blow is counted. It's something that fucking sends death right up my spine"), Guattari makes this comment on the book's reception: "*Anti-Oedipus* is being disseminated like a militant book."[10]

One intuitively knows what Guattari means by this formulation. A "militant book" would be taken up in the arenas of political thought and practice rather than, say, in exclusively academic circles or popular book markets, where its consumption would take an intensive quality, having effects of intervention and consolidation in politicized environments. It is clear that Guattari is not exactly lamenting this mode of consumption. With *Anti-Oedipus,* as is well known, Deleuze and Guattari sought to introduce a breach in "Freudo-Marxism," and this at a practical level; as Foucault's preface has it, "*Anti-Oedipus* (may its authors forgive me) is a book of ethics."[11] Yet there is too I think some ambivalence in Guattari's assessment. Certainly he should not have been too comfortable with the notion of a militant book, because the repressive subjectivity of the "militant"—a subjectivity bound to the semiotic, organizational, and libidinal structures of the social system it nominally opposes—is the object of much critique in *Anti-Oedipus.* Nonetheless, this critique did not reach so far as to overly challenge the *book-form* of militancy. Indeed, the militant consumption of *Anti-Oedipus* might be seen to have some correspondence with its textual form. Notwithstanding the brilliance of its critique of capitalism, *Anti-Oedipus* rather follows the standard structure of a manifesto, critiquing its object through its emergence in historical time and leading in linear fashion to its declared subject of revolution, in this case the nonsubject of schizophrenic desire.

By the second volume of Capitalism and Schizophrenia, however, Deleuze and Guattari had become fully cognizant of the problem. *A Thousand Plateaus* actively attempts to scupper any appropriation of itself in the mode of the militant book, both in its use of a nonlinear structure, where cumulative chapters are replaced with "plateaus" to be read in any order, and in its textual content, proffering as it does a fully developed critique of militant modes of the book, which are shown to be entwined with a religious model of subjection constituted less in the manner of inventive critical politics than in authoritarian monomania. As the image of politics here becomes decidedly complex, immanent to the organic, inorganic, and semiotic conditions of planetary life, it takes with it the form of the book, in a deliciously experimental conceptual turn.

From the first pages, readers of *A Thousand Plateaus* encounter a typology of three kinds of book: the "root-book," the "fascicular root-book," and the "rhizome-book." These are tendencies or organizing patterns in the field of the book, not mutually exclusive categories; in any particular book, one would expect their copresence and interaction, albeit with varying degrees of prominence. But for Deleuze and Guattari, the dominant tendency, such that they call it the "classical" figure of this medium, is the root-book.

The root-book is a signifying totality, an enclosed and sufficient entity constituted as an image of the world—it is a "representationalist recapitulation of a reality external to it," in Daniel Selcer's description.[12] Here the book stands as the agent of truth and location of authority and command, its encyclopedic pretensions attaining spiritual unity with the totalizing word of God. It is a formation immanent to the sacred texts of Judaism, Christianity, and Islam, though Deleuze and Guattari leave much assumed here, and so it is instructive to pursue the lineaments of the concept of the root-book in relation to research on religion and the book. I will limit discussion largely to Christianity, a religion of the book for which spiritual authority is intimately identified with the word ("In the beginning was the Word, and the Word was with God, and the Word was God," in the opening of John's Gospel) and the codex. Here "the book received its highest consecration," as Ernst Robert Curtius puts it, where "Christ is the only god whom antique art represents with a book-scroll."[13] Not that this was a neat and clean relation. For James Kearney argues in *The Incarnate Text,* a work that I rely on in what follows, that Christianity proceeds through a vexed relation to the book that proved to be highly generative.

Picking up again the notion of the book as an image of the world, we can sketch two of numerous sources. For Francis Bacon in his 1605 *Advancement of Learning,* God provided two books: the volume of the Scriptures, which reveals God's will, and the volume of the creatures—more commonly known as "the book of nature"—which reveals his power.[14] These books exist in an imitative relation of complementarity, where the essential forms found in nature are mirrored in the universal book of Scriptures. Earlier, in his 1550 *Primera parte de las diferencias de libros que hay en el universo,* Alejo Venegas conceived of the book as an "ark" and "depository" of divine knowledge. As Walter Mignolo explains, for Venegas, "the human book has two functions: to know the creator of the Universe by reading His Book and, at the same time, to censure every human expression in which the Devil manifests itself by dictating false books."[15]

The essential structure of the root-book is clearly evident in these two influential expositions of the book. As it creates an *imitative* image of nature, the book presides, through the law of reflection, over the *split* between book and world. Severed from the world and, as such, pristine in its spiritual autonomy, the book is also a vector of *authority,* as is clear in Venegas: the "ark" of the book both enjoins subjection to God's Word and ensures against "false books." In this structure of the book as spiritual authority, we can trace also a source for the split between text and material form, and the concomitant denigration of the latter, that has been so persistent a feature of modern book culture. It is very much a story of the Reformation. An influential feature of Christian veneration of the book in the Middle Ages was the Aristotelian coincidence of truth and being, a "quasi-synonymy . . . of *pagina* and *doctrina, liber* and *scientia.*"[16] But with the Reformation, things took a different course. As Kearney shows, Protestantism, with its Lutheran slogan "*solo scriptura,*" was an intensification of the book within a religion of the book, as the word and the medium of the book were reaffirmed, against ritual and the trappings of the Church, as the source and means of Godly authority. And yet the Reformation book contains a "structural ambivalence," in Kearney's formulation, one that exacerbates a tension at the heart of Christian thought.[17] For the physical book was at once the vehicle for spiritual transcendence of the material world *and* part of that fallen world, a sign that humanity had been exiled from direct communication with God's Word. As Martin Luther put it, "if Adam had remained in innocence, this preaching would have been like a Bible for him and for all of us; and we would have had no need for paper, ink, pens, and that endless multitude of books which we require today."[18] The stage is set, then, for the denigration of the book's media form in favor of its textual content, as Protestants negotiate "the impossible position of attempting to overcome their fallen state by placing their faith in an aspect of the fallen world."[19]

The Christian problematic of the book reveals further component parts of the concept of the root-book. It is apparent from Venegas's notion of the book as ark that there is a mundane *subject* constituted in the book's truth and authority, those who would be enjoined to God's Word. It is a subject that is confirmed in its opposition to those who venerated the book as artifact: to Catholics, whose investment in splendid books as devotional objects is vividly illustrated by the sometime practice of incorporating the physical remains of saints into book covers and bindings, and to non-Europeans, in relation to whom the book serves as the "canary in the Enlightenment coal mine," revealing as savages all those who "cannot understand how to read the book as anything but a fetish."[20] Yet if this subject of the Word is structured against the book's sensory and material form, it is certainly not without its own passion, what Deleuze and Guattari call a "monomania" of "the book as origin and finality of the world."[21] They make this point about the book's passional subjectivity through an assessment of the place of this medium in the semiotic system they call the "postsignifying regime of signs." I present Chinese Maoism as an example of this postsignifying regime later, but it is useful first to sketch its principal characteristics.

We make an error in thinking that our linguistic or signifying system, where signs comprise an arbitrary connection between signifiers and signifieds in endless chains of relation, has any particular uniqueness or privilege in the history of expression. In fact, Deleuze and Guattari argue that there are numerous different semiotic systems, or "regimes of signs," of which the "postsignifying" regime (also called the "passional, subjective" regime) is particularly pertinent to discussion of the book.

As analytically distinct from the "signifying regime" (if rarely empirically so; all societies have a mixed semiotics), the postsignifying regime of signs is an "active" rather than "ideational" semiotic system. That is to say, it is characterized not by the endless cycle of interpretation of signs but by "concise formulas" conducive to passional, subjective action. In the *signifying regime,* the radiating network of signification is anchored in centers of interpretive authority (priest, despot, learned elite, political leader, media institution), its points of breakdown heavily coded with the negative value of the scapegoat. By contrast, in the *postsignifying regime,* this signifying network is loosened, and the scapegoat, he or she who is excluded, takes on a positive value of active flight or betrayal. In place of the centers of interpretive authority, local "points of subjectification" emerge that are constituted through the betrayal of dominant social relations and semiotic codes, a "monomania" that leads the subject on a passional vector through a series of finite linear proceedings, each drawn, as if to a "black-hole," by the pursuit of its end. This is the semiotics of the Israelites' exodus from Egypt, the semiotics of Cain and Jonah, where the relationship to God is constituted through flight and betrayal, "in which the true man never ceases to betray God just as God betrays man."[22] Jesus, Deleuze and Guattari write, takes this furthest: "he betrays the God of the Jews, he betrays the Jews, he is betrayed by God who turns away ('Why hast though forsaken me?'), he is betrayed by Judas, the true man."[23] But we are not dealing here only with God, for there are many instances of passional flight: the betrayal of food by anorexic subjectivities; the passional flight of the fetishist, the shoe, say, as his point of subjectification; the monomania of the amorous couple, "a cogito built for two" (indeed, Deleuze and Guattari identify the Cartesian cogito as the quintessential instance of passional subjectivation, a line of flight ever recharged by methodological doubt, that possibility of betrayal by a deceitful God or evil genius).[24] As to the speaking subject of the passional regime, it is constituted through a doubling or enfolding of the "subject of enunciation," the emitter of signs, the prophet (as distinct from the sedentary and signifying priest), and the "subject of the statement," the people in flight, where the latter is bound to the utterances of the former and acts in a "reductive echolalia" as its respondent and guarantor.[25]

Figure 3. The Ark of the Covenant, a portable packet of signs, eighteenth-century depiction at the Battle of Jericho. Artist unknown.

Set off on flight, signification is now unmoored and mobile and so needs a mobile ground: the Ark of the Covenant containing Moses's tablets of Law—"no more than a little portable packet of signs"—and no longer the Temple (Figure 3).[26] By extension, in the action-oriented formulas of the postsignifying regime, the book emerges as the quintessential object of mobile signification—a development apparent in the movement from the Ark of the Covenant in Figure 3 to the tablets in Figure 4, and subsequently to the codex, as the vessel of the Ten Commandments diminishes in volume and gains in portability. Deleuze and Guattari argue that at this point the book moves away from an essentially oral, "nonbook" character with external referent in God or despot and instead comes to internalize the world as the origin and source of truth and authority:

> in the passional regime the book seems to be internalized, and to internalize everything: it becomes the sacred written Book. It takes the place of the face and God, who hides his face and gives Moses the inscribed stone tablets. . . . *The book has become the body of passion.* . . . It is now the book, the most deterritorialized of things, that fixes territories and genealogies. The latter are what the book says, and the former the place at which the book is said.[27]

Figure 4. God hides his face and gives Moses the inscribed stone tablets, 1877 lithograph. Artist unknown. Courtesy of the Library of Congress.

I have elaborated on much of this passage already, but we need a little more reconstruction to ground the formulation of the book here as the mobile "body of passion." I noted that the Reformation approach to the book held an ambivalent relation to matter that accompanied Christianity at origin, and it was not put to rest with the rise of Protestant veneration of scripture. As this ambivalence is worked over in Catholic and Protestant writing and teaching, the book as artifact and medium takes various forms, many of which suggest empirical referents for Deleuze and Guattari's thesis. Let me take two instances. As much as it is a religion of the book, Christianity is a religion of the *codex*; though nearly all the books named in the Old Testament are in the form of the scroll, the codex replaced the scroll as the dominant medium of textual inscription in Christian cultures as early as the second century of the Common Era (and, in turn, the rise of Christianity played no small part in the gradual supplanting of the scroll as the socially preferred medium of textual inscription).[28] Intriguingly, Christianity actively adopted here a somewhat humble and lowly object, an ephemeral medium of little economic or cultural value. Whereas the scroll was associated with elite culture, with sacred, literary, and juridical texts, the codex was the medium of trade and everyday transactions, familiar, that is, to more plebeian classes—associated with women and slaves more than citizens.[29] As well as a means of differentiating this religion from others through its chosen medium, the codex simultaneously, then, articulated the central Christian values of identification with the excluded and debased, taking its pivotal place in the "repertoire of symbols" of Christian value: "just as a criminal executed by the state was revealed as the godhead, so the humble codex was exalted over the prestigious scroll."[30]

The Christian symbolism of the book does not stop there; it is most acute in the common conceit of identifying the codex with a symbol of no less importance than Christ himself. In one instance discussed by Kearney, Christ is described as a "book written within the skin of the virgin," and the subsequent arc of his life, passion, death, resurrection, and ascension are mapped onto the processes of production and reception of this medium.[31] In another example, John Fisher, Bishop of Rochester, narratives Christ's crucifixion through the parts of a book, pursuing the metaphor in boards, pages, lines, text, and including this image of Christ's splayed body: "First I saye that a booke hath two boardes: the two boardes of this booke is the two partes of the crosse, for when the booke is opened & spread, the leaues be cowched vpon the boardes. And so the blessed body of Christ was spread vpon the cross."[32]

There is some evidence, hence, for understanding the Christian book as the mobile "body of passion." How about Deleuze and Guattari's point that the book becomes the locus of authority and command? We have seen God hide his face in the Christian trope of betrayal and, with Luther, the book replace the Church as the location of authority—a book whose independence from the Church is given material proof in the Protestant trope of the book as a simple, somewhat abject artifact, and affirmed as such against the ornate, illuminated books of the Catholic Mass. Granted, the turn to scripture is not immediately appreciable as the "pure and literal recitation" without commentary or interpretation that Deleuze and Guattari see as characteristic of the root-book and its commanding formulas. And yet Luther saw God's Word as truth without history, leaving Catholics like Thomas More to see this as bibliolatry and radical Protestants such as Thomas Müntzer to claim it to be a reification of scripture, worthless without spiritual transformation: "The man who has not received the living witness of God . . . knows really nothing about God, though he may have swallowed 100,000 Bibles."[33] As to Catholic teachings, there is a clear seam that links passion for the book with devotional practice in direct contrast to reading and interpretation.

All that said, if the root-book is religious in origin, it is not limited to such formations. As Curtius shows, metaphors of the total book, as mimetic complement to "the book of nature," are found first in the Latin Middle Ages and soon cross over from the pulpit to philosophy, where they have featured in Montaigne, Descartes, Galileo, Bacon, Voltaire, Rousseau, Hume, and Goethe. More pertinent for our purposes, the leading edge of culture and politics has often proven to be especially receptive to the "strangest cult" of the book, a point Deleuze and Guattari make in the strongest critical terms: "Wagner, Mallarmé, and Joyce, Marx and Freud: still Bibles."[34] Mallarmé's formulation of the book as "spiritual instrument"—"all earthly existence must ultimately be contained in a book"—is the clearest expression of this tendency.[35] But the degree to which Marx is subject to the passional form of the book is questionable; indeed, in *The German Ideology,* Marx and Engels themselves make a direct critique of the religious mode of the book that is remarkably resonant with that of Deleuze and Guattari.[36] Nonetheless, this defense of Marx cannot always be made of Marxism, for the regimes where Marxism became state doctrine were often characterized by a considerable cult of the book. It is to one of these regimes that I now turn to discuss a specific instance of a political root-book.

MAO ZEDONG'S LITTLE RED BOOK

It would be hard to find a book more enmeshed in its immediate environment than *Quotations from Chairman Mao Tse-tung,* otherwise known as the Little Red Book. It has claim to be the second best selling book in world history, and although it trails far behind the Bible, it makes up for this in the astonishing concentration of its production: 1 billion official copies were published in a period of five years, between 1966 and 1971, with the second year of the Cultural Revolution, 1967, accounting for 350 million.[37] The Little Red Book was not a *cause* of the Cultural Revolution, yet—as is indicated by its frequent and central presence in the iconic posters and photographic records of the period—it was an object with a considerable agential role in inspiring, distributing, and consolidating the collective passions of that upheaval (Figures 5 and 6; Plate 4).[38] These posters and images also speak to the significance of its material qualities, as does its popular name, which foregrounds less the content, the "quotations," than the physical dimensions of the book and its color.

Quotations was principally a means for the transmission of the politico-philosophical system officially known as "Mao Zedong Thought," of which it is no contradiction to say that the book was at once an oversimplified distillation and an articulation of its essence, insofar as the book handled and extended the passional semiotic of Maoism. This semiotic was manifest in concentrated fashion in the Cultural Revolution, the mass movement with which the book's fate was intertwined and the context of my discussion here. For brevity's sake, in what follows, I have taken

Figure 5. "Mao Zedong Thought is the magic weapon to victoriously combat all enemies at home and abroad!," circa 1967. Courtesy of IISH/Stefan R. Landsberger Collections, http://chineseposters.net/.

Figure 6. Red Guards holding aloft Mao's Little Red Book: "Chairman Mao is the reddest red sun in our hearts," 1967. Courtesy of the University of Westminster Chinese Poster Collection, http://chinaposters.westminster.ac.uk/.

the passional structure of Mao Zedong Thought to be the principal "content" of *Quotations,* though I make occasional comment about its textual instantiations in particular works.

Whereas Mao's China comprised various semiotic regimes, Mao Zedong Thought presents a clear instance of the dynamics of the word in the passional or postsignifying regime of signs. Žižek is not alone in observing a wholly "cosmic" orientation in Maoism, one that bound the Chinese people to a transcendent trajectory of liberation that Mao's Thought discerned in the movement of human and natural history.[39] In Mao's understanding of dialectics, the world was essentially composed of "two major forces, revolution and counter-revolution," as he put it, a "struggle of opposites [that] is absolute."[40] It was a formulation that Mao might as equally use to appraise particular political conjunctures as he would the likely outcome of nuclear war or the evolution of humanity. For instance: "The life of dialectics is the continuous movement towards opposites. Mankind will also finally meet its doom. When the theologians talk about doomsday, they are pessimistic and terrify people. We say the end of mankind is something which will produce something more advanced than mankind."[41]

This prophetic *reflection* of the movement of human and natural history in Mao's Thought was simultaneously a *separation* from it, one that protected the "purity" of the word against the "ubiquitous contamination" of the everyday, as Robert Jay Lifton describes it.[42] Hence we find that the trope of purity and corruption is liberally peppered through *Quotations.* For example, regarding the practice of "criticism–self-criticism" (an ethicopolitical technique integral to the Cultural Revolution, as I consider subsequently), Mao writes that it "prevents all kinds of political dust and germs from contaminating the minds of our comrades and the body of our Party."[43] And in a variation of the trope, the purity of Mao Zedong Thought is elsewhere conveyed, intriguingly for our purposes, with the aid of a metaphor drawn from the realm of textual matter, as Mao assesses the apparent advantages of the "poor and blank" condition of the peasantry: "A clean sheet of paper has no blotches, and so the newest and most beautiful words can be written on it."[44]

Mao Zedong Thought, then, was a pristine truth in separation from the world, but, in accord with the passional structure of the root-book, it was subsequently returned to the world as authority and action. As such, it constituted the Maoist "point of subjectification," spiritualizing the word as substance, nourishment, and energizer of an immortal revolutionary cause. In the language of a 1966 People's Liberation Army (PLA) newspaper, "the thought of Mao Tse-tung is the sun in our heart, is the root of our life, is the source of all our strength. Through this, man becomes unselfish, daring, intelligent, able to do everything; he is not conquered by any difficulty and can conquer every enemy."[45]

As to the means by which this passional subjectivity was embodied and performed, individual identification with revolutionary immortality was achieved in large measure through proximity with death. This is amply evident in the "three constantly read articles" of the Cultural Revolution period, two of which feature heavily in *Quotations*. "Serve the People," for instance, discourses on a "worthy death," a death of great weight and significance as a consequence of serving the immortal popular cause, in contrast to the insignificant death, "lighter than a feather," that arises from assisting reactionary forces without attachment to the substance of revolution.[46] The point was not to die, exactly, though this had a place as we will see, but rather, as Lifton puts it, "to cultivate such a death and thereby, during life, enhance [one's] individual *sense* of immortality," one's intense affective investment in the cause.[47] A worthy death might be cultivated while facing the enemy in the battlefield, as in "Serve the People" and "In Memory of Norman Bethune," but it also applied to more mundane circumstances, where it evoked selfless dedication to the revolutionary cause even under the most inopportune circumstances. Hence the significance of the third of these articles, "The Foolish Old Man Who Removed the Mountains," the only text that appears in *Quotations* in its entirety. Drawing from folklore, it tells of an old man who strove to dig away by hoe two great peaks that obstructed his home. This impossible task was "foolish" by conventional wisdom, but the man's unshaken dedication to his task, to which he offered his progeny "to infinity," moved God to send two angels to carry off the mountains.[48] In Mao's version, God is brought down to earth, where now "the masses" convert the impossible into the possible.[49] The story displays the intense subjectivism of Mao's Thought, a position that in its extreme taught that the external world was to be appraised only as a function of subjective purity and revolutionary will. As one volume on the study of Mao's Thought put it, a propos the attempted agricultural transformations of the Great Leap Forward, "many living examples show that there is only unproductive thought, there are no unproductive regions."[50]

Mao's Thought also gained traction in its ability to function at the level of personal morality. As is apparent already, Maoism was as much a struggle internal to the self as it was oriented toward collectivity and external goals. In the words of Lin Biao, head of the PLA, "we must regard ourselves as an integral part of the revolutionary force and, at the same time, constantly regard ourselves as a target of the revolution."[51] This application onto oneself of the Maoist principle of "one divides into two" (the universal struggle of revolutionary tendencies against counterrevolution) took the principal form of criticism–self-criticism, but Mao's Thought also presented a set of ethical criteria and ritual practices to evaluate and manage everyday behavior, some of which I consider shortly.

If the revolutionary subject was to embrace immortality through the ethical limit of a worthy death, disregard for death featured more directly in Mao's socioeconomic strategies, as the catastrophe of the Great Leap Forward (1958–62) confirms. Tens of millions died of starvation, overwork, torture, and summary killing as Mao sought an ultravoluntarist route to industrialization via the superexploitation of labor—its aim crystallized in the governing slogan "Catch up with and surpass Britain in fifteen years"—while exporting grain during the famine to fund the import of military and industrial technology.[52] And Mao's words are no less revealing than his policies, as in this framing of nuclear war, for example, from a letter to Nikita Khrushchev: "For our ultimate victory, . . . for the total eradication of the imperialists, we . . . are willing to endure the first [U.S. nuclear] strike. All it is is a big pile of people dying."[53]

Such were the postsignifying characteristics of Mao Zedong Thought that it is no surprise that, while an early essay by Mao called to "oppose book worship," by the time of the Cultural Revolution, Mao's texts had become elevated to a fount of singular truth: "the best books in the world, the most scientific books, the most revolutionary books."[54] Or, in Lin Bao's preface to the second edition of *Quotations,* Mao's Thought was "a spiritual atom bomb of infinite power."[55] Thus sanctified, Mao's words also took on the authoritarian function of the root-book that we saw earlier in Venegas, as is apparent in the command of the Communist Party daily, the *Red Flag,* to "establish with utmost effort the absolute authority of the great Mao Zedong's Thought," "let Mao Zedong's Thought control everything."[56]

From the passional structure of Mao's Thought, we can now turn to the textual and physical form of *Quotations,* a central means of its social articulation. *Quotations* was initially published on a restricted basis in May 1964 under Lin Biao's direction as a vehicle for the political instruction of the PLA. The book comprised extracts from Mao's works in thirty thematic chapters, extending to thirty-three in 1965, with 427 quotations in all.[57] Short and abstracted from the political and tactical contexts of their initial creation, most of the quotations offered not "concrete political analysis" but "moral truths," "trans-historical scripts for revolutionary praxis," as Daniel Leese and Andrew F. Jones characterize them.[58] In other words, the quotations lent themselves to the ungrounded and intensified subjectivations of Mao's passional regime. More concretely, their textual structure enabled a pedagogical practice characterized by group learning and recitation of passages and slogans, an approach long practiced in the PLA that became pivotal to the book's use following mass publication in 1966. Lin Biao described the benefits of such pedagogy thus: "Learning the writings of Comrade Mao Zedong is the shortcut to learning Marxism-Leninism. Chairman Mao's writings are easy to learn, and once learned can be put to use immediately."[59] While such a group-work approach to the "shortcut" of learning clearly has progressive features, its proximity to authoritarian signifying patterns is also apparent. As an "active" rather than "ideational" semiotic structure, Deleuze and Guattari argue that the concise formulas of the root-book require only identification, as interpretation "gives way to pure and literal recitation forbidding the slightest change, addition, or commentary."[60] That this was a feature of Mao's regime is often noted in the critical literature, but it was also actively affirmed, as is apparent from the words of a Shanghai newspaper from 1967: "We must carry out Chairman Mao's instructions whether we understand them or not."[61] One might question the degree to which such rote learning could truly secure enduring identification, but Leese has argued that, combined with efforts to solicit strong emotional response from the text, rote repetition offered certainty and security amid the social disorientation that followed the Great Leap Forward. It may in fact have been the need to in this way contain the impact of the famine that was the impetus for Lin Biao's adoption of this pedagogical practice, and hence for compiling *Quotations* in the first place.[62]

The passional activation of *Quotations* was constituted, then, in the structure of its content and pedagogical mode of reception, but it also took shape in the book's wider material properties. Jones argues that the pocket-sized portability of the Little Red Book, and perhaps even its "talismanic character," was in part "an extension of the underlying logic of the quotation as a literary genre," the promiscuous capacity of quotation to circulate as an integrated and autonomous unity abstracted from specific context.[63] True, there is correlation between the book's quotational and physical forms, but the determinations and effects of the latter, and the social dynamics of its reception and utilization, are not reducible to its textual mode. Designed to fit into soldiers' breast pockets, and vinyl-clad as protection for use in the field, the portability of *Quotations* combines with its *redness,* and this is its most striking and alluring feature. Its red vinyl covers unify the book globally across its translations, perhaps with something of a universal appeal, but in China they carried particular semiotic resonance. Already a prominent signifier of prosperity in Chinese culture, red connoted a commitment to Chinese communism and was elevated into a foundational sign of passional struggle during the Cultural Revolution. One former Red Guard recalls,

> At the time China was engulfed in a permanent red storm. . . . Chairman Mao was our red Commander-in-Chief. We called ourselves "his little red devils." We read and quoted his little red book. Wore his red buttons on our chests. Red Flags. Red armbands. Red blood. Red hearts. . . . We could not tolerate anyone who was of a different color.[64]

In this fashion, the redness of *Quotations* could be experienced as a collective flood of color. Describing Mao's 1966 sunrise audiences with the Red Guards in Tiananmen Square, one biographer writes, "Waved in the air, the red covers [of *Quotations*] made the square resemble a field ablaze with butterflies."[65] But the mass distribution of this compact object—with the rich sensory qualities that are germane to the tactile, portable medium of the book—was such that its compound of redness, struggle, and Mao Zedong Thought could also be experienced at an intimate, personal level. The endorsement leaf in Lin Biao's calligraphy contributed to a feeling of intimacy with the book, a feeling no doubt entrenched by the emotional disjunction associated with the subsequent defacement or removal of this page by each owner, following Lin Biao's death and denunciation.[66] The book could also take part in everyday ritual. At the start of the work and school day, groups would line up in front of Mao's portrait and wave *Quotations* while giving the "three respects and three wishes"; the same practices might also take place immediately on waking or before a meal.[67] Rhythmic waving of the book also had a place in Maoist dance routines known as "loyalty dances," and according to Xing Lu, there was even a correct manner of holding *Quotations* at such ceremonies: with the thumb placed in front and fingers behind, the book would be held over the heart to indicate loyalty and boundless love.[68]

Quotations played a particular role too in the monomania of the Red Guards, the young passional agents of the Cultural Revolution, known for their nomadic mass movement across the country in the "exchange of revolutionary experience" and the violence that followed such injunctions as "Beat to a pulp any and all persons who go against Mao Zedong Thought" and "Long live the red terror" (to quote Red Guard wall posters from two elite middle schools in Beijing).[69] It is a suitable moment to pause and underscore the role of "reception" or the "reader" in the social production of *Quotations*. The Red Guards complete the Little Red Book, but they also *make* it, for it only came to be itself because of the mass consumption associated with the Cultural Revolution and the particular role that it took therein. The Cultural Revolution shows too how complex is the phenomenon of readership, for the productive consumption of this book took many forms other than "reading"—including, as I have suggested, devotion, display, and ritual—as much as the nature of reading here, in the action-oriented semiotic within which it was manifest, was itself highly varied. But what about variation in *interpretation*, the fundamental feature of reader-focused theories of the production of text? There was in fact considerable variation in readers' interpretations of *Quotations,* with different individuals, state functionaries, and Red Guard factions seeking to mobilize meanings in different contexts and to different and competing ends. And yet variation in the interpretation of particular texts (aided by the ungrounded nature of the quotations, as I noted earlier) was perfectly compatible with uniformity in the manifestation of their passional structure, in the monomania of Mao Zedong Thought.

Monomania, this central property of the postsignifying regime, had a specific articulation with the Red Guards' mode of autonomy, an autonomy that was intrinsic to the unleashed brutality of the Cultural Revolution, following Mao's call to "boldly arouse the masses" against the established authorities.[70] This is the somewhat paradoxical autonomy of the passional mode of subjectivity, with its monomania and reductive echolalia, where "the more you obey . . . the more in command you are."[71] As Lifton argues, the autonomy of the Red Guards was characterized by a rare sense of "participating in a great moral crusade" and "of taking matters *into their own hands,* " but in a fashion constituted through a "totalistic attack upon any signs of the independent (non-Maoist) self."[72] Betrayal, that constitutive feature of the passional regime of signs, was endemic: the Chinese revolution was understood to be suffering betrayal by internal "capitalist roadsters"; revolution against this, the Maoist principle of "cultural revolution," was formulated as a *perpetual* betrayal, as the Party and established authorities were figured as that which must be ever challenged and overcome; Red Guards were to betray *themselves,* splitting off any "black" or counterrevolutionary qualities; and traitors and capitalist roadsters were found in every corner of society, ever setting off passional subjectivities on their next proceeding. My interest here is in the monomania set loose, but, given the tremendous appeal the Cultural Revolution had among large sectors of the Chinese population and, indeed, among Western radicals, it is important to register first the particular delusion of this cause.

Though some trends in current philosophy after Badiou still claim otherwise, the Cultural Revolution was not a highpoint of global revolutionary endeavor but a power struggle resulting from a split in the governing class of a demagogic state capitalist regime, as Mao, utilizing his preeminent place in official ideology, sought to reassert his authority (and, ultimately, his recourse to industrialization through superexploitation and terror) following the disaster of the Great Leap Forward. Simon Leys (pen name of Pierre Ryckmans) is most insightful here. An ardent Sinologist, he was, along with the Situationist International (SI), one of the very rare voices on the Left not to succumb to Mao and the ideological representation of the Cultural Revolution.[73] Leys puts it plainly: "The 'Cultural Revolution' had nothing revolutionary about it except the name, and nothing cultural about it except the initial tactical pretext."[74] Indeed, he suggests that the Red Guard phenomenon displayed some striking similarities with the Fascist movement of the Blue Shirts in 1930s Koumintang China, the two sharing the self-declared principles of unconditional allegiance to a supreme leader; anti-intellectualism; fixation on manual labor as a transcendent purpose; cultural conservatism, manifest as physical attacks on perceived decadent Western styles and forms; and the singular value of mass, popular violence.[75] True, the Cultural Revolution claimed to be a revolution against the capitalist corruption of the Party, a movement for communism conceived of as perpetual revolution against establishment stasis and the "Four Olds" (old customs, old culture, old habits, old ideas), but this was merely Mao's ruse to unseat his opponents in the bureaucracy. And it served precisely this aim, a churn of the bureaucracy rather than a challenge to the real conditions of hardship and exploitation, class conditions that Mao, in his efforts toward rapid industrial modernization, in fact sought to entrench and extend. Why, then, did it attract such astonishing emotional investment and mass political support? Leys speculates that it was precisely because the Chinese peasants and workers had every reason to believe the rhetoric, to feel that they were indeed barred from the promised classless society, that they seized the proffered route to revolution so vigorously. He presents his thesis thus:

> The "class struggle" as understood in the Maoist system—that is, the denunciation by the masses of guilty parties who have been singled out for them by the powers that be—is the regime's safety valve, its basic hygiene, a periodic bloodletting that allows it to eliminate the toxins in its organism. For the masses, this ritual exercise gives a very convincing appearance of reality. The violence and the blood that always flows

in these operations, the high positions and broad powers that had once been the preserve of the bureaucrats now found guilty—all this seems to show that a true revolution is occurring. In fact, the double cross is perfect, for the essence of the bureaucratic system is the interchange-ability of bureaucrats, and no mere change of personnel could alter the nature of the regime.[76]

The point is aptly made also in René Viénet's documentary *détournement*, *Peking Duck Soup*, from which I cite a passage that conveys the sudden transformation of the social regime as despotic signification gave way to passional monomania:

> The Orwellian system built up over the years under which everyone had to be aware at all times of the police, the army, the party, the union, not to mention the factory bosses—the Red Guards transcend this system in a matter of hours. What had been jokingly called the "socialist ethic" disappears and is replaced by a new form of politics, which immediately evokes the unbounded admiration of the Western world. The entire population wakes up one morning to find itself subjected, without appeal, to the murderous caprices of Mao's children, who have not yet drunk their Coca Cola. Of course, these kids have every reason to go on the rampage against the bureaucrats, but from the start they are barking up the wrong tree. Instead of doing a number on the bureaucracy, they do one on the proletariat.[77]

Such, then, were the principles and realities of the Cultural Revolution. Its *evaluative criterion* was of course Mao Zedong Thought. Mao's Thought was the means of assaying practice and of stoking the flames of passional flight, as was especially apparent in the technique of criticism–self-criticism (or struggle–criticism–transformation). Originally a formal procedure for confessing and externalizing offending acts, and so developing a redemptive integration of individuals with the Party, in the Cultural Revolution, criticism–self-criticism became entwined with the Red Guards' destructive monomania. In other words, it shifted from an integrating, "collegial" relation to a postsignifying linear proceeding along a "principle of autocracy," as Lowell Dittmer puts it, where "the indeterminacy of Mao's Thought as a calculus of innocence or guilt meant that criticism had no intrinsic limits":

Once someone came under attack, there was an inevitable dynamic to the criticism process which propelled it towards his destruction. The target was isolated, since any contact with him ran the risk of implication. His self-criticisms were indignantly rejected, for to be resolute and merciless was to be "Left," whereas to accept self-criticism was to risk siding with a condemned man. This inherent dynamic vitiated the intended function of criticism as a sort of ordeal by fire for aberrant cadres, simply because no target could possibly "pass the test."[78]

What place did *Quotations* take in this passional monomania? Manifesting the root-book's function as location and guarantor of truth and authority, the mass-distributed object of *Quotations* served to open a direct line of affective integration between Mao and the population that was unmediated by the Party's interpretive authority.[79] Moreover, the "reject[ion]" of "intermediaries or specialists," as Deleuze and Guattari characterize the action-oriented modes of reception of the root-book, here enabled a recoiling of Mao into the masses, the subject of enunciation into the subject of the statement, a point visually displayed in Figure 6.[80] Like a portable packet of signs, *Quotations* thus provided the Red Guards with a distributed and mobile set of points of passional subjectification and enunciation unmoored from, and in betrayal of, established sources of institutional power. If "political power grows out of the barrel of a gun," as Mao's maxim has it, here the gun had a ready companion in the *book*.[81]

The weaponization of words features heavily in Lin Biao's textual packaging of *Quotations* and was taken up at the time in Harun Farocki's early short film, *The Words of the Chairman* (1967). Structured "like a commercial," as Farocki later mused—or, we might say, like a slogan or quotation—a figure wearing a Mao-style hat tears out a page from *Quotations* to the audio accompaniment of Lin Biao's preface.[82] This is fashioned into a dart and launched into a bowl of soup at the dinner table of two characters wearing paper masks of the Shah of Iran and his wife, spattering the Shah as if shot (Figure 7). A literal reading is encouraged by knowledge that the film was made shortly after a critical moment in German militancy when the police killed a student demonstrator protesting the Shah's visit to West Berlin. (That the film's cinematographer was Holger Meins, soon

Figure 7. Screen grabs from Harun Farocki's *The Words of the Chairman,* 1967.

to be of the Red Army Faction, does not discourage this reading.) And yet the blunt clarity of the message also serves to ironize a literal interpretation, as does the rather kitsch scene that opens and closes the film, the close-up of a spinning Little Red Book accompanied by Chinese choral music. This twofold quality of Farocki's film partakes of the Orientalist manner by which Maoist slogans and artifacts were adopted by European radicals as they failed miserably to understand the Cultural Revolution, while at the same time pushing that into parody. Yet this way of framing Chinese Maoism is a very Euro-American story. In China itself, the relation between words and deeds was far from playful; the volitional power of *Quotations* in popular violence (including violence directed against those who defaced or accidentally damaged the book) was clear and apparent. For how else are we to interpret the images of impassioned Red Guards in the heat of upheaval, at mass rallies, in criticism sessions, at beatings, waving aloft, of all things, these diminutive red vinyl books?

True, Mao did not "hide his face" in the direct sense that Deleuze and Guattari mark as constitutive of the passional regime of signs— 11 or 12 million Red Guards came to Beijing for the 1966 rallies with Mao, and his image, as part of the official cult of personality, was famously ubiquitous. But then his role as despot was never far off and was soon to return in the restoration of order, once Mao's position in the Party had been reestablished (and the army was subsequently mobilized to stamp out the movement that it had hitherto protected, curtailing the passional flight of the Red Guards—and the workers and soldiers who had started to strike and mutiny against the Maoist regime and the Red Guards—and reasserting labor discipline). Until then, at these mass rallies, Mao rarely spoke beyond a few words, for to do otherwise would have been to risk the distributed authority of the passional forces set loose: "The leader who used to lecture for hours to persuade his followers of the merits of a new policy now merely appeared before them with an upraised hand and a glassy smile."[83]

THE RHIZOME-BOOK

Moving from the root-book to the rhizome-book, Deleuze and Guattari set out their counter figure by returning to the relation between the book and the world. If, as we have seen, the root-book is in a relation of separation and imitation with the world—"The law of the book is the law of reflection"—it is based on a misapprehension of nature: "How could the law of the book reside in nature, when it is what presides over the very division between world and book, nature and art?"[84] It is a quite different understanding of nature that informs the rhizome-book, a book not characterized by a pristine truth in imitative separation from the world but by an immersive transformation, an "aparallel evolution of the book and the world."[85] In this sense, the "book exists only through the outside and on the outside."[86] Using a related metaphor, the book here is a "little machine" that plugs into its outside not to reproduce the world in the book's image but to construct a discontinuous series of intensive states or plateaus, in relation to which it has no identity, it is always "broken."[87]

The root-book does of course also exist through relations with its outside (as we saw in the Cultural Revolution), but in the rhizome-book, the outside is no longer framed by the book's spiritual autonomy and truth. Rather, the outside floods into the book, as a condition of becoming between the two. Here the distinction between "root" and "rhizome" assists in articulating a certain mode of being qua difference. The root is an arborescent image of thought, as the tree and its root evoke a binary logic of identity and difference, the latter merely a derivation of the former in a series of bifurcations from a primordial unity, whereby "One becomes two" (or "one divides into two," as in the Maoist schema that Deleuze and Guattari reference in this context). The rhizome, by contrast, models the world of grasses and tubers, which have no trunk or unity but grow opportunistically at any point and in any direction. In a rhizome, then, it is not that the one divides into two but that "the One is always subtracted."[88]

A rhizome is an acentered and nonhierarchical system that has "neither beginning nor end, but always a middle (milieu) from which it grows and which it overspills."[89]

In enumerating the qualities of the rhizome, Deleuze and Guattari display a profound feeling for the many materialities of organic and inorganic life, and this is foregrounded in their characterization of its book, whereby the rhizome-book is understood to be a complex and variable arrangement of heterogeneous materials: "A book has neither object nor subject; it is made of variously formed matters, and very different dates and speeds."[90] Yet despite these materialist conceptual framings, Deleuze and Guattari offer little significant insight on *bookish* materials, on how the specificities of textual matter might be expressed in the mode of the rhizome-book. This is understandable, given the radically open process that the concept seeks to name, for the lack of concrete specificity functions to affirm the *proliferation* of specificities, unencumbered by the attractor of a delineated model. And we should register too that a rhizome-book is defined as much by its endogenous characteristics, its mutable encounters, as by any conceptual, formal, or physical features that might inhere within it. However, this lack of attention to the specific materialities of books also has the unfortunate effect of allowing the rhizome-book to appear by default as a rather abstract or metaphorical entity and not something with concrete manifestation in the realms of textual matter. This description of the rhizome-book is indicative: "The ideal for a book would be to lay everything out on a plane of exteriority . . . , on a single page, the same sheet: lived events, historical determinations, concepts, individuals, groups, social formations."[91] For all the powerful evocation here of the immanence of the book to its outside (the "plane of exteriority"), as material form, it features only as a metaphorical "single page."

Skeptical readers might at this point respond that the rhizome-book is fundamentally a figure of *philosophical* production, that it aims to push philosophy from a reflective relation of reciprocal identity with the world to an immanent relation of variation, that *this* is where its materiality lies, not in any serious or sustained relation to the concrete forms of writing and publishing. The preceding identification of the "page" with, for example, "lived events" would seem to indicate as much, and the thesis can also find some support in Deleuze and Guattari's typology, in their concept of the "fascicular root-book." Designating the botched escape from the root-book, the concept is designed to scupper modernist experiments in textual and typographic form. Evoking fibrous or adventitious root systems, clusters of fine radicles without a central taproot, the fascicular root-book has severed its principal root or unity such that it opens out to the world, where the world is now understood to be fragmented and chaotic. But the book remains, in root-book mode, as a totalizing image of the (now chaotic) world. Imitative complementarity persists between world and book, object and subject, matter and spirit, as the book *compensates* for chaos with a secret or supplementary unity of the work amid its fragmentary form:

> The abortionists of unity are indeed angel makers, *doctors angelici,* because they affirm a properly angelic and superior unity. . . . Unity is consistently thwarted and obstructed in the object, while a new type of unity triumphs in the subject. . . . The world has become chaos, but the book remains the image of the world. . . . A strange mystification: a book all the more total for being fragmented.[92]

As I indicated earlier, Joyce's decentered narratives and Mallarmé's book qua "spiritual instrument" are Deleuze and Guattari's main targets, but they also bring William Borroughs's "cut-up" method to illustrate this fascicular figure of the book, and Nietzsche, whose "aphorisms shatter the linear unity of knowledge, only to invoke the cyclic unity of the eternal return."[93] Here the critique of formal experimentation is made in no uncertain terms:

> To attain the multiple, one must have a method that effectively constructs it; no typographical cleverness, no lexical agility, no blending or creation of words, no syntactical boldness, can substitute for it. In fact, these are more often than not merely mimetic procedures used to disseminate or disperse a unity that is retained in a different dimension for an image-book. Technonarcissism.[94]

And yet Deleuze and Guattari are not wholly hostile, for the passage continues:

Typographical, lexical, or syntactic creations are necessary only when they no longer belong to the form of expression of a hidden unity, becoming themselves dimensions of the multiplicity under consideration; we only know of rare successes in this. We ourselves were unable to do it. We just used words that in turn function for us as plateaus.[95]

These quotations amply display Deleuze and Guattari's own tastes in method—"We just used words"—but there is no a priori rejection here of intervention in the book's material form. Neither should we expect there to be. If an "assemblage, in its multiplicity, necessarily acts on semiotic flows, material flows, and social flows simultaneously," then it would be wholly inconsistent to confine the assemblage of the book only to the former.[96] And so, succumbing to their own argument, *A Thousand Plateaus* does in fact make some brief positive comment on concrete experiments in book form. In developing the concept of the rhizome-book, Deleuze and Guattari give some prominence to three modern works on the early-thirteenth-century Children's Crusades, works that generate a nomadic expression in the flow of narratives, movements, and peoples. While these books are still said to be subject to the unity of the fascicular root-book, here there is nonetheless definite appreciation of formal innovation. In Armand Farrachi's *La Dislocation,* for instance, Deleuze and Guattari note enthusiastically that the "sentences space themselves out and disperse, or else jostle together and coexist, and . . . the letters, the typography begin to dance as the crusade grows more delirious."[97] And there is one example of a "rare success" that stands unchallenged: *Absolument nécessaire. The Emergency Book* by Joëlle de La Casinière, which is credited in a footnote as "a truly nomadic book."[98] Deleuze and Guattari make no further comment, but it is a bookwork of graphic poetry, travelogue, and montage, expressive of the itinerant lifestyle and art-practice of its author. As Casinière reports, Deleuze arranged for the publication of this book after she sent him a photocopy of the manuscript, though once it was published, he remarked, revealing a taste for the formal qualities of works without unity, that he preferred the "pale and poorly made photocopy" to the finished book.[99]

The task, then, is to consider the dynamics of the rhizome-book in a way that is attentive not only to the conceptual and textual features of books but to their full materiality, their heterogeneous "working of matters."[100] I attempt this here through concrete cases, for it would run counter to the spirit of this most immanent of concepts to either set out universal criteria for the rhizome-book or consider it outside of its empirical expressions. In what follows, each set of books is initially approached, as was Mao's *Quotations*, through its linguistic structure and/or conceptual content. But against the spiritual autonomy of the word in the root-book, here the word is shown to be enmeshed with, and unsettled by, diverse materials and oriented toward expression that is not constrained by the semiotics of passional authority. I place attention on the singular ways the particular books break with the root-book mode—break, that is, with its encyclopedic pretensions to totalizing knowledge, its imitative relation to the world, its authorial authority, and its sufficiency as an integrated whole. In the course of discussion, I touch on some features of the root-book that I have not thus far considered: its relation to the sensory patterns of the State-form and to the structures of the capitalist commodity. The focus throughout is on how the qualities of the rhizome-book are manifest in the artifact of the book itself, in the context of the aesthetic and political concerns of each book's immediate environment. Since Deleuze and Guattari provide only minimal tools for analysis of the concrete materiality of books, I sometimes draw on concepts that they use to explore material culture in other fields. And to make one more preparatory point, I would underscore that the books are presented here not as a cumulative account of the emergence of the rhizome-book but as a variable field of its expression, each book foregrounding one or more aspects of the rhizomatic tendency in the material form of books.

POLYSENSUALITY AND THE RUSSIAN FUTURIST BOOK

Given the cleavage the root-book enacts with the external world, it is appropriate to start with a set of books within which the physical and sensory properties of matter take center stage: the Russian Futurist books of the 1910s. In their foundational practice of "the self-sufficient word" and "transreason" *(zaum),* the Russian Futurists (or Cubo-Futurists, as they are sometimes known) took the word not as a transparent vehicle of truth and communication but as polymorphous *object,* placing emphasis on the phonic, graphic, hieroglyphic qualities of writing.[101] Here the word as object is unmoored from chains of signification, in relation to which it has only passing and occasional correspondence. Instead, phonetic analogy, rhythm, raw verbal material, and obscure idioms become the substance and organizing principles of expression, as the word "passes into sensation," in Deleuze and Guattari's terms.[102] I made much of the passional dimension of the root-book, but books of the rhizome variety are not without their own kind of passion. In the transrational word, as Aleksei Kruchenykh has it, one of the main exponents of *zaum,* this "not yet frozen" or "melted language" is fundamentally "emotional" in tenor, associated with intensive states: "when the artist wants to convey images not fully defined," "when one loses one's reason (hate, jealousy, rage . . .)," "when one does not need it—religious ecstasy, love."[103]

Hence, while Mao's *Quotations* abstracted the word from the world in the purity of Mao Zedong Thought, in Futurist transreason, the word is drawn back into its many and various material fields. In this one can discern elements of Deleuze and Guattari's "presignifying" regime of signs, a regime that "fosters a pluralism or polyvocality of forms of expression that prevents takeover by the signifier and preserves expressive forms particular to content."[104] But the important point for my purposes is that this Futurist approach to language is interlaced with the form and physicality of the books themselves.

Russian Futurist books were conceived of as active, polysensual objects in a fashion that undoes the root-book cleavage between world and book, as the book becomes a vital entity adequate to the intensive movements of the transrational word. This manifests in a number of ways. It is most immediately apparent in the exuberance of materials that are deployed in Futurist books. Developing from an interest in folk culture, ritual-related art, ideographic text, illuminated manuscripts, and the ornate objects of nomadic peoples, Futurist books have a wild tactility about them. In deliberate contravention of the fine-printing tradition of the *livre d'artistes,* they are often roughly hewn works assembled of cheap, disposable materials—an early example, *A Slap in the Face of Public Taste,* was famously bound in burlap—and diverse print technologies, including lithographed manuscript, handwriting, linocuts, hectography, and rubber stamps. They were not to be read as such but, in all their variability, existed to "see, listen to, and feel."[105]

To this polymorphous array of materials there corresponds a specific aesthetic form, one that is manifest against the principal sensory structures of the root-book. The modern book, as it has developed from the Gutenberg letterpress, intensifies the abstracted optical function at the expense of sensuous complexity. The rigid linear text, uniformity of letterforms, and identical copies produce, in Marshall McLuhan's words, a "visual technology of uniform time and uniform continuous space in which 'cause' is efficient and sequential, and things move and happen on single planes."[106] We might infer from this one reason why Deleuze and Guattari also name the root-book the "State apparatus-book."[107] It not only produces patterns of dogma and authority, as we have seen in *Quotations*, but also imparts a State-form *sensorium*. The Gutenberg book is a microcosm, if you will, of the State function to bind movement to ground and regulate it as such—the "gravity" of the State-form, its production of "striated space."[108] Granted, this case can be overstated. The poetical and philosophical complexity and multivalence of text is not prevented by the linearity of its printed instantiation, and the spatial and temporal dimensions of the codex, in contrast to the scroll, make it a random-access device from the start, suitable for nonlinear, discontinuous reading, as Johanna Drucker and Peter Stallybrass have argued.[109] Still, the Russian Futurists understood the Gutenberg book as presenting much stratification to react against.

In contrast to the optical aesthetic, Futurist books have a strong relation to the "haptic" aesthetic Deleuze and Guattari associate with nomadic art (it is not incidental that a number of the Russian Futurists were heavily influenced by the art forms of the Scythian nomads).[110] I have noted that these books are most tactile, sensual entities, but the haptic is a mode of *vision,* an immersive "close vision" that invests the eye with the property of touch, as it draws vision into a field that dissolves perspective and is grasped only through a local and variable integration of parts, where "orientations, landmarks, and linkages are in continuous variation."[111] In Futurist books, the interweaving and merging of image and text, the use of handwriting, transrational flight of sense, graphic wandering of words, unbounded color, variability of printed materials, and fluctuation in rhythm all pull away from the striated, optical mode of the book and attract an immersive perception, one that allows for an experience of sensory simultaneity in what we might, after Deleuze and Guattari, call "ornamental text," with "weak communication value."[112] Gerald Janecek thus writes of Kruchenykh's work: "a page of 'text' need not be read sequentially in linear time, but can be taken at a glance and absorbed by the same process of free visual exploration used in studying a painting."[113] It is a disorienting sensory experience of which Kruchenykh was well aware: "We can change objects' weight (the eternal *force of gravity*), we see buildings hanging in the air and the weight of sounds."[114]

As can be discerned in Kruchenykh's comment here, the haptic aesthetic combines with a quality of *movement*. For Deleuze and Guattari, the haptic aesthetic comprises a particular kind of graphic inscription or "line," an "inorganic line" that breaks with the "organic" mode of representation. Whereas organic representation, through the principle of symmetry, limits variability in repetition by maintaining the domination of a central point with radiating lines (as in star-shaped figures), haptic aesthetic forms express a power of variation, a "streaming, spiralling, zigzagging, snaking, feverish line."[115] Such art no longer constructs an organic empathy between representation and human subject but articulates a different mode of life — the traits, flows, impulses of an elementary *life of matter,* an "inorganic life."[116] It is an aesthetic form found especially in the animal motifs of nomadic art: "the twisted animals have no land beneath them; the ground constantly changes direction, as in aerial acrobatics; the paws point in the opposite direction from the head, the hind part of the body is turned upside down; the 'monadological' points of view can be interlinked only on a nomad space."[117]

It is no surprise that these motifs find their way into Futurist books, sometimes in simple iconographic fashion, other times in sophisticated adaptations of central Scythian principles.[118] But we might more productively approach the haptic movement of Futurist books through another aspect of nomadic aesthetics, its artifactual form. Deleuze and Guattari argue that the nomadic, inorganic line is associated with certain kinds of mobile objects—jewelry and weaponry. These objects do not "work" in and for striated space, as do tools, component parts of a labor process legally and economically bound to property, but express variable movement undetermined by the striating "gravity" of the State-form.[119] If Futurist books construct a haptic aesthetic, as objects they share also this nomadic quality of movement. For the itinerant property of the medium of the book—this "most deterritorialized of things"—is no longer articulated with distributed authority (as it was in Mao's *Quotations*) or with the striated perceptual patterns of the State-form (as is imparted by the Gutenberg book). Rather, like *paper jewelry,* these "living entit[ies]" that defy gravity and "fly out" on publication serve to distribute a feverish, inorganic life of matter.[120]

The Futurist book also raises a challenge to the root-book's linear or teleological relation to the world. As Nina Gurianova argues, the temporal, spatial, and rhythmic dislocations of these books are such that, to employ the name of one of the most accomplished Futurist works, this is a world *backwards.*[121] But there is still perhaps a danger of the book operating here (in the mode of the fascicular root-book) as an archetype, of "typographical cleverness" propagating a supplementary unity in the fragmented work. It is important, then, that the undoing of the book's teleological relationship to the world is compounded by another aspect of the Russian Futurist book, the persistent troubling of its own unity, as is especially evident in Kruchenykh's work.

Kruchenykh had something of a compulsive passion for publishing and was chiefly responsible for upward of two hundred publications.[122] But it is a passion operative against any principle that would orchestrate a unity or model in the work; true poets, he proclaimed, "should write on their books: after reading, tear it up."[123] This destructive tendency took the somewhat inorganic aesthetic form of an insistence on "the necessity and the importance of irregularity in art."[124] For instance, *Mirskontsa* (Worldbackwards)—a book of poetry by Kruchenykh and Velimir Khlebnikov, and images by Natalia Goncharova, Mikhail Larionov, Nikolai Rogovin, and Vladimir Tatlin—is a highly heterogeneous collection of materials and rhythms. But it is also internally irregular: the order of pages differs between copies; individual lithographed pages vary in the color and weight of paper; rubber-stamped sheets have inconsistent use of letters and decorative symbols; even the covers of the book (by Goncharova, in what is the first example of collage in book design) vary between copies.[125] Kruchenykh was also in the habit of assembling materials across different books: reproducing manifestos and texts in different works; using pages from one book in another; even, in one case, publishing a new book, *Zaumnik,* from an older work, *Iz vsekh knig* (From all books), simply by adding a newly designed cover (albeit one by Aleksandr Rodchenko).[126] In these peculiar practices, the book becomes an interminable shuffling of fragments, a looping movement as pages are assembled and reassembled like the discontinuous folds of the most rhizomatic of organs: "These books . . . smell of phosphorous, like fresh brain curls."[127]

ANTONIN ARTAUD'S PAPER SPELLS

In formulating the figure of the rhizome-book, Deleuze and Guattari make use of a concept they draw from Antonin Artaud, the "body without organs," a concept that is well known to have considerable significance in their philosophical repertoire. If the root-book is one tendency in the field of the book, the book "also has a side facing the *body without organs,* which is constantly dismantling the organism, causing asignifying particles or pure intensities to pass or circulate."[128] That is, as a body without organs, the rhizome-book undoes the sensory and signifying organization of its subject. The haptic materialism of the Futurist book moved in this direction—breaking as it did with the sensory patterns of the striated optical function—but it is in Artaud's paper "spells" or *gris-gris* that we find the most singular concrete experiment in textual matter qua body without organs.[129] Artaud sent these epistolary objects from Ireland and the Sainte-Anne Hospital and Ville-Évrard asylum in France in 1937 and 1939 as protective or imprecatory devices to friends, doctors, and public figures—seven are known to exist, including one that remained unsent to Hitler.[130] Composed of writing, pictograms, and obscure symbols in ink and colored crayon, included with letters or sent alone, these spells are hacked, scored, and burned objects that defy any attempt to separate artifact and text, material form and signifying content (Plates 5 and 6).

As with Futurist books, Artaud's spells are entwined with a particular mode or experience of language, one that Deleuze elucidates in his comparative assessment of surface and depth in the linguistic operations of Lewis Carroll and Artaud. "*I do not like poems or languages of the surface* which smell of happy leisures and of intellectual success," Artaud writes of Carroll.[131] Against Carroll's incorporeal linguistic surfaces, language for Artaud is carved into the body. Yet there is no simple opposition here between surface and depth; the point, instead, is that surface and depth become immanent to each other. It is an experience symptomatic of schizophrenia, where the body is an "involution" of the world around—a "body-sieve," as Deleuze describes it, a "membrane of infinite crevices," for Artaud.[132] "Things and propositions have no longer any frontier between them, precisely because bodies have no surface. . . . Every word is physical and immediately affects the body."[133] It is here, in the schizophrenic breakdown of the division between things and words, that Deleuze and Guattari's claim for the indistinction between what a book *is* and what it *says,* a book as *thing* and a book as *words,* can be taken as a statement of fact, and not as a confounding means of forcing one to think the interplay between divergent textual and sociomaterial means of expression (as I framed it in the preface). But at this moment, one must guard against allowing the loss of distinction between words and things to become the ascendance of words at the *expense* of things. That Deleuze and Guattari make no comment on the specific materialities of Artaud's spells might indicate a failing on that front, though it is quite possible that they knew little of the material form of these works, which only came to public attention in the mid-1980s. But I am getting ahead of myself, for there is a little more to say about Artaud's linguistic practice before we move to its medial inscription.

The experience of Artaud's corporeal semiotic is of language as wounding assault: "One may invent one's language, and make pure language speak with an extra-grammatical or a-grammatical meaning," Artaud remarks on Carroll, "but this meaning must have value in itself, that is, it must issue from torment."[134] And it is to counter such wounding torment that Artaud develops his specific procedures, as Deleuze elucidates. In brief, Artaud isolates words, stripping them of their signifying function, whence they are released as phonetic elements that are singularly wounding, "unbearable sonorous qualities" that affect the sensory organs of the body. Phonetic values are then in turn undone, converted into "breath-words" and "howl-words," overloaded with consonants, aspiration, and guttural sounds, as anyone who has heard recordings of Artaud's performances will not readily forget. Here "all literal, syllabic, and phonetic values have been replaced by *values which are exclusively tonic,*" values that correspond not to a subject of signification but to a disaggregated body, a *body without organs,* "an organism without parts which operates entirely by insufflation, respiration, evaporation, and fluid transmission."[135]

Now, the point for my purposes is that Artaud's spells can be understood as artifactual manifestations of this relation between language and body. To borrow from Stephen Barber's assessment of Artaud's notebooks, the spells are a "prototype," a "testing-ground" for the transformational process of the body without organs. Artaud writes: "I have the idea to put into operation a new re-assembling of the activity of the human world, idea of a new *anatomy.* / My drawings are *anatomies* in action."[136] This operation is at once destructive of the existent corporeal and signifying body and a generative practice—a procedure both "terminal" and "insurgent."[137] And it takes paper not as a mediating substrate but as a material immanent to its procedures; in these spells, Artaud constructs a *paper body without organs.* Let us see how.

Writing in 1947, Artaud conceived of his spells as exorcisms performed on the "objective inertia" of the page, on its striating, organizing gradients: "The goal of all these drawn and coloured figures was to exorcise the curse, to vituperate bodily against the exigencies of spatial form, of perspective, of measure, of equilibrium, of dimension."[138] No inert support for the written word, then, the sheet of paper is fully a part of the procedure.[139] Like a "body-sieve," the *gris-gris* emerges as a dynamic membrane, a field of forces: sign, color, word, lettering, combine with the material of the paper, perforated and frayed with burns, to produce "a surface that is as much active as acted upon," as Agnès de la Beaumelle describes it.[140] And it is, too, a corporeal surface, an extension of Artaud's tormented body in process. Artaud performed incantation in the spells' construction, taken over by convulsive movement as he stabbed, incised, perforated, and burned the page—"he worked in a rage," as an intern at Rodez recalled, regarding the "grinding out" of one of Artaud's self-portraits.[141] In this way, signs were captured and held with the violent force of bodily gesture, so preventing signifying circulation, depriving the word of "its power to draw together or to express an ... ideational event distinct from its present realization."[142]

The subject undone on the body-sieve of the paper was not only its author, if we can use that inadequate word for this visceral and medial procedure, but its audience too. Beaumelle describes the spells as "graphic expulsions," artifacts intended to act physically on their interlocutors, to have an immediate and destabilizing sensory effect.[143] It is an effect well explained by Paule Thévenin:

> Writing no longer has as its sole function that of transmitting a message or a thought; rather, it must act by itself and physically. Everything is studied, calculated so as to strike the eye, and through it the sensitivity, of the person for whom the spell is destined. ... We can scarcely look at these objects without being contaminated by their vehemence.[144]

A trace of this vehement contamination can perhaps be gained from Beaumelle's evocative presentation of the 1939 spells from Artaud's time at the Ville-Évrard asylum:

> Their imprecatory violence now resides more in the physical state of the missive than in the words. Inscribed with a thick ink crayon in purple, the different signs (crosses, stars, triangles, spirals in the shape of serpents, the cabalistic significance of which Artaud knew well) proliferate in all directions, invade the center of the paper itself, break the continuous thread of writing drawn with the same ink crayon: fragments of writing and drawn pictograms henceforth form one body. Not only that: knots, amorphous clusters of crayon, seem to respond in counterpoint, proceeding from the same charge of aggression, to the holes produced by burning the paper (the edges of which are also ravaged); and traces of violent shades of yellow, blue, and red (Artaud also knew the symbolism of colors: these are the colors of death) intensify by their physical presence the imprecatory force of the words. These are no longer simple votive letters but true magical objects, to be handled while making ritualistic gestures ..., which can "illuminate themselves," like "gris-gris."[145]

The medium of the letter served Artaud's graphic expulsions well, for the intimate affect germane to this direct and personal mode of textual communication is compounded by the letter's frail and ephemeral form. If the Futurist book introduced the "worldbackwards" into the teleological dimension of the book's unity and authority, Artaud's spells also refuse existence as coherent and enduring works: "These are not drawings / they figure nothing, / disfigure nothing, / are not there to / construct / edify / establish / a world."[146] The spells are fragments, their audience—the addressees of these artifacts delivered by post—limited and temporary, and they exist, in their asubjective affects, only at the edge of destruction: "And the figures that I thereby made were spells—which, after so meticulously having drawn them, I put a match to."[147]

SANDPAPER *MÉMOIRES*

The last example I will consider emerges from an expressly communist environment, and as such it allows me to consider the material properties of the rhizome-book through a more overtly political lens. There is considerable justification for Guy Debord's claim that his and Asger Jorn's 1959 work, *Mémoires*, was an "anti-book."[148] The textual genre of the memoir typically serves to marshal the identity and historical significance of a public persona, of which General de Gaulle's war memoir was a contemporaneous example, as Karen Kurczynski notes (and as Debord subversively acknowledges by including a snippet from that work in his own).[149] Its adoption by a young avant-gardist was a provocation, clearly, and one that left little of the genre intact, though Debord's anti-book was constructed through many other planes of material text.

Mémoires is at once a fragmentary recollection of Debord's pre-Situationist milieu around the Lettrist International; an exercise in the techniques of *détournement* and *dérive*; and an unworking of its own points of identification, meaning, and narrative coherence. Its pages are filled with scattered text and image fragments usurped and uncredited from disparate medias and sources. Architectural diagrams; map fragments; lines from Shakespeare, Baudelaire, Robert Louis Stevenson, and other literary and popular sources; fragments from Marx—it opens with

Marx's antimemorial statement "let the dead bury the dead"—cartoons, advertisements, scientific treatises, and so forth, all distributed without hierarchy to construct an impressionistic sense of events, atmospheres, ideas, and encounters (Plates 7 and 8).[150] Interlaced with these are the "supporting structures" of lines, splashes, and planes of vibrant color provided by Debord's artist comrade, Jorn. Confirming the anti-book valence of these arrangements, the plain wrappers of *Mémoires* were covered with heavy-grade sandpaper. On one hand, this might exemplify the more self-regarding dimensions of Debord and the SI, typical in this respect of the historical avant-garde; the sandpaper seems to signal a triumphant and self-certain book arrived to damage those against which it was placed. I touch on the limits of the SI later, but I seek here to concentrate on the aspects of *Mémoires* that pushed beyond them. On the other hand, then, the striking effect of the sandpaper covers is the way that when handled they foreground in a heightened sensory fashion the book's physical form and external relations, an enforced appreciation of the book's outside that is complemented by the almost translucent, rather fragile pages encountered within. This interpretation finds some support in the account of the book's production. The material was actually proposed by the book's Danish printer Verner Permild, of the firm Permild and Rosengreen, who also printed Jorn and Debord's earlier bookwork, *Fin de Copenhague*.[151] He was responding to Jorn's request for a binding that would *excite the senses*—sticky asphalt, Jorn suggested, that "should be slightly uncomfortable to the touch but durable."[152]

The critical impact of *Mémoires* on the material field of the book includes two aspects that I have not directly considered in the rhizome-books discussed thus far: a critique of capital and the commodity and a specifically communist intervention in the problem of the root-book's subject. I draw these out through aspects of the book's content, but there is now a reasonable volume of research on the content of *Mémoires,* excusing me to concentrate on paratextual aspects and the sociomaterial forms and relations with which the book was interlaced.[153]

As with Artaud's spells and the Russian Futurist books, *Mémoires* breaks with the prevailing mode of communication, but it does this from a position specifically attentive to the function of language in capitalist society. As Frances Stracey notes in her discussion of *Mémoires,* language for the SI was bound up with an emergent cybernetic mode of production that integrated signification with command in an "informationist" paradigm that sought to eradicate all linguistic redundancies and ambiguous signals.[154] This was a "universal language" of which, "since its advent, the triumphant bourgeoisie has dreamed."[155] More succinctly, "words *work.*"[156] There is a striking relation here with Deleuze's critique of the place of "universals of communication" in contemporary "control society," with its distributed and continuous systems of regulation, as I touched on in chapter 1: "speech and communication have been corrupted. They're thoroughly permeated by money—and not by accident but by their very nature."[157]

For Deleuze, politics cannot resist this situation with an *alternative* communication—a "counterinformation" or a "democratic conversation"—because what is required is a breach in the very modes of subjectivity and exchange constituted in communicational systems.[158] Deleuze's elusive term for such practice is "noncommunication," one that also appears in Debord's 1961 film *Critique of Separation.*[159] Unlike Deleuze, the SI at times held to the future possibility of a liberated communication fully present to itself; in the same year that *Mémoires* was fabricated, the SI journal, for instance, declared that "all forms of pseudo-communication must be consigned to utter destruction, so that one day we may achieve real, direct communication."[160] It is a piece with the other figures of presence that mark the limits of the SI's communism, most notably its notion of "radical subjectivity" (to be liberated and whole again after shucking off the chains of passivity) and the workers' council (the SI's totem of a future communist form of self-directed labor, the collective *management* rather than *abolition* of work). If the SI were only this, there would be little use in returning to it today. But it contains a good deal that pushes against these limits, not least with its politics of noncommunication.

The Situationists found their breach in the informationist paradigm through the method of *détournement.* As in the plundered visual and textual sources of *Mémoires, détournement* is the reuse of existing semiotic and aesthetic materials in new ensembles that seeks, in Jorn's words, a "devaluation" of received patterns of meaning.[161] The association with the category of political economy, "value," is not accidental, for this was a devaluation of language to match that of social production more widely: "words will not cease to *work* until people do."[162] In a *détournement,* the new ensemble derives its "peculiar power" from holding together trace associations of the devalued elements with the new senses created.[163] In Debord and Gil Wolman's words, its effects are "dependen[t] on memory," because "*the main impact of a détournement is directly related to the conscious or semiconscious recollection of the original contexts of the elements.*"[164] Why is this? As information cleanses the communicative channel of redundancies, it performs an individuation of speaker and auditor, consolidating their identities with each repetition, the memory of the auditor-subject serving to condense the repetitions into a coherent center, a subject "immobilized in the falsified center of the movement of its world."[165] *Détournement* introduces redundancy and ambiguity into the communicative channel, making meanings proliferate and scatter. But its effectivity lies in the degree to which this proliferation dislodges the integrating or subject-producing capacity of memory, as familiar and identity-confirming bits of information now appear strange and disarticulated, no longer providing their consolidating effect. If *détournement* is, hence, the first step toward a "literary communism," it is so in its persistent *wrenching* of language from the paradigm of information and its subjective functions. "It is not 'the nadir of writing' but its inversion."[166]

The destructive orientation to language in *détournement* necessarily troubles the textual medium favored by the historical avant-garde. It can establish no unique and unified work in the manner of "some total-izing, Mallarméan Book," as Tom McDonough observes.[167] The works of *détournement* are of a different order, and *Mémoires* is one of these, "entirely composed of prefabricated elements," as the title page notes.[168] Its composition of usurped and devalued words and images undercuts the possibility of a distinct and self-expressive authorial subject, a move all the more powerful for its apparent location in the autobiographical genre of memoir. The referential object of the book, Debord's Lettrist milieu, is similarly undone as a coherent world or political subject, something itemized and foreclosed in linear historical memory. Structured around three dated chapters that indicate significant points in the life of Debord and the Lettrist International—so establishing the book as a prehistory of the SI, which was founded two months before he commenced work on the book—moments of this "memory" come into focus at points. But it is an unstable and virtual historical field, at once charged with potential—comprising, as the first page warns, "lights, shadows, shapes," "fringes of silence," "full of discord and dismay"—and lost, irrecoverable, and resistant as such.[169]

The technique of devaluation operates here not only in the redeployment of existing semiotic materials but also in their singular instantiation on the pages of the book. As the SI journal later noted of *Mémoires,* "the writing on each page runs in all directions and the reciprocal relations of the phrases are invariably uncompleted."[170] Such indeterminacy is compounded by the cumulative effect of the book, with concepts and meanings coming in and out of focus as they resonate, accumulate, and dissipate across its pages. And this is not only an effect of language but is accentuated by the dramatic pattern and spatialization of the work, as text and image are structured, counterposed, and overcome by Jorn's variously lulling, violent, humorous, and vertiginous sheets, pools, and scratchings of vibrant color, what amounts to a "grammar of abstract form," as Kurczynski describes it, "deliberate sensory provocations" that insist on active reading from the viewer.[171] Jorn's technique is in part an instance of his experiments toward an immanent, topological mode of aesthetic expression, what in a later text he describes by marking a distinction with the "Euclidean geometry" of Wassily Kandinsky's paint dripping from a distance: "If you work very close to the manuscript, the flow of colours makes surfaces, blotches"; it is the painterly articulation of a "poly-dimensional cosmos at the surface."[172] As such, Jorn considered *Mémoires,* and the potentials it pushed in lithographic book production, to recall the medieval manuscript, but now in a new, post-Gutenberg form.[173] And yet if *Mémoires* was to be such, it was not as an expression of the creative labors of the heroic artist. As Kurczynski argues, Jorn's drips and pools of printed color, mechanically reproduced in glaring commercial gradients, are something of a pastiche of the abstract painting of Jackson Pollock, of the authenticity and rugged individuality that the American culture industry exported as his politically expedient global image.[174] This is the context within which to understand Jorn's remark to the publisher that the production of *Mémoires*—comprising, remember, entirely prefabricated elements—was to be a work of "total industrialization," that "should be finished without us having anything to do with it."[175]

It should be underscored, and it is an astonishing achievement, that in the midst of these intensive, disorienting characteristics, *Mémoires* maintains a conceptual rigor and force. Indeed, this rigor is inherent to the book's disorienting qualities, for it is found not in the conventional form of philosophical demonstration but in the practical *performance* of its concepts (which is not, as we will see shortly, to say that it sought or achieved the identity of theory and practice).[176] Such performance is not limited to *détournement*; the book also invites its readers to engage with it in the Situationist manner of a *dérive*. Against the spectacular time of capital, the empty succession of equivalent units of time, which, as I argued earlier, the medium of the book models in its linear structure, in *Mémoires,* time is loosened from determination, opened to chance, nonlinearity, and irreversibility, as the reader drifts through its fragments and spatiotextual arrangements, making it anew with each encounter, as one might drift through a city, the more usual domain of the Situationist practice of the *dérive*.[177] In fact, the form here exceeds the content, extending a practice and a sensibility of *détournement* and *dérive* that can work against the limits of their textual articulations in this book, which at one point carries an inexcusable misogyny, an index of the failure of the SI to adequately develop a communist critique of the sexism of itself and its times.[178] One of the trace associations that *Mémoires* holds in its *détournement* is the popular fascination with the nineteenth-century killer of women, Jack the Ripper, the enduring nature of which is a persistent indictment of the sexism that inheres in the modern imaginary of the city. Granted, a *détournement* appropriates to unsettle and destroy, but Debord here merely adopts the misogynistic ambience that is constructed and consumed in the Ripper myth. For as Patrick Greaney has shown, Debord draws a simile between the Ripper's evisceration and arrangement of the organs of his murdered victims and the cutting and montage that comprise a *détournement,* while allowing the Ripper, "that other night prowler," to stand metonymically for himself as practitioner of the *dérive*.[179]

We follow a more critical path when considering the effect of *Mémoires* on the structure of the commodity, a pivotal aspect of its anti-book character. The commodity form of the book is a feature strangely absent from Deleuze and Guattari's assessment, as if on this matter they succumbed to the obfuscating power of the root-book. The book is a form of commodity that is especially effective at hiding its commercial nature, its capitalist structure obscured by its apparently universal value as a transcendent intellectual, moral, and aesthetic good.[180] It is as if the generic capitalist power of commodity fetishism—to produce an autonomous artifact severed in consumers' minds from its relations of production—is given a boost by the spiritual power of the root-book, these dual powers of dematerialization conjoining in something of a perfect commodity.[181] For despite appearances, these industrial "goods which pretend not to be goods at all" have been entwined with the emergence and development of the commodity form.[182] As we saw in chapter 1, not only was printing instrumental in the division of intellectual and manual labor that lies at the heart of capitalist abstract labor, but the book was itself the first standardized and reiterable mechanically produced mass commodity, the book industry being a prime mover in the division of labor, the hourly wage, new technologies, consumer credit, and privatization of language through copyright—and it remains today fully enmeshed in the latest industrial and technological developments.[183]

In this realm of the commodity, or at least of monetary exchange, *Mémoires* has unsurprisingly become something of a rare item, changing hands today for upward of $4,000. But in its time, this anti-book had an intrinsic anti-commodity orientation. Jorn's advocacy of its "industrialization" was aimed at the cult of artistic virtuosity; in the domain of industry proper, the abrasive material of the book's sandpaper covers defies the commodity values of smooth industrial production and circulation, as the printers experienced quite literally, to the cost of the knife in their cutting machine.[184] And the SI explicitly framed the book as a product of "anti-design," an "unpopular book" against the popularity of the mass-market commodity: "There is too much plastic, we prefer sandpaper."[185] Of course, these apparently disruptive qualities could merely indicate a different circuit of commercial value, that of the *livre d'artistes* or artwork proper. It is significant, then, that Debord describes *Mémoires* as a book created not to be sold but to be a splendid or excessive gift, a "potlatch." In his preface to the 1993 reedition, Debord explains, "Thus for thirty-five years my *Mémoires* were never put on sale. Their celebrity comes from only having been given out in the form of the *potlatch*: that is to say of the sumptuous gift, challenging the other party to give something more extreme in return."[186] Practiced by certain American Indian tribes on the Northwest coast, the potlatch is a circuit of inequivalent exchange where the prestige of each party is a function of the extravagance of its gift to the other, a gift that challenges the receiving party to outdo its extravagance in return. Exchange here does not obfuscate social relations, as it does in commodity circuits, but intensifies them, where relations are based not on scarcity and command but on abundance and waste, of giving without guarantee of return, the circulation of objects bearing an evental force of disequilibrium.

The practice gave the title to the Lettrist International's bulletin, *Potlatch,* which was true to its name in being "sent gratuitously to addresses chosen by its editors, and to several people who asked to receive it. It was never sold."[187] *Potlatch* was an inexpensive, mimeographed typed text bulletin, not untypical of its time, though it has certain formal effects particular to its aims nonetheless. When contrasted with the experimental extravagance of much avant-garde publication, its stripped-back form evokes something of a clandestine newsletter, as Grail Marcus describes it, and its unauthorized break with official discourse was made all the more urgent and necessary by the apparent powerlessness of its medium, as compared with the "elegance of print," which "empowers the most impossible of sentences" and thus delivers them to order:

> In 1985 Debord republished the complete run of *Potlatch* in a brightly typeset, cleanly designed book with a purple cover; it gave a sheen of likelihood, of investment and return, to words that first trumpeted their messages of destruction and rebirth in a realm outside apparent possibility, dim and smudged on loose sheets of mimeo.[188]

But notwithstanding these formal qualities, the gift nature of *Potlatch,* as Debord put it in 1959, concerned more its textual content than anything especially artifactual: "the non-saleable goods that a free bulletin such as this is able to distribute are novel desires and problems; and only the further elaboration of these by others can constitute the corresponding return gift."[189] *Mémoires,* by contrast, was a decidedly more multifaceted and material gift in the round. That said, it was in fact put on sale—the last page of *Mémoires* informs that it was distributed in the United States by Wittenborn and Company, a renowned New York art publisher and book shop, and Debord's letters show efforts to secure distributors elsewhere. His 1993 recollection is inaccurate or a little disingenuous, then, but there is indication that the book's place in commodity circuits was a function of the need to finance the SI's activities, an inherently contradictory endeavor, and no suggestion that *Mémoires* did not also circulate as a potlatch.[190]

If gift economies break with commodity exchange, they can introduce social relations that are themselves constraining, as the gift serves to bind and consolidate relations of obligation.[191] And it is true that the circulation of printed matter had a significant role in maintaining (and breaking) the interpersonal and organizational relations of the SI, as Debord's correspondence attests.[192] But this is only part of the story, for the SI's reading of the potlatch economy was more that of Georges Bataille than Marcel Mauss; if the excess affect or intensity associated with the gift-circulation of *Mémoires* was directed toward establishing relations of *association,* such relations were to manifest as a destructive effect on associational *identity.*[193] That is to say, the patterns of association of the root-book—with its orientation toward establishing or molding an integrated collective subject within its regimes of truth and authority—have little presence in *Mémoires,* which in this sense we might characterize as something of an antimanifesto. Debord writes,

> This anti-book was only offered to my friends, and no-one else was informed of its existence. "I wanted to speak the beautiful language of my century." I wasn't too worried about being heard. . . . I proved my sober indifference to public opinion straight away, because the public were not even allowed to see this work.[194]

His willful disregard here of this fundamental feature of the classical political book, its subjectivating function, has a somewhat aristocratic air to it, but it is by no means an apolitical move. Indeed, with a little work, we can interpret Debord's remark in the context of what David Banash considers to be the *most* radical feature of *Mémoires,* namely, the breach it enacts in the instrumental passage of conceptual and aesthetic production into "activist" practice.[195] The interlacing of theory and practice is foundational for political Marxism, and radical politics more broadly, and yet is too often ordered by a very limited understanding of both terms, whereby theory is to be applied in practice and valued to the degree that this is achieved. Rather than allowing theory to hold open a disruptive orientation to the social world, including to "practice," the latter overwhelms the former, under the political imperative of "what is to be done?" And so practice, unproblematized, risks reproducing established identities and political forms, confirming the present rather than accentuating its limits.

The breach *Mémoires* enacts in such instrumental approaches to theory and action is enacted through the qualities I have been considering, qualities that make it a political book—intervening across linguistic, sensory, subjective, and associational conditions of being—in large measure to the degree that it is not an *activist* book. As to the specific theme of the "public," to which I turn now, the breach works against the instrumental relation between a writer and his group, a group and its public or subject, where a political text more normally serves to confirm each pole and bind them in a relation of identity. The point can be teased out through reflection on another Situationist antiwork, the Hamburg Theses of September 1961, which Debord later recalls, not without some drama, as "the most mysterious and most formally experimental text in the entire history of the SI."[196]

The Hamburg Theses, which were evoked several times in SI publications, were the result of a theoretical and strategic discussion between Debord, Attila Kotànyi, and Raoul Vaneigem concerning the future conduct and critical orientations of the SI, held over a few days in Hamburg bars en route from the SI's fifth conference in Gothenburg. There is nothing unusual in this, except that, though the Hamburg Theses are said by Debord to have "authors," *they have no existence as a text.* They were never published, nor was any written record made, as Debord first publicly revealed in a 1989 letter to Thomas Y. Levin:

> With the intention of not leaving any trace that could be observed or analyzed from outside of the SI, nothing concerning this discussion and

what conclusions it reached was ever written down. It was found that the simplest summary of its rich and complex conclusions could be expressed in a single phrase: "The SI must now realize philosophy." Even this very phrase wasn't written down.[197]

The content of the Hamburg Theses was pivotal in the group's move away from the practice and self-conception of an artistic avant-garde to more overtly political–theoretical concerns (as came to a head in the 1962 split in the SI, with the exclusion of Gruppe SPUR and the associated exclusions and resignations of the Scandinavian artists, including Jorn, who resigned the year earlier, albeit while continuing for a period under the pseudonym of "George Keller").[198] But in its noninscription and nonpublication, the "striking innovation" of the Hamburg Theses, as Debord asserts, was not in their content but in their *form,* and in the relation between the two.[199] In a letter to Vaneigem that revels in the paradoxical quality of this nontext, Debord writes, "We agreed *not to write* the Hamburg Theses, so as to impose all the better the central meaning of our entire project in the future."[200] How so? The political nature of this form is not to be explained only by the value of secrecy and confusion, though this is no doubt a feature. The "experimental originality" of the Hamburg Theses lies, rather, in their negative act of nonrepresentation, a blow against the informationist regime, against a society of incessant representation and communication. And this, moreover, took shape in the specific arena of revolutionary politics. The Hamburg antitext was a break with the expressive norms of the historical avant-garde, as Debord maintains, "which until then had given the impression of being avid to explain themselves."[201] Such eager self-representation, what Jacques Camatte calls "racketeerist marketing," serves to perpetuate the capitalist psychological and organizational values of competitive self-promotion in nominally anticapitalist scenes, while also confirming and consolidating political identities as established in the present, for competition entrenches the secure boundaries of the competing parties.[202] Against this self-marketing, the antitext of the Hamburg Theses performs a much more reflexive and elusive task of *self-undoing*—as Kotányi put it, in oblique reference to the Hamburg Theses, "if, in spite of every appearance and all evidence to the contrary, the sweeping away of our existence is a possibility, then we will be the first to commit ourselves to this dissolution."[203] Here we come to this antitext's deployment of Marx, for the undoing of group identity takes shape through the nonidentity of the proletariat.

Debord notes that the "single phrase" summary of the Hamburg Theses ("The SI must now realize philosophy") evokes Marx's formula in "A Contribution to the Critique of Hegel's Philosophy of Right: Introduction" of the realization and suppression of philosophy, thus binding this antitext to the negativity of the proletariat, as Anthony Hayes elucidates.[204] For in Marx's formulation, philosophy will not be realized until it becomes adequate to the critique and overcoming of capital, becomes adequate, that is, to the proletariat. Until it does so, philosophy merely has a relation of *identity* to the world, it "belongs to this world and is its *complement,*" as Marx's text has it.[205] To be adequate to the proletariat is not to represent it but to be adequate to a form that has no identity to represent.[206] The proletariat is "the *total loss* of humanity," encountering itself only through the domination of labor—and the domination of the absence of labor, for those without paid work, and of reproductive labor, which only *appears* not to be determined by capital. As such, it can realize itself only in its own abolition. It is not a collective subject in a face-off with the bourgeoisie but a class that must fight *against itself,* against the identities—of work, industrial sector, gender, "race," nation—by which it is bound to and reproduces capital, a class that realizes itself only in its own suppression: "When the proletariat proclaims the *dissolution of the existing world order,* it is only declaring the secret of its own existence, for it *is* the *actual* dissolution of that order."[207]

How can a text be adequate to this nonidentity? As we have seen, the Hamburg Theses are one response, embodying in expressive form the nonidentity of the proletariat, its "restlessness within its very self."[208] For this antitext develops the theoretical critique of capital as that which must be unbound from workers' identity; it undoes the avant-garde group as privileged agent of revolution, refusing its identity-forming mechanisms of self-marketing; and it negates its own identity as a text by subtracting the means of inscription and publication by which it might otherwise become established in the world. The Hamburg Theses are a text that is not a text for "a class of civil society which is not a class of civil society, a class [*Stand*] which is the dissolution of all classes."[209]

It might seem fitting that a text pivotal to the shift in the SI's center of gravity from intervention in culture and the production of artworks took the form of a non-work, a text without physical presence. But if it is indeed apt, it reveals a flaw, a tendency in the SI after the split to magically solve the proletarian problem—of acting in nonidentity with society—by retreating into theory, transcending the awkward materialities of everyday life in the pristine clarity of the concept. As Howard Slater argues, it is an approach that, ironically, binds the group back into identity, as precision in its conceptual negation becomes the condition of its "idealized self-image," "a self-image nurtured by the pursuit of written coherence."[210] And yet the physical absence of the Hamburg Theses is still an intervention in form, and their paradoxical quality is dependent on the fact that texts are in the main physically instantiated, as was the case for SI texts before and after the 1962 split. Here artful intervention in material form persisted. It is not only that the SI, despite the declared move away from art, continued to focus on the cultural arena and on the production of film—as others have noted—but it also directed considerable artistic effort toward the physical and formal manifestations *of its theory*.[211] There are numerous instances, regarding which we can note in passing that the SI reflexively deployed a range of textual forms and mediums, including a photo-romance (Ralph Rumney's 1957 psychogeographic report *The Leaning Tower of Venice*); a "filoform tract" (as Debord described the 1958 *Adresse aux producteurs de l'art moderne,* a single line of text printed on a band of paper 2 × 90 centimeters); telegrams (as used to great poetic effect in May 1968, most especially the telegram sent to the Politburo of the Chinese Communist Party, which began, "Shake in your shoes bureaucrats"); a deluxe edition (Gianfranco Sanguinetti's 1975 *The Real Report on the Last Chance to Save Capitalism in Italy,* under the pen name "Censor," whose success as a fake—in revealing the social elite's credulity of the book's theses concerning the state's false flag operations against the workers' movement, for example—was achieved by its convincing mimic of the cultured and lucid cynicism of a high bourgeois, among other textual means, but was aided by its appeal to bourgeois bibliographic vanities with its luxury paper and numbered edition); and encompassing leaflets, posters, maps, graffiti, cartoons, postcards, pamphlets, journals, and books.[212] Then there is the carefully crafted page design of the SI's self-published text, its spatial arrangement and graphic style by turns classical and modernist, and, of course, the metallic-look, colored covers to *Internationale situationniste,* regarding the material qualities of which Debord exercised close attention.[213] It was a design coup that, as McKenzie Wark notes, packaged the journal as a rare and elusive entity even as — or *because* — the content was open to free and profligate appropriation, the journal defying the property form of text with the prominent anticopyright notice that readers encountered upon turning the title page: "All texts published in *Internationale situationniste* may be freely reproduced, translated and adapted, even without indication of origin."[214]

On the Scandinavian side of the split, the political aesthetics of print were given more autonomy by the nondisavowal of art. In Jorn's impressive repertoire of aesthetic mediums, the book had a not inconsiderable presence, as Ruth Baumeister has shown, but print media took an especially inventive form in Jacqueline de Jong's journal *The Situationist Times* (1962–67).[215] A plus-A4 format comprising paper stock in varying textures, colors, weights, and opacities; fold-outs; and, in issue 6, lithographic art prints, *The Situationist Times* is flooded with diagrams, sketches, topological figures, and photographic images that break out from the confines of illustration to play a leading role in the journal's morphological experiments and concepts.[216] Indeed, in issues 3, 4, and 5, on labyrinths, rings, and knots, text often cedes its place entirely to the comparative juxtaposition of forms, "visual essays," as Slater describes the method, "best suited to reveal the differences, the variabilities within similar forms and motifs," and that could "override and draw attention to the overlooked ambiguities and unsuspected authoritarianisms of language" (Figure 8).[217] One text in the first issue of *The Situationist Times* is of especial note here, de Jong's "Critique of the Political Practice of Détournement" (Plate 9).[218] It narrates and challenges the couplike manner of the 1962 exclusion of the German and Scandinavian sections and does so in a way that at once articulates and refuses the declared terms of that split by bringing art and

Figure 8. *The Situationist Times,* no. 5, 1964, showing images from disparate sources of the issue theme of "rings."

text together, in an expressionistic, handwritten, graphic work of published writing. This intensive material text flows, spirals, tightens, and eddies across twelve pages, barely readable in many points, and is charged with a heightened emotion, with laughter and rage, as is the narrative and conceptual content of the work—quite the opposite of the SI's ice-cold politico-aesthetics of exclusion, of "No Useless Indulgences," as the title of Michèle Bernstein's text on such matters has it.[219]

Returning to *Mémoires,* it shares with the Hamburg Theses the SI's enduring and deliberate political aesthetics of textual form, while making its own anti-book intervention in both textual *and* physical planes, the summit in book-form of the moment when the SI could confidently hold art and theory together. However, my discussion of the Hamburg Theses had a different initial purpose, to bring their formal critique of the self-present subject of revolution to shed light on the antipublic form of *Mémoires.* If the potlatch quality of *Mémoires* disrupted the community-binding circulation of objects, the unbound community to which it was offered was the proletariat—*Mémoires* was a proletarian gift. We can now say with more conceptual clarity that the aim of *Mémoires* was not to be "heard" by a public or existent political subject but to problematize such relations between book and public, and their respective identities, including the identity of avant-garde authors or groups who would present themselves as achieved embodiments of that problematization (and so are nothing of the sort). Here the disaggregating property of the rhizome-book—considered thus far in the form of the Futurist "worldbackwards" and Artaud's unproductive body without organs—has a direct impact on the communist thematic of revolutionary subjectivity. *Mémoires* aborts its unity as a concentrated bloc of semiotic authority and relinquishes the role of group attractor—as site and means of self-marketing and subjectivation—all the better to affirm distributed, emergent, and self-critical composition as the proper substance of communist politics.[220] If "literary communism" is a move against information, it is, then, also a move against community, to allow this shared trope of Jean-Luc Nancy and Debord to momentarily place them in proximity. Literary communism enacts an "inoperative" community that affirms the reciprocal constitution between writing and community only on the condition that identity be cut away from both, where literary communism is the "undoing"—or "interruption, fragmentation, suspension"—of any total "work" and any consummated collectivity.[221]

There is also a *temporal* dimension to this antipublic form, on which I will draw this discussion to a close. In repelling the certainties and seductions of political subjectivity, *Mémoires* simultaneously suspends its temporality, the nonlinear and broken flow of the book's pages unsettling the "now" of instrumental action—a necessary move if politics is not to be exclusively determined by the limited parameters of the present but remain open to the unforeseen, to the event. This point, which, as I have argued, is handled in the aesthetic form of *Mémoires,* is developed conceptually in *The Society of the Spectacle* and in relation to the theme of revolutionary subjectivity. The last lines of the latter book take the rather standard, manifesto-like form of an upbeat appeal to the final victory and its agent, in this case the organizational form of the workers' council.

But the penultimate passage has a decidedly more exploratory bent, suggesting that the demand for political immediacy serves in fact to excise the political from the immediate and leave it conditioned by the past, by what is already, rather than what may become. Here the "restlessness" of the proletariat combines with a certain *revolutionary waiting*, together constituting a communism not of action, as such, but of the event:

> The abstract desire for immediate effectiveness accepts the laws of the ruling thought, the exclusive point of view of the *present,* when it throws itself into reformist compromises or trashy pseudo-revolutionary common actions. Thus madness reappears in the very posture which pretends to fight it. Conversely, the critique which goes beyond the spectacle must *know how to wait.*[222]

A précis of my argument in this chapter may be helpful in underscoring what Deleuze and Guattari's typology enables us to say about political books. Their approach requires that people of the political book recognize, and extract themselves from, the essentially religious structures and passions that regulate the book's field. Each time a political book declares or implies its unique truth and total access to the world, the concept of the root-book invites us to consider how this truth is created from a *cleavage* with the world, truth as spiritual dogma that is then returned to the world as authoritarian passion. This critical approach suggests that we explore such formations with attention to the full materiality of books, even if Deleuze and Guattari do not quite do so themselves. I have done this here with Mao's *Quotations.* Mao's book was a wholly material entity, but its material qualities—color, portability, textual structure—fed into, and were governed by, the book's spiritual autonomy and authoritarian regimes of truth.

If the political book is to break with this root-book structure, it needs a different relation to matter, a relation Deleuze and Guattari elucidate through the concept of the rhizome-book. This concept is useful less as a mechanism of classification than for what it encourages us to see in the experimental field of political books. As such, it is best approached through the properties of specific books, in their rich "working of matters." It is possible to set out some shared characteristics of the specific rhizome-books considered in this chapter. In these works, language is unmoored from signifying chains and dogmatic compulsions, be that in the mode of Futurist transrational sensory blocs, Artaud's howl-words, or Debord and Jorn's devalued informational patterns. And this language is enmeshed with variable material fields in a remodeling of the object of the book: as a haptic sensory arrangement of eclectic printed materials; as a dynamic membrane of body-sieve paper; as an anti-book of appropriated materials, nonlinear structures, and virtual images. Just as the material world floods into these books, breaching their boundary with nature, so also is the book's subject undone, most radically in Artaud's spells, which operate as involutions of body and word in paper membranes of sensory intensity. Each set of books, too, undoes the book's teleological authority and coherence: a "worldbackwards" of irregular and refolded materials; a fragment put to fire; an antimanifesto with an inoperative public.

Yet it is also clear that these books emerged from singular political and aesthetic contexts and problematics. In *Mémoires,* for instance, the conjunction of communication and authority is approached explicitly as a dimension of capital, unlike in the other works considered here, and this book's disruptive properties are a unique aesthetic modulation of the nonidentity of the proletariat and the communist critique of avant-garde organization. These situated variations are such that the concept of the rhizome-book cannot describe a cumulative set or itemized aggregate of appropriate techniques. To take seriously Deleuze and Guattari's "taste for matter" requires that the concept operate immanently to the concrete field it surveys.[223] In any particular instance, one would expect the inter-action of both root and rhizome tendencies. The books considered in this chapter push either tendency to extremes, so indicating the singular possibilities and variations of political books, but even here one could no doubt also find aspects of the opposing tendency, especially if these books were considered also in terms of their relations of reception—there is nothing exhaustive about my treatment.

The political book emerges from the works considered in this chapter, then, as a highly complex entity, where politics is operative in a book's concepts and textual content, as one expects, but also in its passions and authority and in its physical, sensory, temporal, and spatial proper-ties. If radical politics concerns transformation of the very conditions of being—not the "*merely* political revolution, the revolution which leaves the pillars of the building standing," against which Marx posits communism proper—then evaluation of these latter properties is as important as attending to a book's more overt political expressions.[224] Indeed, it is attention to the breadth of the materiality of books that has enabled me to argue that some of the most apparently radical aspects of books can often be their most reactionary.

4

What Matter Who's Speaking?

THE POLITICS OF ANONYMOUS AUTHORSHIP

> It is the attribute of the bourgeois world that all commodities
> bear their maker's name, all ideas are followed by their author's
> signature, every party is defined by its leader's name.... Work
> such as ours can only succeed by being hard and laborious and
> unaided by bourgeois publicity techniques, by the vile tendency
> to admire and adulate men.
> —AMADEO BORDIGA, *Sul Filo del Tempo*

> It was the printing press that finally was to kill Anon. But it
> was the press also that preserved him.
> —VIRGINIA WOOLF, "Anon."

I begin this chapter with an epigraph attributed to Amadeo Bordiga,
cofounder of the Italian Communist Party, but it has an uneasy presence
here, for its content clashes with its form.[1] While the illuminating effects
of epigraphic text are in part secured by their authorial designation, it
is precisely to such forms of legitimation and authority attendant on
the author's name that Bordiga's text stands opposed. The fault for this
contradiction does not lie with Bordiga, however. If we had read these
sentences in their original context, attribution to a particular individual,
or indeed to an individual at all, would have been less straightforward,
because Bordiga published his considerable contributions to communist
thought anonymously, declining to sign his name to most of his work.
Pause to consider how singular that intervention is, both in its time, for
here is the one-time leader of a political party willingly relinquishing
the prestige and authority that he would otherwise have garnered from
his writings, and now, because the identification of creative textual expression with an author, and the marketing of text on that basis, shows

every sign of continuing apace, or intensifying, whether one looks to popular book markets, academic research, or social media. Even as I seek here to champion anonymous authorship, *Anti-Book* carries my name on its covers.

"Hard and laborious" is perhaps not the formulation I would choose, but in this characterization Bordiga conveys a useful impression that authorial anonymity is something to be *achieved,* repelling the "vile tendency" to adulate individuals in an open set of acts and procedures. There have of course been numerous communist interventions against the power and degenerative effects of the possessive individual, often in concert with moves toward anonymous collective practice, from Ned Ludd onward.[2] And, in recent times, anonymous political practice has had a place in the realm of the popular political imaginary, with the Russian activist group Pussy Riot and the hacker movement Anonymous being signal instances.[3] Nevertheless, Bordiga's communist pursuit of the capitalist structure of identity into the form of the *author* is a rare move, thus electing his revolutionary anonymity, paradoxically, as an emblem for this chapter.

In chapters 2 and 3, I concentrated on particular publishing platforms, and I will do so again in chapter 5, but here my interest lies in a media form, the author, which is embedded in the range of platforms as the lynchpin to the property forms and subjectivities of writing and publishing. I first present the critique of the author-function in Foucault and Marx before indicating the opening of a countertendency in Foucault's occasional comments on anonymous writing. The discussion then turns to two empirical cases of anonymous or pseudonymous authorship, the Luther Blissett "multiple name" (1995–99) and Bernadette Corporation's novel *Reena Spaulings* (2005). As will be clear shortly, Marx and Foucault show that the central problematic of experiments in anonymous authorship is the author's relationship to her "outside," to social relations broadly conceived. In *Reena Spaulings,* the outside is figured as a relation to the city but also, in its broader context of production, to another novel, Michèle Bernstein's *All the King's Horses,* whereas in the case of Luther Blissett, the outside is modeled through Marx's formulations of "communal being" and "general intellect." These latter featured in Bordiga's theoretical pursuits, but his deployment of authorial anonymity was made in relationship to a different problematic, that of the "party." It is to this dimension of the communist author's outside that the chapter moves next, prompted by the notion of the "imaginary party" in the French journal *Tiqqun* and "The Invisible Committee," pseudonymous author of *The Coming Insurrection*. In this discussion, I set out the anti-identitarian qualities of Marx's theory of the party through his twofold formulation of the "ephemeral" and "historical" party, though I do this not to take up the question of political organization but to draw out features of writing practice that arise when anonymity and the party come into relation, with regard especially to questions of textual authority and dogma, practices I pursue through three journal publishing projects: *Comité*, the revue of the May 1968 group, Comité d'Action Etudiants-Ecrivains; Marx and Arnold Ruge's *Deutsch-Französische Jahrbücher*; and the communization journal *Endnotes*.

FOUCAULT AND MARX ON THE AUTHOR-FUNCTION

In his dissection of the features of the modern "author-function," Foucault famously associates its emergence, from the late eighteenth century, with texts that came to function, through the mechanisms of copyright law, as units of property. The modern author arises from the polymorphous field of discourse as a means to confer authority and distinction on a discrete share of text, a work, and is concurrently projected back onto that work as its sole and unique source, whence arises his proprietary rights. Quite the contrary, then, to our customary picture of the author as exceptional fount of refined signification, "the author does not precede the works; he is a certain functional principle by which, in our culture, one limits, excludes, and chooses."[4] Or, as Jeffrey Nealon underscores the property dimensions of Foucault's construction, this is the "author-function [as] a creator of scarcity, an interior space introduced into an exterior field of discourse to create privileged nodes of value."[5] In the history of textual production, then, the coming into being of the author-function "constitutes the privileged moment of individualization," an individualization that is bound to the property form of writing.[6] (We should note too that this property form is understood as an *immaterial* entity, the "work" abstracted from any physical medium that may carry it, and so the author-function is a central dimension of the text–matter distinction we have been following throughout *Anti-Book*.)

This late-eighteenth-century arrival of the author into the dominant social order of property is not, however, the author's first appearance; it is historically secondary to authorial identification via penal law, where named authorship was a mark of, and deterrent to, transgressive discourse. Foucault explains:

> Texts, books, and discourses really began to have authors (other than mythical, sacralized and sacralizing figures) to the extent that authors became subject to punishment, that is, to the extent that discourses could be transgressive. In our culture (and doubtless in many others), discourse was not originally a product, a thing, a kind of goods; it was essentially an act—an act placed in the bipolar field of the sacred and the profane, the licit and the illicit, the religious and the blasphemous. Historically, it was a gesture fraught with risks before becoming goods caught up in a circuit of ownership.[7]

For example, an English parliamentary edict of 1642, responding to a flood of anonymous publications, required "that the Printers do neither print or reprint any thing without the name and Consent of the Author."[8] The first inkling of the rights of the author are apparent here, certainly, but, as Mark Rose argues, this edict does not index a "regime of property," of the author–work conjunction, but a "regime of regulation," its aim to prevent transgressions of public discourse.[9]

This transgressive dimension to writing does not of course vanish with modernity; Foucault argues that it carries over into the property regime of the author, but it does so predominantly in a *domesticated* fashion as a propensity toward transgressive literary content, as if the author were in this way "compensated" for her entry into the social order of property, literature becoming a field of sanctioned transgression.[10] Hence, in this essay, Foucault finds that literary content offers little for a politics of writing. What is required, instead, is a more structural intervention, as he hints at in "What Is an Author?" and later goes some way to formulate, namely, that the politics of writing might be developed in direct *opposition to the author-function.* I leave that point in Foucault hanging for a moment to introduce Marx's interventions on this front of the author, interventions that allow us to tentatively raise the question of anonymous authorship.

The strange interplay of textual property and penal law in the constitutive field of the author is evident also in Marx, in his earliest pieces of journalism on censorship and freedom of the press in the *Rheinische Zeitung* (Rheinish newspaper), though this time censorship and property constraints are more directly enmeshed. In the first of these articles, an 1842 text on the occasion of a new censorship law, Marx argues that the Prussian censor's function of conferring and securing the identity of its authors effected precisely the inverse. Far from a protective act, this state-sanctioned form of literary identity *stripped* authors of their real individuality, subject as they now were to write within the established limits, at pain of censorship or prosecution. Marx thus declaims, "The law permits me to write, only I must write in a style that is not mine! I may show my spiritual countenance, but I must first set it in the *prescribed folds!*"[11] Somewhat confirming his point, the text was summarily banned. I will continue with the object of Marx's critique here a little more, but let me indicate, to pick up again shortly, that another dimension to Marx's critique of the author is also introduced here. Marx makes no direct case for anonymity in this text, but it was part of the text's construction and effect, for Marx signed it pseudonymously, by "a Rhinelander."

Not that censorship stood as an evil alone, as it did for bourgeois critics. If Marx's sight points back against the feudal model of press censorship, the prohibition against transgression, it also points forward against that which the bourgeois critics of censorship were ushering in. For Marx in these articles on press freedom made trenchant attacks also on the commodity form of writing, where the press "degrades itself to the level of a *trade*," subject not to the rigors of thought and critical debate but to the market laws of free trade.[12] Under these conditions, censorship is merely an exceptional moment of "unfreedom" in a press that is unfree *in its very structure,* such that, as he quips, "The writer who degrades the press into being a material means deserves as punishment for this internal unfreedom the external unfreedom of censorship."[13] All the same, the modern property form of writing was not yet fully formed, and neither was Marx's communist insight, for his formulation of the writer's expressive individuality overlaps with a trope that helped to *facilitate* the property regime of writing. While the emergence of copyright was bound up in liberal discourses of the natural right to property—a right resultant, in John Locke's foundational formulation, from the proprietor having "mixed his *Labour*" with nature—it found a ready companion in the romantic conception of the author as creative individual.[14] A properly communist construction of the source of writing must hence look elsewhere than to a supposedly unalienated creative subject, as Marx himself signals in other texts on the matter.

Ten years after these texts on press freedom, a French decree that all journal articles bear their authors' signatures prompted Marx in *Class Struggles in France* to underscore the association of state-sanctioned authorship with the debasement of the critical field, only this time he indicates also the interplay between textual property and named authorship (as text becomes self-advertisement). Here it is less the author's creative individuality than an *amorphous public discourse* that is Marx's valued party, and now a political value is accorded anonymity in the argument itself:

> So long as the press was anonymous it appeared as the organ of a public opinion without number or name; it was the third power of the state. With the signature of each article a newspaper became merely a collection of journalistic contributions by more or less well-known individuals. Every article sank to the level of an advertisement.[15]

This can be taken as part explanation for why Marx himself penned hundreds of periodical articles and reports without signature, a fact rarely noted but confirmed by the bibliographies to almost all the fifty volumes of the Marx and Engels collected works. It is not quite a communist theory of writing, for the press–public conjunction is here understood to be a condition for a functioning bourgeois polity, as is indicated by the metaphoric association with the circulation of money in the continuation of the preceding passage: "Hitherto the newspapers had circulated as the paper money of public opinion; now they were reduced to more or less worthless promissory notes, whose value and circulation depended on the credit, not only of the issuer, but also of the endorser."[16] Nonetheless, the "public" in Marx's writings on press freedom has a radical dimension. It is posited against those social roles that are *approved* to speak, academics ("learned men by profession, guild or privilege," with "their distinguished pedantry and their petty hair-splitting dissertations, interposed . . . between the people and the mind, between life and science") no less than journalists. In their stead, it is the "*unauthorised* writers" who carry the true commitment to writing, who feel a "*vital need*" of the press.[17]

If anonymity here pertains to individual and collective expression against the twin debasements of the state-sanctioned and bankable author, Marx makes an enticing claim that anonymous text has a destabilizing effect also on the psychic economy of the state, a point developed by Margaret Rose. The censor experienced unsigned works, in Marx's words, as an "uncanny anonymity."[18] For, having taken away authors' singular qualities through the conferral of state identity—having rendered them anonymous, in other words, in the sense of being generic and interchangeable—the censor was then faced with an anonymity that undermined his intentions, a critical and collective writing without name that was the alien product of his own action. The censor, as Rose puts it, was "psychologically and tactically confronted by the very anonymity [censorship] would abolish, as 'uncannily' its own now alienated and foreign creation."[19]

Marx's construction of uncanny anonymity here is especially useful in stressing that anonymous authorship impacts not only the author herself but also the social nexus more broadly—in this case, the psychic economy of the censor and the discursive structures of censorship. That said, though in these texts Marx poses a challenge to the state-sanctioned form of the author and makes the opening moves to a critique of the modern author-function, anonymous authorship was for him more a tool to aid in the emergence of bourgeois polities than it was a textual feature of their communist overcoming. I suspect that the deliberate adoption of anonymity as a communist practice would have been viewed by Marx to be in too close proximity to the conspiratorial forms of Masonic and Bakuninist politics, a fetter to his move to publish communism "openly, in the face of the whole world."[20] And yet the very text where Marx makes this declaration of nonclandestine openness, *The Manifesto of the*

Communist Party, was in fact published anonymously, where it opens an enticing dimension to anonymous authorship, as we will see later on.

TO CONQUER THE ANONYMOUS

If Marx was at the limit of affirming anonymous authorship as an anti-capitalist textual form, Foucault tips over it, with forays into anonymity as a deliberate counter to the modern author-function. We should keep in mind here that Foucault's critique, in contrast to Marx's pseudony-mous intervention, is made not only against censorship but against the conditions of *all* discourse, or all discourse within which one encounters authors, and that this is part of a carefully constructed ethics of writing. In "What Is an Author?" anonymity takes two forms. At the essay's close, Foucault imagines a culture where discourses would circulate in a "perva-sive anonymity," evaluated not in terms of their authenticity, originality, and subjective density (that is, as governed by the author-function) but in terms of their structural patterns and functions, a direction encapsu-lated in his quotation, at the essay's close, from Samuel Beckett's *Texts for Nothing*: "What matter who's speaking?"[21] But while Foucault here imagines a world without the author-function, this formulation is more a condensed presentation of his archaeological method for the analysis of discourse than it is an indication of a specific practice of anonymity. That is not the last word, however, for the text also contains resources for a more concerted ethics of written anonymity. If the author-function is internal to the privatization of discourse, there are indications that the *author,* the writer of a text, may have a different role. This is not quite the writer as empirical person. The author-function does not merely mold and block the individuality of the writer, as the young Marx had it; for Foucault, there is *nothing* of the real individual in the "game of writing," the writer exists here as a "dead man."[22] But in this absence lies the au-thor's potential force, the trace indication of a life that can in no way be reconstructed, a "mark of the writer [who] is reduced to nothing more than the singularity of his absence."[23]

This is enigmatic indeed, though it opens out to a rich stream in Foucault's ethics of writing, where the politics of the author arises in the author's absence or, given its necessary combat with the author-function, in *techniques for producing that absence*. It is in this direction that I now move.

Foucault gave an interview with *Le Monde* in April 1980 in which he declined to reveal his identity, describing the deliberate choice of authorial anonymity as a means to a better "surface of contact" with the reader, one "unrippled" or no longer distracted by the author's name.[24] This is for a chance of better "being heard," for sure, but also, more significantly, for a dynamic life of the work beyond authorial intent: "The effects of the book might land in unexpected places and form shapes that I had never thought of."[25] Such attention to opening the foreclosed work in the realm of its *readers* is complemented by Foucault's thoughts on what anonymity might bring to the *author*. In another interview, Foucault comments that a work "does not belong to the author's project" or "existence"—it is, rather, a desubjectifying experience of the "outside": "It maintains with [the author] relationships of negation and destruction, it is for him the flowing of an eternal outside."[26] To "conquer the anonymous," as Foucault puts it, is to construct and affirm this relation of authorial erasure in the opening to the author's outside. This, not the individuation of the author-function, is the *real* mark of singularity:

> What gives books like those which have no other pretension than to be anonymous so many marks of singularity and individuality are not the privileged signs of a style, nor the mark of a singular or individual inter- pretation, but the rage to apply the eraser by which one meticulously effaces all that could refer to a written individuality.[27]

At this point we should draw a distinction that is often blurred in Foucault's comments on anonymity. In certain places, such claims to the erasure of written individuality occur *under this author's name,* most famously in Foucault's declaration in *The Archaeology of Knowledge* that his writing prepared a labyrinth into which he could lose himself: "I am no doubt not the only one who writes in order to have no face. Do not ask who I am and do not ask me to remain the same: leave it to our bureaucrats and our police to see that our papers are in order. At least spare us their morality when we write."[28] These moments are of limited help to us. For as Nealon observes, such declarations of faceless singularity emanating

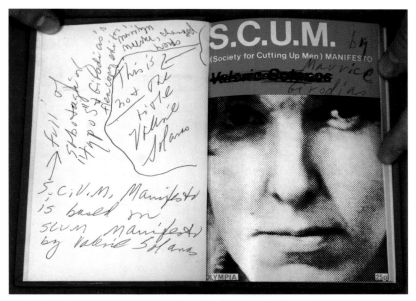

Plate 1. New York Public Library's copy of Valerie Solanas, *S.C.U.M. Manifesto,* defaced by Solanas. Photograph copyright Hiroko Masuike / The *New York Times* / Redux / eyevine.

Plate 2. Conrad Bakker, *Untitled Project: Commodity [Capital],* 2007. Courtesy of Conrad Bakker / www.untitledprojects.com.

Plate 3. Pamphlets by Unpopular Books, including Asger Jorn, *Open Creation and Its Enemies,* 1994.

Plate 4. Mao's Little Red Book as spiritual atom bomb. "Turn philosophy into a sharp weapon in the hands of the masses," circa 1971. Courtesy of IISH / Stefan R. Landsberger Collections, Chineseposters.net.

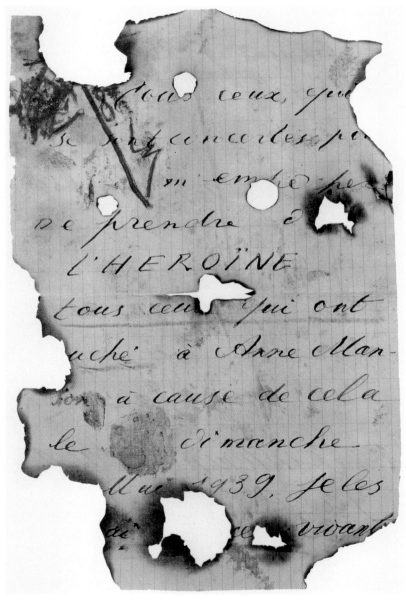

Plate 5. Antonin Artaud, *Spell for Roger Blin,* circa May 22, 1939, recto. Copyright ADAGP, Paris and DACS, London 2015.

Plate 6. Antonin Artaud, *Spell for Roger Blin,* circa May 22, 1939, verso. Copyright ADAGP, Paris and DACS, London 2015.

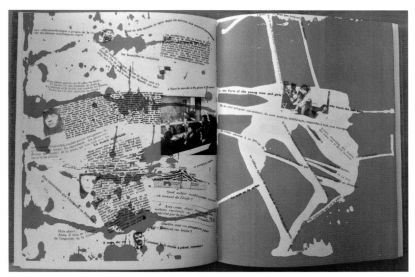

Plate 7. Inside pages from Guy-Ernest Debord, *Mémoires* (Copenhagen: Internationale situationniste, 1959), "supporting structures" by Asger Jorn. Photograph by Mehdi El Hajoui. Courtesy of Alice Debord.

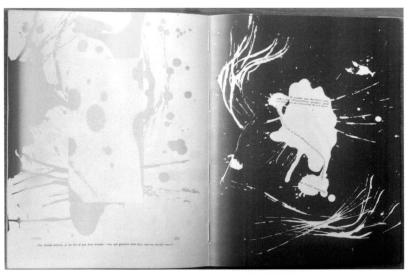

Plate 8. Inside pages from Guy-Ernest Debord, *Mémoires* (Copenhagen: Internationale situationniste, 1959), "supporting structures" by Asger Jorn. Photograph by Mehdi El Hajoui. Courtesy of Alice Debord.

Plate 9. Jacqueline de Jong, pages from "Critique of the Political Practice of Détournement," *The Situationist Times* no. 1 (1962).

Plate 10. "Ceci n'est pas un magazine," artwork concept by Quim Gil, drawn by Damian Jaques, *Mute* 1, no. 19 (2001).

Plate 11. The *Mute* broadsheet, no. 2 (1995), featuring artwork from BANK's "Zombie Golf" exhibition combined with stock golf landscape.

Plate 12. The *Mute* Print on Demand booklet. Cover of 2, no. 0 (2005), features *Maternita,* a Chainworkers' poster by Angela Rindone. Cover of 2, no. 4 (2007), is by Pauline van Mourik Broekman.

Plate 13. Wu Ming's portrait, 2001–2008.

from a named author and posited against the bureaucrats of the norm have the unfortunate effect of charging the author with a power of scarcity and transformation that invokes and intensifies the very structures and privileges he claims to overcome, Foucault here borrowing the not-so-rare trope of the author as unique point of transvaluation.[29] Fortunately, as we have seen, this was not Foucault's only route to anonymity.[30]

TRANSINDIVIDUAL AUTHORSHIP

I turn now to concrete practices of anonymous authorship, first to Luther Blissett. Of the different strategies to conquer the anonymous, Foucault comments favorably on the use of collective pseudonyms, saying this of Nicolas Bourbaki, the pseudonymous collective mathematician: "Bourbaki is at bottom the model. The dream for all would be, each in his own domain, to make something like this Bourbaki, where mathematics is elaborated under the anonymity of a fantastic name."[31] This is the broad direction taken by Luther Blissett, though with an important difference. Unlike Bourbaki, whose name functions as the signature of a delimited collective, Luther Blissett was a "multiple name" without border, an enunciative function, as I will explain in depth shortly, that was *open to anyone.*[32] This multiple name was first established in Bologna, Italy, in the mid-1990s, as a project oriented toward scandals and pranks of communist hue and making tactical use of the cityscape and diverse mediums, from radio and Internet to music and the novel. The politics of authorship was by no means Luther Blissett's only concern, but it was a central constitutive feature and is the aspect of his composition and practice on which I focus here.

Luther Blissett was no less interested than Foucault in a form of anonymous writing that arises from the author's "outside," though he approached it in a way that brings Marx back into our discussion, for Luther Blissett at times understood himself to be an articulation of "communal being" and "general intellect," terms developed by Marx to conceptualize sociality against the dichotomy, so foundational to capitalist modernity, between the individual and the social, a political sociality of the communal or the common.[33] Taking "communal being" and its direct cognates first,

Marx famously shows in "On the Jewish Question" how the bourgeois individual of the modern state—the "citizen," the subject of the "rights of man," the "possessive individual" as we know it since C. B. MacPherson—is premised on an opposition between individual and social existence. In this oppositional relation, the social appears to impinge on the primary autonomy of the individual, but the real delimiting power is actually the social form of the individual itself, the "*confined* individual, confined to himself."[34] A *product* of the capitalist social, the individual masquerades as its *ground* and *cause,* constraining expansive social being into the isolated subject of private property:

> In the rights of man it is not man who appears as a species-being; on the contrary, species-life itself, society, appears as a framework extraneous to the individuals, as a limitation of their original independence. The only bond which holds them together is natural necessity, need and private interest, the conservation of their property and their egoistic persons.[35]

Bourgeois politics partakes of and enforces this structure, such that social being experiences a double degradation, not only excised from the confined and partial individual but reduced to a mere support for the latter, as "the [political] sphere in which man behaves as a communal being [*Gemeinwesen*] is degraded to a level below the sphere in which he behaves as a partial being."[36]

By contrast, Luther Blissett's politics of the collective pseudonym seeks to break the bounds of the partial individual by founding itself on, or bringing into expression, the communal being that traverses and exceeds the individual. As Stathis Kouvélakis points out, the whole bearing of Marx's critical philosophy, which for shorthand we can call his anti-utopianism, prevents him from stipulating the positive determinations of communal being.[37] The concept is instead more a means of immanent critique, whose conditions can be observed only negatively, in revealing the proclaimed universal community of the bourgeois individual to be in fact one of *a-social isolation,* as we have seen, and to be premised on a series of *exclusions.* For the structure of the bourgeois subject placed slaves, racialized others, women, the working class, with their tenuous relation to property, or *being* property, as outside of the political community, their social conditions of life naturalized as prepolitical. That lack of positive determination does not mean, however, that we cannot gain faint glimpses of communal being, if we understand it less as a resource available to be tapped than as a construction that arises in practices that undo the partial individual and the social forms that produce and sustain it. Here the individual and the collective are no longer placed in a dichotomous relation, for the dichotomy is undone along with the terms that it produces, as each individual or, as we can now call it, *singular* instance is a product of collective relations, and each collectivity is constituted through its singular and various manifestations. As Luther Blissett puts it, the collective pseudonym is the production of a "multiple single" within and against the partial mode of being of the individual.[38] Let us be clear, there is no unanimity here. The multiple single is collectivity in difference and discontinuity, collectivity that is without bounds or that exists insofar as it undoes its bounds. As Jean-Luc Nancy has it in his formulation of the "singular plural," which is not uninformed by Marx, the *"common,* having-in-common or being-in-common, excludes interior unity, subsistence, and presence in and for itself. Being with, being together and even being 'united' are precisely not a matter of being 'one.'"[39]

Bringing the now communist Marx to bear on his Young Hegelian self, we might make a leap to say that the "multiple single" is the real individuality that Marx was groping toward in his critique of the state-approved author, if communal being can take the place of the author's "spiritual countenance." From the standpoint of the multiple single, the source of the written word ceases to be subjective interiority and becomes instead the immersion in an individual's outside qua polymorphous communal being, an operation with words against the borders of the individual. Here authorial originality gives way to a kind of primary "creative plagiarism," a molding of that which is always prior to and in excess of the individual—a "continual recombination and variation" of cultural and existential materials that deny "any dichotomy between 'collective' and 'individual.'"[40] As one Luther Blissett veteran later put it, with regard to a writing project we will encounter in chapter 6, "I work with other people, we write fiction by using words, images, colors and sounds that we pick up from everyday life, history and the media landscape. A whole, open community writes along with us, albeit unconsciously or semi-consciously. This has always been true for *every* author and cultural artifact."[41]

There is a certain universality here ("every author"), yet the ontology of expressive communal being is not a timeless abstraction but something located in features of collective production particular to contemporary capitalism—hence the centrality of the second of Marx's concepts, the "general intellect," of which Luther Blissett has characterized himself as a "paradoxical anthropomorphisation."[42] In the concept of the general intellect, Marx seeks to account for the effects of an expansive "general social knowledge" become "*direct force of production.*"[43] General intellect is a fundamentally social formation that exists both transindividually—circulating and multiplying in what Marx suggestively calls the "social individual" and the "social brain"—and machinically, in its immanent articulation with science and technology.[44] It is an astonishingly prescient concept that projects from the early days of industrial production to grasp a great deal of the capacity of contemporary capitalism to generate social wealth outside of direct labor time, from the properties of communal being existent across the social whole, incorporating the cognitive, linguistic, corporeal, and affective dimensions of association.[45] But as an analysis of tendencies in capitalism, general intellect is as much a concept of destabilization and crisis as it is a description of a set of emerging powers and relations. For instead of leading to the progressive overcoming of work, the powers of general intellect serve to intensify its imposition, as per usual for the function of technology in capitalism, while accentuating the "general law of capitalist accumulation," as Marx has it, namely, the tendential reduction in the proportion of variable to fixed capital, leading to the growth of surplus populations and crises of overaccumulation.[46]

Amid these features, I would draw attention to three points of special relevance to the multiple name. First, the terrain of communal being qua general intellect is wholly technocultural: there is no naturalism to it. Second, as an articulation of general intellect, the multiple-name author is not a point external to capitalist patterns of association but is enmeshed within them, her substance—cognitive capacities, technological and linguistic virtuosity, the cultivation of collective affects—increasingly central to the preferred ethico-aesthetic regimes of neoliberal subjectivity. Hence, third, the multiple name must now not only affirm communal being against the partial individual (an ever vital political task in our intensely individuated societies) but also critically orient herself against the ways that communal being, or a certain modality of it, has itself become a key capitalist resource and championed as such. The latter is a particularly acute fault line of collective, anonymous practice. As the anonymous collective authors of the book *Speculate This!* observe, many of the favored expressive and organizational characteristics of anonymity are now celebrated business values of the post-Fordist enterprise, in its paradigmatic models of the "work team" and the "project."[47] Anonymous collectivity cannot, hence, be affirmed in and of itself; for *Speculate This!,* and, I would concur, the communist potential of anonymity, depends in large measure on the degree to which it interrupts the corporate articulation of anonymous collectivity in "work," in both the senses of labor and of proprietorial product.

LUTHER BLISSETT'S *Q*

If the multiple single is the ontological condition of Luther Blissett's anonymity, it is not reached merely by dropping one's name. Anonymity must be *actively constructed,* as can be observed in Luther Blissett's practice of the multiple name. I approach it here through four imbricated aspects: the transindividual agency of the proper name in the novel *Q,* the subjective and temporal disaggregation of the author-function, its immanence to mass media, and the changed status of the author's property. In a subsequent section, I address *Q*'s interventions in the medium of the book through consideration of *The Benefit of Christ Crucified,* a book that functions in *Q* as a self-reflexive double to draw out a number of specifically medial themes.

To reiterate, the multiple single is not an undifferentiated whole but an open field where singularity is an expression of collectivity, and vice versa. It is at this juncture of collectivity and difference that the peculiar function of the proper name is located in Luther Blissett's novel, *Q.* Keeping with our conceptual terms, Sabrina Ovan makes a compelling case that the narrative motor of *Q* is precisely the transindividual property of the general intellect, a motor set in motion by the name.[48] Narrating the turmoil of peasant insurgency, radical heresy, and nascent capitalism in sixteenth-century Reformation Europe, the novel follows two characters in their itinerant movement across the European terrain, paying special attention to the social and technological webs of authority, political alliance and intrigue, banking and trade, and production and distribution of early printed matter. One character, the eponymous Q, is an austere papal spy and heretic hunter, agent of Giovanni Pietro Carafa, who was soon to become Pope. The other, the object of Q's pursuit, remains nameless. Or rather, his name is in continual variation, changing as he traverses the sociopolitical terrain—from Gustav Metzger in the Peasants' War to Gert-of-the-Well in the Münster Rebellion and to Ismael-the-Traveller-of-the-World when he leaves at the close for Istanbul, to note three of his incarnations. Of his many names, a number are taken from actual historical figures in the Radical Reformation, whereas others are laced with wider cultural associations, so augmenting the collective effects of the name. For instance, Metzger is a clear homage to the stateless exponent of "autodestructive art" of the same name, and Ismael is no doubt a nod to the disinherited figure in the Hebrew Bible and the Qur'an, and to Herman Melville's traveler in *Moby-Dick*.

In suspending the consistent name, the subjective continuity that would normally orchestrate the narrative field is unsettled, allowing instead for *communal being* to come forth as protagonist, in all its discontinuous, variegated, and antagonistic complexity. This is the abiding experience of reading the novel, where subject and social relations operate on the same plane in an often disorienting swirl of forces, relations, and tumultuous events. The narrative leaps about from the bloody massacres of the Peasants' War to the plotting of a banking fraud and the trade flows of early capitalism, all the while—no doubt with allegorical purpose—enmeshed within, driven by, and testing the limits of assorted apparatus of power and paradigms of resistance. Yet this narrative of social complexity is nonetheless populated or enacted by (momentarily) named subjects, singularities in the communal field of practice. As Ovan argues, with this function, the name is not an identity in separation from the collective, or even a momentary *share,* but the *passage* of the collective, its putting into play as singularity.

Q is a novel about mass movements and revolutionary social events, though I am arguing that its critical intervention on this front is not in representing such collective forces or in giving them voice in its content; *Q*'s experiment lies in its *form,* in the way the collective, qua multiple single, takes over the expressive voice, whose impact is found most intensely in the narrative's points of discontinuity and contradiction. For despite initial appearances, it is not a story of the autonomous movement of the masses in history but of the constraints, limits, errors, that mass movements face and fail to face up to. There is irony, then, that *Q* became something of an activists' bedside book over the arc of the alter-globalization movement, for its allegorical lesson here was not wholly absorbed, the book providing the movement with mobilizing images of the victorious masses that were unencumbered by its more unsettling insight concerning the traps of direct confrontation with power and the limits of activist subjectivity. Then again, perhaps those lessons are always hard to hear in the swell of struggle, in which case *Q*'s allegorical power is more salient to the retreat of the radical wave; indeed, its authors have described it, and their subsequent novels, as *lessons in defeat,* in how to live in crisis, how, against all odds, to find ways beyond defeat, where allegory must be seen now not as an integrating subjective mechanism suturing past and future but as a fragile and exploratory series of "unpredictable rebounds."[49]

Turning to the character Q, while the many-named protagonist emerges through immanence to social events, the papal agent, by contrast, exists at an abstraction from the social field—"Carafa's eye," as Q is first introduced, looking in and reporting on, even as his spycraft seeks and finds direct effects that approximate to the historical record. He features in the novel in the form of diary entries and letter-reports to Rome that convey a sparse and solitary subjectivity, driven across the novel by his facilitation of Carafa's nefarious "Plan" of utilizing the Radical Reformation to modernize and entrench Church authority. In a sense, keeping with the epic form, Q and his nemesis are held in a Manichaean struggle, their different styles—collective/solitary, immanent/abstract—being expressive of two political orientations and sensibilities that arise from, and put into play, the same conflictual social field. It is thus all the more poignant that when Q finally betrays his master, it is to an unnamed constituency of agents—the "anonymous architects" of the Plan—and the aleatory forces of the social to which he delivers himself: "There is nothing you can do," he writes to Carafa near the close of the narrative, "you cannot even reproach yourself for your failure to predict the defection of your finest agent on the last mile: the minds of men move in strange ways, and no plan can take account of them all."[50]

While it is Q who sets out for us the established historical terrain of the story, its named protagonists and factual events, it transpires, then, that he is no more an identity than his heretic opponent. The point is well observed by Ovan, quoting these lines from Q's diary: "Throughout my life I have never written one word for myself: there isn't a page from the past that could compromise the present; there is no trace of my passage. Not a name, not a word. Only memories that no one would believe, since they are the memories of a ghost."[51] And yet this is no moment of synthesis and overcoming, where Q would succumb to a nameless multitude as subject of historical change, for Q's revelation of nonidentity indexes less the dynamics of resistance than a quality of power—the unnamed agents of the conspiratorial Plan, yes, but also the anonymous and impersonal force that is *capital,* to whose place in the story I now turn.

Though the first half of *Q* presents a social field rooted in the swell of peasant insurgencies and Anabaptist efforts to live heaven on earth, at a decisive stage this ground is pulled away, as Stewart Home emphasized in an incisive early review, when direct confrontation between opposing subjective forces, peasant and state, is substituted with an immanent diagnosis, critique, and intervention in the ungrounded ground of emerging capitalism—of money, banking, global trade, and new media.[52] From now on, the *banks* are the new Antichrist. As the many-named protagonist declaims, overcome at the point of the novel's shift in gear, "Why has no one ever talked to me about banks before?"[53] We know from Marx that the subject of the capitalist mode of production is neither the bourgeoisie nor the proletariat but *capital itself,* the classes of capitalist and worker being merely subjective forms born of the conjunction of capital and labor: "The capitalist functions only as *personified* capital, capital as a person, just as the worker is no more than *labour* personified."[54] Mass social movements can of course change history, but they are no less caught up in these impersonal forces of capital and need to understand themselves as such. Hence in *Q*'s decisive scene, as the second part of the novel tips into the third, the multinamed protagonist receives this instruction about the turn from feudalism to the new world of capital:

> "We were born in two different worlds, Lot. On the one hand you've got the lords, the bishops, the princes, the dukes and the peasants. On the other the merchants, the bankers, the shipowners and clerks. . . . Here there is no ancient and unjust order to turn upside down, no yokels to sit on thrones. There's no need for an apocalypse, because it's already been underway for a while." . . . Eloi pulls out a coin and turns it round between his hands, throws it in the air and catches it a few times. "You see? You can't topple money: whichever way you turn it, one side always shows."[55]

And so, our protagonist has now lost his faith, after the bloody slaughter of the Peasants' War and the mounting evidence that theological positions and passions are entwined within and conditioned by the machinations of state power, the maneuverings of the Church, and the leverage of credit money, "rivers of money lent in exchange for a percentage of the profits."[56] It is a vertiginous condition, for where to locate the standpoint of revolution? Now the movement of the multiple single is undecidable, ever compromised, and without subject or purity of position. In this part of the book, struggles must take a different form. They are organized primarily as an attempt to counterfeit the bills of credit of the Fugger family of mercantile bankers and, as I return to later, the production and distribution of a seditious and anonymous book, *The Benefit of Christ Crucified*. Such struggles are not millenarian, they are not even cumulative, but exist immanently to social relations as points of singular emergence, disruption, and dissipation. The communist sensibility of the novel is revealed less, then, in *Q*'s desertion than in this formulation by *Q*'s nemesis, his nonidentity indexed to the proletariat as nonsubject:

> Details are escaping, the minor shades who populated the story are slipping away, forgotten. Rogues, mean little clerics, godless outlaws, policemen, spies. Unmarked graves. Names which mean nothing, but which have encountered strategies and wars, have made them explode,

sometimes stubbornly, as part of a deliberate struggle, at other times purely by chance, with a gesture, a word.... With each defeat we tested the strength of the Plan. We lost everything each time, so that we could stand in its way. Barehanded, with no alternative.[57]

One would not want formal experiments in expressive communal being to be without their own points of tension, impasse, and failure. What, then, are *Q*'s limits? In putting the collective into play through the singular, *Q*'s many-named protagonist certainly presents a strong, practical critique of many of the received truths of radical politics; the novel, I have suggested, is certainly no naive celebration of the masses in history, of the onward march of the collective. And yet this protagonist has an omniscient ability to diagnose and critique the problems with these movements, presenting the reader with a point of identification that is too comfortable—if not an all-knowing subjectivity, then something of an infallible "reason of the revolution," if you will. As the writers of *Q* later came to reflect on this quality of their protagonist, "it is too easy to be empathetic with him because even if he makes a mistake he is always on the right side."[58] The omniscient narrator is a bourgeois literary device when in the shape of an individual character; she is probably also that when figured as a singular instantiation of communist critique, because a true instantiation of a multiple single in struggle, one who has no identity as such, neither as individual nor as collective, must experience the contingency of the social through impasses and breakdowns in ways that she, and her readers, can never fully comprehend or articulate.

In more concrete terms, this problem with figuring the collective as an all-knowing reason of the revolution can be observed in what it omits or obscures. In this instance, as the authors of the novel were soon made aware by their readership, the omniscience of the protagonist in his immanence to the discontinuous constraints and struggles of the social field does a violence to that which should necessarily be a central feature of what he encounters in this field, namely, the social relations of *gender*. With women largely a supporting cast for a male adventure, the representation of gender in *Q* has rightly become an object of self-criticism.[59]

OPEN REPUTATION

In moving from the novel to the terrain of Q's author, the wider practice of the multiple name with which the novel was interlaced, the processual and discontinuous property of the name, becomes considerably more pronounced. The central feature of this multiple name—as others before it, from Ned Ludd to Karen Eliot—is its disaggregation and dispersal of the self-identical expressive subject. Although access to the pseudonym of Luther Blissett was no doubt limited in part by competence in certain kinds of cultural capital, anyone could in principle adopt the name and in so doing become Luther Blissett (with a few provisos: efforts would be made to prevent him from propagating racist, sexist, or fascist material). Luther Blissett was an "open reputation" that conferred a certain authority and capacity to speak—the authority of the author, no less—on an open multiplicity of unnamed writers, activists, and cultural workers, whose work in turn contributed to and extended the open reputation. In this sense, the author-function is magnified and writ large. But it is such in breach of the structures that generate a concentrated and unified point of rarity and authority, because the author becomes a potential available to anyone, and each manifestation of the name is as original as any other. In this fashion, a different kind of individuation emerges, the individuation of the multiple single: Luther Blissett is at once *collective*, a "co-dividual" shared by many, and *singular* or *fragmented*, a "dividual," an infinitely divisible entity composed of multiple situations and personalities simultaneously.[60] That Luther Blissett had his own portrait—a vaguely androgynous icon created of overlaid male and female photographic images—only confirms this new modality of individuation, invoking the paradox of a multiple single author (Figure 9).

The subjective disaggregation and dispersal of the author also has a temporal dimension. The name "Luther Blissett" was borrowed from the Jamaican-born British footballer who played an ill-fated season at AC Milan in 1983, contrary to great expectation. But no explanation is provided as to the reasons for the adoption of the footballer's name. Indeed, after a fabricated identification of the Luther Blissett multiple name with the conceptual art practice of one "Harry Kipper" (a tactic intended to

Figure 9. Luther Blissett's portrait. Reproduced under a Creative Commons Attribution-ShareAlike 2.5 License.

divert from the start any association of the multiple name with its origi-nators), the proliferation of origin stories became a part of the multiple name itself: "Anyone who makes use of the name may invent a different story about the origin of the project."[61] Luther Blissett was thus set loose from the unifying effects of linear temporality and the biographical arc, allowing history to become a fragmented and multiple resource for each instantiation of the name.

Enabled by this relation to history, one telling of the Luther Blis-sett story is especially enticing, projecting as it does the multiple single structure of a "negative hero"—and something of a zerowork stylist of sport—back into the footballer's media image at AC Milan. Our Luther

Blissett writes, "Only the blindness of a young fan led me to hate him, then, for those badly-treated footballs," for he came to recognize that the footballer's erratic performance was in fact a calculated act.[62] Sensing in the interactive and communicative game of football the dynamic structure of general intellect, the striker "revealed himself to 80,000 consumer-producers" as a *saboteur* of capitalist valorization:

> [He] refuse[d] to be an interface in this system. He decided to stop com-municating, to be a living short-circuit. So he started to move around the field at random, appearing not to care about the game. . . . He became invisible, he could not be represented as part of a social system: he was a drifting mine ready to explode every Sunday in unexpected ways, with strange gestures which broke the cold normality of the football-system. . . . Luther, the black bomber, one of us.[63]

Recall that the concept of the general intellect allows for no autonomy from capital, that even as Luther Blissett's multiple single is posited as an overcoming of capitalist relations, it is enmeshed within them. Such is apparent in this story of the negative hero, which succeeds only insofar as it is interlaced in the reader's mind with the high-value, mediated im-ages of commercial sport. This intermediated quality took on a further dimension when the retired footballer was invited onto the U.K. television program *Fantasy Football* to read lines from Luther Blissett's manifesto, where he showed himself to be rather tickled by the multiple name.[64] If this helps allay understandable concerns about the possible racism of the appropriation without consent of Luther Blissett's name, I would add too that there were clear antiracist resonances in the adoption of his name in a national culture riddled with racism.

Just as the multiple name puts into play an expressive communal being in breach of the author-function's effects of individualization, it unsettles too the author's twin pole of the unified *work*—"the solid and fundamental unit of the author and the work"—which here becomes as fragmented, variable, and layered as the multiple name itself.[65] It is in this sense that we should understand the cultural output of Luther Blissett (at least until Q) as less of the order of "product" than of "action" (to repeat Foucault's designations for texts of, respectively, authorial property and unnamed dissent). Through the skillful orchestration of hoaxes, pranks, and fakes, Luther Blissett's practice was characterized by scandalous disruption of mass media across the platforms of television, newspaper, book publishing, radio, and Internet—his initial venture was, appropriately, a hoax on a prime-time "missing persons" television show.[66] This is mass-mediated culture in its most contemporary manifestation, what we can call the media expression of general intellect: mass media as the technological mobilization and fashioning of transindividual moods or affects, as has become closely associated with the spread of punitive legal instruments and political regimes of security, albeit that in Luther Blissett's 1990s, this was manifest in moral panics against Satanic ritual abuse and the like, before it was succeeded by "terrorism" and "illegal immigration."[67] In this media environment, Luther Blissett was less an external agent operating through an autonomous regime of truth than a practice immanent to the technocultural formations of the media—comprising the same materials and forms but working through mimicry and exposure of the media's orchestration of truths and affects. It is a point well made by Wu Ming 1 while reflecting on one of Luther Blissett's media hoaxes: "by using the tools of traditional counter-inquiries, we had gotten no results. The 'homeopathic' effect of one single lie cured the illness better than the traditional media medicines administered to the public opinion."[68]

Actions rather than products, Luther Blissett's interventions also challenged the specifically commodity form of the book. If no one person or group owns the name of Luther Blissett, the name owns none of its output, which, in keeping with the approach to a primary plagiarism of collective cultural production, was protected from the encroachment of property by anticopyright mechanisms. In a more offensive move, Luther Blissett also impinged on the copyright of others. In one case, he published a book under the name of the popular anarchist writer Hakim Bey, a book comprising a slapdash mix of old Bey writings, fabricated texts, and speeches by Stalin attributed to Bey.[69] The book was greeted—here is the power of the author-function—with praise from leftist reviewers, until the prank was revealed and the publisher threatened, in a most un-anarchist fashion, to sue for copyright violation. Luther Blissett's move to the form of the novel complicates matters, for Q is a recognizable commodity (with international distribution and sales of upward of 250,000 units). But this book was soon made available for free download and circulation, a very early instance of this now not uncommon practice; in its published form, *Q* at least indicates and allows for circuits of distribution not immediately constrained by commercial exchange. Clearly Luther Blissett's communist composition is considerably more complex than could be assessed with a judgment on how "free" is his textual product. The crucial question of open access publishing is not one I pursue in *Anti-Book*. But let me side with those, notably Gary Hall, who argue that today, as open access becomes a plank of the metrics-led marketization of research in neoliberal government and commercial agendas, free access, though an important political terrain, is not in itself enough to constitute radical media formations.[70]

As a particular expression of the multiple single that wells up in and against identity, Luther Blissett's name, like the names in *Q,* was not destined to endure. Modeled according to a Five Year Plan, at the end of 1999, many of his Italian founders abandoned the name, committing seppuku, or ritual suicide. As always, others remain free to propagate Luther Blissett's open reputation, but this act of the "veterans" of the multiple name was a means against habit of returning to the generative basin of communal being: "[seppuku] is one way like another to get rid once again of an identity, to be reborn open to new experiences of social warfare and new mad passions."[71] This subtraction of the veterans from the "uncontrollable golem" of Luther Blissett simultaneously clears room for the development of his potential new styles, or those of other multiple names, where seppuku is an articulation of the decidedly non-Soviet impetus of his Five Year Plan; Luther Blissett's Bolognese founders later described themselves as "the only central committee whose aim is to lose control of the party."[72]

THE BENEFIT OF CHRIST CRUCIFIED

The second epigraph to this chapter, taken from "Anon.," Virginia Woolf's haunting late meditation on anonymous expression, draws attention to the relationship between anonymity and forms of textual inscription and reproduction. Reprising some of our concerns with anonymous authorship,

Woolf here locates creative expression not in a self-present subject, and in the correlated separation of a creative subject from an audience, but in a foundational, transindividual anonymity:

> The voice that broke the silence of the forest was the voice of Anon. Some one heard the song and remembered it for it was later written down, beautifully, on parchment. Thus the singer had his audience, but the audience was so little interested in his name that he never thought to give it. The audience was itself the singer.[73]

Having broached the question of inscription here, Woolf sees little to champion in the textual mediation of anonymity. To Anon., print is a destructive medium. Printed books can record the past existence of anonymous texts in published works of fable—they can "preserve" anonymity—but they cannot create it. "Anon.," then, is a lament to the loss of anonymity. Woolf is not wrong; under the dominance of the author-function, most creative textual media abhor anonymity. But as we have seen, this is not the whole picture. Thankfully, printed and now digital media can also sustain and engender anonymous authorship, shifting our appreciation of anonymity from a foundational, premediated condition to a wholly mediated mode of expression, one that is often lodged, indeed, in the leading edge of such mediation. Luther Blissett was born of the Internet; his founders were early adopters of international bulletin boards such as FidoNet and describe their work and modus operandi as having been shaped by the Internet.[74] We are obliged to ask, then, why did *Q* take the apparently backward media form of the printed codex, and why did the narrative feature a book? As a book within a book, and one with uncertain authorial provenance at that, we can expect *The Benefit of Christ Crucified* to have allegorical value, an expectation that is only heightened when it is recalled that in *Q*'s sixteenth-century setting, the printed book—like the Internet in Luther Blissett's late 1990s—was a new media form.

    Q invests the cultures and forms of mechanical printing with considerable political significance. In the early parts of the novel, the printed word is a veritable agent of the Radical Reformation, where books are "projectiles fired in all directions by the most powerful of cannons," platforms "for sending messages and incitements further and faster to reach the brethren, who have sprung up like mushrooms in every corner of the country."[75] And it is not only books. The pamphlet has its place here, a medium of low-cost and often anonymous writing that was common to the Reformation, and at one point the unnamed protagonist invents the flier, or *Flugblätter,* a by-product of paper wastage in the printing process, which becomes for some peasants their first encounter with the printed word. There is undoubtedly much veracity in this account of the reach and politicizing capacities of early print media, but the first parts of *Q* play heavily on bourgeois tropes of the democratizing power of information, tropes about which Luther Blissett had some ambivalence. Hence the picture becomes more complicated in the third part of the book, in keeping with the shift in focus from revolutionary peasant subjectivity to the internecine world of capital. *The Benefit of Christ Crucified,* which plays a pivotal role in part three, is not the Word of the revolution. If the allegorical value of this book is in drawing attention to the political dimensions of media, it is less to do with the democratizing effects of the broad and speedy distribution of textual content than with displacing and unsettling the perceived value of such, in favor of critical appreciation of the sociomaterial relations and capacities of media form. Let me consider these points in more detail.

Along with his loss of faith, *Q*'s nameless protagonist soon develops circumspection about Lutheran formulations of the purity of the Word.[76] The radical Anabaptist wing of the Reformation is by turn condemned for a similar fixation:

> Your vision of the struggle made you divide the world into black and white, Christians and non-Christians.... That kind of vision will help you win a just battle, but it isn't enough to realize the freedom of the spirit. On the contrary, it can construct new prisons in the soul, new morals, new courts.... The only disagreement between a pope and a prophet lies in the fact that they are fighting over the monopoly of truth, of the Word of God.[77]

The point is made most dramatically with a scene of book burning, as the Münster Anabaptist commune goes awry: "An obscene altar raised to oblivion, the Word of God erasing that of men, spewing forth its triumph over our bent backs, burying our eyes beneath an impenetrable blanket of smoke."[78]

If not primarily a question of content, then, the political dimensions of *The Benefit*—this small book, "handy, clearly written, fits in a pocket"— lie in its textual materialities, in its social and economic forms, relations, and effects. It is an orientation toward text that is condemned in Lutheran formulations, where, as I noted in chapter 3, the Word must transcend the fallen materiality of its platform.[79] As if to confirm this focus on materiality against the Word, we are told that the content of *The Benefit* is rather mundane, it is a "mediocre book" (insofar as *The Benefit* presents the reader with a critical double to *Q* itself, this is an amusing comment on the literary significance of the latter text).[80] It transpires to be the work of a moderate Catholic, a book whose watered-down Calvinism seeks rapprochement with Lutheran theology by making justification through faith alone compatible with Church doctrine—content that is objectionable to the Inquisition and papal rectitude, certainly, but it is hardly on the order of Thomas Müntzer's cry of *Omnia sunt communia*, "everything in common." The politics of the book lie, rather, in a plot to sew discord amid the dominant powers, to unsettle and contain the advance of the Inquisition by attracting numbers of moderates to its thesis. If it is a "cunning little book," this should hence be understood in terms of its seditious relations rather than its identity as a work and thus has little to do with authorial intent.[81] While Carafa's agent, Q, seeks to discover and impose authorial responsibility for this anonymous text, somewhat in the manner of the feudal author-function in prosecuting literary transgression, in the unfurling of the plot the author has little significance. Instead, the scandal is nested in the book's relations of clandestine production, distribution, and reception, arenas from which authors make way for printers, financers, publishers, itinerant booksellers, smugglers of the printed word, and affluent men of letters (where these latter, who would usually be accorded significance in literary history, are merely "useful idiots": "It doesn't matter a damn that they don't know what they're talking about, what's important is that they go on talking about it").[82]

Q's turn to the materialities of text is not, however, to accord them the purity of cause previously reserved for the Word. Just as the Word here has no purity, no less innocent are the objects, networks, and relations through which the scandal unfurls. Granted, there are lapses. *Q*'s dramatic book-burning scene of the triumph of the Word of God has sound historical backing—ensuring the purity of the Word through the burning of opposing books was common to all sides in the Reformation. But this scene trades rather heavily on the trope of the book as singular agent of reason and enlightenment that is so central to the self-representation of bourgeois culture. Notwithstanding the weight of association between the burning of books and Nazi anti-Semitism, Luther Blissett may have missed an opportunity here in his deployment of Gustav Metzger. For Metzger's autodestructive art, with its critical handling of industrial capitalism's "obsession with destruction, the pummeling to which individuals and masses are subjected," appears to have allowed for book burning, having included in his 1996 Destruction in Art Symposium one of John Latham's "Skoob Tower" book-incendiary ceremonies.[83] Nonetheless, it is clear that the plot of *The Benefit,* ultimately unsuccessful, is made on ambivalent terrain; this book, as the other books that circulate in the novel, features first and foremost as a *commodity,* a commercial opportunity for merchant capital. And so the itinerant bookseller who first enrolls the many-named protagonist in the life of *The Benefit* outlines its critical intent and formal innovation in the same breath that he appeals to its potential market value—even suggesting a certain codetermination between the two. "No one likes frontal attacks, hair-splitting arguments, accusations any more." "Heterogeneity" in literary form and uncertainty of authorship are the taste of the day. The content of *The Benefit* "is fine for bores," but it is written by a Catholic friar: "That's a scandal, don't you see? And scandals mean thousands of copies."[84]

The playful self-critique of *Q*'s formal innovations that is implicit in this quotation reminds us that *The Benefit* is in critical interplay with *Q* itself. Therefore, my discussion of *The Benefit* serves to illustrate some of the formal interventions of *Q* as a printed book, though not in a way that aggrandizes or elevates the latter. *Q* emerges from association with the qualities and contours of its fictional double not as a great literary work, an avant-garde masterpiece, but as a minor critical intervention in the materialities of text—in the authorship, authority, and commodity form of publishing—a "masterpiece of dissimulation" and a "mediocre book" in one.[85] And its techniques carry no assurance of continued critical effect. It might be an allegorical warning of the ambivalence of such interventions in media form that the papal agent Q considers the possibility that *The Benefit* could serve as a net to capture those cardinals who looked favorably on the reformers: "A book passing from hand to hand, from library to library and contaminating everyone who touches it. And when you haul in the net, you get all the big fish all in one go."[86]

Still, I have not yet directly addressed the reasons why Q took the particular form of the printed book. Almost without exception, reviewers of Q pointed to its allegorical exchange with emerging Internet culture, but in a way that substituted allegory with cliché, namely, the common story of a comparable experience of transformation in the mass reproduction and democratic dissemination of texts, a sloppy association that reduces the singular characteristics of these different media forms and contexts to a relation of resemblance.[87] Against this, I have suggested that the allegorical value of Q is actually in *challenging* the myths of Internet technophilia—the liberatory power of the unfettered word, the intrinsic democratic effects of the mass reproduction of text—and in developing a feeling for the particular and complex materialities of media, not least of which are relations of the commodity. In this lies one explanation for Q's adoption of the medium of the book. The allegorical relation is founded on the *difference* of the printed codex from digital media. Its brute physicality, apparently outmoded quality, and particular sensory forms, when inserted into a political milieu associated with digital and online media, have a jarring or estranging effect that opens a susceptibility to the themes we have been observing—it is a countersomnambulism, to speak like Marshall McLuhan.[88] Put otherwise, the adoption of the codex displays something like an early post-digital feeling for this medium, whereby the printed book retains its particular medial qualities while developing new capacities and effects in a media sphere transformed by digital technology. As much as Q's allegorical story pertains to our experience of the Internet, it also concerns, then, our experience of the post-digital book.

REENA SPAULINGS MEETS MICHÈLE BERNSTEIN

Pursuit of pseudonymous authorship through the form of the novel is a feature too of Bernadette Corporation's *Reena Spaulings*. Published five years after *Q*, the author of this novel is also a collective pseudonym, just as anonymity or impersonality is a dominant theme of its content. Again, we encounter a book within a book, or the construction of a book through a resonance with another book. The serial translation of this latter book, Michèle Bernstein's 1961 novel *Tous les chevaux du roi*, published as *All the King's Horses* in pamphlet form one chapter at a time, doubled as a gallery program for Reena Spaulings Fine Art, which shared the fictional name of the protagonist of Bernadette Corporation's novel. John Kelsey, of Bernadette Corporation, describes his translation as a slapdash affair, based on source text that was a photocopy of a photocopy of the original edition, so lending the endeavor an aura of samizdat publishing, befitting the nonprofessional nature of the gallery. And its serial publication had a particular purpose, as the gallery sought to "create a line in time that would cross through the various, fleeting exhibitions, some of which were installed and deinstalled in a single afternoon, and in a highly improvised manner," the pamphlets providing linear progression to an otherwise more chaotic entity.[89] As such, the novel might have served as a conservative force, but the narrative coherence it offered was loose and episodic, and it operated, moreover, to draw proximities between the dissimulation of Bernstein's narrated world and that of Reena Spaulings, less grounding than fictionalizing the gallery, which, as Kelsey suggests, "was also a sort of fiction, operated by several people under a made-up name, without a business plan or any prior experience in dealing art."[90]

Bernstein's novel, set in spring 1957, shortly before the founding of the Situationist International (SI), is itself a fictionalization of a social entity, that of daily life with her comrade and husband, Guy Debord. It is a dispassionate drift through Parisian literary and artistic circles and the sexual liaisons and strategies of their open marriage, interlaced with occasional allusions to the politico-aesthetic orientations of their Lettriste milieu. Of the latter, one exchange—between the characters Carole, Gilles, and the narrator Geneviève—stands out for its reference to the practice of the *dérive* (and for the fact that it later achieved notoriety when adopted in *The Return of the Durutti Column,* the 1966 comic strip flier by André Bertrand that promoted the SI pamphlet *On the Poverty of Student Life*). Carole asks Gilles:

> "What are you working on, exactly? I have no idea,"
> "Reification," he answered.
> "It's an important job," I added.
> "Yes, it is," he said.
> "I see," Carole observed with admiration. "Serious work, at a huge desk cluttered with thick books and papers."
> "No," said Gilles. "I walk. Mainly I walk."[91]

The pleasures of recognition that this passage offers are such that it is invariably cited by commentators on the book and is prominent in the back cover promotional text of the Semiotext(e) edition. But the identity-effect, on the reader and the SI, of such recognition is otherwise an object of Bernstein's more subversive practice. As Kelly Baum describes the novel's dissimulating effect on character, "identity is consistently figured as an act of bad faith," the self as "indulgent and polymorphous," "flexible, contingent, and highly performative," and while there is some emotion at stake in the narrative, desire here is instrumentalized and deflated, testing heteronormativity, and the limits of sexual liberation, if by no means scrambling their coordinates entirely.[92] As for its subversive impact on the Situationist scene, it is instructive to reflect a little on the set of contrasts Bernstein's novel—whose writing and publication is broadly contemporaneous with Debord's *Mémoires*—presents with Situationist theory and textual practice. Like *Mémoires, All the King's Horses* is a *détournement,* a *détournement* of the form of the novel that makes use of the redundancy of that form, deploying all the clichés of the then fashionable fiction of the young, beautiful, and free-wheeling and the broader culture of lifestyle publishing. And yet, unlike *Mémoires,* it is also a product of Bernstein's *paid labor,* or at least of a wager that it might generate income, as indeed it did. She explains,

> I was still a member of the lumpensecretariat, working for tuppence ha'penny at a humdrum publishing house. Guy Debord, naturally, wasn't

working. The journal of the Situationist International sold five or six copies, and we sent the rest to people we found interesting. . . .

So, to make ends meet, to earn our bread and butter, I decided to write a novel. . . . At that time the situationists, including myself, had an ironclad belief that the classic novel was past its sell-by-date. It had to be surpassed, overturned, exploded. Why not? Because in this case, no editor: no dough. The solution was simple: I would fabricate a "fake" popular novel. Load it with sufficient clues and irony so the moderately observant reader would realise that they were dealing with some kind of a joke, the steely gaze of a true libertine, a critique of the novel itself.[93]

All the King's Horses has been largely put aside in the reception of the SI as an insignificant work, no doubt in part because of its commercial impetus. Yet it is this quality, that of a hack work, wherein Bernadette Corporation found its appeal:

We had heard that Bernstein quickly disowned her own novels as minor commercial ventures, as not serious (in comparison to her husband Guy Debord's theoretical texts, for example), but this was exactly what interested us: writing under the sign of commerce, but also disowned writing. What can we make of a text that insists on both its own commercialism and its refusal of authorship?[94]

What can we make of it? As implied already, *All the King's Horses* shows Debord's refusal to take a job—framed as a decidedly avant-gardist gesture in his early Left Bank graffiti "Ne travaillez jamais" ("Never work") but otherwise not unappealing—in a less than favorable light, for it is now revealed to have been achieved in part on the back of the labor of his wife.[95] More broadly, this text, contaminated by commerce and fictionalizing Bernstein's life with Debord and comrades "as if it were a breezy but jaded romance for teenaged girls," troubles the decidedly heroic and masculine pose of her avant-garde milieu and its theory of action.[96] Indeed, the book's *détournement* might exactly be operating on this register: not only a joke on fashionable youth fiction but, as Debord, Jorn, and others emerge as "flimsy parodies" in the style of a *Gossip Girl* paperback, it may also be "an ironic *détournement* of the SI itself," as Kelsey puts it, "a glamorization and a critique of the very milieu [Bernstein] was participating in."[97] A self-critique of the heroism of the SI and its theory, perhaps it is only in fiction that this could have emerged, for fiction, as Bernadette Corporation has it, is an especially suitable vehicle for such acts of distancing and critique, a means of disidentification, "of putting oneself and one's problems at a distance, of getting rid of oneself."[98]

In their own novel, *Reena Spaulings,* this "getting rid of oneself" is developed in critical exchange with one of the novel's protagonists, New York City—or New York City as imagined against the "patriotic ghost of the city" installed after 9/11, imagined, like Bernstein's Paris, "as a means of rewriting and reinhabiting the city itself."[99] To draw a thread to my earlier discussion, this city plays a role not dissimilar to Luther Blissett's "communal being," at once the condition and the product of the writing: "Like its authors, the New York City depicted herein finds itself constantly exposed to the urges of 'communism'—that is, to a chosen indifference to private property, a putting-in-common of the methods and means of urban life and language."[100] The exposure to communism here takes the dual form of a certain plenitude and (as I turn to later on) an absolute evacuation. If authorship is to be adequate to the fractal quality of the city, the city necessitates the plenitude, the putting-in-common, of collective and unnamed composition: "If you look at a city, there's no way to see it. One person can never see a city. You miss it, hate it, or realize that it's taken something from you, but you can't go somewhere and look at it and just see it empirically. It's an everyday group hallucination. This novel is modelled on that phenomenon."[101] And so, to compose the novel, as the preface informs, apparently 150 professional and amateur writers came together in the model of the Hollywood studio system, "each assigned specific functions within the overall scheme."[102]

As to its content, Bernadette Corporation describes *Reena Spaulings* as a novel of images, "a book written by images, about images, to be read by other images."[103] The description recalls Henri Bergson, for whom matter is an aggregate of images, the image being "an existence placed halfway between the 'thing' and the 'representation,'" neither reducible to the sense impressions it creates in the mind nor being wholly independent of mind, entirely different from what we perceive of it.[104] In this respect, New York City comes on the stage of the novel as Bergson's "universe" of "universal becoming," the perpetual interaction of images, without cause or effect, without beginning or end.[105] But we encounter it through a second protagonist, a young woman named Reena Spaulings, who serves as an image to perceive the city's universe of images. For Bergson, the universe of interacting images is encountered through perception-reaction circuits that break the infinite play of interaction by reordering the images according to the utility of a subject, a delimiting effect:

> To the degree that my horizon widens, the images which surround me seem to be painted upon a more uniform background and become to me more indifferent. The more I narrow this horizon, the more the objects which it circumscribes space themselves out distinctly according to the greater or lesser ease with which my body can touch and move them. They send back, then, to my body, as would a mirror, its eventual influence; they take rank in an order corresponding to the growing or decreasing powers of my body. *The objects which surround my body reflect its possible action upon them.*[106]

But this is not the only story, for "memory," the past collection of images, offers the possibility that a "rift," a "zone of indetermination," is inserted between perception and reaction to allow other images to seep in and unsettle that circuit of subjective utility, opening to other, less automatic or more desubjectified relations to images.[107] And it is this that is Reena Spaulings's promise and potential, her *communism*. If the impossibility of grasping the city necessitates collective authorship, the disidentification of writers, such techniques of writing undo Reena Spaulings, who, no longer "spanned by any author's mind," loses her subjective coherence as a character to the interactions of the city, or she may do.[108] Granted, the perception–reaction circuits of New York City are orchestrated by capital in self-entrepreneurial and individuating apparatus: "Buy a Dyptique candle for the bathroom. Moisturizer, bananas, toilet paper. Walking in this city is more like work on the way home from work."[109] And yet there may be "a walking that would be more like giving it all away."[110] At moments New York City comes to Reena Spaulings like Clarissa Dalloway drifting through London's West End, becoming imperceptible as a subject as the universe of interactions—the impressions, sensations, varying magnitudes, colors of the city—are extended through her and she in turn extends them, beyond the perception–reaction circuit of subjectivation. The city "sucks her up and grows through her. In the spine, in the brain, in the guts," "walking in the wavelengths of color beyond color."[111] "I'm addicted," says Reena, "to maximum exposure and maximum identification with whatever touches me, a conspiracy involving myself and everything."[112] "What if nothing belonged to anybody?"[113]

If the idiom here borrows from Bergson and Woolf, the book's proximity to Bernstein's novel leaves little doubt that it does so also as an inflection of the Situationist *dérive*. In this context, especially, it is striking that Reena Spaulings is no avatar of radical subjectivity but absolutely generic, a woman of our mass-mediated time, evacuated of any particular qualities—Bernstein's influence again. "How is she? Young and ugly and beautiful. All-in-one vehicle. A sponge, a vacuum," "she could be just about anybody."[114] Reena Spaulings is a security guard at the Metropolitan Museum of Art become star underwear model. With her, writing under the sign of commerce has become a world *only* of commerce—this is also *capitalism* of the image:

> Why is it that when you do so little for it, no amount of recompense is enough. Holy shit this is six months' worth of standing guard at the Met. I just think that when you're serving time for it, a sense of reality allows the dollar amount to remain small and still seem OK, to trickle in at the same pace as the hours do, whereas when you're selling nothing you're selling an essence which is priceless. Why is it that essences are so light? Holy shit it's my economy, an economy of essences.[115]

In an economy of images, work and leisure have reached indistinction: "Is there a dream of ongoing creativity directly connected to, inclusive of all your activities—like dancing, writing, bleeding, social obligations? Are there priorities? If there is no designated 'leisure' time, but everything is work, even non-work becomes work."[116] It seems that Marx's communist vision of variable activity delinked from identity has been colonized.[117] Reena Spaulings suggests that communism instead is a kind of *inaction*— here is the "evacuation" I signaled earlier. Communism does not appear to be emerging in any concrete sense, certainly not as an active subject. It is only glimpsed as the negative of capital, perceived in the most capitalized subjects—the undecidability of Reena Spaulings's "boredom," her immanence to the images of the city, a "state of grace providing zero payoff." "Communism, [New York City] seems to say, is the only thing we share today, besides our extreme separation."[118]

By definition, such undecidability presents no guarantees. Indeed, Bernadette Corporation might be as revealing of new tendencies in our contemporary "separation" as they are of resistance to them. Anonymity is not an inviolate communist tactic. It has always had a certain cachet for the avant-garde individual, but it now has broader appeal, lending a functional quality to the self-entrepreneurialism of the neoliberal culture industry. The point is acutely made in a recent upbraiding of Bernadette Corporation's John Kelsey, which took the form of an illicit appropriation, pornographic doctoring, and online distribution of Kelsey texts in a PDF called "Monsieur Roubignoles presents *The Kelsey Collection Artforum 2004–2012.*" While Kelsey's scene looks very much like communist anonymity, this anonymous critique found Kelsey's cultivated personal anonymity to be a mechanism of self-marketing.[119] Here the ultraleft artist, in the manner of a brand, looses *himself* to emerge as a robust *constellation of parts*. It is an instance of what Kelsey's assailants call the "advertised personality," whereby the artist is all the more able to accrue reputation and hence brand value the less his personality is tied to any one particular quality:

> Interested in the way the reticence of our subject in his personal behavior (in essence, who he *was*) paired with the verve of his branded *persona*—as a prolific member of the artworld's *enfant terrible* collective Bernadette Corporation, as well an athletic collector of associations with subcultural signifiers via his gallery (Reena Spaulings Fine Art), writings, and flirtations with the far left—we hypothesized that the two were indelibly connected. When one was redeemed—the other was near at hand, and vice versa.[120]

INVISIBLE, EPHEMERAL, HISTORICAL: ANONYMITY AND THE PARTY

A good deal of Bernadette Corporation's development of the theme of anonymity arises from engagement with the French journal *Tiqqun* (1999–2001), including the Invisible Committee's book *The Coming Insurrection* (an anonymous body of text for which "Tiqqun" can stand as the collective name). The biography of *The Coming Insurrection,* first published in 2007 and in English in 2009, illustrates a renewed mobilization of the author-function by penal law, in the mode of security measures against a catch-all "terrorism." For it was a principal piece of evidence in the case of the "Tarnac 9," the high-profile arrest in November 2008 of a group associated with *Tiqqun,* then living in a communal farmhouse, accused of a relatively minor act of sabotage on the French railway.[121] The emphasis in *Tiqqun* and *The Coming Insurrection* on legal infraction must have encouraged some awareness of the *tactical* value of anonymity, but anonymity arises here in relation to the problem of identification more broadly conceived, including the individuating apparatus at play in textual media.

As the French state in its prosecution of the Tarnac 9 disregarded the authorial anonymity of *The Coming Insurrection,* Fox News's ever exercised Glenn Beck was unhindered by its claims (as I will come to in due course) to decenter the authority of the medium of the book, repeatedly returning to *The Coming Insurrection* as the root, agent, and program of any number of leftist, liberal, and world historical outrages. It was a strange turn of affairs, with the trope of the "total book" alive and well in the mass medium of right-wing televisual talk—part knowing neocon entertainment, part delusional paranoia. Not that Tiqqun needed this publicity, for its theses struck a chord with radical milieu in the wake of the alter-globalization movement and the move into economic crisis, especially in the 2009 California student struggles and elements of Occupy.[122] These political scenes were served in part by Semiotext(e), which published *The Coming Insurrection,* three books of texts taken from the *Tiqqun* journal, and the Invisible Committee's sequel, *To Our Friends,* though unlike the "little black books" of Semiotext(e)'s early Foreign Agents series, these volumes have a rather tame and establishment feel, at least when placed against the welter of small press and no-press translations and editions that compose the broader English-language reception of Tiqqun. It is a media field that elects Tiqqun as one of the first born-post-digital phenomena in communist publishing, with print, online, and e-pub versions interlaced— it includes, for example, PDFs designed for self-printing as pamphlets rather than online reading, a specialism of the Zine Library forum, and a print edition in English of *Tiqqun* 1 in the form of a facsimile translation.

As I indicated, if Tiqqun has a *principium individuationis,* it is a politics of anonymity and desubjectification launched against the constraint and isolation of imposed identity, a situation where "personalization" feels "a lot more like an amputation."[123] I trust that something of the orientation and style can be conveyed with a brief quotation, from the Tiqqun text "How Is It to Be Done?"

> The experience of my desubjectivization. I *become*
> a whatever singularity. Some *play* opens up between
> my presence and the whole apparatus of qualities
> that are ordinarily attached to me. . . .
> All that isolates me as a *subject,* as a body endowed
> with a public configuration of attributes, I feel it
> Founder.
> . . . .
> I need to become anonymous. In order to be present.
> *The more I am anonymous, the more I am present.*
> I need zones of indistinction.
> In order to reach the Common.[124]

Rather than pursue this construction of anonymity in itself, I intend here to step from Tiqqun and consider the articulation of anonymous authorship with the communist formulation of "the party." My prompt is Tiqqun's notion of the "imaginary party," which appears in various guises in their texts, including in the subtitles of the two issues of the journal: "Conscious Organ of the Imaginary Party" and, in number two, "Organ of Liaison within the Imaginary Party." This relatively high-profile articulation of the notion of the party notwithstanding, returning to this theme today will prompt some surprise with more circumspect readers. Has the communist party not been long proven a dead end? Surely, in an age of networks and disaggregated labor, this organizational model is an anachronism? I am certainly not interested in reviving the theory of the party associated with Lenin, Trotsky, or Mao—that is, the party as state-form (whether in waiting or in power), as obscure sect, or as mechanism of *churn* in bureaucratic echelons. Indeed, I am not seeking any kind of revival, or even making the case for a particular model of organization.

I touch on the organization question, but my purpose, instead, is to consider the party as a field of anonymous textual expression and to draw out a set of additional qualities in communist writing with which such anonymity is articulated, qualities that circulate around the problematization of textual authority and certainty, antididacticism, and an immanent but critical relation to struggles (which are not—spoiler alert—qualities I find in abundance in Tiqqun).

The word *tiqqun,* Hebrew for "salvation," lends pseudonymous attribution to a body of texts, but it has other functions and domains of application. As the translators of one of the Semiotext(e) editions describes it, "'Tiqqun' can refer to an anonymous collective, the journal in which these texts appeared, a subjective process, or to the historical process to which these same texts bear witness."[125] One effect of this construction is the substitution of the authorial voice with that that of the social, a book's contributors becoming merely "scribes" of a situation, as is apparent in the opening of *The Coming Insurrection*:

> This book is signed in the name of an imaginary collective. Its contributors are not its authors. They were content merely to introduce a little order into the common-places of our time, collecting some of the murmurings around barroom tables and behind closed bedroom doors. . . . They've made themselves scribes of the situation. . . . It's enough just to say what is before our eyes and not to shrink from the conclusions.[126]

This is a textual trick, certainly. It may well serve to arrogate the persuasive weight that comes with mass phenomena to an otherwise idiosyncratic standpoint, and so intensify rather than diminish the authority of the author, who is all the more able to pass himself off as a universal in being unnamed as a particular. I assess that possibility later. But it also suggests more productive moves, which I pursue here initially through Marx.

While Marx was disinclined to adopt anonymous authorship as a communist value in its own right, one of his unsigned texts places anonymity at the heart of the history of communist writing, where it presents the possibility of developing a communist anonymity in relation to the theme of the party. In the first edition of *The Manifesto of the Communist Party,* the most famous and widely read of all Marx's works, you would look in vain for attribution to its authors.[127] Commissioned by the Communist League, the recently founded organization of émigré radicals in London, what little accreditation it has only appears in the preamble, and then in a way that is decidedly noncommittal. Toward the goal of meeting the bourgeois "Spectre of Communism with a manifesto of the party itself," the preamble informs that "Communists of various nationalities have assembled in London, and sketched the following manifesto, to be published in the English, French, German, Italian, Flemish and Danish languages."[128] This apparently casual sentence belies the considerable complexities and ramifications of the text's authorship. But before proceeding to consider these, let me reflect for a moment on why I am engaging with a "manifesto," given the critique I made of this textual form in chapter 1. While I am developing the theme of anonymity here from a manifesto, I do so by shifting from the manifesto qualities of Marx and Engels's text, which it seems critics cannot but remark upon, to the textual qualities of the party form that its content evokes, which are much less commonly considered (the party's marginal nature in discussions of this text seemingly confirmed by the fact that that it has largely dropped out of the title of this work, which is usually printed as the *Communist Manifesto*).[129] In thus decentering the manifesto structure of this work, my exploration of anonymity and the party also leads into other nonmanifesto textual forms and mediums—letters, journals, textual fragments—and some indication that these forms have particular salience for the construction of anonymity and the party.

If one was inclined to diminish the significance of the *Manifesto*'s anonymity, it could be accounted for by the convention of group attribution for a collective statement of principle, with Marx and Engels writing on behalf of the Communist League. That is partly true, though the Communist League is not mentioned by name. But the *Manifesto*'s authorial anonymity is not best understood as a means of substituting the proprietorial voice of individual authors with that of a group. Certainly the *Manifesto* was commissioned and published by a communist organization, but it was not to be the exclusive preserve of that organization nor a textual mirror to consolidate its identity and promote its leadership role. On the contrary, the text's anonymity served to *decenter* the role of its commissioning organization as much as it did the role of its authors and, instead, to place the text immanently to the anti-identitarian terrain of the party.

To understand the nature of this party, before moving to develop the ramifications of anonymity therein, we can start a little while after the *Manifesto* and the dissolution of the Communist League, with Marx's reflections on the theme in an 1860 letter to Ferdinand Freiligrath. Here Marx challenges the notion that his noninvolvement in political organization during the unfavorable conditions of the 1850s was the result of "'doctrinaire' indifference," and in so doing he indicates a twofold analytic of the party: the party in an "ephemeral sense" and in a "broad historical sense."[130] The *ephemeral party* or *formal party* (I will use the latter, Bordiga's rendering of Marx's term) is any particular communist organization situated in time and space, an organizational articulation of specific conjunctures.[131] And the *historical party,* of which the former is "simply an episode," is the set of conflicts and struggles that are immanent to the social relations of capital as a whole, throughout time—for capital is inherently antagonistic—and in any one time; the historical party is that which "is everywhere springing up naturally out of the soil of modern society."[132] As such, it is not historical in the sense of determination by the past; quite the reverse, the historical party is that which leans into the future, it has an evental quality, immanent to the mutating and antagonistic limits of capitalist social relations.

The two modes of the party intersect—one is an organizational articulation, concentration, and, potentially, extension of the other—but they have different qualities and effects. The first point to stress in delineating their specific qualities is that the historical party is not a cumulative composite of formal parties, and neither does it designate a linear historical thread through select communist organizations (such that the Communist League, for example, has no privileged role; as an episode of the historical party, it is only one of "a hundred other societies").[133] Indeed, there is considerable theoretical basis for arguing that the historical party plays a *disruptive* role in formal organizations.

We can develop this point about the historical party through Marx's earlier comments on the party in the *Manifesto,* this time formulated in a period of upswing in struggles, the revolutions of 1848 just around the corner. Though the concept of the party developed in the *Manifesto* seeks to forward certain modes of thought and association—notably, internationalism and the critique of capital—it is not a concentrative entity but a distributed one: "The Communists do not form a separate party opposed to other working-class parties. / They have no interests separate and apart from those of the proletariat as a whole. / They do not set up any sectarian principles of their own, by which to shape and mould the proletarian movement."[134] The party is stretched across the social, dependent on social forces and struggles for its existence or its substance—"the proletariat as a whole"—and, in an anticipatory and precarious fashion, oriented toward social contingencies and events. As Badiou puts it (albeit for rather different purposes to mine), it is not only the case that for "the Marx of 1848, that which is named 'party' has no form of bond even in the institutional sense." More than this, there is here a positive stipulation of the party's evental quality: "the real characteristic of the party is not its firmness, but its porosity to the event, its dispersive flexibility in the face of unforeseeable circumstances."[135] Rancière sheds light on this too. Given the precarious and anticipatory orientation of the party, there is considerable insight in his thesis that Marx's party—for all its universality, or *because* of it, its opening to the becoming of social relations, the nonidentity of the proletariat—is directed not toward unity but toward *division* that "first of all the purpose of a party is not to unite but divide."[136]

How does this party as evental division relate to the theme of organization, the theme of the formal party? In moments of uprising and revolution, the party names those organizations that play the necessary role of organization and coordination, pushing toward revolutionary rupture as it "cleaves its way" through organizations based on sectional interests, developing forms of coordination that undo the distinctions and identities through which such sectional organizations stand against revolutionary change.[137] In other words, the formal party plays the role of evental division outlined in the *Manifesto,* but in *organizational* terms. In less favorable conditions, however, the features of the formal party can be rather different. In these conditions, formal organizations provide a certain affective solace and institutional memory—if only of impasses and failures to be overcome—that can be put back into play and contestation in a new upswing. But in such periods of abeyance, formal parties also have a reactionary tendency to direct efforts and resources toward maintaining their organizational identity against a now hostile environment, substituting this for diffuse struggle as the object of communist politics or arrogating such struggle to the project of the party's endurance. We should register here the significance of context to Marx's letter to Freiligrath. For his concept of the formal party is at least in part an articulation in theory of his practical *withdrawal* from such parties, from "meddling with associations which had now had their day." It is a concept that seeks to prevent identification of the party with such limited organizational entities and, perhaps, with organizational questions only, rather than questions concerning the antagonistic content of capitalist daily life (hence his remark about the historical party "springing up naturally out of the soil of modern society," something immanent to social relations as a whole and not the exclusive preserve of formal organizations).[138]

Drawing these strands back into our thematic, I am arguing that the *Manifesto*'s anonymity is the authorship form most adequate to its theory of the party, a speech without identity to match the party's immanence to social relations and porosity to the event. Anonymity displaces the author-function, the privileged and integrated site of proprietorial discourse, with the organization (formal party). But that alone would not be adequate to the evental nonidentity of the party, for it risks a unity of its own, and a certain "doctrinal monolithism," the subsumption of different and various contributions to the dictatorship of a unified theory determined by the pursuit of party identity—as Camatte puts it, while explaining why *Invariance* chose to *end* its use of the Bordiga epigraph I take for this chapter. Hence Marx's theory of the party requires a *second* displacement, whereby the authorship of a text opens out also to the disruptive force of the historical party, sometimes through the formal party (in periods when the formal party operates against sectional interests and self-integrated groups) and sometimes *against* it (when, in periods of abeyance, the formal party becomes itself such an integrated group). Anonymous authorship, in short, is a refusal to separate an expressive identity from the open terrain of organizational forms and social antagonisms and a means to allow that terrain to undo the author-function. And vice versa: to bring the party and anonymity into proximity is to extend the open antagonism of the party in and through the practice of writing, an experience for writer and reader alike.

That is a conceptual formalization, but the point can also be pursued through particular features of the social life of the *Manifesto*, notably the role of *translation* in its geographical dispersal, to pick up again the peculiar self-presentation of its collective authorship. As Martin Puchner has shown, the *Manifesto*'s announcement that "Communists of various nationalities have assembled in London, and sketched the following manifesto" in six languages intimates the proletarian internationalism that the text seeks to meet and evoke, and, more intriguingly, it does so in a fashion that seems to place each language on a par, with the German in which it was written appearing in the middle of the list as merely one language among others. It is as if the proposed editions were to exist without translation, or *only* in translation, a text without an original language. One may yet be concerned that this suggests the "universal language" that I have challenged elsewhere in this book, but that is not the best way to read it. Puchner argues that the *Manifesto*'s "total translatability," where all its editions in all languages "are equivalent," is a proletarian enactment of the "world literature" described in the *Manifesto*'s pages.[139] "Equivalence" does of course evoke the leveling equivalence of the commodity form, the means by which value emerges and commands, but here equivalence serves less to homogenize the text than to affirm the particularity of its adoption and consumption, such that translation *improves* the work, as it is taken up by formal parties in different antagonistic sites, linguistic communities, and geographical contexts (which the émigré experience ensured were frequently incongruous, as Puchner notes). Discussions concerning the great contribution of Chartist and early feminist Helen Macfarlane (who first translated the *Manifesto* into English, serialized in four parts in the Chartist weekly the *Red Republican* in November 1850), or Samuel Moore's 1910 translation (with his line "all that is solid melts into air" that bears only a passing relation to Marx and Engels's German), are hence more than of bibliographical and biographical interest—they are textual expressions, in place of the author, of the distributed and disruptive form of party that this one-time anonymous text bears and produces.[140]

As this comment on translation indicates, anonymity and the party do not come into proximity all by themselves as two independent forms.

Rather, their interplay takes shape in conjunction with critical orientations and practices in writing and publishing that ramify their effects and that, indeed, are often necessary to determine their successful achievement. The remainder of the chapter seeks to draw in some of the these dimensions of writing and publishing with reference to particular projects that have directly or indirectly handled the problematic of anonymity and the party. The first of these serves as a crystalline example of the discussion thus far, though this time we have an explicit assertion of anonymity as an intrinsic value of communist writing.

COMITÉ AND THE COMMUNISM OF WRITING

Blanchot lived 1968 through the Comité d'Action Etudiants-Ecrivains (Student-Writer Action Committee), in the company of Marguerite Duras, Dionys Mascolo, and some twenty others, which, along with a number of tracts, published a single issue of a journal, *Comité,* shortly after the end of the events. Among the journal's short, conjunctural, and philosophically intense texts is "Communism without Heirs," a text that posits communism against the binding effects of identity and the latter's didactic and imperial valences. That is, communism is against everything that "roots men in a time, in a history, and in a language," against "the principle of alienation constituting man as privileged in his particularity, . . . imprisoning him in a contentment with his own reality, and leading him to propose it as an example or to impose it as a conquering affirmation."[141] Patriotism is the particular target, or its adoption by so-called communist parties, though the text can also be read against tendencies to identity in the aftermath of May, tendencies toward prolonging its formal parties— their tactics, organizational structures, theories, rhetorics, and aesthetic styles—beyond their event. As a ruptural event, Blanchot writes in December 1968, the May movement must now "renounce itself," and not, as he observed all around, establish and sanctify a "new tradition," a false fidelity that negates the event it claims to affirm.[142]

If communism is against identity in this way, it is apparent that *Comité* understood nonidentity to be the *very condition* of communism, an understanding that here takes an exquisite formulation: "Communism is what excludes (and excludes itself from) every already constituted community."[143] This is communism as porosity to the event, as division, as "rupture," in Blanchot's idiom, bound to the proletariat as nonidentity— the passage hence continues: "The proletarian class, community without any common denominator other than penury, dissatisfaction and lack in every sense of the term."[144] All this we have seen earlier, under the theme of the historical party, but Blanchot's formulation is an opportunity to move more directly into the terrain of anonymity. We know from Mascolo that Blanchot penned "Communism with Heirs," but the writings in *Comité* were published anonymously.[145] This was not an incidental move. For *Comité,* the unworking of the identity of communism, in its immanence to the proletariat, was to be necessarily also an unworking of the identity of the *author,* a condition for a "communism of writing," as the project was characterized in "The Possible Characteristics."[146] This editorial text is a striking departure from the "what we stand for" editorial statements that usually accompany collective political publishing, and which are so often catalysts for the passage to identity in formal parties—totemic sets of principles through which groups seek to "project an impressive image on the social screen," in Camatte's phrasing, and so mark their self-delimitation and perpetuation of capitalist patterns of self-marketing.[147] By contrast, this piece concentrates less on *Comité*'s political ideas and principles than on its *form of writing and publication,* what it calls the journal's "possible characteristics" in the task of conjoining the "rupture" of communism to "breaking with the traditional habits and privileges of writing."[148] Of these, one characteristic, set out at the top of a list of seven, announces the journal's anonymity (where, to clarify, the first two points are the negative conditions entailed in the production of the third, which, as we must understand from Blanchot's writing on communism, is a collective speech without identity, or, as Kevin Hart puts it, a speech formed on the "contestation of unity"):

> The texts will be anonymous. Anonymity aims not to remove the author's right of possession over what he writes nor even to make him impersonal by freeing him from himself (his history, his person, the suspicion attached to his particularity), but to constitute collective or plural speech: a communism of writing.[149]

AGAINST THE ROAST PIGEONS OF ABSOLUTE KNOWLEDGE

For all its immanence to the social field, our formulation of the party thus far still hazards the risk, as I registered previously, of a certain identitarian and authoritarian closure, whereby a text arrogates the authority of mass social forces to pass off its own partial truth as a universal condition—an instance of Blanchot's alienated particular, identity at once self-contented and commanding, though now cloaked by anonymity. To avoid this, displacing authorship into the eventual becoming of the party and proletariat necessitates also displacing its *authority* into the same milieu. Marx says as much. In an early letter to Arnold Ruge, Marx makes the case for a communist form of writing that is to be adequate to the theory of the party: unconstrained by identity; leaning into the future, into the uncertainty of the event; and oriented toward division. As the necessary complement to this, Marx adds an additional feature. Unlike idealist models of abstract thought, where ideas are introduced from one particularity but claim universality, this communist writing immanent to conflictual social relations necessitates that it drop any "dogmatic banner." As Marx explains (in a passage I will also pick up later, and so reproduce here at length),

> Not only has a state of general anarchy set in among the reformers, but everyone *will* have to admit to himself that he has no exact idea what the future ought to be. On the other hand, it is precisely the advantage of the new trend that we do not dogmatically anticipate the world, but only want to find the new world through criticism of the old one. Hitherto philosophers have had the solution of all riddles lying in their writing-desks, and the stupid, exoteric world had only to open its mouth for the roast pigeons of absolute knowledge to fly into it. Now philosophy has become mundane, and the most striking proof of this is that philosophical consciousness itself has been drawn into the torment of the struggle, not only externally but also internally. But, if constructing the future and settling everything for all times are not our affair, it is all the more clear what we have to accomplish at present: I am referring to *ruthless criticism* of all that exists, ruthless both in the sense of not being afraid of the results it arrives at and in the sense of being just as little afraid of conflict with the powers that be.[150]

In this construction, "mundane" communist thought does not *impose* itself on struggles—does "not confront the world in a doctrinaire way with a new principle: Here is the truth, kneel down before it!"—rather, it emerges *from* struggles, from critical relationship to their torment, and with such torment it must remain ever articulated. The role of communist writing is thus diminished; it does not offer the communist equivalent of the Word of salvation but merely adds a little shape, reflection, and synthesis to knowledge that "already abounds in the world," as Jasper Bernes characterizes the antididactic role of theory in this letter.[151] Yet in this diminishing, writing becomes all the more salient and intensive, because it no longer basks in self-importance, beached and bloated with its own clichés, but seeks as best it can to operate immanently to the evental unfurling of social relations. Marx's formulation here is all the more pertinent in that its context and medium of inscription performs its content. For it is a text written to explain not communist thought in the abstract but the particular purpose of publishing a journal, the *Deutsch-Franzöische Jahrbücher* (German-French annals, published February 1844), whose one (double) issue was coedited by Marx and Ruge and includes the full series of their letters, as if the epistolary form were especially suited to such textual formulations of an immanent, antidogmatic communism. The series concludes with a clarion call for this antidogmatic mode of writing and publishing, proposing "the trend of our journal" as "self-clarification (critical philosophy) to be gained by the present time of its struggles and desires. This is a work for the world and for us."[152]

Such antidogmatic writing, immanent to contingent social relations, is simultaneously an embrace of uncertainty. As is apparent at the start of the preceding quotation from Marx's letter to Ruge, whereas bourgeois thought is unsettled by uncertainty (when it "has no idea what the future ought to be"), communist thought, as it leans into the future, is *necessarily* uncertain and speculative, it even holds uncertainty as its condition. This point can be teased out from *Endnotes* (2008–), where communist uncertainty, if I can put it like that, is interlaced with the media form of the journal. The first issue of *Endnotes* carries part of the same letter to Ruge on its back cover, where it plays a somewhat paradoxical role. A text now 170 years old, written and published to explain the rationale of a nineteenth-century journal, here assists in delineating and confirming a publishing project that actively seeks to *sever* itself from the past, from communism understood as tradition and historical subject, and orient instead only to the mutating limits of capitalist social relations. For *End-notes,* communist theory arises in the "immanent horizon" of the class relation, "it is produced by—and necessarily thinks within—this antagonistic relation," a relation "that is only insofar as it is ceasing to be," for it is an "*impossible* relation," based on the ever-repeated effort of capital to overcome the irresolvable problem of labor, namely, the general law of capitalist accumulation.[153] As regards the journal's relation to concrete struggles, if communism arises in the mutating horizon of capitalist social relations, it encourages attention not to the identities and certainties of political movements and ideas as they have sedimented through time but to encounters with the *limits* of these identities, as they approach what it is at each moment that continues to bind them to capital and the attendant rifts and conflicts that might push them beyond such limits. It is an approach that is at once antidogmatic or "mundane" in its immersion in social struggles and founded as far as possible on the uncertain and contingent unfurling of those struggles. At the same time, the anti-identitarian quality of the party necessitates that the journal here take a *critical* form, the displacement of authority from communist writers to struggles themselves being by no means an *identification* with the latter, for their self-certainty must be problematized too. The journal, hence, "tries to fashion tools with which to talk about present-day struggles—in their own terms, with all their contradictions and paradoxes brought to light, rather than buried."[154]

This has effects also on the practice of journal publishing, if we turn from the critical orientations of this journal to its media form. The group that publishes *Endnotes* explains that its commitment is to rigorous and open-ended "internal debate," to the journal "as a place for the careful working out of ideas," "in which no topics would be off-limits."[155] But if this is to take place at the limits of struggles, against rather than within their identities, then it must hold at a distance attempts to take political positions "or other matters in which the Ego—collective or individual—would necessarily take centre-stage."[156] And here we return to the theme of anonymity, for the published outcomes of these discussions appear in *Endnotes* without author attribution—guest contributions excepting, from writers who are "outside the core group."[157] The inference is that authorial anonymity is a product and index of collective, internal debate, where the collectivity in question is bounded by the group, such that the identity of the author is displaced by the group.[158] It is a commonplace explanation of authorial anonymity and is often accurate in this. But here it would be more in keeping with the ungrounded ground of *Endnotes*'s communist critique, of the historical party, to understand anonymity as indexing less a group production than the exposure of the group to the limits of bounded collectivity. Camatte and Collu get at something of this with their formulation that "the correct sense in which anonymity is posed" is when communists recognize themselves "in a theory that does not depend on a group or a review, because it is an expression of an existing class struggle."[159]

Writing at the limit impacts too on the thematic content and temporal structure of *Endnotes*'s publishing practice. The editorial to the third issue explains that the more abstract theoretical content of the first issues was in part a result of the low ebb in struggles but also "because we didn't know what we wanted to say about the struggles that were ongoing, and we thought it best not to pretend otherwise."[160] This declaration of uncertainty is a striking counter to the textual construction of authority and self-certitude that characterize the writing of conventional parties and sects as a condition for their effective self-delimitation and public marketing. It inclines the journal to avoid "rush[ing] to conclusions for the sake of being topical" and for "concerns about publishing," which I take to mean the latent compulsion of the journal platform to periodicity. What the editorial to the unpunctual *Endnotes* 3 frames as an "explanation for the delay" could also, then, be an articulation of the communism of writing.[161]

Readers acquainted with *Endnotes* may think me insincere. After following the journal's complex turns through value-form theory, systematic dialectics, and communization, one is not left with the overriding feeling that its texts lack certainty. And the visual design of the journal is similarly redolent of a project that is sure of what it means. A wariness toward the demands of periodicity was also a feature of *Comité,* but here it played in tandem with a concern to ward off the constraints of regular physical and textual form, for the list of *Comité*'s possible characteristics claims that the journal was to be an "essentially irregular publication, bound to a temporal irregularity, just as much as an irregularity of format and formulation."[162] That is not so for *Endnotes,* which has a stripped-down and rigorously ordered page layout and format size, sans serif fonts, and cover aesthetic that is uniform across issues, save for variation in the color of the covers, issue title, and back cover epigraph and in the small sketch of a part-concealed lurking urban monster that accompanies the postal address on the back flap (Figure 10). It seems some distance from the experiments with publishing form that feature elsewhere in *Anti-Book.* Indeed, the temptation is strong to follow the anonymous writer of the blog *Insipidities* and conclude that something of the unruly materiality and vitality of communism is missing here; that, at least for those attuned to the "cultic objects" of communist print, the "socialist-minimalism" of *Endnotes*'s compositional and aesthetic form operates in "sublated life registers."[163]

The *Insipidities* review of *Endnotes* 3 could be described as a counteractualization of this "socialist minimalist" condition. What can be gained by reviewing the journal without reading it, as is this writer's wont, bypassing the "business of serious reading and analysing and writing" and instead perceiving it as an experience of immediate encounter? What are the effects of imagining *Endnotes* 3 "without the corrections, say in its first draft[?]" How is "the slag of it all, to be discerned from the pure ore? What is filtering what? What is excluding what?" What does "*carefulness,* as illustrated in the group editing of collective thinking, [*do*] to the outcome of that thinking, I mean *politically*[?]" What is opened or closed in our conceptualization of the social and affective qualities and domains of communism when the word "struggle" is used forty-one times in a journal's introduction alone? These are some of the fecund or "maximalist" possibilities of a communist review (an antireview, perhaps) of a communist journal, from which there is much to learn.[164] And yet the content of *Endnotes* is not without generative interplay with its aesthetic form.

We might approach the journal as a typographic and aesthetic articulation of the communization problematic, where communism is so stripped down to the thin horizon of self-overcoming—without subject, tradition, teleology, dogma, or guarantee—that its published articulation looks like

Figure 10. *Endnotes,* cover of no. 1 (2008) and inside pages of no. 3 (2013).

printed alienation, and may necessarily be so, given the impossibility of proletarian autonomy from capital. But this is not quite a surrender of design, for *Endnotes* holds *nonidentity* in its tight-laced form, its preference for austere design being in part a rigorous nonpreference for any one design in particular, a nonpreference that lends the journal, almost despite itself, an anomalous aesthetic allure. Is it a clue that this journal makes such an intervention at the level of its aesthetic form, or a lapse in the regimen of nonidentity, or overkill, that, hiding in plain sight, *Endnotes* 3 contains a *flipbook*? In an article titled "The Holding Pattern" on the 2011–13 struggles that spread from the Tunisian uprising to Occupy, half the page numbers have been substituted with small black squares that spin around as one flips through the journal.[165] It is a modeling of the abiding weakness of this "movement of the squares," which had the not inconsiderable power of heightened collectivity, and visibility as such, but, in the very form that its collectivity took, was disembedded from the concrete situations of everyday life whence the movement might otherwise have gained enduring leverage.

Having considered the interplay of anonymous authorship with the party, and with the associated decentering of textual authority and the place of critical uncertainty, I will return briefly to Tiqqun. There are certainly points in Tiqqun's notion of the "imaginary party" that articulate the conjunction of anonymity and the party thus far discussed. Some features are ably apparent, for instance, in "Sonogram of a Potentiality," from *Tiqqun 2*, which seeks to draw gender and sexuality out into the social realm—subjecting the "private" and "intimate" "to the intensity of politics"—and frames the move as a critique not only of the interiorized and unitary subject but also of the self-bolstering certainty that accompanies that subject in writing. Here we read, then:

> I wanted a text that wouldn't cry, that wouldn't vomit sentences, that wouldn't give premature answers just to make itself look unquestionable. And that's why the following is not a text written by women for women, because I am not one and I am not just one, but I am a many that says "I." An "I" against the fiction of the little "me" that acts as if it were universal and mistakes its own cowardice for the right to erase, in the name of others, everything that contradicts it.[166]

This reflexive and anti-identitarian orientation is manifest also in relation to the mediums of communist writing. A preface to Tiqqun's book edition of *The Theory of Bloom* informs the reader that, despite appearance to the contrary, "it does not behave like a book," for it resists that medium's closure and its function as complement to the subject: "The Book is a dead form, in so far as it was holding its reader in the same fraudulent completeness, in the same esoteric arrogance as the classic Subject in front of his peers."[167] This text, it suggests, is instead an "editorial virus." It "exposes the principle of incompleteness, the fundamental insufficiency that is in the foundation of the published work."[168] The formulation recalls comments on communism and the book in *Comité*, where the medium of the book—as described in a text concerned with the plethora of books about May 1968 that followed immediately upon its demise—serves to close down the rupture of communism:

> Everything that disturbs, calls, threatens, and finally questions without expecting an answer, without resting in certainty, never will we enclose it in a book, which, even when open, tends toward closure, a refined

form of oppression. . . . No more books, never again a book, so long as we maintain our relation with the upheaval of the rupture.[169]

To prolong "the arrest of history" that was May 1968 requires instead writing in "fragments," in mural writing, tracts, posters, bulletins, and journals. For sure, the fragment is not the only means to politics in writing. The *Comité* text "Reading Marx" draws out three modes of composition in Marx's writing—pertaining to his subversive pursuit of philosophy, politics, and science—only one of which is fragmentary, though all have salience: "Communist speech is always *at the same time* tacit and violent, political and scientific, direct, indirect, total and fragmentary, lengthy, and almost instantaneous."[170] These modes of writing do not "live comfortably" in Marx, they interplay and come apart, an "example [that] helps us to understand that the speech of writing, the speech of incessant contestation, must constantly develop and break away from itself in *multiple* forms." Fragmentary forms, then, "do not say everything," but in that is their particular effect and power: "on the contrary, they ruin everything; they are outside of everything. They act and reflect fragmentarily. . . . Like words on the wall, they are written in insecurity, received under threat; they carry the danger themselves and then pass with the passerby who transmits, loses, or forgets them."[171]

Tiqqun's "editorial virus" appears to suggest such directions in media form, but it is not the derailing of identity that it at first seems, for Tiqqun substitutes the reciprocal identity of book and *subject* with that of book and *community*—the book as agent of community, the book, in other words, in the most classical mold, what chapter 3 identified as the "root-book." As the preface to *The Theory of Bloom* has it, the "great books have never ceased to be those which succeeded in *creating* a community," and this one, apparently, is no different:

With the most explicit mentions, with the most crudely convenient indications—address, contact, etc.—it increases itself in the sense of realizing the community *that it lacks,* the virtual community made up of its real-life readers. It suddenly puts the reader in such a position that his withdrawal may no longer be tenable, a position where the withdrawal of the reader *can no longer be neutral*. It is in this sense that we will hone, sharpen, and clearly define *The Theory of Bloom*.[172]

This formulation of the book is illustrative of a tendency evident throughout Tiqqun, where articulations of the nonidentity of the party are overwhelmed by—or serve to *cloak*—a politics of identity. Especially in texts like *The Coming Insurrection, Call,* and *Introduction to Civil War,* the declared process of becoming anonymous takes the form and injunction of identification with a "we" or an "us" against a "they." Ejecting capitalist relations by force of will and acts of marginal lifestyle—externalizing the "they," in other words—this "us" becomes a privileged subject or party, despite protestations to the contrary and however various and fragmented its composition. This community of "us" finds the conditions of communism not in the diffuse and emergent field of lives and struggles immanently determined by the value forms of capital—the nonidentitarian field of the historical party—but in its own present existence, and in the confirmation and preservation of this through community with others who hear the "call" and "join us" in federations of "friendship."[173] The following example is too easy a target, but it has the merit of setting out this aspect of Tiqqun's position with clarity:

> Us—it is neither a subject, nor something formed, nor a multitude. Us— it is a heap of worlds, of sub-spectacular and interstitial worlds, whose existence is unmentionable, woven together with the kind of solidarity and dissent that power cannot penetrate; and there are the strays, the poor, the prisoners, the thieves, the criminals, the crazy, the perverts, the corrupted, the overly alive, the overflowing, the rebellious corporealities. In short, all those who, following their own line of flight, do not fit into Empire's stale, air-conditioned paradise. Us—this is the fragmented plane of consistency of the Imaginary Party.[174]

In contradistinction to the ruptural quality of the historical party, immanent to social relations, the emancipated "us" described here—associations of all those "who do not fit," where "power cannot penetrate"—cannot but posit and ever renew a *demarcation* from the social, because the latter necessarily places the autonomous association under threat. That is the imaginary party's outward facing effect, the boundary produced by the "they." Facing inward, the considerable risk of this demarcation is that it constitutes a collective identity in which social hierarchies, psychological dependencies, and reified thinking are intensified in associations that tend toward homogeneity based on the equivalence of their members to the particular feature that defines them. As such, the particularity of the "us" apparently outside of capital becomes the very product *of* capital, a mechanism for the reproduction of its subjective modalities. This is far from the communist anonymity we have been pursuing.

5

Proud to Be Flesh

DIAGRAMMATIC PUBLISHING IN *MUTE* MAGAZINE

> For those capable of attention, [diagrams] are the moments
> where being is glimpsed smiling.
> —GILLES CHÂTELET, *Figuring Space*

> To publish a magazine is to enter into a heightened relationship
> with the present moment.
> —GWEN ALLEN, *Artists' Magazines*

What is a political magazine? Or to give that question contemporary
purchase, what can a political magazine be and do today, in our time of
ubiquitous media, when the intermediation of communicative platforms,
user-generated content, wikis, blogs, and social media have so thoroughly
transformed the publishing environment? This chapter addresses that
question through a study of the London-based art, technology, and politics magazine *Mute,* an experimental "hybrid publishing" venture that
tests the limits and potentials of Web, e-publishing, and print platforms
alike.[1] As with all the writing and publishing projects discussed in *Anti-
Book,* the politics in question resides not only in the magazine's content
but throughout its media form, for *Mute*'s signal feature is that since its
inception in 1994, it "has regarded message and medium, content and
carrier as inherently linked."[2] *Mute*'s coverage of the evolving political and
aesthetic capacities of digital and online media (among a welter of other
topics) has thus intersected with a continual remodeling of its publishing
form, a "self-differing" orientation, to use Rosalind Krauss's term, that is
apparent in the title of its 2001 hybrid publishing document: "Ceci n'est
pas un magazine" (Plate 10).[3] This chapter pursues the specific ways that
Mute has undertaken its critical remodeling, so building up a picture of
what I call its "diagrammatic publishing," an immanent and self-differing

media form that operates through the magazine's publishing platforms, participatory mechanisms, aesthetic styles, editorial and commissioning paradigms, temporal modes, and commercial structures.

The term *diagram* features in this chapter in two interrelated senses: as a visual means of modeling and as a material form or process. First, diagrams are schematic orderings of graphic and textual materials that seek, through the arrangement of lines, images, and words, to describe and model dynamic relationships. One such visual diagram was developed by *Mute* to plot, convey, and provoke its move to hybrid publishing, a diagram called "The Magazine That Mistook Its Reader for a Hat!"[4] The chapter concentrates on this publishing diagram; it was incited by *Mute*'s diagram and takes many of its cues from it. Second, the diagram, as I use it, is a concept developed by Deleuze and Guattari that, in concert with the concept of "assemblage," seeks to grasp the emergent consistency and agential effects of singular sociomaterial formations, in their concrete and abstract scales, and the means by which these articulate mutually sustaining relations between content and form. It is a concept used to research social phenomena in a manner that wards off the trap of reifying its field, insofar as it attends to breaks as much as to continuities, and seeks at once to map sociomaterial formations and intervene within them. As I plot *Mute*'s media form, I come to describe it as a diagram in Deleuze and Guattari's sense, with this aspect of the chapter emerging out of discussion of the magazine's visual diagram into empirical analysis of its concrete publishing practices. In *Mute*'s visual diagram, then, there is an indistinction between the two senses of *diagram* as I use it—graphical modeling and diagrammatic form. If it does not scramble this schematic picture too much, we might say that *Mute*'s publishing diagram, the central organizing object of this chapter, is a diagram of the magazine becoming a diagram.

The particular features and qualities of *Mute*'s diagrammatic form will become apparent in due course, but I would like to commence analysis of the magazine with a picture of its general character, for which I will use not a diagram but two metaphors. Metaphors court cliché, but in their capacity to evoke forms, they can also be a first step toward diagrammatic rendering (a thesis I will develop later). The character I want to convey here is one of the political magazine as an *immanent* mode of publishing, for which I draw first on a metaphor supplied by Antonio Negri, a political philosopher and militant whose work in both domains has been closely associated with periodical publication.[5]

MAGAZINE IMMANENCE

In recounting his experiences in collectively publishing the political journal *Futur Antérieur* (1989–98), Negri offers a striking appraisal of the nature and purpose of this medium:

> A good journal is like an octopus, continually reaching out and pulling in the theoretical and historical happenings in the environment in which it lives. This journal had a soul—a passionate soul which tried to absorb everything in the world around it which offered theoretical interest, a political choice, an ethical dimension, or simply a joy of life. The soul of a journal is its radical determination to give meaning to everything it touches, to build it into a theoretical tendency, to embrace it within a mechanism of practical activity.[6]

From this one can draw out three interrelated traits of magazine immanence. First, the magazine's "soul" resides in its *politicizing content*—in conceptual, ethical, and practical dimensions—and, second, in a manner always open to the environment in which it lives, "to everything it touches," what I will call a passionate *immanence to the social world*. Elsewhere in this essay, Negri also sketches a number of important if more mundane features, not least of which is the considerable labor and cost involved in production and the theoretical and political conflict that fires editorial practice. In so doing, he starts to take us into the nitty-gritty of magazine publishing, indicating that its immanence to the social world is far from smooth and uncomplicated but rather is produced through assorted and conflictual practices and structures. But for now, let me simply draw from this the third key trait: that the political magazine is very much a textual medium of *collective production*.

Politicizing content, immanence to the social world, collective production—these are broad traits that will feature throughout my discussion of *Mute*'s diagrammatic form. But at this stage of the picture, we come up short, for Negri's metaphors only take us so far: "octopus" and "soul" help convey the reach and passions of a political magazine, yet neither of these metaphors of organic and spiritual life is especially helpful if one seeks to evoke the many and various materialities involved in the composition of a magazine. Moreover, they give the impression of a centralized and integrated entity, an image of the political magazine that I seek here to move away from. Rather than "pulling in," "absorb[ing] everything" into the magazine's center, as the image of the octopus so vividly evokes, I want to convey a stronger sense of magazine immanence, something flatter and decentered. To that end, a better metaphor of the magazine can be borrowed from Deleuze and Guattari's figure of the book as "single page":

> The ideal for a book would be to lay everything out on a plane of exteriority ..., on a single page, the same sheet: lived events, historical determinations, concepts, individuals, groups, social formations. ... [A] broken chain of affects and variable speeds, with accelerations and transformations, always in relation with the outside.[7]

As with Negri's characterization, this single page is a figure of immanence with the social, but unlike the octopus, the page as "plane of exteriority" is radically decentered. They call it a "single" page, but this is in no way unified; it is a *broken* plane, comprising the outside with no interiority or identity of its own—a plane crisscrossed by concepts, events, groups, peoples, and social formations, it operates "in the middle, between things, interbeing, *intermezzo*."[8] Yet, still, the metaphor comes up short, because although we have shifted from octopus to the writerly inorganic material of paper—and achieved a compelling image of the magazine as a decentered immanence along the way—this single page offers little purchase on the concrete dimensions of magazine form, the page being only a metaphorical field of encounter or, at most, the field where the encounter is written. Neither have we gained any understanding of the nature of the mutually sustaining exchange between content and form that is so central to *Mute* and any other self-differing magazine.

   We need to move, then, from the metaphors of magazine immanence— octopus and single page—to its concrete practice in *Mute* magazine, the plotting of which will show how complicated such immanence can actually be.

THE EUROPEAN ANTI-*WIRED*

The document that first announced *Mute*'s move into hybrid publishing, "Ceci n'est pas un magazine," sets up something of a slogan that conveys the extent and manner of its experimental interest in magazine form. This *is* a magazine; even in *Mute*'s post-digital incarnation of print, Web, and e-publishing platforms, the editorial group continues to use this category to describe the publishing project as a whole (a convention I adopt here). The declaration "this is not a magazine" does not, then, signify a negation of that medium but rather a self-reflexive critique and problematization of the magazine as media form. It conveys too a critique of identity that pervades the magazine as a whole, a critique that *Mute* has maintained since inception, and which is a necessary first step in any move to publishing immanence, repelling a center of attraction that would otherwise deter its persistent opening to its outside. In due course I will move to discuss the nature and effects of this reflexive, anti-identitarian critique on *Mute*'s media *form,* for that is my primary concern in this chapter, but by way of introduction to *Mute,* I come to this after some initial reflection on how its anti-identity has been manifest in the magazine's remit and textual content.

Mute's long-term editor, Josephine Berry Slater, accounts for the magazine's rather unusual self-critical orientation by reference to the fine art backgrounds of its founders, Pauline van Mourik Broekman and Simon Worthington, an orientation she describes as a "concerted battle against the dominant logic of specialisation or static identity," a "refusal to unconditionally embrace a genre, discipline or political position."[9] But if *Mute*'s resistance to static identity is driven by a critical sensibility derived from art practice, it is also a product of the particular remit of the magazine, as constituted in mutual exchange with its early textual content. Initially focused on mid-1990s digital arts and the impact of the Internet on the art establishment, *Mute* quickly came to concentrate on the nature and effects of new technologies across society as a whole, an orientation apparent from the magazine's early strap line, "Culture and Politics after the Net." Fascinated by the dramatic changes associated with pervasive computing and digitization, *Mute* distinguished itself by remaining resolutely critical of the explanatory frameworks, conceptual figures, and inflated political claims of early Net culture—it emerged somewhat as "the European anti-*Wired,*" in Berry Slater's crisp formulation.[10] Tracing the now familiar themes of digital democracy, information commons, the prosumer, the creative economy, immaterial labor, and such like, *Mute* resisted the seductions of identity offered by these conditions and concepts. The magazine preferred instead to position itself—necessarily precariously—on the fault line between the transformative communicational and associational capacities of digital technologies and their proclivity for extending and perfecting the marketization of social relations. Indeed, the dynamics of neoliberal capitalism have increasingly come forward in *Mute* as a principal focus and explanatory framework. This could have produced a dogmatic or ideological orientation, but rather than a totalizing intellectual structure, the concern with contemporary capitalism has been pursued through an eclectic range of its empirical instantiations. As van Mourik Broekman contends, *Mute* sought to "treat capitalism as a governing global condition without losing out on the specificity of its manifestations."[11]

This empirically routed focus on capitalism is the ground—an immanent, mutable, ungrounded ground—for *Mute*'s critique of identity. For whether concentrating on the class-cleansing "regeneration" of east London, Web 2.0 social media, the commercial deployment of "culture," precarious labor, the financialization of the art market, or the security structures that underpin liberal models of citizenship, *Mute*'s understanding of the rapacious dynamics of capital allows for no secure point of critical identity. Indeed, *Mute*'s common observation is that critical identity tends to perpetuate the structures of domination and exploitation that it nominally opposes. For instance, with regard to the possible role of the artist as critical outsider, an influential *Mute* article by Anthony Davies and Simon Ford, "Culture Clubs," traced how, in the period prior to the dotcom crash, art had become one element, along with music, fashion, design, clubbing, and political scenes, that could be "brought together, mediated and repackaged in a range of formats" conducive to entrepreneurial capital. In this neoliberal structure of culture, the "topographical metaphor of 'inside' and 'outside'" upon which much critical art practice has been founded is now not only untenable as a critical paradigm, it becomes a *constitutive part* of these new commercial mechanisms, for here an apparently critical "outside" actually provides the "marginal" and "socially engaged" art practice upon which culture industries thrive.[12]

Yet *Mute*'s aim has not been to substitute the subjectivity of the outsider artist with one of an apparently more radical hue: precariat, multitude, cognitariat, self-organized autonomy, the 99 percent, to name some of those who have had ascendancy during *Mute*'s publishing span. These have some potential to assist in opening critical attention, but they are no less bound to relations of identity and exclusion, as Angela Mitropoulos's *Mute* essay "Precari-Us?" astutely observes. While warning against the assumption of "precarity" as a vanguard point of political aggregation under the impetus of a newly precarious middle class, Mitropoulos explains,

> Names confer identity as if positing an unconditional presupposition. Like all such assertions, it is not simply the declaration that one has discovered the path to a different future in an existing identity that remains questionable. More problematically, such declarations are invariably the expression and reproduction of a hierarchy of value in relation to others.[13]

Returning from the particular content of *Mute*'s articles back to its broader remit, it would be a mistake to imagine that the magazine's critique of identity indicated a pristine critical position abstracted from the messiness of the social world. It is quite the contrary, for interlaced with *Mute*'s critique of neoliberal social forms is something of a joyous materiality, an orientation held in its longtime strap line "Proud to Be Flesh." Here we start to make the initial moves from *Mute*'s critical orientations into its publishing form, from its critique of identity into its critical immanence with the sociomaterial world. *Mute*'s affirmation of "flesh" may sound a little peculiar, even reactionary—Siegfried Zielinski's reading of *Mute*'s term in this way is understandable, though incorrect.[14] It has a particular point of origin, posited against the bloodless myths of "immateriality" that populated the early field of technoculture, be it in Gibsonian notions of cyberspace, Charles Leadbeater's visions of "living on thin air," the "frictionless" circuits of finance capital, or postautonomist formulations of immaterial labor. Flesh, here, is sensate matter, an association of bodies, needs, affects—not an ontological opposition to digital technology or a humanist assertion of an inviolate organism but an open biosocial plane with which technology is irrevocably enmeshed. "Flesh," as van Mourik Broekman confirms, is a stand-in for "material substrates of all kinds."[15] It is a formulation that was realized aesthetically to great effect on the cover of *Mute*'s 2009 anthology *Proud to Be Flesh,* with its highly mediated image of a map of the world rendered in marbled raw red meat (with the book's spine modeling the meat's fat layer, thus integrating the book's codex form with the meat of its cover image). If Negri's octopus reaches out *into* its environment, this metaphor of flesh, then, has *Mute* wholly *enmeshed* within it; flesh is the substance of the magazine, the material flux of the world with which *Mute* is fully immanent.

FORM AND CONTENT

Mute's publishing form has undergone six major transformations. It began as a broadsheet using the same salmon pink paper stock as the *Financial Times* and printed on the latter's London Docklands presses during the machinery's nighttime test run (Plate 11).[16] The broadsheet presents us with an initial instance of the immanent and anti-identitarian sensibility of *Mute*'s content and remit becoming expressed in its *media form,* its understanding of "flesh" taken up in its publishing paradigm. The immediate impression this first manifestation of *Mute* conveyed was of a disjunction between its "new media" content and graphics and the "old" and establishment media form of the broadsheet, an effect that was accentuated by the deliberate styling on the first British daily newspaper, the *Daily Courant* (est. 1702), going so far as mimicking the font and presenting the latter's editorial (concerning the difficulties of launching a new publication) as *Mute*'s own.[17] This "retro-futurist" gesture served to deflate the technoboosterism of emerging Net culture and sought to "escape a simplistic homologue between 'radicality' and cut-up, contemporary design."[18] More particularly, the broadsheet presented a formal critique of the prevalent rhetoric of immateriality, a move underscored by the paper's fleshy pink tones, a clear resonance with the paper's strap line. If *Mute* was, thus, "Proud to Be Flesh," this format also drew attention to the socioeconomic structures within which *Mute,* as any other publishing project, was enmeshed. It is abundantly clear that the *Mute* broadsheet was only possible by piggybacking on the capital-intensive production process of the *Financial Times,* and its proximity to such an iconic source of business information produced unsettling associations for any reader who might have imagined that this artifact of new media critique had escaped from the world of capital.[19] For all its inventive and singular style, the *Mute* broadsheet was, then, very much enmeshed in a world not of its own making and saw its role at a formal level to foreground the material complexities and contradictions of such an existence.

Now that we have an initial example of *Mute*'s interplay between form and content, this relation can be theorized a little more, and in a way that can be taken up later into the concept of diagrammatic publishing. A first approximation of the form–content relation can be developed with the aid of Krauss's concept of the "self-differing medium" that I proposed in chapter 1 to be a central dimension of any anti-book. A self-differing medium is constituted when the conventions and structures that determine the medium of a particular artwork are themselves taken up in the work in a fashion that alters those determinations, such that the work comes to specify its own medial conditions and hence becomes self-differing.[20] The medium, then, "is something made, rather than something given," or made as much as it is given.[21] Significantly for our understanding of *Mute,* the medium in Krauss's formulation is not confined to a work's physical substrate but can also take an epistemic form, including rules, logics, and paradigms. Hence, in *Mute*'s case, as we will see, the medium might include publishing platforms but also, for example, editorial paradigms and logics of user participation. Moreover, for Krauss, the aesthetic work tends not toward a progressively more refined adequacy to its medium but toward an open and recursive emergence through successive loops of interaction between the work and its medium. There is no direct correspondence, hence, between work and medium but more a *baggy fit,* allowing for an uncertain determination between the two and a degree of latitude in the way a work responds to its material forms, even as it succeeds only insofar as it constitutes the necessity of their resultant relation.

As the broadsheet clearly exemplifies, *Mute* embodies a strong self-differing orientation, but it diverges from the kinds of work that Krauss analyses in ways that suggest this concept may apply here only in general terms. For *Mute* is not a single work, or a series of works by a single artist, but a polymorphous and discontinuous aggregate, emerging over a twenty-year time span across the many different dimensions and features of content and form that have come into relation; its analysis calls for concepts that can handle that discontinuity and variation. Second, while the concept of the self-differing medium is useful in foregrounding the aesthetic and medial dimensions of *Mute*'s experimental form, *Mute* is of course a *publishing project* rather than an artwork. As such, its textual content—as with Negri's characterization, the leading feature of this political magazine—has greater significance in its own right and more autonomy with regard to its media form.

To develop an approach that addresses these points and offers a more adequate theorization of *Mute*'s content–form relation, I turn to Deleuze and Guattari's concept of "assemblage" and, later, to that of "diagram." For Deleuze and Guattari, textual content and material form—or "discursive multiplicities" and "non-discursive multiplicities"—exist in relative autonomy. Between content and form "there is neither a correspondence nor a cause–effect relation nor a signified–signifier relation"; instead, they are drawn together in assemblages where they interact in relations of "reciprocal presupposition," an assemblage being at once product and cause of this interaction.[22] Much of the time, such assemblages reproduce standard patterns, where the product of the reciprocal presupposition of content and material form is unremarkable and the fact of this relation is largely unnoticed. We can think of a commercial lifestyle magazine as such an assemblage. It tends to reproduce standard patterns of format, editorial, page layout, modes of address, journalism, manufacture, and so on, as textual and visual content and magazine form interact in unremarkable fashion, and where cultures of consumption have little feeling for how much all this interpolates particular kinds of subjectivity. But in more experimental magazines like *Mute* (and only some of the time and in particular instances, for the standard patterns endure here also), the interaction between content and form intensifies, the two interfere with each other, causing mutual transformation and, hence, transformation in their aggregate, the magazine assemblage.

A particular assemblage's mix of content and form will be highly various. As we will see in *Mute,* sometimes the relationship between content and form is explicit and clearly expressed in a particular work; other times, the relation is less directly identified with a particular work but rather is a quality of the magazine as a whole, or a quality of a delimited sequence in its publication. Likewise, sometimes the interplay between content and form is expressed in ways where text takes a dominant role (the kind of works N. Katherine Hayles calls "technotext," "where a literary work interrogates the inscription technology that produces it"); other times, more in accord with Krauss's concept, text may have little presence, and instead paradigmatic, organizational, or medium-specific features of the magazine may articulate its agendas.[23] It may even be the case that brute physical materials come to express the magazine's critical agendas, what Guattari calls the "mute redundancies" that too often suffer "overcoding" by linguistic text.[24] Of this, the salmon pink broadsheet is a clear instance—a "'mute,' visual, encoded" articulation of the magazine's critical concerns, as van Mourik Broekman describes it.[25] Whichever manifestation it takes, the concept of assemblage teaches that while content and form are in relations of reciprocal presupposition, there is always a "gap" between them, irreducible as they are to each other, such that an assemblage functions "out of balance" and always open to its outside.[26] As I will show shortly, it is in this gap that the "nonplace" of the diagram operates, at once "swallowed up" in particular assemblages and operating as their agential pilot.[27]

MINIFESTO AND DIAGRAM

We can now return to plotting *Mute*'s publishing form. Leaving the broadsheet behind in 1997, between issue numbers 9 and 24, *Mute* took a more recognizable magazine format (saddle-stitched, then perfect bound) before adopting a lavish coffee-table format with issues 25–29 (2002–4). The design experiments, aesthetic qualities, and publishing practicalities of this period of the magazine are addressed in considerable depth in *Mute*'s graphic design anthology, so I will largely pass over discussion of these.[28] Instead, from here on, this chapter focuses on the subsequent period from 2005, when *Mute* fully embarked on its "hybrid publishing model."[29] At this point the magazine comes to take on what I call a diagrammatic form. I mostly focus here on the period between 2005 and 2011, known as "Volume 2," which I take to be the height of *Mute*'s hybrid and diagrammatic publishing, before the immanent financial limits I discuss toward the end of the chapter necessitated a climb down to a more Web-based model.

The immediately apparent feature of *Mute*'s development at this stage is the changed role and status of its online publishing, as the Metamute website (first instituted in 1995) shifted from being an adjunct to the printed magazine to taking a central place. Yet this is not that well-rehearsed story of a simple move from print to online but a reconfiguration at a more infrastructural level, a change in the magazine's publishing form and paradigm. It was a change introduced in a highly original manner through two visual diagrams, published in the magazine itself, which graphically modeled the dynamics and directions of its transformation. I will spend some time working through the second of these diagrams before turning from its abstract modeling and the diagrammatic form that it reveals to consider the concrete features of the magazine's form with which the diagram is in interplay, as map, provocation, and product.

I have mentioned the self-critical orientation held in the title of the first of these diagrams; the same is true for its sequel, which is our focus here: "The Magazine That Mistook Its Reader for a Hat!" It riffs on neurologist Oliver Sacks's account of a patient who was so unable to recognize the world around him that he mistook his wife for a hat, so metaphorically signaling the perceived rift between the magazine and its outside and the radical "perceptual change involved in moving from a traditional magazine . . . to a hybrid publishing model."[30] The rather unusual character of this document warrants some explanation before I attend to the specific publishing form that it plots. *Mute* playfully describes the two diagrams as "minifestos," encouraging us to approach them at a tangent to the textual form of the manifesto. Like the manifesto, these

diagrams mark explicit points of radical departure, diagnosing and projecting a future that in turn—and this is the peculiar mode of authority
of the manifesto form—reacts back upon the present of the magazine to
force and channel transformation.[31] However, as I argued in chapter 1, the
performative structure of the manifesto is heavily invested in the exterior
presentation of a strong and coherent group subjectivity, the successful
projection of its vision in large part necessitating that it conjure away the
cracks, discords, and instabilities of political existence. *Mute*'s diminutive
designator *mini*festo signals a movement away from such self-inflation.
The minifestos work rather differently, turning their gaze *internally* to
the normally "invisible processes" of self-critique and development and
projecting *these* to the outside.[32] That is to say, they serve a function
of critical self-analysis, what van Mourik Broekman calls a reflexive
"autopoetic criticality," which is now brought to the "surface," no longer
hidden behind a puffed-up subjectivity but laid out for readers on the
magazine page.[33]

If this document is a minifesto, it takes the form of a visual *diagram*,
a schematic ordering of graphic and textual material—lines, pictograms,
words, arranged in space. Gilles Châtelet's *Figuring Space* offers much
insight here, and in terms that are especially pertinent for considering
Mute's media form, for he sees diagrams as modes of scientific inscription particularly germane to experimental and inventive projects that
break with identity—that proceed through "blind spots," "problematics,"
"fogs"—as the complexity of life is "take[n] up again in the flesh."[34] It is
an argument that can be best approached through the contrast Châtelet
draws between diagrams and metaphors. He writes, "Diagrams are in
a degree the accomplices of poetic metaphor. But they are a little less
impertinent—it is always possible to seek solace in the mundane plotting of their thick lines—and more faithful: they can prolong themselves
into an operation which keeps them from becoming worn out."[35] Both
metaphors and diagrams work to describe and evoke relations—they
"leap out" to figure space—but metaphors risk becoming "worn out"
clichés, with passifying effect, as they dissolve the "cold" technical specificity of a particular operation with the "warm confusion" of relations of
resemblance.[36] Diagrams, on the other hand, with their modest plotting
and sketching—as they struggle in uncertainty to grasp elusive abstract

relations and make connections across disparate realms—are extended or prolonged in contact with the world (or the "flesh") that they map. Not that metaphor is entirely dismissed (helpfully for me, since I began this chapter that way and will have recourse to other metaphors yet). While metaphors tend toward cliché, we can think the relation the other way around and see them also as proto-diagrams, or nursemaids to diagrams, understood as the process of shifting from clichéd representations to an awakened critical intervention: "metaphor begins the process of shedding its skin that will metamorphose into operation, and hence it is that this nook swarms with clichés that strive to invite us to view a rediscovered operativity."[37] Yes, diagrams inevitably arrest movement too, abstracting a figure from the complexity of sociomaterial relations, but they do so in a manner that remains open to—indeed, "solicits"—the indeterminate potential of matter to take other form, its "virtuality."[38] Diagrams, then, both illustrate and engender; that is their specific function:

> [If the diagram] immobilizes a gesture in order to set down an operation, it does so by sketching a gesture that then cuts out another. The dotted line refers neither to the point and its discrete destination, nor to the line and its continuous trace, but to the pressure of the virtuality . . . that worries the already available image in order to create space for a new dimension: the diagram's mode of existence is such that its genesis is comprised in its being.[39]

DIAGRAMMATIC PUBLISHING

Having assessed "The Magazine That Mistook Its Reader for a Hat!" as minifesto and visual diagram, it is time to turn to its specific content. What does *this* diagram engender, as it puts "metaphors aside" and "turn[s] felt into flesh," in *Mute*'s rather Châteletian formulation of the task?[40] The specific problematic the minifesto addressed, as with its precursor, was the opening of *Mute*'s previously closed editorial structure to user participation, as *Mute* came to recognize the radical changes under way in the publishing environment and made a move toward user-generated content. But it does so by posing the problem as one of *the media form of the magazine as a whole,* as *Mute* transformed into a diagrammatic entity. We can follow the transformations through the minifesto itself (Figure 11).

THE MAGAZINE THAT MISTOOK ITS READER FOR A HAT!

Towards a 'Participatory Publishing Model', Part II
(Part I, 'Ceci n'est pas un magazine', Mute 19, May 2001 [http://www.metamute.com/ceci01.pdf])

WHERE ARE WE NOW?

The title of this second part of *Mute*'s publishing plan is a play on *The Man who Mistook his Wife for a Hat*, the title of neurologist Oliver Sacks's anthology of case studies. In his book, Sacks gives compassionate accounts of various neurological disorders and the demands placed on patients forced to reorder their sensoriums after severe accidents. In the cases he selects, these accidents created nearly unbridgeable rifts between the victim and 'reality'. In the most famous one, he relates the experience of patient 'P' whose bearing on reality has been so seriously reshuffled that he... mistakes his wife for a hat.

Without wishing to venture a completely untenable analogy, the perceptual change involved in moving from a traditional magazine (with plans, pitches and commissions), to a hybrid publishing model (where a network of readers, contributors and editors starts to co-determine the publishing process), could be said to force a comparably radical shift in perception. How do you turn your wife from a hat into a woman?

Behind the scenes of the psychiatric ward that is *Mute*, we've been going through momentous changes, taking important preliminary steps towards decentralisation. We've implemented a content management system to fully automate our web publishing and allow for multiple, distant contributors. We've started working internally and externally with a 'Wiki' (a collaborative tool for working asynchronously across the net) – for instance on the production of this issue. And we've readied our network architecture for a host of different types of decentralised communication (ranging from lists to webforums) and media.

But none of this matters if there is no reason to participate: as we said in our previous 'minifesto' ('Ceci n'est pas un magazine'), decentralisation for its own sake – or, worse, for the sake of product expansion – is one of the most suspect phenomena to have emerged in online culture. Opening up the relationships between producer and consumer as often as not stands for some form of direct technocracy and the co-optation of individuals' freely given productivity for private gain. In such cases, the hat remains stubbornly a hat. But to shift the perception of the production process to turn felt into flesh, or a closed creative process into an open one, it must of course be based on something more than a mere conjuring trick. Metaphors aside, below is a description of how and what we propose to achieve – a proposal that blends one part unrepentant optimism with two parts practical engineering.

B. THE MUTE PROJECT CLUSTER
More than the sum of its parts

ATTRACTION   INVITATION
DISCUSSION / NETWORKING
SELECTION
KNOWLEDGE   KNOWLEDGE

WE ARE NOT ALONE...
Random inspiration, context and family

http://www.boollab.org
http://orang.orang.de

http://www.consume.net
http://www.thing.net
http://www.open-organizations.org
http://www.rhizome.org
http://www.indymedia.org
http://www.openflows.org
http://www.nettime.org

F/OSS
http://opensource.mit.edu/online_papers.php
http://slash.autonomedia.org
http://www.infopool.org.uk
http://desdeamericaconamor.org
http://radioqualia.va.com.au/freqclock

http://www.sarai.ne
http://www.oekonux.org

A. WHAT'S THIS BUG BRAIN THINKING ABOUT?

While opening up *Mute*'s brain to collective tinkering, and having learnt from the experience of building our complementary platforms, we have recognised the importance of making clear our key areas of interest (as they stand at present):

- New forms of cultural expression
- The impact of technologically-driven change on culture and society
- Participatory and decentralised publishing and communications models
- Sustainable and alternative economies of cultural production
- The anti-capitalist movement
- Community owned and run wireless networks
- Alternative means of visualising cultural/political/social systems (e.g. cartography)
- Autonomous modes of organisation

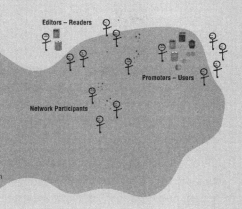

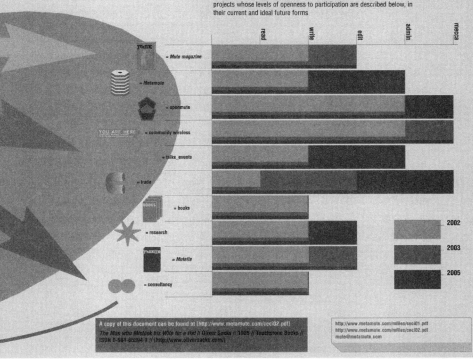

Figure 11. "The Magazine That Mistook Its Reader for a Hat!" Artwork concept by *Mute* based on an earlier concept by Quim Gil, art direction by Simon Worthington, *Mute* 1, no. 25 (2002). Courtesy of Skyscraper Digital Publishing.

Starting with the image titled "B. The Mute Project Cluster," it is apparent that the new publishing model was less a shift from print to digital than a move from identification with a single platform to a hybrid "cluster," an open set of *many* platforms and practices, where a hybrid is "anything derived from heterogeneous sources, or composed of elements of different or incongruous kinds."[41] These clustered platforms are represented here pictographically, but in concrete terms, as it stood at the height of *Mute*'s diagrammatic form, the magazine comprised the following: the Metamute website; a quarterly print-on-demand (POD) booklet; the OpenMute consultancy and training in open source tools, design, and e-publishing (with associated speculative initiatives in independent and peer-to-peer publishing tools and distribution: More Is More and Progressive Publishing System); Mute Books; solo and collaborative workshops, talks, and events (a notable instance was the November 2008 Forever Blowing Bubbles walking tour through London's financial City with Peter Linebaugh and Fabian Tompsett); occasional pamphlets; and *Mute* LISTSERVs (including Mute-social, a public notices list, and, if we include the nonpublic aspects of the magazine, Mute-edit and Mutemag-production, closed lists where the intellectual and practical dimensions of editorial are hammered out).[42]

Where exactly is *Mute* in this hybrid cluster? We see in section (B) that the platforms circle the perimeter of a vortex, suggesting that *Mute* is at once to be found in each of its clustered platforms, as I have suggested, and—"more than the sum of its parts," as the accompanying text has it—*in the vortex itself,* a metaphor for a particular kind of process. *Mute,* in other words, takes both *concrete* and *abstract* form. If we develop this with Deleuze and Guattari's terminology, *Mute*'s media form comprises at once a series of concrete publishing assemblages (the clustered platforms, interlacing content and form in particular situations) and an "abstract machine" or "diagram" (pictographically represented as a vortex). This addition of "diagram" to our already elaborated account of the assemblage is significant, for it allows us to grasp what gives consistency to the cluster of publishing platforms. A diagram "pilots," or governs and potentializes, a set of assemblages, where the latter are particular and various expressions of the former's "abstract formula," its general orientation. As an abstract entity, a "nonplace," a diagram does not stand over the assemblages but is immanent to them.[43] And it has no form and content of its own—it is "almost blind and mute," manifest only through the assemblages, and in turn becoming transformed by their particular and various handling of its abstract formula.[44] So, although I suggested earlier that a magazine can be understood as an assemblage, in *Mute*'s case, that was true only until it was displaced from identification with *one* publishing platform onto a *cluster* of platforms, at which point it was no longer only an assemblage, or even a set of assemblages, but became also a diagram, where the diagram both governs its assemblages and is in a relation of mutual presupposition with them. These are the bare bones of diagrammatic publishing, of which *Mute* from this point on is a singular exemplar, but we need yet to understand the way that it produces magazine immanence and to tease out the concrete specificities of this diagrammatic form.

To these ends, the minifesto continues to be instructive, where the vortex has additional valence as a modeling of immanence. It is a metaphor still, but one that is considerably more operational, in Châtelet's sense, than Negri's "octopus" and Deleuze and Guattari's "single page." If we follow the movements, the vortex (B) conveys a strong processual quality to *Mute* that avoids the twin problems of a closed and bounded entity and an undetermined flux. It suggests instead an immersive or immanent entity whose inside is an involution of its outside, a process operative through a permeable boundary. The vortex, indeed, is *constituted* on this boundary. What does that mean? It is to say, first of all, that the magazine is defined by its ever-changing boundaries, the encounters of outside and inside— the magazine *is* these encounters. Yes, a vortex is a site of concentration, intensely so, but unlike Negri's image of the octopus, it is concentration without a center, or with a very different kind of center. It is something of a paradoxical space, both inside and outside simultaneously—"an inside copresent with the outside," as Deleuze describes it—where the inside and outside are continually exchanged, twisted, and doubled together.[45] Or to speak with Châtelet, this is an immanent "horizon" ("one always carries one's horizon away with one") that, insofar as it is driven by the outside, is experienced as a certain involuntarism of the intensive encounter: "corrosive like the visible, tenacious like a smell, compromising like touch, [the horizon] does not dress things up with appearances, but impregnates everything that we are resolved to grasp."[46]

How does this immanent, vortexlike process actually occur? The focus of the minifestos is on the process of generating textual and visual *content,* for the editorial team framed the hybrid publishing model as a reprioritization of content, a return to what was "'always already' *Mute*'s main interest."[47] This could sound like a move away from the experiments with magazine form that I have been pursuing, but it is actually through such refocusing on content that *Mute* began its *most* experimental engagement with media form. For it was characterized by a redoubled attention to the diversity and effects of the medial means by which content is produced, circulated, and consumed. Returning to follow the movements in the minifesto, the border of the vortex is constituted, then, through the parameters of "attraction" and "invitation" that, in centripetal fashion, draw content out from the environment and into a point of concentration, *Mute* itself. As we have seen, this point of concentration is experienced only in and through the magazine's clustered publishing platforms, so the magazine's border, its immanent horizon, is multiple, layered, and discontinuous. And at each of these borders, magazine content is solicited, handled, and problematized in terms that are conditioned by the particular technical and epistemic qualities of that platform. These platform qualities are not politically inert, of course, but are interlaced with sets of political problematics of their own (as we will see).

With this picture, we have a much richer sense of the sociomaterial "flesh" of the magazine, and we have too a diagrammatic explanation of *Mute*'s reflexive practice of self-critique. For insofar as the magazine's vortex-movement folds and unfolds its environment, the critique that it develops of that environment is necessarily also turned against itself as a product *of* that environment. This dimension of self-critique is crucial to the immanent, diagrammatic form of the magazine, because without it, *Mute*'s center would lose its paradoxical copresence with its outside, its vortex would slow down and settle into an identity separated from that which its content surveys.

There is a further quality of magazine immanence to the movement described in the minifesto, whereby the attraction of content works alongside a decentering redistribution of the magazine's participants, in regard to content provision and publishing infrastructure, what it terms "participation." This is critically described by text (C) (as I will discuss shortly) and partially assayed on the right of the diagram, where the distinct media platforms are represented according to a calibrated scale of openness to user participation—for example, limited involvement in the commissioning of Mute Books, but a goal of participation in the editing and administration of Metamute—and this changing according to the progression of time.

Moving around the remainder of the minifesto, the bottom left quadrant (A) sets out the magazine's principal research interests and critical orientations. In our now near-complete plotting of *Mute*'s diagrammatic form, we can take these to be itemized expressions of the magazine's abstract formula, what I outlined earlier as its immersive and self-critical fascination with technosocial "flesh," which is at one and the same time its insistence on the nonidentitarian critique of capital. This abstract formula—which at the "blind and mute" level of the diagram is not yet differentiated into media form and textual content—passes through each and every point of the magazine's platforms or assemblages as something like *Mute*'s dynamic equilibrium. And last, to the right of quadrant (A) is a selection of other vortexlike organizations with which the magazine is in intellectual and practical exchange, both extending its reach and further displacing its center through relations of collaboration.

The minifesto is, then, a visual diagram of *Mute*'s diagrammatic publishing, a particular and operational instance of magazine immanence. The point now and for the remainder of the chapter is to consider how this diagrammatic form is manifest in concrete specificity. My account is not intended to be totalizing—that would run counter to the unfinished virtuality of the diagram as visual model and sociomaterial process—but rather is a sampling of key dimensions and features. Each feature I discuss is a concrete articulation of *Mute*'s diagrammatic publishing as it is manifest in specific aspects of the magazine *and* in relation to particular political problematics, problematics that are associated with these specific aspects and are, in this, also those of *Mute*'s self-differing "flesh" more broadly conceived. The first two sections, on *Mute*'s website and its

POD quarterly, focus primarily on particular platforms. After that, the discussion considers dimensions of the magazine's diagrammatic form that pertain to the magazine as a whole, some of which are explored in relation to specific technological mechanisms, such as the affordances of distributed media or the "tag" capacity, whereas others are discussed in more abstract terms, such as its mode of editorial voice. Let me stress that all of the platforms and publishing problematics that I discuss here have their own particular qualities and effects, which push and pull in various discontinuous directions such that the diagrammatic aggregate is more a broken bricolage than a mushy whole.

INOPERATIVE PUBLIC: METAMUTE, OPENMUTE, USER PARTICIPATION

Of the different media platforms that compose *Mute*'s publishing cluster (as listed previously), I will focus primarily on Metamute, OpenMute, and, in the subsequent section, the POD quarterly. Running on the open source content management system Drupal, Metamute moved from an adjunct to the printed magazine to become the "editorial engine" of *Mute* content as a whole, working in concert with the other platforms of its publishing cluster.[48] As one might expect, given the distributive capacities of digital and online media, Metamute has been a significant vehicle for *Mute*'s vortexlike opening to a more "participatory" publishing model—through the comment function, news sections, blog imports, and the submission of more substantial user contributions, including artworks. Participation, here, is presented in the text of the minifestos as a "non-vampiric" set of relationships "where a network of readers, contributors and editors starts to co-determine the publishing process."[49] It could sound like a new media cliché, except that this assertion sits amid an array of reflexive assessments (in the minifestos and elsewhere) of the complex pattern of participation that can emerge and follows a keen sense that participation is a fraught and contradictory process rather than a self-evident good that requires merely a technical fix.

In certain instances, most notably around J. J. Charlesworth's critical exposé of the neoliberal arts agendas and governance structures of London's Institute of Contemporary Arts, Metamute has succeeded in weaving distributed user-generated content—from various sites and political positions, in assorted textual modes, and at different institutional scales—with top-down editorial commissioning and research-based writing.[50] And yet this participation has been at best fitful, especially when contrasted to the high volume of Metamute's traffic (averaging 12,500 unique visitors per month in 2013–14). The significant feature of *Mute*'s intervention in the terrain of participation is located elsewhere—first, in the magazine's reflexive and critical relationship to the discourses of participation and the public and, second, in its practical orientation toward the technologies and paradigms of small-scale publishing, both of which I consider here.

There has been a strong tendency in contemporary discourses of media decentralization and participation to treat them solely as issues of technology and to sideline the socioeconomic relations within which digital and networked media are embedded, what *Mute,* in the accompanying document to the second minifesto, calls the "mode of . . . social inscription."[51] When attention is paid to the social inscription of participatory media, one sees how its apparently democratic features can actually serve to *mask* and *entrench* inequalities of access and power, for user participation and its discourses of empowerment are in fact central to the emerging business paradigms and valued subjective dispositions of commercial media. *Mute* was an early critic of what is now a commonly recognized condition: that participation and decentralization function in Web 2.0 social media as a source of accumulation and control, as public production is incited, channeled, formatted, data mined, and monetized for private gain.[52] *Mute* was thus clear in its minifestos, at the same moment that it opened to a more participatory paradigm, that "decentralisation for its own sake— or, worse, for the sake of product expansion—is one of the most suspect phenomena to have emerged in online culture."[53] *Mute* resisted such tendencies by displacing the problem of participation from an exclusive concern with expanding the field of user-generated content onto a broad critical assessment of relations between the magazine and its readership, and in a manner that sought to transform both terms.

The resolute criticality of *Mute*'s engagement with fledgling and now full-blown digital media scenes has meant that it has tended to repel, as much as attract, its potential readership, so warding off the identitarian closure attendant on efforts to construct and mirror a delineated audience or market niche. Van Mourik Broekman reflects, "At the point this seemed a distinct possibility (around 1998/99) we were loathe to turn *Mute* into a kind of sector journal servicing the needs of a nascent art-and-technology/digital-art/new-media community."[54] There is a similar problematization of the broader figure of the "public." *Mute*'s default understanding of the capitalist structure of social relations is of course contrary to the notion of a generic public that preexists its construction in any one (more or less exploitative and exclusionary) social configuration—nation, citizen, "local community," and so on. The destructive deployment of the trope of the public in speculative urban development has, for example, been a long-standing interest of the magazine, of which Laura Oldfield Ford's pithy formulation of its art modality is indicative: "public art, as we think of the term since the '80s, seems to be about making colonial totems that say, 'it's ok, we've tamed the natives, it's safe to come in.'"[55]

We can say, then, with Jean-Luc Nancy, that there is an "inoperative" quality to *Mute*'s understanding of its public, readership, or community, where community, in Nancy's terms, is constituted in self-critical exposure to its limits, its outside, to what it is *not*: the "socially exposed particularity" that undoes the "socially imploded generality" of community in its identitarian mode.[56] To this *Mute* adds in something of community's *affective* fault line. *Mute*'s inoperative community is not that *attraction to the same,* which drives the "like" function of Facebook and is coded into Google's search algorithms, but a "connection-engine with 'strangers,'" as van Mourik Broekman describes it.[57] It is "not just about recognizing and being semi-narcissistically drawn to an image of oneself, one's own subjectivity and proclivities," but is an experience of "'alien' ideas that are nonetheless compelling, troubling, or intriguing" and that attract people into the "reader- and potentially even contributor-circle," a "connection-engine [that] draws people in, propels people out, in a continual, dynamic process, which, due to its intensity, very effectively blurs the lines of professionalism, friendship, editorial, social, political praxis."[58]

To be clear, this inoperative orientation is as much a critique of the notion of a *counter*-public. On this front, *Mute* has engaged significantly with radical trends in "open" organizations, at once embracing horizontal and collaborative modes of organization while challenging their tendencies to nurture informal hierarchies and cloak the "predicating inequities of the wider environment in which [an organization] is situated," as J. J. King argues, much as Jo Freeman's essay "The Tyranny of Structurelessness" did for the libertarian politics of the 1970s, though now with special attention to the digital media environment, open source communities, enterprise culture, and the affective and linguistic qualities of political association.[59]

However, all this critique of participation, public, and counterpublic by no means absolves the magazine of the need to address the practicalities of association, for it has made intriguing moves toward a model of the public adequate to its diagrammatic form. OpenMute is especially interesting in this regard, a "network resources project" that was established to provide Web tools, training, and publishing resources to cultural and community groups at low or no cost.[60] A project that began with *Mute*'s efforts to share its own experience of automating its Web publishing activity, OpenMute displays again the magazine's centrifugal practice of "pushing outward" its internal organizational dynamics and capacities into the wider social arena, now to the extent of them becoming public resource.[61] Crucially, the public domain is posed here not as a distinct social body but rather as a question of *infrastructure,* of "public knowledge architectures."[62] So framed, *Mute*'s formulation of public participation is an attempt to breach the divide between the often utopian political claims for digital publishing and the less impressive reality of its use, given the common skills gap and financial constraint that prevent marginalized groups from full utilization of open source and other Web and e-publishing tools.

These aspects of OpenMute coalesced into a distinct "Technology" stream of the magazine and its consultancy work, where a core focus has been the development of open source and e-publishing tools and initiatives to aid small publishers and independent arts organizations. The driving problematic is apparent in Worthington's assertion that the "interesting questions" about the future of the book concern not the tired cliché of whether books are an endangered species but "the composition of the publishing market—irrespective of whether that is for digital or print," where fantasies of democratic user participation disguise the consolidation of media monopolies and small publishers face prohibitive barriers to financially viable production and distribution in e-publishing environments.[63] To meet this problem, Worthington's *Mute*-developed Progressive Publishing System, for instance, was an experimental software engine for the easy conversion of published materials across POD, short-run press, e-book, mobile, and tablet platforms, aiming to circumvent the prohibitive barriers to production and distribution that are so debilitating for small publishers.[64] It is a project that has since fed into his research on open source publishing infrastructures at the Hybrid Publishing Lab at Lüneburg's Leuphana University.[65]

THE AESTHETICS OF PRINT ON DEMAND

I want at this stage to bring in the print product of *Mute*'s diagrammatic form and therein open to more discussion of the place of art and design, concentrating on the POD quarterly booklet that ran to seventeen issues between 2005 and 2010. Known as Volume 2 to mark the extent of the departure from previous formats, the POD booklet arose as a solution to two problems that burdened *Mute* at the time of its move toward hybrid publishing. First, POD helped overcome a persistent Web–print dichotomy in *Mute*'s publishing practice, offering a platform that is something of a hybrid of print and digital technologies, a clear instance of post-digital publishing.[66] Flexible and cheap, POD is a publishing platform somewhat in the mode of the post-Fordist mainstay of just-in-time production. It combines high-speed photostatic print with perfect-bound full-color covers in book editions of any size, from one copy upward: a point of considerable contrast to *Mute*'s broadsheet format, where the minimum print run had been ten thousand.[67] POD allowed *Mute* to spread the costs of printing, so drawing expenditure and revenue into greater sync, and to distribute production to global locations closer to points of purchase so as to reduce shipping costs. It also held the promise of a large degree of automation in the publishing process, with design and content management tools enabling easy to-and-fro movement between Web and print platforms (a platform convergence capacity that OpenMute has tested through its speculative initiatives, such as Progressive Publishing System, as aforementioned, and the Web2POD tool, for collating and outputting personalized article collections). These are all significant developments in the economic struggles of small publishers.

The second problem addressed by the POD quarterly concerned a growing imbalance in the relative emphasis the magazine placed on its media form as against its content—the coming apart of this precarious interrelation. The product of POD technology in Volume 2 is a rather stripped-down printed object; it has a "simplicity" and "sobriety" that could not be more different from the "pinnacle of print luxuriousness" that was the immediate print predecessor of *Mute* 25–29.[68] It is true, the magazine at that time was a beautiful print artifact, with, among other features, its experiment in high-absorbency art paper (which required drying out for days after printing, indicative of *Mute*'s difficulties at this time) and the free rein the format gave to *Mute*'s taste for cartographic visual technique, experiment with page design, and the interplay of image and text. It is the *smell* of the magazine's paper stock that marks the rarity of *Mute* in that period, considerably more evocative of the alchemy of ink and paper than any commercial book. But the magazine's immersion in design is probably best illustrated by the cover of *Mute* 29, where the feature themes of oil, war, and finance are synthesized in spectral images produced by pouring molasses on a scanner bed, which was then backed with silver foil to drive an intense reflection through the molasses and so produce an eerie, oil-like quality.[69]

These numbers of *Mute* were "high-end design's last stand," as the editors later reflected.[70] By contrast, the POD quarterly could be seen as a marked failure, given, as I have been arguing, that a "heightened sense" of experiment with magazine format and design has been a fundamental characteristic of *Mute* since its inception.[71] Yet high-end magazine aesthetics can tip the subtle relation between form and content out of balance, as a "format-fetishism," in *Mute*'s assessment of the problem, comes to task the medium alone with the magazine's political agendas.[72] By the time of *Mute* 29, certain format and design preferences had indeed gained an agential autonomy that risked distorting the magazine as a whole, burdening its precarious form with the unsustainable labor- and design-intensive values of the coffee-table format. POD enabled a rebalancing, but unlike its use in commercial publishing, where it is merely an economy, a poor imitation of offset lithography, in *Mute,* the properties of POD were taken up in its self-differing orientation toward design.

To some extent, the design focus of Volume 2 shifts from the visual form of the magazine page to the design of Web, e-pub, and software facilities—the latter, in Progressive Publishing System, for instance, has a clear aesthetic dimension—but that is not the only story. However much *Mute* by issue 29 had come to be an extraordinarily beautiful print artifact, as the POD quarterly pushed at the limits of Web–print hybridity, it handled a more *diagrammatic* aesthetic than its print predecessor, more immersed in the sociomaterial flesh of publishing. The quarterly's strange and seductive combination of book format and magazine page structure contains echoes of the Xerox styling of 1970s self-publishing, with its stark photostatic ink, simple line drawings and vector graphics, and pared-back urban and landscape photography, most effectively seen in the full-bleed, double-page spreads that can give a rather haunting aspect to the booklet, notably in Pam Worthington's image (in the first POD issue) of Morecambe Bay, site of the death of nineteen Chinese cockle pickers in 2004. But this is less a retro repetition of past visual forms than an aesthetic product of the sociotechnical relations of post-digital publishing, as the benefits of decentralization, automation, and low cost that came with the photocopier are found again in the unique capacities of a new print medium.[73]

With the POD quarterly, *Mute* continued the practice of commissioning new artwork for each issue. The "Living in a Bubble: Credit, Debt and Crisis" issue (which, with impeccable timing, was published in September 2007, just as the banks' liquidity troubles tipped into full-blown economic crisis) included a number of artworks on the issue theme solicited from an open call to readers, so posing the problem and possibility of nontextual modes of representation of that which is so difficult to cognitively map. But perhaps the most successfully realized of the commissioned works in Volume 2 is David Osbaldeston's "Out of Time" in number 13, for it takes advantage, in the manner of an artists' book, of the structure of the POD booklet. Here press photographs of "iconic" world events—the 1992 LA riots, the Iraq 1991 "Highway of Death," among others—are combined with text cutouts and dates in degraded, rephotographed images. The effect is to problematize the tendency of such images to take on a life of their own, as they now circulate in the booklets in a reified and desolate state.

There is something also rather singular to the POD cover design (Plate 12). Prior to the adoption of this format, *Mute* had often toyed with the design conventions of lifestyle publishing, especially in its period as a saddle-stitched magazine. The experimental fashion photography of Richard Dawson's "Shelf Life" series is a case in point, a remarkable set of variously humorous and unsettling images and scenarios that both convey and trouble the stylistic repertoires that might be encountered in an "edgy" commercial fashion magazine, the uncanny effect of these images accentuated by their somewhat incongruous presence in a magazine with anticapitalist orientations. Another example is *Mute*'s teasing approach to the convention of ensuring consumer attraction by adorning the magazine cover with a face, here with the decidedly *non*-individual faces of a Borg, Furby, or clip-art businessman.[74] The glossy magazine also made use of the advertising facility of the insert (which provides publishers with additional page space at a fraction of the cost of bound pages) to publish not adverts but artworks, or artworks on the back of adverts— *Mute*'s *Metamap* (insert to *Mute* 21) is a case in point, a vast cartography of global communications surveillance modeled on Buckminster Fuller's Dymaxion Map. But in leaving the glossy magazine format behind, and so no longer dependent on consumer seduction via the newsstand shelf (where want of a more appropriate marketing category had *Mute* placed somewhat incongruously in "men's lifestyle"), the POD quarterly freed up *Mute*'s experimental attitude, allowing for "increasingly baroque" and stylistically eclectic covers that encompassed, among other things, ad-busting, artists' commissions, and neo-Dada collages.[75]

These brief comments on the design and art content of Volume 2 touch a point of (not unproductive) tension in *Mute*'s publishing practice. The magazine's movement over time toward a more concerted intervention in the broad sociopolitical terrain of neoliberal culture has been perceived by some, including its longtime part-funder Arts Council England (ACE), as a disquieting departure from its core remit, while other more recent readers from activist circles sometimes challenged the magazine for failing to maintain an overtly political focus. The problem with these criticisms is that they miss the distinctive nature of *Mute* as a hybrid site of conjunction, where perceptual and intellectual repertoires and orientations derived from art and politics brush up against each other in an open and critical space that resists collapsing the two together. It is notable, in this regard, that *Mute*'s particular conjunction of art and politics is quite different from what we might call the "activist aesthetic" that emerged with the alter-globalization movements of the 1990s. Though certainly making good use of agitprop traditions—witness the *Mute*-commissioned flyposters from "We Are Bad" that opposed the class-cleansing urban effects of the London 2012 Olympics—the magazine maintains a commitment to the capacities of art to have transformative effects particular to its own forms and structures of composition, with regard to sensory affect, aesthetic autonomy, open composition, and so on.[76] Howard Slater's *Mute* essay on Ghédalia Tazartès is a striking illustration, with its evocative encounter with the timbres, local affects, temporal thickness, and "lessness" of a musician who invites the listener into a dislocation of the unified self with "personified emotions made dissemblingly sonorous."[77] One might even go so far as to suggest that it is in these kinds of works that *Mute* locates the true politics of aesthetics, given the instrumentalization of "engaged art" that the magazine has so carefully tracked.

DISTRIBUTED COMMISSIONING

If the low-intensity participation of user comments proved to be relatively inconsequential to *Mute,* the magazine's commissioning practices have enabled its immanent relation with its environment to proceed with considerably more success. *Mute* has gathered a number of regular contributors more or less closely associated with the editorial group, but the vast majority of its content is commissioned from new or occasional writers. The commissioning structure has two main aspects. First, it is dependent on an immersion in distributed communication networks. Web-based mailing lists have been central, as Berry Slater explains: "for a long time Nettime supplied a large proportion of our writers. So we're on the list, we might be participating, we might be lurking, but we're logging, you know, voices and research agendas and so on."[78] Second, such everyday tracking of communication networks is complemented by the effect of atypical events (for instance, the 2008 financial crisis or the 2010–11 U.K. movements against student fees and austerity) that throw up fresh and various sets of writers as they allow the magazine to encounter a new "density of social relations": "then there are also these wonderful, kind of, events that come down and you don't see happening, and that really alter things again."[79]

This commissioning structure brings into view a dimension of *Mute*'s diagrammatic form that is not so clearly rendered in the minifestos. If the writing in *Mute*-as-vortex is, in this way, a product of distributed networks and events, then it is less an entity located in one place—the impression that one could gain from the minifesto's representation of the single vortex—than a process that occurs across social space. It is this that lends *Mute* the quality of being ever-decentered that is key to Deleuze and Guattari's metaphor of immanent publishing, the "single page." I noted that this page was a "broken" field of composition; we can now see a practical way in which that is so. Insofar as the magazine comprises such distributed commissioning, it is a decentered and fragmented entity that emerges concurrently at each of the sites where contributor, writing, and publishing platform come into encounter.

Mute's distributed commissioning impacts also on the mode of *authorship* of the magazine's writers. *Mute* takes some pride in assembling content from an eclectic mix of artists, cultural workers, data programmers, activists, academics, research students, musicians, independent researchers, novelists, and others, in various combinations, who are not confined to a particular sector or school, nor chosen by an abstract specialism in writing, but are selected by the adequacy of their relation to the problem or event at issue. There is a certain *impersonalism* at play, then, where the site and source of expression are shifted from the self-expressive subject to an individual's particular and temporary condition amid mutable social relations. This tendency toward distributed authorship is not to say that *Mute* is a fully inclusive global forum. In its content, the magazine has made significant interventions in critique of the racialized, gendered, and classed patterning of violence and exploitation in global regimes of production, consumption, and control, but the makeup of its contributing writers has continued to be predominantly first world. Nonetheless, in *Mute*'s awareness of the barriers to participation (where, as numerous articles have investigated, racialization, gender, and class are interlaced with constraints that are territorial, legal, linguistic, technological, and financial), one can again observe the magazine's self-critical sensibility, its refusal to accrue satisfactions of identity from its current media form.

The significance of this kind of distributed commissioning was noted as early as 1921 by the Hungarian communist Adalbert Fogarasi, whose argument helps bring into view its political dimensions. For Fogarasi, the communist press needed not only to distribute communist content but to challenge the capitalist press in its form also.[80] Similarly to *Mute,* the promise of such intervention in publishing form was an immanent relation to social events, a relation that could undo the bar between reader and writer:

> Getting the readers to work with the press is a crucial means in this regard. The reports written by workers on events in the plants which are published in *Ordine Nuovo* ("The New Order," the Italian communist paper edited by Antonio Gramsci) represent a successful effort at transcending the untenable distance between communist reader and writer, or at least occasionally reversing the roles.[81]

This has obvious benefits for workers' education, political empowerment, and the emergence of collective enunciation, but Fogarasi understood its role also as a move toward overcoming the specialist role of the journalist, an alienated personification of abstract labor, in this respect just like any other form of capitalist work:

> It is not the [journalists] who have produced the capitalist press, but the other way round. . . . Just as capitalist production transforms the workers into simple accoutrements of the products of their labor, into mere things, so the press transforms the journalists. . . . The journalist is a specialist with unique qualifications. These do not consist in special knowledge in a specific, substantive realm of human intelligence and ability, but in the ability to write about anything. Under the journalist's pen theories, facts, opinions, counter-opinions, and news are transformed into an undifferentiated mass of printed matter. . . . The laws of reification insure that the

journalist himself, as a simple personification of journalism, follows the laws, carries out his functions mechanically and unconsciously. Under his pen every intelligible structure is remade *into a commodity.*[82]

A century on, we now know that the commercial paradigms and narcissistic compulsions of social media trouble any neat notion that the breakdown of the division between reader and writer has an inherently progressive orientation. But that by no means invalidates Fogarasi's impulse toward critique of the commodity form of the specialist writer and her textual product or the importance of contemporary intervention on this front. In *Mute*'s case, distributed commissioning is an effort toward remodeling the form of the magazine writer through critical appropriation of the decentralizing capacities of online media, not a *surrender* of the magazine to the dominant commercial structures of the latter.

FREE INDIRECT EDITORIAL

There is an impersonalism also in *Mute*'s diagrammatic approach to editorial. The point of *Mute*'s distributed commissioning is not, as in the Web 2.0 model of user-generated content, to abdicate editorial control but to interlace distributed commissioning with editorial intervention, an approach that the minifestos call "hybrid editorial." To come to an appreciation of the nature and novelty of this form, it is instructive to contrast it to Lenin's canonical formulation of political editorial in *What Is to Be Done?* Here Lenin accords the party newspaper a singular political significance, as the preeminent means of generating and training party organization and inculcating political consciousness and will. As such, "'paper' work" *is* political work, of which the key function is to convey the party's "design, dimensions and character" and to inculcate a "complete and all-embracing line."[83] Here editorial voice has a structural resemblance to the centralized, integrated, and hierarchically ordered form of the Leninist party, with its Taylorist structure of governance, the split between management and execution whereby consciousness is introduced to the workers from the party center. There are no doubt also structural resemblances and some common cause between centralized editorial and the formal features and industrial paradigms of the print newspaper more generally, such that (recalling my discussion of Debray in chapter 1) class structure, organizational form, and editorial voice were held together in a mutually sustaining "media ecology." As I have remarked already, the time of this media ecology is over; regardless of one's views of the Leninist publishing model, the demise of the workers' movement, class fragmentation, and the prosumer capacities of distributed media and user-generated content are such that it would be a delusion to think that the Leninist media form could be potentialized today.

This is not to say, however, that there is no place for strong editorial voice. We must ask, then, what might a diagrammatic editorial paradigm look like, one that no longer seeks to be the external projection of a centralized party line but has, instead, a distributed and emergent quality? *Mute*'s experience helps tease out an answer. Van Mourik Broekman comments that changes in the editorial board, development of editors' interests, and their more and less subtle differences of political position are such that both "across time" and "in time," there is "no unitary, collective 'voice'" to the magazine.[84] And yet there are clearly regularities or consistencies to *Mute*'s positions, something of a critical orientation or voice of sorts, and the magazine certainly makes no claim to be a transparent channel for the voices of the social world: "any notion of unmediated editorial contact with a sort of virgin non-local 'voice' must continue to be regarded as another (colonialist?) phantasm.... (The figure of the lone 'Third World' or 'conflict zone' blogger that is a firm favourite of the UK press comes to mind here.)"[85]

Neither unitary nor unmediated, then, *Mute*'s editorial voice is instead a product of the magazine's weave of voices over time and space. It is constituted not only of the similar and different interests, relations, and biographies of the editorial group—as fashioned in their editorial LISTSERVs and biannual meetings—but also of the contributors that the magazine channels, the events with which it becomes associated, and the projections and associations that readers bring to the magazine, for the editorial voice exists as much in the imaginations of its readers as it does in the magazine's pages. It is, in other words, a voice of the *magazine itself*, which, drawing from Maurice Blanchot's reflections on the collective and volitional capacities of magazine form, has an "intermediary status."[86] This is not simply an amalgam of parts; the point I wish to make is that as the magazine's editorial voice emerges across its constituent parties, it has a *quasi-autonomous* existence. Indications of this condition can be detected in Berry Slater's reflections on the theme, where she introduces the intriguing notion that editorial voice can operate *against the will* of the editorial board: "We have a really complicated relationship to that voice. It sometimes happens against our will, sometimes it's consciously driven, and sometimes it's held up in an accusatory manner—'How can *Mute* think or do such a thing?'—as if *Mute* were some kind of unified entity, an editorial brain."[87] Displaced from any one subject position, the editorial voice takes on a life of its own, with a character close to Deleuze's notion of "free indirect discourse," a discourse dislodged from any one speaking subject that hence carries a desubjectified, somewhat uncanny quality.[88] To adapt Deleuze's words to our context, the model we have here is of the magazine's editorial voice as "monster," it "*has a life of its own*: an image that is always stitched together, patched up, continually growing along the way."[89]

I will avoid preempting the fuller discussion of free indirect discourse that I undertake in chapter 6, but what is important about this concept here is that free indirect discourse has a volitional or catalytic capacity. A *product* of the multiple voices that compose it, free indirect discourse, in its quasi-autonomous condition, reacts back upon them to become a *cause,* as it draws out or induces associations, affects, ideas, and critical orientations from its milieu. This catalytic quality can be clarified with reference to a concept with closer proximity to our topic. In the "institutional psychotherapy" practiced by Jean Oury and Guattari at the psychiatric clinic La Borde, a central role was taken by the collective production and publication of journals, not merely as a matter of linguistic expression but as a means of assembling diverse components—semiotic, affective, practical, technological—in an entity that was at once product and catalyst of institutional practice, self-critique, and therapy, where, in Gary Genosko's words, "the institution is in part a product of a journal's collective elaboration and refinement over time."[90] This model breaks with the therapeutic dyad of analyst and analysand by enabling the journal itself to function as a mediating "third object" or "transversal tool," as Genosko describes it. Writing and being read, editing, printing and the enchantment of the print product, allocating and reordering tasks, distribution, and so forth, all become immanent to the testing and refashioning of individual and collective subjectivity.[91] No doubt *Mute*'s editorial board would have things to say about the place of this magazine in their psychosocial and institutional relations, but my point is that something of the volitional effects of the "third object" will feature in the broader milieu of readers, writers, and participants who find themselves taken up in intensive relations with *Mute*'s voice, however fleeting or occasional these may be.

Judged by Lenin's criteria of socialist editorial, that it inculcates and projects an "all-embracing political line," such an unfettered or monstrous editorial will appear wanting. But for a magazine constituted of a vortex-like weave of contributors and events in *opposition* to a delineated subject or political line, this quasi-autonomous editorial voice is an indication of the vitality of the magazine, as an overdetermined, precarious, and yet agential collective enunciation. The role of the editorial group and its other contributors is to nurture the quasi-autonomous voice, to contribute to the quality of its critical interventions and aggregations, but also to be dazzled by it, to be taken unawares and swept up in its movement. No doubt, free indirect editorial will sometimes go awry, lose its critical edge or its aggregating and volitional powers, but as it operates at and on the limits of collective identity, this is the necessary wager of monstrosity, its lurching and fitful quality an indication of open, diagrammatic form.

MAGAZINE TIME AND THE ARCHIVE

I have thus far approached *Mute*'s diagrammatic publishing in predominantly spatial terms, but the magazine also has a significant *temporal* dimension. Periodicity is of course an intrinsic feature of the modern political newspaper and magazine, orchestrating the time of writing, the labor of production, and the patterns of consumption, just as these in turn impart a temporal pacing to the generation and circulation of political ideas. It is in reference to this temporal structure that *Mute,* with all its anomalous qualities, could most convincingly ground its claim to be a "magazine," albeit that the regularity of the print product has been somewhat elastic: initially a quarterly, a one-year period of the saddle-stitched magazine reached a six-issue target, while in its coffee-table format, it slowed to a biannual. This elasticity has a certain appeal as an aspect of *Mute*'s self-differing sensibility, but there is no great challenge here to the formal structure of publishing periodicity, which subsumes the complexities and conflicts of social experience in "the steady onward clocking of homogenous, empty time," as Benedict Anderson writes of the daily newspaper.[92] There is, however, a more profound and critical temporal dimension to *Mute*, as can be developed from the way that time is inflected in the magazine's different platforms.

Mute's diagrammatic cluster holds together both "fast" and "slow" publishing platforms.[93] Metamute allows for turnaround from commissioning to publication in sometimes as little as two weeks, producing a "stream of content," in Worthington's description, as compared to up to six months with the coffee-table format, where articles were "banked" for simultaneous release, and the POD quarterly, where a selection of online articles were collected around an editorial theme.[94] The benefits Web publishing provides of fast responsiveness to events are obvious, but in this mix of fast and slow, speed is not given absolute priority. Though *Mute*'s distributed commissioning has shown a tenacious ability to stay at the leading edge of cultural and political events, the magazine's singularity lies elsewhere, as can be discerned from this comment by Berry Slater:

> We don't have the resources to be the first at the scene of the crime—we don't have that kind of facility. What we *can* do is to come at something with an analysis that tries to shape the thing harder, or drive further under the surface of appearances of what is happening. And maybe that's the sort of thing that we do slightly pride ourselves on, and the ability also to be long range. I think the pieces that we've published by people like Anthony Davies on the neoliberalisation of culture in cultural institutions, for example, are almost future-casting.[95]

This formulation of critically "shaping" the world can be productively approached through the theme of time, where it is possible to discern a temporal sensibility of a Bergsonian kind, picking up on a point I made in a different context in chapter 4. Unlike simple forms of life that react to perception with immediate action, in complex nervous systems, a pause or "rift"—a "zone of indetermination"—is inserted between perception and reaction as perception forces a recall of memory, of past perceptions, which combine with the current perception to modulate action. Thought and action hence no longer react automatically to stimulation, so reproducing the past, but combine with these past perceptions so as to act differently, to open up new dimensions in the future.[96] It is not an overly metaphorical reading of this formulation to suggest that a political magazine operates in much the same way. The magazine is a forum, a zone of indetermination, where perception of the world is channeled through political memory—memory of the contributing author, of the reader, of the magazine's archive—in writing that critically shapes that perception and wrenches it from the narrow frameworks and automatic responses of the immediate present. In this way, the magazine's politicizing content (as with Negri's account of *Futur Antérieur*, *Mute*'s driving force) carries and imparts a polytemporality, and one with an orientation toward the new. It is a temporality that operates in the midst of, and in opposition to, the flattened temporal structure of contemporary capitalism, with its obsession with immediacy and the "now"—a structure that, for all its apparent modernity, actually impedes the truly new, for it isolates the present from the resources necessary to open it to anything other than a repetition of the same, a "tautological manoeuvre whereby what is already present is endlessly represented because it is already present," as Berry Slater describes it.[97]

Yet memory is not in itself enough to enable critical intervention in temporal form, for it can have a decidedly conservative function, swamping the current perception with the past. Bergson continues: "With the immediate and present data of our senses, we mingle a thousand details out of our past experience. In most cases these memories supplant our actual perceptions, of which we then retain only a few hints, thus using them merely as 'signs' that recall to us former images."[98] This possibility is apparent in van Mourik Broekman's remark about the risk of an "elephantine memory problem," where the editorial voice, political orientations, or aesthetic styles of *Mute* can be constrained by the magazine's "sediment of history."[99] If *Mute* is to stay vital, then, the archive must itself be treated as an arena of the magazine's self-critique and structural remodeling, a practice that is exemplified by the difference between *Mute*'s two anthologies. These books register the publishing transformation of Volume 2. One book, *Mute Magazine Graphic Design,* assembles the magazine's image, page, and graphic design, along with an extensive history of *Mute*'s publishing models, while the other, *Proud to Be Flesh,* compiles eighty-one articles from the magazine's history (a stock of six thousand plus), each stripped of images and overt design features. At close to six hundred pages, *Proud to Be Flesh* is a hulk of a book, with an austerity that its sumptuous covers and glossy inserts only confirm by their stark contrast with all those words. And yet it is this anthology that is the truly inventive of the two. *Mute Magazine Graphic Design* has the air of a swan song to *Mute* as a lavish print work, whereas *Proud to Be Flesh* is fully part of *Mute*'s diagrammatic form, where it serves as something of an agential object in its own right. As van Mourik Broekman and Worthington stress in the foreword, the book is not a conventional anthology, a "Best of *Mute,*" but a critical working on the archive. It "treats the entire back catalogue of *Mute* as its critical arena," putting accumulated text back into motion, drawing out the editorial themes that have "crystallized" from the magazine's multiple voices, and projecting possible routes of future inquiry.[100] With this crystallizing aim, it is fitting that *Proud to Be Flesh* takes the form of a dense and compact book, a media object tangential to *Mute*'s flatter, more magazine-like platforms, in relation to which the book works as a condensing and refracting agent.

Proud to Be Flesh was compiled by *Mute*'s editorial group; a second initiative toward revitalizing *Mute*'s archive placed more emphasis on the participation of the *user.* A significant feature of the Metamute rationale has been maximization of the data storage and retrieval capacities of the Web so that it can transform the archive sedimented in linear fashion—the strata, if you will, of magazine issues—into a more horizontal or immanent plane, a disaggregated data set ever leaning into the present. Using three hundred plus "tags," users can assemble multiple pathways through Metamute on topics ranging from sound art to oil and border activism. The promise of this and related metadata functions is that Metamute can act not only as a medium of the "now," as is the shrill rhetoric accompanying the field of publishing under the shadow of social media, but as a membrane that multiplies the critical resources of the past in the present toward an expanded future.

DOCUMENT, FRAGMENT, FALLOUT

It would be a great mistake to think that *Mute*'s diagrammatic form coheres in an integrated and smooth-running publishing entity, to allow the modeling of the minifestos—or, indeed, the mapping undertaken in this chapter—to produce retroactive effects of unity on what is in fact a highly contingent and unstable entity. As a product of numerous and different contents and forms with competing agential valences, *Mute*'s continuity and relative coherence are only just achieved, and only then in a fashion characterized as much by false starts and loose ends as by publishing achievements—and so we encounter a second instance of the "broken" quality of *Mute*'s magazine immanence. This makes logical sense; if an entity is constituted on the many horizons of its outside, immersed in the "flesh" of the social field, it is necessarily subject to disruptions and changes in that field. What is enticing about the diagram and assemblage as concepts and forms in this context is that they bring such contingent and broken composition into the foreground as a principal dynamic, where, as Deleuze and Guattari put it, they "work only when they break down, and by continually breaking down."[101]

The six major transformations of *Mute*'s publishing model illustrate this, with each remodeling more or less the result of a particular problem, event, or contingent encounter rather than some unfurling of a publishing teleology. The point is casually made in the comment that it "was only a small and seemingly incidental experiment" with POD technology that brought it into view as a "possible solution" to the problem of a Web–print dichotomy.[102] And this dimension of diagrammatic publishing is not only expressed in such points of major transformation; it also inheres in *Mute*'s everyday functioning, where the magazine's vortexlike opening out of its internal structures is accompanied by a deliberate attention to, and foregrounding of, its fringes, failures, and long tail.

This is most apparent in *Mute*'s approach to documentation, where documents serve to hold the groping and fragmentary developments of the magazine's publishing models on its public surface. This is of course true of the minifestos, which emerged as an attempt to publicly document *Mute*'s efforts at transforming its publishing paradigm (a move that was prompted, appropriately, not by the editorial board but by a reader of the magazine).[103] If these are self-problematizing documents, as I have argued, they are also accounts of blockage and breakdown. Van Mourik Broekman notes that "The Magazine which Mistook Its Reader for a Hat, is the story of what happened when this promise [of the first minifesto, "Ceci n'est pas un magazine"] meets the harsh realities of the material world, where resources, time and human behaviour cause things to slow down, or not work."[104] And yet these documents of breakdown and transformation have also passed a threshold to become achieved aesthetic works, central instances of the magazine's published form. Hence we need examples that are closer to the unfinished, working quality of documentation. One of these is an early set of speculative consultancy documents by Saul Albert on the possible development of a Metamute "Collaborative Review Library." These allowed interested parties to observe, online, *Mute* probing the publishing potential of such sociotechnical entities as trackbacks, social bookmarking, cross-publication strategies, wikis, barter schemes, micropayment structures, and so on, in a project that was itself concerned in part with documenting *Mute*'s transition to open source.[105] More recently, *Mute*'s interventions in the field of publishing technology find documentary articulation in an "R&D" section of the Metamute web pages, open for perusal, beta phase testing, and participation by readers of the magazine.

Such foregrounding of the magazine's fringes and margins has even taken the form of a work of commissioned art. The collaborative sound project "Fallout" (1999–2001) that *Mute* undertook with the artist Kate Rich had as its very object the excluded fragments of publishing practice: the "fertile material" of the "office conversations, ambient sounds and 'surplus' interview material that get excised in the production of a print magazine."[106] Released online over the work's duration and then included as an audio CD with *Mute* 21, three tracks are especially noteworthy: sound clips of an interview with the systems artist Steven Willats, an interview previously published as "King of Code" in *Mute* 17. In this part of "Fallout," the listener does not so much encounter an audio version of the interview as a breakdown in conversation, *an interview going wrong,* and in a way that not only foregrounds the margins of the otherwise neatly fashioned and contained printed interview but also reveals something of its suppressed content. For the breakdown arises in large measure from dispute between interviewers and interviewee about the liberal assumptions inherent to systems theory and its model of consensus, that from which the artist makes his work. What is experienced, then, is a piece of fallout reacting back on the published interview to bring a new entity into view, an entity that in its breakdown performs the conflictual and overdetermined nature of all systems, including the system of the magazine interview itself.

CHOREOGRAPHY OF COMMERCE

It may come as a surprise that *Mute*'s editorial group has been explicit in describing the magazine as a "business," since the cultivation of *anti*-business organizational forms has been a long-standing sine qua non for political publishing projects. The latter orientation is not without problems, in recognition of and response to which the case has occasionally been made for the adoption of business practices in radical publishing, most influentially by the Comedia group in the 1980s. Comedia's argument in essence was that if alternative media were to achieve longevity and escape the activist ghetto, they needed to transform their organizational structures along capitalist lines, with a professionalization of management, marketing, and accountancy and the development of an entrepreneurial attitude.[107] The critique was intended to be comradely and claimed not to favor the "blind extension of management ideas into organizations with social goals," but the weight of the argument could not help but push just that, as each encounter with experimental publishing was assessed by conventional criteria of publishing success, against which, of course, it came up short.[108] And yet Comedia's preparedness to critically assess the financial paradigms of radical publishing is significant. It is a direction taken by *Mute* also, though on a different tack to Comedia. It is true, as van Mourik Broekman and Worthington wryly note, that from a certain angle, *Mute*'s story could indeed appear to resemble the "clichéd image" of the creative "do-it-yourself entrepreneurial venture" lionized in the neoliberal imaginary.[109] However, *Mute*'s standing as a business is located in relation to a somewhat different set of concerns to those propounded by Comedia, containing none of the latter's implicit sense of the organizational superiority of business forms.

The politics of *Mute*'s commercial structure is best considered through the magazine's critique of the much-touted radical publishing principle of "independence" or "autonomy." If independence is defined as economic self-sufficiency in a negative relation to state and corporate bodies, *Mute* as longtime recipient of an ACE grant (£68,912 in 2011–12, the year before funding was axed) is not an independent entity. Yet it is questionable whether "independence" on this axis is really so progressive. The reach of capitalist forms of value is such that very little stands outside its powers of mobilization and capture; the linguistic structures and perceptual habits by which we experience text, let alone modern publishing technologies and communication infrastructures, are all thoroughly permeated by capital. To proudly declare media independence under such conditions is to be at best naive and, at worst, to disguise (however unintentionally) the real structures of capital and power. The point is clear in van Mourik Broekman's rhetorical question: "if the price of a Western European country's culture is disguised by social welfare, mature technological infrastructures and a history of imperialism, does this elevate its 'independence' over global production cultures that appear more compromised?"[110]

In this light, *Mute*'s self-designation as a "business" is an ironic display of its thorough implication in capitalist social relations, a condition of its immanent "flesh" that requires not declarations of independence, which would merely obfuscate social relations with progressive sounding rhetoric, but an ever compromised "choreography of situation": "the only viable methodology is to be alert and totally engaged in the contradictions of our position/ing, never presuming an organisational innocence."[111] There are also more practical considerations. Central to *Mute*'s experimental publishing has been a concern at each stage of its transformation to find a financial model that allows the magazine to endure and staff and

writers to be paid. *Mute* here shares with Comedia an interest in priori-
tizing financial viability and avoiding the self-exploitation of "free labor"
that plagues independent media initiatives.[112] But there is an important,
if subtle, difference. The Comedia model is predicated on an uncritical
notion that business structures and commercial media practices are neutral
sets of tools that, if well handled, can be repurposed for leftist content.
It is an approach that jettisons the politics of media form in favor of an
accommodation to commercial norms on the wager that this can result
in relative success—understood as commercial viability and audience
reach—for radical media. Experience suggests that it is actually far from
clear that commercial success in these terms is so readily achievable by
small press media.[113] Regardless, *Mute*'s self-critical financial form is
somewhat different, characterized not by accommodation with commerce
but by a struggle *against* it.

A detour through Deleuze's analysis of the place of money in cinema
is helpful in elucidating the nature of *Mute*'s intervention on this front.
In a brief and enigmatic comment, Deleuze places capital at the heart
of cinema, arguing that cinema is an "industrial art" not, as one might
assume, because of its technological form but owing to its "internalized
relation with money," "an international conspiracy which conditions [cin-
ema] from within."[114] For cinema is subject to money's "harsh law" that
"a minute of image . . . costs a day of collective work."[115] To this law there
can be no independence, no escape, only one rejoinder, as Deleuze quotes
Fellini: "When there is no more money left, the film will be finished."
But if cinema cannot escape money, neither does it accommodate itself.
For any cinema worthy of the name, the internal relation with money is
a relation of *struggle*: money is cinema's "most intimate and most indis-
pensable enemy."[116]

Now, the struggle that characterizes *Mute*'s production is not dissimilar. The magazine's efforts toward a financially sustainable publishing
model are not premised on achieving a point of happy accommodation with
money; how could they be, when the structural antagonism of capital is
such a persistent theme of *Mute*'s content? The effort, rather, is to *wrench*
sustainability from the fundamentally hostile structure of commerce, a
task with an ever-receding horizon of success. Accommodation would

of course make things easier (as it does in the bulk of banal industrial art), but that would be to abdicate the magazine's critical aims, because a condition for commercial success is to make any number of changes to form and content (as set out by Comedia, for example). *Mute* is left, then, in a relation of intimate and irresolvable struggle, one that is manifest in the paradoxical and contradictory combination of efforts to pursue commercial sustainability—subscriptions, advertising, micropayment structures, devolved sales, grant moneys, consultancy, crowdfunding—with the decidedly noncommercial practices of refusing to build a stable profile or court a market niche, the adoption of free-content and anticopyright mechanisms, and direct critique of the governance agendas of funding bodies. As a "business," *Mute* is a strange commercial and anticommercial hybrid; in the struggle against money, it could not be otherwise. It is a paradoxical condition, born in the relationship to money, that traverses the magazine as a whole, as is apparent in van Mourik Broekman's reflection on the transformations in *Mute*'s publishing paradigms:

> We told ourselves the changes we made in the magazine were smart adaptations, determined by market conditions like distribution, that could allow us to sell more copies and increase our chances of being successful enough to stay around. But I now wonder whether these changes in the form weren't a very elaborate way of avoiding—or perhaps safeguarding—the central project of working out a certain critical framework, *without* the interference of the market, institutional requirements, etc.[117]

My account of *Mute*'s diagrammatic publishing has been largely kept to the period between 2005 and 2011, but the theme of the magazine's business form warrants extending the analysis to after that date. The moving tangle of contradictions that is *Mute*'s business model hit a brick wall in spring 2011, when the magazine's ACE grant was axed, a fate *Mute* shared with a disproportionately large slice of the digital arts sector. This has combined with the severe difficulty of sustaining itself in the free-content economy of the Internet—where, in a familiar story, readership has increased and diversified in inverse proportion to sales and subscriptions—to leave *Mute* in a more than usually precarious situation. Nonetheless, the ACE cut was met by *Mute,* in typically combative fashion, with a new publishing

paradigm, its sixth. Alongside a restructured Metamute that more effectively foregrounds the diversity of *Mute*'s publishing cluster and routes to
sales, the print product of the magazine, dubbed "Volume 3," is something
of a hybrid of the high production values of the coffee-table format and
the automated editorial facilities of the POD quarterly. Volume 3 comes
packaged with a new strap line, "We Gladly Feast on Those Who Would
Subdue Us," which is rendered also in Latin, should the swagger of *Mute*'s
response to austerity be in any doubt. But my concern at this stage of the
chapter is with the way *Mute* responded to the ACE cut with a practical
critique of the business paradigms of such cultural funding bodies and the
insidious effects of these on experimental arts and publishing.

In two pithy responses, both published in the first issue of Volume 3,
van Mourik Broekman and Berry Slater drew on ten years of *Mute* research
into the governance agendas of arts funding to dissect the conservative
reflux of ACE's decision. These texts detected an emerging tendency
to redefine digital media merely as resource for extending the reach and
organizational development of conventional art practice rather than as
a "highly self-reflexive area of work with a long and rich history linking
into video, performance, independent publishing, installation art, software development, literature and more."[118] And this occurred precisely at
the moment when critical intervention in the digital media field is most
needed, as the Web becomes increasingly locked down and instrumentalized through capitalization and corporate consolidation. It is, however, the
critical reflection in these texts on the insidious neoliberal effects of ACE's
governance agendas that is most compelling for our analysis of media
form. *Mute* approaches these agendas as vehicles for the backdoor introduction of corporate practices into the critical arts sector, undermining
it from within, at the level of organizational form. And so the designators
of success—"risk taking," "excellence," "innovation," and the ubiquitous
"creativity"—are to be found only in bodies that adapt their organizational
structure to corporate norms. The claim, in what Berry Slater aptly describes as a Darwinism of the arts, is that the cream will rise; the reality
is that ACE agendas and organizational requirements strangle criticality
and experiment in favor of crowd-pleasing forms, distinctive brands,
and solid business plans: "It is the bad faith of conflating capitalism's

transformation of the cultural field with the criteria of so-called 'cultural excellence.'"[119] In textbook neoliberalism, these organizational structures also introduce self-interest and competition for scarce resources, along with mechanisms of self-subjection, a "slavish gratitude" for funds that induces complicity with ACE values and agendas even among those bodies who are denied funding. It is why *Mute* responded to its funding cut with such a strong public critique and the establishment of a critical and organizational forum, "ACE Digital Uncut," within which a diverse range of digital arts groups opened a new collective front on the financial politics of digital media.

Taking leave here of *Mute*'s ongoing publishing transformations, I will conclude with a sketch of the principal features of *Mute*'s diagrammatic form. Returning to the model of magazine publishing that I drew from Negri, *Mute,* like *Futur Antérieur,* is driven by its politicizing content, its critique of neoliberal capitalism across the latter's myriad empirical manifestations. And, still in accord with Negri, *Mute* is radically open to its environment, to the social field within which it exists and to which it seeks to contribute political insight and association. There is a resolute materialism to *Mute*'s understanding of this social field, a materialism that foregrounds the technomaterial character of human life and sociality—the "flesh" of the world. Indeed, it is a materialism that sweeps up even the medium by which the critique is made, for *Mute*'s very *form* as a magazine is subject to political critique and experimentation, a reflexive and anti-identitarian process diagrammed in its publishing minifestos. In all this, *Mute* makes the same move toward magazine "immanence" that was articulated in the metaphors of "octopus" and "single page" employed by Negri, Deleuze, and Guattari, but it moves our understanding of the political magazine considerably beyond these, at the level of its organizational modeling *and* its practical construction.

Here politics is not located only in the magazine's politicizing content, the empirically routed critique of neoliberal capital, but also in its media form, where content and form, in relations of "assemblage," constitute mutually sustaining and transforming relays. *Mute* is a hybrid cluster of parts and processes, some of which are technological (open source software, POD), others aesthetic (the design affordances of the magazine's print platforms), content generating (distributed commissioning, user-generated content), temporal (the archive as critical intensification of the present), communal (OpenMute's public knowledge architectures, its monstrous editorial), and financial (the paradoxical business form of this forum of anticommerce). In each of these parts and processes, there is no determined relation between content and form. Rather, these two modalities of media production come together in zones of experimentation—which may be an apt description of *Mute* as a whole, except such a description risks sounding somewhat loose and metaphorical, whereas my aim here has been to map abstract and concrete dimensions of the magazine's publishing practice *in their specificity,* in the components that compose this experimental publishing venture. The assemblages, paradigms, and problematics of which the magazine is formed are many and various, but they all operate in a vortexlike manner of critical immanence to the sociomaterial flesh of the world, to the social relations of neoliberal capitalism. *Mute,* one might say, is the faltering pilot of the magazine's assemblages—their "diagram." Together, all these components and characteristics constitute a model and practice of diagrammatic publishing.

Mute's diagrammatic form is precarious, for while the parts of its publishing cluster contribute to the magazine as a whole, they also pull in various directions with competing capacities and effects. The risk is that the magazine will "go entropic," as the editorial group have evocatively put it, losing coherence and collapsing into its environment.[120] But this precarious character is also a sign and source of *Mute*'s vitality, for it is self-critical experimentation at the horizons of each aspect of its publishing cluster, in its contingencies and breakdowns, that drives change in the magazine's form.

If *Mute* indicates a possible future for the political magazine, it is not that future mapped by the pundits of technological teleology but one comprising such contingencies and media hybridities, where the assessment and development of media form—in post-digital fashionings of "old" and "new"—is always interlaced with an appreciation of, and challenge to, its social inscription. *Mute* suggests a publishing practice that is driven in part by an experimental attitude that comes from a deep commitment to the properties and potential of diverse mediums—a little "format-fetishism" is no bad thing. In the end, however, what is most singular about this art, technology, and politics magazine is that its media form becomes a more vital site of aesthetic and political experimentation the closer it attends to the production and circulation of its content. Unlike many self-declared "independent" publishing projects, *Mute*'s financial arrangements are just as much internal to its self-critical mutations as any other dimension of its diagrammatic form. That is just as well, for these arrangements, and the culture and economy they carry, may prove to present the greatest threat of entropy. When there is no money left, the magazine will be finished.

Or not. In May 2014, as I complete this chapter, *Mute* has responded to its funding cuts with another major transformation in its media form: "Volume 4," Web and e-pub publishing as-lean-as-you-can-get.[121]

6

Unidentified Narrative Objects

WU MING'S POLITICAL MYTHOPOESIS

> What is opposed to fiction is not the real; it is not the truth
> which is always that of the masters or colonizers; it is the
> story-telling function of the poor, in so far as it gives the false
> the power which makes it into a memory, a legend, a monster.
> —GILLES DELEUZE, *Cinema 2*

> When we talk about "myths," we mean stories that are *tangible.*
> —WU MING, "Why Not Show Off about the Best Things?"

It is reported that Mao never forgave Nikita Khrushchev for his 1956 "Secret Speech" on the crimes of the Stalin era.[1] Of the aspects of the speech that were damaging to Mao, the most troubling was no doubt Khrushchev's attack on the "cult of personality," not only in Stalin's example but in *principle,* as a "perversion" of Marxism.[2] After all, if the cult of personality was an "invariant feature of communist states and parties," as Alain Badiou has remarked, it was soon to be brought to a point of "paroxysm" in China's Cultural Revolution.[3] And so it should be no surprise that Mao retorted two years later with a defense of the axiom as properly communist. In delineating "correct" and "incorrect" kinds of personality cults, Mao insisted, "The question at issue is not whether or not there should be a cult of the individual, but rather whether or not the individual concerned represents the truth. If he does, then he should be revered."[4] Not unexpectedly, Mao presents Marx as an example of an individual who should be "revere[d] for ever," along with Engels, Lenin, and "the correct side of Stalin."[5] Yet Marx himself was most hostile to such practice, a fact from which Khrushchev sought to make mileage, quoting from Marx's November 1877 letter to Wilhelm Blos:

From my antipathy to any cult of the individual, I never made public during the existence of the International the numerous addresses from various countries which recognized my merits and which annoyed me. I did not reply to them, except sometimes to rebuke their authors. Engels and I first joined the secret society of Communists on the condition that everything making for superstitious worship of authority would be deleted from its statute.[6]

Not only hostile to the cult of personality, Marx *coined* this pejorative construction in the political domain, so presenting its Soviet practitioners with quite a bind.[7] The cult of Stalin was consciously put into play in 1929 on the occasion of his fiftieth birthday, though this affective structure of Soviet leadership first emerged with Lenin around 1920 and was consolidated with the preparations for conserving his body and memory, when the founder of the Cheka, Felix Dzerzhinsky, declared, "In regards to the cult of personality, *this is not a cult of personality,* but in a certain manner a cult of *Vladimir Il'ich.*"[8] The contortion is impressive, but this formulation is logically untenable of course, and so it was the first and last time any Bolshevik spoke publicly of a "cult" of their leader. In any case, it transpired that the personality cult was *aided* by its disavowal, "denied in speech precisely so that it could be better constructed under the cover of denial."[9] A popular cult must look exactly that, popular and spontaneous, and not appear driven by the object of the cult himself.

If I quote Khrushchev favorably, it is not to accord with his broader thesis or the aims of his speech, which, in elevating the personality cult to an all-encompassing explanatory principle, sought to inoculate the state against criticism of Stalin's era and of its enduring social, industrial, and agricultural polices. Keeping such social relations out of his critique, focusing instead on the all-powerful individual, Khrushchev was deploying a bourgeois explanatory schema, such that Althusser was correct in this regard to call the cult of personality a "pseudo-concept," with only superficial explanatory value.[10] And yet, while the personality cult was not an adequate explanation for Stalin, as a structure of affective investment cultivated in Communist regimes, it nonetheless had considerable force in binding populations to leader, party, and state. It is also the mythical form most commonly associated with the history of communism. That is not to say that the cult of the individual is exclusive to this arena. As Badiou remarks, devotion to a particular individual is commonplace in established religions and in bourgeois culture, notably the reverential framework of artistic "genius," without it being dismissed as a pathology.[11] To this we can add that the avowedly capitalist states have not been averse to venerating their own political leaders, through the Cold War opposition to Communism and since. The cult surrounding Narendra Modi's 2014 ascension to power in India is a recent case in point, to which the unseemly speed by which *The Economist* gave its endorsement—"Strongman: How Modi Can Unleash India," declared one front cover—is a disturbing repetition of capital's seemingly natural inclination in times of crisis to champion the strongman savior.[12] We should note also Beppe Grillo and the Italian Five Star Movement, where right-wing populism has been assisted by repurposed leftist rhetoric and a structure of leadership that might best be described as the cult of personality filtered through the entertainment complex of "Late Berlusconism," as Wu Ming has put it.[13]

These are important reminders that it is not only state Communist regimes that have suffered from superstitious worship of individual authority. But this is not the lesson Badiou draws from his observation, for the continuity of such veneration of exceptional individuals seems for him to help *validate* the cult of personality, although the point lacks his normal force of affirmative declaration: "it is neither more nor less inappropriate to sacralize political creators than it is to sacralize artistic creators. Perhaps less so, all things considered, because political creation is probably rarer."[14] Actually, he can be more forthright. In a later text, "The Idea of Communism," toward the task of articulating the possible parameters of a communist sequence for the new century, Badiou describes the positive role of the cult of personality as projecting "the exception" into the otherwise mundane life of individuals, "to fill what merely exists with a certain measure of the extraordinary."[15] In revolutionary "proper names," what he at one point calls "different versions of the 'cult of personality,'"

the ordinary individual discovers glorious, distinctive individuals as the mediation for his or her own individuality, as the proof that he or she can force its finitude. The anonymous action of millions of militants, rebels, fighters, unrepresentable as such, is combined and counted as one in the simple, powerful symbol of the proper name.[16]

Any doubt that Badiou's construction of the proper name here does indeed include in its domain the historical phenomenon of the cult of personality is put aside if we consider his curious interpretation of the Secret Speech. Badiou appears to accord with Althusser's reading, that Khrushchev's critique of Stalin lacked "the perspective of revolutionary politics," as he puts it.[17] And he repeats Althusser's intriguing suggestion that Khrushchev opened the door to reactionary politico-philosophical positions in the West—Marxist humanism for Althusser, the reactionary humanism of the "new philosophers" for Badiou. But the reasons given for the latter are different. While Badiou initially sounds like Althusser, he sees the fault not in the analytic frame of the cult of personality qua bourgeois explanatory schema but in challenging the cult of personality at all, which he views not as a defective explanation but as a structure to be defended. The Khrushchev episode thus provides Badiou with "a very precious lesson: even though retroactive political actions may require that a given name [e.g., Stalin] be stripped of its symbolic function, this function as such cannot be eliminated for all that."[18]

The lesson to draw from *Marx*'s formulation is rather different: the presence of the cult of personality in communist scenes is an indication that they were still bound to capitalist structures of identity and authority, to the "great man" theory of bourgeois history, namely, the indexing and referencing of social phenomena to individual actors, a specifically capitalist culture of leadership and representation that developed across the globe from the 1890s and became an entrenched feature of the twentieth century.[19] With Amadeo Bordiga, as Jacques Camatte presents his position, the "cult of the great men and messiahs," of "bourgeois personalism," was a "pathogenic element" in the workers' movement.[20]

There is a curious feature of the media component of state Communist cults of personality, a feature that draws this discussion into the orbit of the anti-book. The Sino-Soviet personality cults were complex products of pastoral, psychological, visual, linguistic, architectural, artifactual, and bureaucratic forms and relations, where broadcast and filmic media had a central place. But they all also found some ground in the considerably less image-centric media forms of writing and books, not only in the textual production of the public image of the leader, which in the state art of biography was considerable, but also in sharing a common proclivity toward projecting the leader as *author*.[21] From Stalin to Ceaușescu, each racked up a sizeable set of bound and sanctified "collected works," as, in Debray's words, "the most philistine despot found himself wreathed in the laurels of knowledge" (Figure 12).[22]

The leader cult of Nazism, its concrescence of "race," nation, and struggle, which was famously bound up with developments in the cinematic image—the regime of "information" and automatic response, as Deleuze and Benjamin describe it, "Hitler as filmmaker"—also took the book as an integral component.[23] There is a patent mythical dimension to the Nazi spectacle of book burning, initiated with the German Student Association's "Twelve Theses" (which self-consciously recalled Martin Luther's "Ninety-Five Theses" and an earlier book burning associated with an anniversary of the latter). Cleansing culture of the "un-German Spirit" and "Jewish intellectualism," book burning signified to the Nazis, in Joseph Goebbels's words to the forty thousand assembled for one such spectacle in Berlin, that "the future German man will not just be a man of books, but a man of character."[24] Yet the burning of books hardly displays *indifference* to this medium; from colonial burning of the textual matter of non-Europeans through Catholic burning of Protestant texts, and vice versa, book burning affirms the body of textual work that is not so consumed. It is no surprise, then, that Goebbels's "German character" also found a ready *complement* in the book, in the figure of Hitler as author, crafting his vision of German character in *Mein Kampf*—in its content, yes, but also in the myth of its *writing*, of Hitler entirely devoting his prison time to the production of this work—a copy of which was given free to every newlywed couple and every soldier at the front, a distribution that symbolically bound the Nazi tenets of family, "race," and war.[25]

Does critique of the personality cult mean that communism should be opposed to mythical structures of association *in total*, to the energizing value of images of the "extraordinary," in Badiou's phrase? Creating distance from the cult of personality and pursuing instead a communism

ВЕЛИКИЙ СТАЛИН-СВЕТОЧ КОММУНИЗМА!

Figure 12. "Great Stalin—Beacon of Communism," Viktor Ivanov, 1952. A volume of Lenin's collected works in his left hand, Stalin is framed by the works of Marx and Engels, Lenin, and Stalin.

immanent to the social relations of capital would seem to encourage a move away from myth. But myth also has modalities more in tune with the communism I have been exploring in this book, and that is the direction I take here, through the understanding and practice of political mythopoeis developed by the collective writing project Wu Ming.[26]

POLITICAL MYTHOPOESIS

Wu Ming, Luther Blissett's most prominent successor, comprises the participants of that "multiple name" project who wrote the novel *Q* discussed in chapter 4 (with one addition and, later, one departure), but instead of an open multiplicity, Wu Ming is a discrete collective author, now comprising four people, whose work is more directly focused on textual production, in narrative fiction, including five novels, and nonfictional critical interventions.[27] There are continuities between Wu Ming and some of the features of Luther Blissett that I set out in chapter 4: the critique of property persists; the Wu Ming collective retains an opacity toward the mechanisms of the author-celebrity; and, though the group is limited in number, certain qualitative benefits of the "multiple single" still prevail, such that they characterize themselves as both a distinct entity and a body that is different and greater than the sum of its individual parts. Some of this is held in Wu Ming's name, which is Mandarin for "nameless":

> The name of the band is meant both as a tribute to dissidents ("Wu Ming" is a common byline among Chinese citizens demanding democracy and freedom of speech) and as a refusal of the celebrity-making, glamorizing machine that turns authors into stars. "Wu Ming" is also a reference to the third sentence in the Tao Te Ching: "Wu ming tian di zhi shi," "Nameless is Heaven's and Earth's Origin."[28]

All the same, as a closed multiplicity, Wu Ming's mode of authorship is considerably less inventive and exploratory than Luther Blissett, as the collective is happy to admit. It is Wu Ming's approach to *myth* that interests us here. The textual production and interrogation of myth is a prominent feature of Wu Ming's novels and critical writing, finding one of its fullest elaborations in an essay reflecting on the mythical value of Thomas

Müntzer, a central presence in *Q*. As "Spectres of Müntzer at Sunrise" explains, myths are narratives that are circulated and reiterated socially, generating affective bonds, shared meanings, and volitional capacities. Despite a common misconception, the function of genuine myth is not to bind a community to the past but to open the parameters of the future in the present by multiplying the resources of the past:

> Ongoing narration makes [myth] evolve, because what happens in the present changes the way we recollect the past. As a result, those tales are modified according to the context and acquire new symbolic/metaphorical meanings. Myths provide us with examples to follow or reject, give us a sense of continuity or discontinuity with the past, and allow us to imagine a future.[29]

These symbolic effects combine with a certain shamanic or event-inducing capacity to "summon supernatural powers" toward a transformation of the present. For Wu Ming 1, it is no accident that "myths and folk tales [are] populated by demons, witches, magicians, gods etc."[30]

That said, any attempt at a progressive evaluation of myth is immediately confronted by the knowledge that myths can have a decidedly conservative, even destructive, function in political environments: "Revolutionary and progressive movements have always found their own metaphors and myths. Most of the times these myths outlive their usefulness and become alienating. Rigor mortis sets in, language becomes wooden, metaphors end up enslaving the people instead of setting them free."[31] This is what Furio Jesi calls the "technification of myth," when the mythical image overwhelms conscious and subconscious processes, dulling critical capacities and narrowing the individual's relation with the transformative field of communal experience.[32] The cult of personality is readily understandable in these terms, but this prominent historical instance of communist myth is not the only example of the way that political myth can go awry. Much of Wu Ming's reflection on myth has emerged from a critical relation to activist currents in the period around the 2001 anti-G8 events in Genoa, from where they identify specific problems in the linguistic and subjective modalities of myth. Referring more or less directly to the Italian Disobedienti group (in a text accompanied by a satirical image of the group's spokesperson, Luca Casarini, morphed with Stalin), Wu Ming 1 comments on the way mythical language can operate as clichés and slogans abstracted from the ethical and affective conditions of communal life:

> The problem is not merely the language being "outdated," because it can even sound new, it can include a lot of neologisms. No, the problem is that the "wooden language" ... is *ethically* unacceptable, it is a jargon made of slogans and clichés that keep experience away, it never establishes any contact with sorrow or pain, love and delight, feelings, emotions. It only accompanies boredom. What good is an annoying sequence of words in a vacuum? Think of those stupid, ultra-rhetoric propaganda speeches filled with "the Movement of movements," "disobedience," ... "we're going to disobey," ... "we are the multitude."[33]

This reflection on the linguistic "sclerosis" of the Italian activist milieu after 2001 is especially striking because it is in part a critical self-assessment of Wu Ming's own political practice, having themselves been involved in the Tute Bianche (White Overalls) movement, the remnants of which established the Disobedienti. And it raises a second problem with political mythopoesis: not only its lifeless and clichéd language but its overly integrated and self-sacrificial subjective force. Wu Ming's early approach to myth has some debt to Georges Sorel's formulation of the "general strike." For Sorel, the power of socialist myth is its capacity for "evoking instinctively" a coordinated set of feelings at a "maximum intensity" such that an instantaneous "intuition of socialism" is achieved "which language cannot give us" and that enables proletarians to "always picture their coming action as a battle in which their cause is certain to triumph."[34] Wu Ming's mythopoetical practice through stunts and performative texts in the buildup to Genoa clearly bears signs of this framework, as is most evident in their text "From the Multitudes of Europe."[35] This "edict" constructs a narrative movement of a historical subject focused on Genoa, a transhistorical confrontation between the class of property and the multitude: "We are new, and yet we are the same as always" (Figure 13). But Sorel's "certainty of triumph" is a delusion that can have dire consequences, and Genoa turned out to be a police-orchestrated "bloodbath"—with

Figure 13. Wu Ming media stunt toward the anti-G8 events in Genoa 2001, utilizing a monument to the Resistance fighters in the Battle of Porta Lame, Bologna. Reproduced under a Creative Commons License.

the Carabinieri's killing of Carlo Giuliani and their torture and assault of detained demonstrators.[36] It was a bloodbath with which Wu Ming considered themselves indirectly complicit: "We were among the most zealous in urging people to go to Genoa, and helped to steer the movement into the ambush."[37] Caught up in the wave of mobilization, it appears that they lost sight of *Q*'s critique of political subjectivity. As Wu Ming comment on the popular weaving of features of *Q*'s world—Thomas Müntzer, the Peasant's War, the Münster Rebellion—in the mythopoetical "general metaphor" of the Genoa movement, "although it was inspiring and effective, the metaphor was a misrepresentation. . . . Thomas Müntzer spoke to us, but we couldn't understand his words. It wasn't a blessing, but a warning."[38] This recognition has prompted a critical reassessment of Wu

Ming's relation to myth, central to which is an effort to refound political mythopoesis without or against a unified subjectivity. It is in this direction that this chapter moves.

Wu Ming's work on mythopoesis is traversed by an abiding sense of crisis in political subjectivity, of the tenuous possibilities of politics, and by a pervasive feeling of defeat. But it is crisis made productive, as dis-aggregated style, roving affect, and fragmented iconicity become the parts of an experimental mythopoesis unconstrained by the unifications of a political subject. It is a perspective Wu Ming broadly share with Deleuze, who argues that we are living through the demise of the unified subjective form of "the people"—as was principally expressed and corrupted in U.S. "universal immigration" and Soviet "universal proletarization"—such that politics need not seek a new subjectivity but refound itself upon the anti-identitarian condition that "the people are missing."[39] It is true that Deleuze talks also of a "people to come," but that formulation blunts his intervention on this front, namely, that it is in "impossible," "cramped," and radically disaggregated conditions that politics arises, a politics that is unable to achieve *and ever wards off* the unifications of a people, a position that Deleuze and Guattari closely associate with the nonidentity of the proletariat that I have been picking up throughout this book.[40]

This is not an easy condition to bear, given how grounded modern politics has been in the image of collective identity, from the citizen to the traditional Marxist subject of labor. Bereft of serviceable images of the people, we are left only with saturation of the political field by clichés, information, and order-words. In this situation, as Deleuze has it, we are severed from our being in the world, from our ethico-political capacities: "The modern fact is that we no longer believe in this world. We do not even believe in the events which happen to us, love, death, as if they only half concerned us."[41] The terms are rather grandiose, but the sense they convey of crisis, dislocation, and incapacity is salient.

The task under such conditions is to construct means to believe in the world, *this* world, not as a programmatic set of principles, "beliefs," but as an affirmation of the world against its constraints and closures, and from this belief to open orientations to the future, to "precipitate events, however inconspicuous," to "engender new space-times, however small their surface or volume."[42] The privileged vehicle for Deleuze in this regard is cinema. In what follows, I touch on some of the techniques of cinematic narration that he sees as actualizing new ways of being and believing in the world. But I do so through a particular feature of Deleuze's argument, namely, his account of the place and politics of storytelling or myth, as it appropriates the role of generating political association and imagination on the conditions of their absence. The counterintuitive nature of this intervention needs underscoring. Myth arises not in recip-rocal presupposition with a people—a tradition, a culture, a historical calling, and one that is placed under threat from an outside—as it does for the Right, but on the absolute evacuation of political subjectivity, on the nonexistence of a people.

Here too Wu Ming share the diagnosis, though their formulation is more directly situated in contemporary conjunctures, and with less of the grandiose quality to Deleuze's "belief in the world." It arises with particular attention to the Italian context of mass media's final abdica-tion of any democratic claim to inform and challenge the polis and of the "eternal present" of media narratives, as Marco Amici puts it, that foreclose relations to the past and, hence, capacities to act differently on the future.[43] But myth also pertains to the interlaced structures and con-ditions of property and ecological crisis. These are the conditions of the "*political* necessity" of myth, where "art and literature cannot just sound late alarms: they must help us to imagine a way out. They must heal our gaze and strengthen our capacity to visualize."[44]

We can say, then, that Deleuze and Wu Ming share Badiou's concern for a politics of the "extraordinary" that brings political vitality to a debased and prostrated everyday life, but the cult of personality would for them, clearly, be part of the problem. Instead, they begin the task of developing a *desubjectified* mythopoesis, which in Wu Ming operates through three features, which structure the following discussion: first, a technique of "falsifying narration" that puts into play a conception of time as bifurcat-ing and nonlinear; a concern, second, not with transcendent judgment and integrated subjectivity but with immanent evaluation of fragmented modes of being; and third, the agency of a desubjectified enunciative voice, the "unidentified narrative object."

FALSIFYING NARRATION

Under the generalized condition of defeat, the loss or inherent corruption of the model of a historical people, the temporality of "progress" has nothing to offer. Wu Ming's mythopoesis responds to Benjamin's diagnosis of the temporal dimension of the integration of the workers' movement with capital: "Nothing has corrupted the German working class so much as the notion that it was moving with the current."[45] Instead, Wu Ming's historical fiction is premised on an understanding of time as a "fractal" field, one neither linear or cyclical but composed of "bifurcations," "conflicts," "discontinuities," and paths not taken, the value of which resides in the capacity of the past to "retroact on the present, which is contradictory as well."[46] Fiction is uniquely placed to mine, overlay, and accentuate these bifurcations, practicing what Deleuze calls "falsifying narration." Deleuze locates the emergence of falsifying narration in postwar cinematic images and literatures that break with determination by linear movement to express time as a labyrinth of forking paths. In these conditions,

> narration ceases to be truthful, that is, to claim to be true, and becomes fundamentally falsifying. This is not at all a case of "each has its own truth," a variability of content. It is a power of the false which replaces and supercedes the form of the true, because *it poses the simultaneity of incompossible presents, or the coexistence of not-necessarily true pasts.*[47]

To be clear, this is not a negation of the real but its enrichment and intensification; as narration falsifies its object and generates incompossible worlds, it "constitutes the layers of one and the same . . . reality," "sheets of past [that] coexist in a non-chronological order" where a "single event can belong to several levels."[48] Falsifying narration is thus better seen as a *politicization* of the real, allowing art to make a direct and transformative intervention in and against the reified images of established history, of the "true." The point is well made by Timothy Murphy in his account of falsifying narration in the work of William Burroughs:

> Narration is freed from the despotism of compossibility and multiplied, producing a fertile network of potential trajectories through time. . . . This

is the role that artworks can play in the present, the role of fantasmatic structures that alter the direction and speed of the present moment by altering the past trajectory on which the present would have to travel.[49]

And yet there is also a certain realism at play here, what Dimitri Chimenti describes as a "thematic" realism, a "manipulation of the real . . . which represents determinant aspects of how individuals inhabit their world."[50] This is central to Wu Ming's falsifying narration and to the "nebula" of contemporary works they have characterized as the "New Italian Epic."[51] The writer's standpoint is displaced, "adjusting the periscope to the horizon (and to the immense horizon of phenomena) rather than the horizon to the periscope," in a phrase from Pasolini (who plays a key role in Wu Ming's understanding of falsifying narration, as he does for Deleuze).[52] In its place, at this "horizon," falsifying narration brings *structures* and *systems* into expression; these are narratives of capital, at once empirically grounded and unrepresentable in their totality. This, then, is the strange condition of falsifying narration: it undoes the distinction between the real and the imaginary to gain a better, visceral, and structural grasp on a reality understood to be ever escaping the possibility of representation, "a non-totalizable complexity, 'non-representable by a single individual.'"[53] And so Valerio Evangelisti describes this narrative form as "speaking through systems," through "historico-geographical frameworks, visions of entire societies, cosmic impulses, as long as the outcome is achieved: making people think, in a realistic or metaphorical way, about the collective perception of an alienated everyday."[54]

There are numerous formal aspects to this mode of narration. To take only one, these works of New Italian Epic commonly graft historical documents into the fiction—newspaper articles, legal documents, letters, and other extraliterary texts, even, on occasion, fictional works masquerading as factual documents. Such grafts lend plausibility to the representation of the real, intensifying the reality effect by "allowing the real to slide into its own textual reconstruction."[55] Concurrently, this technique destabilizes the textual methods by which the true is established, further unsettling the distinction between the real and the fictional to allow falsifying narration to take hold. It is not always achieved; such works are "often unsuccessful," as Wu Ming describe it, suggesting that an opening to failure is a condition of the experimental nature of mythopoetical production.[56]

Turning now to the specific content of Wu Ming's falsifying orientation, it seeks not exactly to take an alternative path through the labyrinth of forking paths, a reasonably common science fiction practice of "ucrony," but to explore worlds *at their evental points of potential,* worlds layered, discontinuous, and heated with the force of impending change. As Wu Ming describe it, "we prefer to investigate the 'possibility' of a bifurcation in history, the moment when history 'might have gone' in a different direction. We are not interested in depicting the bifurcation itself, or its consequences."[57] This is "the moment that precedes the fork in the road," a fiction "balanced on the edge of ucrony without ever practicing it."[58] Wu Ming's novel *Manituana,* for instance, is located in the overdetermined field of the American War of Independence and written with allegorical intent in our time of crisis, instability, and neoimperialism in the geopolitics of the United States. Against the state-myth of the birth of U.S. democracy, which hides a reality bathed in the blood of Native American peoples and enslaved Africans, it depicts the Six Iroquois Nations (Mohawk, Oneida, Cayuga, Onondaga, Tuscarora, and Seneca) forming an alliance with the English Crown in self-defense against the genocidal territorial ambitions of the rebels. Here, through multiple narrative voices, the novel is tasked with imagining the hybrid indigenous and settler cultures that would soon be crushed by the emergent structures of the newly independent nation.[59] But the mythical effect of the novel does not stop with this upbeat image. If *Manituana* constructs an antinational culture, a true hybrid against the state-myth of U.S. universal immigration, it is a construction at one and the same time flooded with violence. Violence, as Emanuela Piga well observes, is here a *protagonist,* one that "overwhelms and possesses both the victors and the vanquished."[60] The most affectively binding scenes convey the hybridity of peoples and, conversely, the atrocities committed on both sides, a violence that viscerally articulates how bound is the past and the present to the slaughter of the nation-state and its model of the people. As such, myth serves at once to open potentialities *and* to foreground the feeling of being blocked, so intensifying our relationship to the limits of the present, what Deleuze describes as "putting into a crisis" among those who come up against "an impasse in every direction."[61] Without forcing our gaze on the latter, on our "impossibilities," myth would merely serve an escapist or utopian function, a storytelling of "cardboard people and paper revolutionaries."[62]

Churning up a past that is not past, imagining possible worlds, multiplying perspectives, foregrounding our impasses, *Manituana* is a historical hallucination, a falsifying narrative that reacts back on the "true" of American exceptionalism, past and present.

BROKEN HEROES, SHATTERED STATES OF EMOTION

Wu Ming's feeling for the protagonism of violence—an amorphous, asubjective, structural agent—leads into the second feature of mythopoesis. In holding history in an intense and labyrinthine state of potential, falsifying narration resists attraction to a political agent and transcendent frame of judgment. *Manituana* displays a clear empathy with the Iroquois, but it produces no privileged standpoint: "we're not interested in the cliché of the 'innocent' Indian who's in harmony with nature."[63] In one scene at an aristocratic London party, Philip Lacroix, a Mohawk raised by French missionaries, posits his *empirical hybridity* as answer to the Enlightenment problem of whether he is Voltaire's "*ingénu,* the natural man," or "a latecomer . . . yet to attain a state of civilisation?" "I like the fairy tales of philosophers," Lacroix adds, wryly quoting Voltaire, but they "have never set foot in America and have never met an Indian."[64] If the Iroquois are, then, as existentially complex as the Europeans, they are also as implicated in the brutal and insidious violence, "drunk on blood" as the visionary character Molly Brant warns in the prologue.[65] From this hybrid and compromised position, the Iroquois do come forward as heroes of a sort, but only while simultaneously carrying along their failures, "characters who are at times strong, at times crushed by limited prospects and suffocating binary options, while at other times they are butchers themselves."[66]

Without a valorized subject, falsifying narration concerns itself instead with the immanent evaluation of the ethical and aesthetic capacities of the lives—variously blocked, hobbled, and resistant—that populate its narrated systems. For Deleuze, "it is a matter . . . of evaluating every being, every action and passion, even every value, in relation to the life which they involve."[67] This is an evaluation that complements the bifurcating image of history in concerning itself with a *disaggregated* field of being—affects, images, values as so many raw materials or part-objects of political imagination. Deleuze observes this in the concerns of 1970s U.S. black cinema, after the failure of Black Power:

> instead of replacing a negative image of the black with a positive one, [black American cinema] multiplies types and "characters," and each time creates or re-creates only a small part of the image which no longer corresponds to a linkage of actions, but to shattered states of emotions or drives, expressible in pure images and sounds.[68]

Wu Ming's literary creations are not this radical in form, maintaining a close relation with action-driven narrative structures. But modes of sociality, collective affects, and ethical evaluation of different capacities of life are central constituent operators in their novels. *54,* a novel much concerned with ethical and aesthetic styles of life in mid-1950s Italy, is a case in point. Set in "peacetime," this is no less a conflictual terrain than that of *Manituana,* as the opening lines inform: "'Postwar' means nothing. / What fools called 'peace' simply meant moving away from the front. / Fools defended peace by supporting the armed wing of money."[69] Against the backdrop of Cold War maneuvering in a land of strategic importance and the dashed hopes of the Resistance, here working-class popular culture—most especially the *filuzzi* dance and the neighborhood bar—brushes up against new consumer desires, global trade and communication networks, and the charmed life of Cary Grant in a manner that posits *style* at the foreground of experience. This is style as the direct expression and handling of the complexities and impasses of situated existence, the way a time is affirmed, a *belief in the world* constituted—where "ethics and aesthetics coincide and become act."[70]

Cary Grant is the privileged figure. Born Archibald Alexander Leach in Bristol to a poor proletarian family, Grant toured the United States as a circus acrobat, tackling a number of low-paid jobs in New York City before undertaking in California what his biographer Graham McCann calls the "invention of Cary Grant."[71] In Wu Ming's assessment, Grant was "a *class apart*": the first star to work independently of the Hollywood studios; a transatlantic character with an unmistakable masculinity but graceful and relaxed, very different from Clark Gable or Gary Cooper, with a certain "lightness," one that assists flight "from the world's sloth and dullness," and the sartorial skill by which the dispossessions of class—as well as of racialization and gender—have long been mediated and symbolically challenged.[72] Certainly Grant's "class apart" is integral to his bankability for Hollywood, to his suturing of the audience to an image that hides and reproduces the exclusions of race, gender, and class, but it is an image that *54* seeks to repurpose. In Wu Ming's novel, Grant is courted by Alfred Hitchcock to return to acting, in what would become 1954's *To Catch a Thief,* and by MI6 to act as covert emissary to Yugoslavia to discuss, of all things, Tito's ambitions for a biopic. But what interests me here is that alongside these narrative arcs, wherein Grant's character is loosened from self-identity, he has a particular mythopoetical function. Indeed, he is introduced with a rave evaluation from an omniscient narrator that elevates him to a decidedly unorthodox figure of *communist overcoming*: "In classless society, anybody could be Cary Grant."[73] This is the passage at its most exuberant:

> Who had never yearned for such perfection, to draw down from Plato's Hyperuranium the Idea of "Cary Grant," to donate it to the world so that the world might change, and finally to lose himself in the transformed world, to lose himself never to re-emerge? The discovery of a style and the utopia of a world in which to cultivate it.[74]

Grant functions in the novel, then, as an "Idea" or icon—but an Idea without transcendent judgment, without judgment of *any* kind. It is an Idea based solely on his immanent affirmation of life, the singular style of which this transatlantic star was famed. To partake of his style, to *become* Cary Grant, is not to imitate him but to practice no less of an immanent affirmation of one's conditions of life. The Idea of Grant must hence disaggregate in the very process of its affirmation, because to affirm Cary Grant is to project oneself back into the manifold of one's social existence: Pierre, the star *filuzzi* dancer, "crossed the [dance] floor as though it were

Piazza Maggiore on a Sunday morning, keeping his hand in his trouser pocket, under his jacket, more Cary Grant than ever."[75]

The structure of immanent style sketched here is such that the selection of Grant for this role must itself be somewhat arbitrary, contingent on local taste and preference. And this preference in turn must retain a certain immanence and not be aggrandized. Wu Ming 1 thus comments elsewhere that the passage in *54* that introduces Grant's myth is also in part a parody of efforts by leftists to rationalize and constrain their affective investments according to higher political values, "the temptation ... to force that passion or preference back under the umbrella of your ideology."[76] By contrast, he offers a more immanent, local explanation for their choice: "We included Grant ... because we like him, we find him intriguing, we like his style." And even here contingency works its ways, for it seems that the choice of Grant was also something of an accident, when Wu Ming 2 mistook the initials of Gary Cooper for those of Cary Grant in his research notes on 1950s Hollywood sex symbols.[77]

UNIDENTIFIED NARRATIVE OBJECTS

What happens to political agency in this field of incompossible worlds and fragmented modes of being? The agency of desubjectified myth is generated through its peculiar form of enunciative voice, myth's third characteristic. We can come to an appreciation of this through further consideration of the place of the real in falsifying narration. If myth is an ethico-aesthetic evaluation of situated lives, it should be clear that it cannot be an arbitrary imposition by a writer on a historical or social field. Examples of the cinema of falsifying narration with which Deleuze engages tend to be documentary and ethnographic in genre, and Wu Ming's mythopoesis emerges only after prolonged periods of historical research. In other words, their characters are meticulously located—indeed, the likeness of Wu Ming's Cary Grant to the actor is such that a comparative review of *54* with a contemporaneous Grant biography found the *fictional* portrayal to be the most convincing.[78] It is, then, "real and not fictional characters" that are put "in the condition of 'making up fiction,'" as Deleuze has it.[79] The effect is to produce a blurring or contamination of the point of view of the author (external to the world presented, hence in cinematic convention "objective") and that of the characters and world portrayed (internal to the scene, hence "subjective"). Wu Ming call the resultant enunciative form an "unidentified narrative object" or UNO.

The concept refers to the disorienting blend of fiction and nonfiction that I touched on above, but its effects are felt on the enunciative voice, where it bears association with Deleuze's particular understanding of "free indirect discourse": narration between subjective and objective viewpoints that sweeps up both in an utterance that is loosened from determination by either.[80] The result, as Wu Ming 1 describes it, is somewhat "hallucinatory" or "uncanny," an at once seductive and disconcerting feeling of familiarity and strangeness that arises as one loses the ability to locate the enunciative voice and the "reality," or not, of the world being portrayed.[81] It is an effect he considers most successfully achieved in Roberto Saviano's *Gomorrah,* the devastating work of reportage, fiction, and political economy on the intimacy between global capital and the cruel and nihilistic world of Neapolitan organized crime. Here, "the 'narrating I' frequently hallucinates and 'hijacks' the points of view of other people, intentionally playing on the confusion between the author, the narrator and a 'narrating I' that doesn't belong to any of them."[82] As *Gomorrah* blends and confuses the apparently objective and the literary, the autobiographical and the journalistic, the novel presents scenarios through the author's "I" that, on reflection, stretch plausibility to its breaking point. Readers are led to object that they have been duped—*he could not have witnessed that*—at the very moment that their experience of the world represented is at its most intense, disturbing, and critically salient. Rachel Donadio's *New York Times* review is revealing of such effects, in complaining that Saviano's readers are not informed that he "took liberties with his first-person accounts," while at the same time commenting that "I could not get this brave book out of my head."[83]

It is the autonomy of this unidentified roving voice—between the real and the fictional, between the perspective of the writer and a particular historical or social body—and its disorienting, hallucinatory, and alluring affect that provides myth with its agential, catalytic force. An *effect* of its telling, UNO or myth gains autonomy and folds back on its field of emergence to become a *cause*. As Deleuze has it, myth is a "monster," it *"has a life of its own*: an image that is always stitched together, patched up, continually growing along the way."[84] Referring back to chapter 4, one might think of Luther Blissett in exactly these terms—not only a collective author but an unidentified myth, a catalyst, an "uncontrollable golem."[85] Of course, it is the agential, catalytic property of a distributed myth—to gather diverse affects and relations in an intensity that projects into action—that also makes the cult of personality so effective. The intensity of the popular cult of Mao, for example, did indeed assist people in accomplishing extraordinary feats, be it in industry, sport, or popular violence. The difference in Wu Ming's conception is that here myth provides no fusion of belonging determined by a transcendent subject or truth. Fragments of association, imagination, ideas, moods, are woven together through myth, but—if it avoids becoming technified—these emergent arrangements remain constituted around an absent center, with a processual openness to their outside. If Luther Blissett and a certain reading of Cary Grant are examples, and Malcolm X too, as we will see shortly, it is only insofar as they play a role in the more everyday dynamics of myth to intensify one's desubjectifying and critical encounter with, or belief in, the world.

To dispel any Arcadian images that may have been conveyed with all this talk of storytelling, it should be underscored that these unidentified and fragmented qualities of myth are facilitated by its relation to artifice and technology. Just as Luther Blissett was immersed in media forms, free indirect discourse is for Deleuze a fully mediated mode of expression, characterized by a taste for "making the camera felt": obsessive framing, alternation of lenses on the same image, bizarre angles, abnormal movements, excessive zooming. The novel has fewer technological affordances, but it is productive to regard Wu Ming's literary practice as similarly concerned with foregrounding and testing the capacities of the medium, albeit in a manner that seeks at one and the same time to have a popular quality ("We wanted to give our contribution to popular culture, we wanted to bring conflict and contradictions into it, not condemn it from the outside looking in").[86] Here we can note the aforementioned incorporation into the novels of nonliterary textual forms such as historical documents, diaries, newspaper articles; the insertion of Wu Ming's own interviews with historical figures into the mouths of fictional characters in *Asce di guerra* (Hatchets of war); experimentation with unusual and unexpected points of view—the "oblique gaze," as Wu Ming have it— where nonhuman entities can take on narrative functions; the cross-media storytelling, Web-based reader interaction, and fan fiction of *Manituana,* all encouraged by the online publication infrastructure of the novel; and the attention to the way that linguistic structure itself can express political forms, sensibilities, and relations of power.

To illustrate only the last of these features, the one that is most pertinent to this chapter's discussion of the tangible qualities of mythical language, *Manituana* is especially attentive to the politics of expression that subtends more formal political structure. In one illuminating scene, Joseph Brant, Iroquois protagonist and sometime translator, contemplates the tensions of political negotiation, reflecting on the disjunction between the visceral, expressive language of the Mohawk and English, the language of clarity, order, and Empire. Interlaced with the particular narrative role of the scene, this is a staging of the distinction between information and myth and the latter's affective, visceral, and nonlinear qualities:

> English was a rougher, more concise language; in the journey from eyes to mouth the words shrank, leaving part of their significance on the page. In the language of the Empire, every cause was followed by a consequence, to every action there was a single corresponding purpose, to every action the most appropriate reaction. On the contrary, the language of the Mohawk was full of details, run through with doubts, refined by constant adjustments. Each word stretched and expanded to capture every possible meaning and ring in the ear in the most consonant manner.[87]

Given the historical conjuncture, it goes without saying that this difference in expressive form was also a relation of domination and struggle, the mechanisms of which include additional media specificities. I mentioned the colonial effects of the codex in chapter 1, to which we can add the role of the *page,* taking a cue from the preceding passage. If the page was immanent to the reduction of polyvocal meaning to order and linear sequence, as Wu Ming here suggest, its integration in colonial power also had particular medial features, a point well made by L. M. Findlay. The forced encounter of Native American populations with treaties, ledger books, schoolhouse lessons, and so on, was such that the "colonizing and assimilating page was to affect almost every aspect of Indigenous life."[88] Even the apparent tabula rasa quality of the pristine blank page was an expression of colonial value and dispossession, for its adoption in indigenous image making bore witness to the systematic extermination of buffalo, whose hide had provided the traditional medium of inscription. Findlay has pursued such effects through discussion of the ways that writing and the page feature in "ledger art," drawings by Native American men on the backs of surplus ledger books, produced while in stockades or reservations in the late nineteenth century. In one, whose visual narrative features the distribution of treaty goods, the rectangular shape of the Stars and Stripes flies over the scene, performing the symbolic work of colonial rule that the page on which it is drawn reiterates:

> The page, in the very rectangularity it shares with the flag, functions as a kind of cultural or semiotic stockade, having the very shape that Chief Joe Mathias would later have in mind when, after the collapse of the fourth Canadian Conference on Aboriginal Self-Government, he told his people that they would never "be contained within the four corners of a history book."[89]

THE STYLES OF MALCOLM X

There is little doubt that Wu Ming's tastes are for the marginalized, the defeated, the minor shades of history—this body of writing unfurls as an "epic of the *ex-centris*," a "mythology of the excluded," to borrow from Angelo Petrella's characterization of *Q*.[90] Yet Wu Ming also engage with established and enduring iconic examples of political myth, another instance of unidentified mythopoesis interfering with the broad terrain of popular culture. Wu Ming's mythopoetical encounter with Malcolm X is especially enticing in this regard, on the occasion of the fortieth anniversary of his assassination.

In keeping with the nonlinear, falsifying approach to history, this is Malcolm X as a historical figure *and* a most contemporary myth, a roving and mediated power: "When an actor—any actor—plays the part of

Malcolm X, it's as if Malcolm possesses him."[91] This time slip typical of myth is here given contemporary purchase by the persistence of property relations, as carried by Malcolm's last name—or, rather, by its substitution with an X:

> Renouncing the surname of a slave, the stigma of an ancient violation, pulls the present into the discussion, the imposed identity, the role that is assigned to us by the script of the winners. Putting into play a radical discussion, this is to say, one that descends to the roots to reconquer negated memory. Your ancestors were merchandise.[92]

Here the property form of the name that Foucault identified in the author-function takes a different shape in modern capitalism's alloyed power of primitive accumulation, where the name designates not privatization of discourse but existence as fungible property—the structural terror of chattel slavery and its repercussions in the brutal architecture of racialized dispossession today:

> Malcolm—freed from the racist doctrines of Elijah Muhammad— understands even better that the horrors of slavery, of segregation and inner colonialism of the USA don't depend on the "evilness" of the whites (the "devils with blue eyes"), they're not gratuitous nor unjustified, and what's more, they're necessary for the defence of property relationships. Those who maintain the memory of slavery in the center of their own reflection will arrive more easily at criticizing property.[93]

Malcolm's "X," then, recalls across time the violence of property—just as it shatters the property relation of the name, constituting a nonfilial and nonlinear field of struggle: "George Washington exchanged his slave for a barrel of molasses, but your grandfather wasn't a barrel of molasses. Your grandfather was Nat Turner. Your grandfather was Toussaint L'Ouverture."[94]

Constructed on this terrain of property and its negation, the myth of Malcolm X lives as an affective pattern—"Malcolm X became imprinted upon my neurons"—and as a style.[95] I noted earlier that for Deleuze, mythical affect comprises "shattered states of emotions," "pure images and sounds" without linkage to historical action, making reference in particular to 1970s U.S. black cinema. But he has commented also that from time to time, one does find a conjunction of such aesthetic qualities with political struggle, a conjunction manifest in the gestures or styles of historical personas: "a coincidence of poetic acts and historical events or political actions, the glorious incarnation of something sublime or untimely. Such great coincidences are Nasser's burst of laughter when he nationalized Suez, or Castro's gestures, and that other burst of laughter, Giap's television interview."[96] In the big scheme of things, these are "tiny events," but as fragmented blocs of style, image, and affect, they have a joyous and untimely quality that works as a mythopoetical catalyst for "new worlds," for new patterns of political being.[97] To expand on one of Deleuze's examples, it is reported in Chris Marker's *A Grin without a Cat* (a film that is as concerned as Deleuze is with the politics of the missing people) that Castro's habit of punctuating his oratory with nervous adjustment to his microphone became a central affective operator of his speeches, a part-object joyously anticipated by his audience. As the film's narrator comments, displaying an acute appreciation of the dynamics of mythopoesis, it displayed Castro's skill in "turning the accidental into the legendary." For Wu Ming, Malcolm X too has this untimely aesthetic power, and in a way that underscores its fragmented quality, that which might be lost in Deleuze's reference to Nasser and Castro, associated as they are with the cult of personality. Malcolm communicates today—in a manner "so direct that it breaks the barriers of time"—as a disaggregated style, a layered and discontinuous arrangement of bodily and sonorous parts: "husky sounds [that] grab you by the shoulders," "parables and stories," "rhetorical questions," "body language," "'call and response' passages," "close-cropped hair," "the rims of his glasses," and the "dazzle" of his smile.[98]

Granted, there are serious risks with this kind of focus on style, as is apparent from the experience of another black radical icon of the period, Angela Davis. In an essay reflecting on the multiple and contradictory semiotic and political functions of her 1970s Afro or "natural" hairstyle, which carried considerable mythopoetical force, Davis shows how this complex aggregation of style and body politics was reduced over time to a decontextualized fashion item, a unit of "revolutionary glamor."[99] Her principal example is a 1994 "docufashion" re-creation in *Vibe* magazine of her 1970s image, titled "Free Angela: Actress Cynda Williams as Angela Davis, a Fashion Revolutionary." An eight-page spread, one image is a re-creation of her FBI Wanted poster, of which Davis comments: "The way in which this document provided a historical pretext for something akin to a reign of terror for countless young Black women is effectively erased by its use as a prop for selling clothes and promoting seventies fashion nostalgia."[100] Davis especially attends here to the destructive power of photography, a power to arrest agency and atrophy memory, even in the midst of social struggle. Though the stakes of Wu Ming's intervention are significantly less, it is a concern that they share. Wu Ming make no at-tempt to hide their given names, but they refuse to appear on television or allow their photographs to be taken, providing instead (until spring 2008) a publicity image of a 1950s dance troupe devoid of faces and captioned "this revolution is faceless" (Plate 13). They explain,

> No photos, no filming. Once the writer becomes a face that's separate and alienated . . . , it's a cannibalistic jumble: that face appears everywhere, almost always out of context. A photo is witness to my absence; it's a banner of distance and solitude. A photo paralyzes me, it freezes my life into an instant, it negates my ability to transform into something else. I become a "character," a stopgap used to quickly fill a page layout, an instrument that amplifies banality.[101]

This assessment of the closure attendant on facial representation does not, however, extend to the public display of other component parts and expressions of the human body, parts that can enfold and project experi-ential and associational vitality:

> On the other hand my voice—with its grain, with its accents, with its imprecise diction, its tonalities, rhythms, pauses and vacillations—is wit-ness to a presence even when I'm not there; it brings me close to people and doesn't negate my transformative capacity, because its presence is dynamic, alive and trembling even when seemingly still.[102]

The fate of bodily images, parts, and styles is not only, then, to integrate and paralyze political composition. Malcolm X does of course circulate in culture as a unified photographic image. But Wu Ming's engagement suggests that in a *disaggregated* state, his style can maintain a propulsive and critical vitality, "alive and trembling" at the borders of the facialized subject.[103] Malcolm is a fragmented set of affects, refrains, sounds, and rhetorics constituted in the open and nonfilial community of the critique of property, a mythical field evoked with an X.

With this single letter *Anti-Book* draws to a close. It may seem perverse to end a book on the many materialities of political writing and publishing with a solitary letter. But this is a *visceral* unit of mythical writing, a textual mode where "each word *carries with it a world*."[104] Text has of course been the focus of much attention in this book, but if there is a central argument to *Anti-Book,* it is that the particular political qualities of texts are only grasped when approached in relation to the media forms that carry them, codetermine their meaning, collide with them, or leave them aside in the pursuit of effects of an extratextual nature. As to myth, the fragmented, partial "world" that it carries, *its* materiality, this operates against the reactionary powers of technified myth, from the cult of personality to the wooden language than can consume activist culture, with its linguistic clichés and integrated subjectivities. Through certain textual procedures, it posits instead a peculiar kind of unidentified and roving myth that is generated through the investigation and circulation of affects, styles, values, across the divide between fiction and the real. In this, one finds the imaginative, exploratory, and catalytic force of myth to call forth new associations, new worlds, worlds born on the condition that the people are missing, that inhere in a fragmentary, experimental state. Not that this practice is devoid of purchase on the concrete conditions of life, on the dynamic systems within which we are bound; what is perhaps most ingenious in Wu Ming is their interlacing of a politics of mythical invention with the critique of the intolerable of capital, as is especially apparent in the engagement with Malcolm X.

In contrast to the concentrative and authoritarian function of the cult of personality—premised, at least in Mao's case, on the singular "truth" of the integrating leader—here myth is a collective endeavor without a determined subject, not a "people" but a processual "monster," stitched together and patched up through its situated, variable, and incompossible iterations. Wu Ming's not infrequent encounters with orthodox left icons should be approached with this understanding—it is as if these highly

Figure 14. Wu Ming's portrait, 2009. Reproduced under a Creative Commons License.

integrated images of concentrated state-myth call out to be rerouted and potentialized through the disaggregating powers of the unidentified narrative object. Something of this is apparent in Wu Ming's later self-portrait (Figure 14). Gamal Abdel Nasser provides a key component of the image, but it is a strange montage, where Nasser's face is multiplied fourfold and placed on the heads of a *filuzzi* dance band. As fragments of pan-Arabist icon, Mediterranean basin, Italian working-class musical culture, and a certain 1950s proletarian style swirl together, the effect is "uncanny" indeed—quite the reverse of an integrated and subjectifying image, yet all the more generative for it.[105] But I will conclude with a similarly irreverent image, one that takes us back to the personality who opened this chapter. If Mao himself is not directly subject to such treatment, the iconography of Chinese Maoism is. Identifying the link to the free digital downloads of their books, Wu Ming's English language website carries a familiar socialist realist image of a triumphant worker holding aloft a copy of Mao's Little Red Book. But an addition to the image makes it a rather less common communist montage: floating in the sky above is the disarming face of Cary Grant, doubling the cult of personality and its transcendent regimes of book-bound truth with an icon of a rather different order.

Notes

PREFACE

1 Franco Moretti, "Style, Inc.: Reflections on 7,000 Titles (British Novels, 1740–1850)," in *Distant Reading* (London: Verso, 2013), 181.
2 For further details about this 2006 artwork by Paolo Cirio, Alessandro Ludovico, and Ubermorgen, see http://www.amazon-noir.com/. The political, technological, and aesthetic dimensions of the project are critically considered in Michael Dieter, "Amazon Noir: Piracy, Distribution, Control," *M/C Journal* 10, no. 5 (2007), http://journal.media-culture.org .au/0710/07-dieter.php.
3 Saree Makdisi, *William Blake and the Impossible History of the 1790s* (Chicago: University of Chicago Press, 2003), 8. William Blake, *Visions of the Daughters of Albion,* cited in ibid., 152. My gesture toward Blake's political aesthetics of the book is indebted to Saree Makdisi's wonderful writing on the theme. See also his *Reading William Blake* (Cambridge: Cambridge University Press, 2015), where he describes Blake's illuminated books as "un-books."
4 William Blake, *Europe,* cited in Makdisi, *William Blake,* 41. William Blake, "The Marriage of Heaven and Hell," in *The Complete Illuminated Manuscripts* (London: Thames and Hudson, 2000), 414.
5 Gilles Deleuze and Félix Guattari, *A Thousand Plateaus: Capitalism and Schizophrenia,* trans. Brian Massumi (Minneapolis: University of Minnesota Press, 1987), 4.
6 Leah Price, *How to Do Things with Books in Victorian Britain* (Princeton, N.J.: Princeton University Press, 2012), 35–36.
7 Guy Debord and Gil J. Wolman, "Methods of Détournement," in *Situationist International Anthology,* ed. and trans. Ken Knabb (Berkeley, Calif.: Bureau of Public Secrets, 1981), 11.

1. ONE MANIFESTO LESS

1 Andrew Murphie, "Ghosted Publics: The 'Unacknowledged Collective' in the Contemporary Transformation of the Circulation of Ideas," in *The Mag.net Reader 3* (London: Mute Publications, 2008), 102.

2 Lisa Gitelman, *Paper Knowledge: Toward a History of Documents* (Durham, N.C.: Duke University Press, 2014), 3.

3 N. Katherine Hayles, *How We Think: Digital Media and Contemporary Technogenesis* (Chicago: University of Chicago Press, 2012), 2.

4 Michele Zappavigna, "Ambient Affiliation: A Linguistic Perspective on Twitter," *New Media and Society* 13, no. 5 (2011): 788–806.

5 Kenneth Goldsmith, *Uncreative Writing: Managing Language in the Digital Age* (New York: Columbia University Press, 2011), 25.

6 Michele Moylan and Lane Stiles, eds., *Reading Books: Essays on the Material Text and Literature in America* (Amherst: University of Massachusetts Press, 1996), 12.

7 See Ann Burdick, Johanna Drucker, Peter Lunenfeld, Todd Presner, and Jeffrey Schnapp, *Digital_Humanities* (Cambridge, Mass.: MIT Press, 2012).

8 N. Katherine Hayles, "Translating Media: Why We Should Rethink Textuality," *Yale Journal of Criticism* 16, no. 2 (2003): 276.

9 N. Katherine Hayles, *Writing Machines* (Cambridge, Mass.: MIT Press, 2002), 25.

10 Ibid.

11 Ibid., 33.

12 I discuss the role of the reader at certain points, but not to a great extent, so allow me to contribute to this dimension of a book's materiality in a different way, and in this open to the extratextual dimensions of the readership of material text. *Anti-Book* is still a book, all too much of a book, so I invite readers to perform an anti-book operation with it, upon it, against it. Should you be willing to send me the new artifact or some form of documentation, I will endeavor to respond in kind. I can be contacted at my work address.

13 Roger Chartier, "Languages, Books, and Reading from the Printed Word to the Digital Text," *Critical Inquiry* 31 (2004): 133–52.

14 For a compelling example, see Hanna Kuusela, "On the Materiality of Contemporary Reading Formations: The Case of Jari Tervo's *Layla,*" *New Formations* 78 (2013): 65–82.

15 Benedict Anderson, *Imagined Communities: Reflections on the Origin and Spread of Nationalism,* rev. ed. (New York: Verso, 2006). Robert Darnton, *The Forbidden Best-Sellers of Pre-Revolutionary France* (London: HarperCollins, 1996).

16 Elizabeth L. Eisenstein, *The Printing Press as Agent of Change* (Cambridge: Cambridge University Press, 1980).

17 Daniel Selcer, *Philosophy and the Book: Early Modern Figures of Material Inscription* (London: Continuum, 2010), 13–14.

18 Ibid., 15.

19 Regarding the specifically technical aspects of fixity, Johns notes that the "first book reputed to have been printed without any errors appeared only in 1760." Adrian Johns, *The Nature of the Book: Print and Knowledge in the Making* (Chicago: University of Chicago Press, 1998), 31. It is an appealing confluence that the theoretical self-identity of the book qua commodity became true to its word at about the time William Blake's "illuminated books" introduced error or variability into the production process as an intrinsic feature of the practical overcoming of that commodity.

20 Ibid., 2–3.

21 Ibid., 28.

22 Johanna Drucker, *The Century of Artists' Books* (New York: Granary, 2004), 2.

23 Clive Phillpot, *Booktrek: Selected Essays on Artists' Books (1972–2010)* (Zurich: JRP Ringier and Les presses du reel, 2012), 148. Before this aesthetic field arrived at a name, Phillpot remarks that he would describe the earliest instances he encountered in the late 1960s as "odd pamphlets," a term I rather wish had stuck. Ibid., 12.

24 Rosalind E. Krauss, *"A Voyage on the North Sea": Art in the Age of the Post-Medium Condition* (London: Thames and Hudson, 1999). Rosalind E. Krauss, *Under Blue Cup* (Cambridge, Mass.: MIT Press, 2011).

25 Krauss, *Voyage on the North Sea*, 7.

26 A self-differing medium can hence displace and cut across any particular material support. For instance, the "medium" of work by Ed Ruscha, whose *Twenty Six Gasoline Stations* (1962) is usually taken as the founding instance of the artists' book, is for Krauss not the book as such but the automobile. See Krauss, *Under Blue Cup*, 20, 73–78.

27 Ulises Carrión, "The New Art of Making Books," in *Book Art: A Critical Anthology and Sourcebook,* ed. Joan Lyons (Rochester, N.Y.: Visual Studies Workshop Press, 1985), 31, 32, 40, emphasis added. I would downplay the place of artists' *intention* at the end of Carrión's sentence, for the agency here is complex and emergent.

28 Félix Guattari, *Schizoanalytic Cartographies,* trans. Andrew Goffey (London: Bloomsbury, 2013), 253, 255.

29 Richard Kostelanetz, "Why *Assembling,*" 1973, http://www.richardkostelanetz.com/examples/whyassem.html.

30 Richard Kostelanetz, "Book Art," in Lyons, *Book Art,* 27, 29.

31 Lucy R. Lippard, *Six Years: The Dematerialization of the Art Object from 1966 to 1972* (London: Studio Vista, 1973).

32 Lucy R. Lippard, "Conspicuous Consumption: New Artists' Books," in Lyons, *Book Art,* 50.

33 Krauss, *Under Blue Cup,* 32. Alexander Alberro, *Conceptual Art and the Politics of Publicity* (Cambridge, Mass.: MIT Press, 2003). Many thanks for this point to Stephen Zepke and one of the anonymous readers of this book in manuscript.

34 Gwen Allen, *Artists' Magazines: An Alternative Space for Art* (Cambridge, Mass.: MIT Press, 2011), 219.

35 For more on the political dimensions of the artists' book, see Janneke Adema and Gary Hall, "The Political Nature of the Book: On Artists' Books and Radical Open Access," *New Formations* 78 (2013): 138–56.

36 See Drucker, *Century of Artists' Books,* chapter 11.

37 Lippard, "Conspicuous Consumption," 50.

38 Phillpot, *Booktrek,* 5, 22.

39 Michael Hampton, *THEARTISTSBOOKANEWHISTORY* (London: Banner Repeater, 2011). Kostelanetz makes a related point with regard to the accepted nomination for this genre of work as "artists' books." It focuses attention on the artist rather than the object (whereas the "art at hand is *books,* no matter who did them") and serves to isolate them as "artworks" from other media forms ("the term 'artists' books' incorporates the suggestion that such work should be set aside in a space separate from writers' books"). Kostelanetz, "Book Art," 29–30.

40 Allen, *Artists' Magazines,* 241.

41 Richard Kostelanetz, "Why *Assembling.*"

42 Allen, *Artists' Magazines,* 241. Richard Kostelanetz, "Why *Assembling.*"

43 Richard Kostelanetz, "Assembling," http://www.poetrymagazines.org.uk/magazine/record.asp?id=18202.

44 Karl Young, "Foreword to *Assembling* 12," http://www.spunk.org/texts/art/sp000177.html.

45 Richard Kostelanetz, "Why *A Critical Assembling,*" in *A Critical (Ninth) Assembling (Precisely: 6789),* ed. Richard Kostelanetz (New York: Assembling Press, 1979).

46 Young, "Foreword to *Assembling* 12."

47 Richard Kostelanetz, "Why *A Critical Assembling.*"

48 Kostelanetz, cited in Allen, *Artists' Magazines,* 241.

49 I take the formulation, with thanks, from one of the anonymous readers of this book in manuscript.

50 Régis Debray, "Socialism: A Life-Cycle," *New Left Review* 46 (2007): 5. The essay is extracted from his 1991 work, *Cours de médiologie générale.*

51 Ibid., 5.

52 Ibid., 6.

53 V. I. Lenin, "The 'Plan' for an All-Russian Political Newspaper," in *What Is to Be Done? Burning Questions of Our Movement,* 149–74 (Peking: Foreign Languages Press, 1973).

54 Debray, "Socialism: A Life-Cycle," 8.

55 Vilém Flusser, *Does Writing Have a Future?,* trans. Nancy Ann Roth (Minneapolis: University of Minnesota Press, 2011), 40.

56 Ibid., 26.

57 Troploin [Gilles Dauvé and Karl Nesic], "What's It All About? Questions and Answers," *Troploin Newsletter,* no. 4, April 2007, 2, http://libcom.org/library/whats-it-all-about-questions-answers-troploin.

58 Kevin Gilmartin, *Print Politics: The Press and Radical Opposition in Early Nineteenth-Century England* (Cambridge: Cambridge University Press, 1996), 65.

59 James Vernon, *Politics and the People: A Study in English Political Culture, c. 1815–1867* (Cambridge: Cambridge University Press, 1993), 105.

60 Ibid.

61 Ibid., 106.

62 Iain McCalman, *Radical Underworld: Prophets, Revolutionaries, and Pornographers in London, 1795–1840* (Oxford: Clarendon Press, 1988), 152.

63 "We can and must immediately set about founding the Party organ—and, it follows, the Party itself—and putting them on a sound footing." V. I. Lenin, "An Urgent Question," in *Lenin Collected Works* (Moscow: Progress, 1964), 4:221.

64 Debray, "Socialism: A Life-Cycle," 14, 18, 15.

65 Ibid., 22.

66 Ibid., 24.

67 Ibid., 9.

68 Ibid., 5.

69 Théorie Communiste, "Much Ado about Nothing," *Endnotes* 1 (2008): 155.

70 Karl Marx and Frederick Engels, "The Holy Family; or Critique of Critical Criticism," in *Karl Marx and Frederick Engels Collected Works* (London: Lawrence and Wishart, 1975), 4:36.

71 Moishe Postone, *Time, Labor, and Social Domination: A Reinterpretation of Marx's Critical Theory* (Cambridge: Cambridge University Press, 1996), 8.

72 Ibid., 9.

73 Théorie Communiste, "Much Ado about Nothing," 156.

74 Ibid., 174.

75 Ibid., 157.

76 Gilles Dauvé, "Leninism and the Ultra-Left," in *The Eclipse and Re-Emergence of the Communist Movement,* rev. ed., by Gilles Dauvé and François Martin, 63–75 (London: Antagonism Press, 1997).

77 "Afterword," *Endnotes* 1 (2008): 214.

78 *Endnotes,* "What Are We to Do?," in *Communization and Its Discontents: Contestation, Critique, and Contemporary Struggles,* ed. Benjamin Noyes (New York: Minor Compositions, n.d.), 29.

79 Ibid., 28.

80 *Comité* [Maurice Blanchot], "[Communism without Heirs]," in Maurice Blanchot, *Political Writings, 1953–1993,* trans. Zakir Paul (New York: Fordham University Press, 2003), 93.

81 Eric Hobsbawm, "The Communist Manifesto in Perspective," http://www.transform-network.net/journal/issue-112012/news/detail/Journal/the-communist-manifesto-in-perspective.html.

82 Martin Puchner, *Poetry of the Revolution: Marx, Manifestos, and the Avant-Gardes* (Princeton, N.J.: Princeton University Press, 2006).

83 I have approached the question of the manifesto's subject in relation to the subject of modern revolution, but the manifesto has a broader and intrinsic relation to the emergence and self-representations of the bourgeois subject of the modern nation-state, a point well made by Janet Lyon, *Manifestoes: Provocations of the Modern* (Ithaca, N.Y.: Cornell University Press, 1991).

84 Alain Badiou, *The Century,* trans. Alberto Toscano (Cambridge: Polity Press, 2007), 139, 138, emphasis added.

85 Badiou quotes Mallarmé to illustrate this convulsive conjunction of "action" with "undoing": "the drama takes place all at once, just in time to show its undoing, which unfolds like lightning." Ibid., 136.

86 Ibid., 140, 139, 136, 139.

87 Guy Debord, "Document beyond Debate," trans. Ken Knabb and Not Bored!, http://www.notbored.org/orientation36.html.

88 Gilles Deleuze, "One Manifesto Less," trans. Alan Orenstein, in *The Deleuze Reader,* ed. Constantin V. Boundas, 204–22 (New York: Columbia University Press, 1993). Deleuze uses this formulation to describe Carmello Bene's subtractive approach to theater, where constants of character, subject, and text—that which orchestrates and dominates the narrative and performative field—are subtracted to allow a-subjective dimensions and conditions of expression to emerge, what he calls "minor" theater.

89 Kathi Weeks, "The Critical Manifesto: Marx and Engels, Haraway, and Utopian Politics," *Utopian Studies* 24, no. 2 (2013): 216–31. Lyon, *Manifestoes.*

90 Valerie Solanas, *SCUM Manifesto* (1967), 1. This passage includes scare quotes around "Life" and "society" that were removed in the Olympia Press edition. I quote from the copy held by the Dobkin Family Collection of Feminism, with thanks.

91 Melissa D. Deem, "From Bobbitt to SCUM: Re-memberment, Scatological Rhetorics, and Feminist Strategies in the Contemporary United States," *Public Culture* 9 (1996): 527.

92 Solanas, *SCUM Manifesto*, 13. Deem, "From Bobbitt to SCUM," 531.

93 Lyon, *Manifestoes,* 175.

94 The defaced edition was discovered by Laura Winkiel.

95 Laura Winkiel, "The 'Sweet Assassin' and the Performative Politics of *SCUM Manifesto*," in *The Queer Sixties,* ed. Patricia Juliana Smith (New York: Routledge, 1999), 74.

96 Sara Warner and Mary Jo Watts, "Hide and Go Seek: Child's Play as Archival Act in Valerie Solanas's *SCUM Manifesto*," *TDR: The Drama Review* 58, no. 4 (2014): 91. I am grateful to Sara Warner for answering my questions about the finer points of Solanas's publishing practices.

97 Ibid.

98 Warner and Watts argue that Solanas's very first references to something called the "SCUM Manifesto" were actually to a different text, titled "SCUM (Society for Cutting Up Men)," a one-page A4 flier comprising only two paragraphs and a notice for a SCUM Forum. This time it included an image, though nothing like a reader-seducing face, but a pen-line sketch of a hand flipping the middle finger, which Solanas had also used as the cover art to *Up Your Ass.* A reproduction of this proto-edition is included in Warner and Watts, "Hide and Go Seek," 81.

99 Mary Harron, cited in Dana Heller, "Shooting Solanas: Radical Feminist History and the Technology of Failure," *Feminist Studies* 27, no. 1 (2001): 171.

100 Ibid., 175, 171.

101 Ibid., 186.

102 Sara Warner, *Acts of Gaiety: LGBT Performance and the Politics of Pleasure* (Ann Arbor: University of Michigan Press, 2012), 66.

103 "SCUM will become members of the unwork force, the fuck-up force; they will get jobs of various kinds and unwork." Solanas, *SCUM Manifesto,* 17.

104   Warner, *Acts of Gaiety.*

105   Girodias advanced Solanas $500 for an autobiographical novel, with the promise of a further $1,500. When the novel failed to appear, he accepted Solanas's manuscript of "SCUM Manifesto" in its place.

106   Valerie Solanas, cited in Breanne Fahs, *Valerie Solanas: The Defiant Life of the Woman Who Wrote SCUM (and Shot Andy Warhol)* (New York: Feminist Press, 2014), 299, 297.

107   Solanas's copyright applications are detailed in Warner, *Acts of Gaiety.*

108   Ibid., 52.

109   Solanas, cited in ibid., 35.

110   Valerie Solanas, cited in Mary Harron, "Introduction: On Valerie Solanas," in Mary Harron and Daniel Minahan, *I Shot Andy Warhol* (London: Bloomsbury, 1996), xxvi.

111   Lyon, *Manifestoes,* 10.

112   See Nick Mirzoeff, "On Hardt and Negri's 'Declaration,'" http://www.nicholasmirzoeff.com/O2012/2012/05/09/on-hardt-and-negris-declaration/. Jason Reed, "Revolution in Theory/Theorizing Revolution: On Hardt and Negri's Declaration," http://www.unemployednegativity.com/2012/05/revolution-in-theorytheorizing.html. A print edition of *Declaration,* at a more typical price, was issued at a later date.

113   This echoes the design of *Quaderni rossi,* a journal foundational to the Italian Operaismo movement with which Negri was of course closely associated. As Mario Tronti recalls: "*Quaderni rossi* was a beautiful title for a journal, with an evocative simplicity, eloquent in itself. 'Notebooks' expressed the will for research, analysis and study. The red of the cover was the sign of a decision, a commitment to be *this.* To start the writing, and therefore the reading, on the front cover—black on red—was a brilliant idea on Panzieri's part." Mario Tronti, "Our Operaismo," trans. Eleanor Chiari, *New Left Review* 73 (2012): 123. For discussion of the materiality of publishing in Operaismo, see the excellent essay by Steve Wright, "'I Came Like the Thunder and I Vanish Like the Wind': Exploring Genre Repertoire and Document Work in the Assemblea Operai e Studenti of 1969," *Archival Science* 12, no. 4 (2012): 411–36.

114   Michael Hardt and Antonio Negri, *Declaration* (n.p.: Argo Navis Author Services, 2012).

115   Ibid.

116   Paul Mason, "Why Israel Is Losing the Social Media War over Gaza," http://blogs.channel4.com/paul-mason-blog/impact-social-media-israel gaza-conflict/1182.

117 I have discussed this in Nicholas Thoburn, "Vacuoles of Noncommunication: Minor Politics, Communist Style, and the Multitude," in *Deleuze and the Contemporary World*, ed. Ian Buchanan and Adrian Parr, 42–56 (Edinburgh: Edinburgh University Press, 2006).

118 Gilles Deleuze, *Negotiations 1972–1990*, trans. Martin Joughin (New York: Columbia University Press, 1995), 175.

119 Gilles Deleuze, *Cinema 2: The Time-Image*, trans. Hugh Tomlinson and Robert Galeta (London: Athlone Books, 1989), 269.

120 Ibid., 262.

121 Deleuze, *Negotiations*, 129.

122 Jodi Dean, *Blog Theory: Feedback and Capture in the Circuits of Drive* (Cambridge: Polity Press, 2010), 95.

123 Jodi Dean, "Communicative Capitalism and Class Struggle," *Spheres* 1 (2014): 6.

124 Dean, *Blog Theory*, 95.

125 Beverley Skeggs and Simon Yuill, "Capital Experimentation with Person/a Formation: How Facebook's Monetization Refigures the Relationship between Property, Personhood and Protest," *Information, Communication, and Society* 19, no. 3 (2016).

126 Robert W. Gehl, "The Archive and the Processor: The Internal Logic of Web 2.0," *New Media and Society* 13, no. 8 (2011): 1232.

127 Skeggs and Yuill, "Capital Experimentation with Person/a Formation," 5.

128 Ibid. Ippolita, *The Facebook Aquarium: The Resistible Rise of Anarcho-Capitalism*, trans. Patrice Riemens and Cecile Landman (Amsterdam: Institute of Network Cultures, 2015).

129 Dean, "Communicative Capitalism and Class Struggle," 9, emphasis added.

130 Jodi Dean, *Publicity's Secret: How Technoculture Capitalizes on Democracy* (Ithaca, N.Y.: Cornell University Press, 2002). Dean, "Communicative Capitalism and Class Struggle."

131 For extensive critique of activist use of social media, see Lina Dencik and Oliver Leistert, eds., *Critical Perspectives on Social Media Protest: Between Control and Emancipation* (London: Rowman and Littlefield, 2015), and Natalie Fenton, "Left Out? Digital Media, Radical Politics and Social Change," *Information, Communication, and Society* 19, no. 3 (2016): 346–61.

132 For a communist critique of this body of work, see Nicholas Thoburn, "Do Not Be Afraid, Join Us, Come Back? On the 'Idea of Communism' in Our Time," *Cultural Critique* 84 (2013): 1–34.

133 Jodi Dean, *The Communist Horizon* (London: Verso, 2012).

134 Dean, *Blog Theory*, 126.

135   Ibid., 1, 3.

136   Dean, "Communicative Capitalism and Class Struggle," 11.

137   Dean, *Blog Theory*, 3.

138   Ted Striphas, *The Late Age of Print: Everyday Book Culture from Consumerism to Control* (New York: Columbia University Press, 2009), 6.

139   For an excellent recent account of the neoliberal uses of "culture" and "creativity" with regard to governance and literature, see Sarah Brouillette, *Literature and the Creative Economy* (Stanford, Calif.: Stanford University Press, 2014).

140   "Culture is bound to the book. The book as a repository and a receptacle of knowledge becomes identified with knowledge." Maurice Blanchot, "The Absence of the Book," in *The Infinite Conversation,* trans. Susan Hanson (Minneapolis: University of Minnesota Press, 1993), 423.

141   Trish Travis, "Ideas and Commodities: The Image of the Book," MIT Communications Forum, 1999, http://web.mit.edu/comm-forum/papers/travis.html.

142   Laura J. Miller, *Reluctant Capitalists: Bookselling and the Culture of Consumption* (Chicago: University of Chicago Press, 2007), 28.

143   Lucien Febvre and Henri-Jean Martin, *The Coming of the Book,* trans. David Gerard (London: Verso, 1997), 109.

144   Marshall McLuhan, *The Gutenberg Galaxy: The Making of Typographic Man* (Toronto: University of Toronto Press, 1962), 125. Anderson, *Imagined Communities,* 34.

145   Abbott Payson Usher, *History of Mechanical Inventions,* cited in McLuhan, *Gutenberg Galaxy,* 124.

146   Ibid., 132.

147   D. F. McKenzie, "Printers of the Mind: Some Notes on Bibliographical Theories and Printing-House Practices," *Studies in Bibliography* 22 (1969): 1–75. I take this reference from Gitelman, *Paper Knowledge,* 85.

148   See Makdisi, *William Blake and the Impossible History of the 1790s,* 146.

149   Febvre and Martin, *Coming of the Book,* 248, 350.

150   Tim Ingold, *Lines: A Brief History* (London: Routledge, 2007), 127, 128.

151   Ibid.

152   Ibid.

153   Febvre and Martin, *Coming of the Book,* 22, 29.

154   Luther's works represented approximately one-third of all German-language books sold between 1518 and 1525. He was "the first writer who could 'sell' his *new* books on the basis of his name." Anderson, *Imagined Communities,* 39.

155 N. N. Feltes, *Modes of Production of Victorian Novels* (Chicago: University of Chicago Press, 1986), 7.

156 Ibid., 8.

157 Pierre Macherey, *A Theory of Literary Production,* cited in ibid., 8.

158 Miller, *Reluctant Capitalists.* Claire Squires, *Marketing Literature: The Making of Contemporary Writing in Britain* (London: Palgrave Macmillan, 2009). Striphas, *Late Age of Print.*

159 Striphas, *Late Age of Print,* 8, 102.

160 Ibid., 43.

161 George Steiner, "After the Book?," in *On Difficulty and Other Essays* (Oxford: Oxford University Press, 1980), 188–89.

162 See Hayles, *How We Think,* 55–79.

163 Janet Duitsman Cornelius, *When I Can Read My Title Clear: Literacy, Slavery, and Religion in the Antebellum South* (Columbia: University of South Carolina Press, 1991).

164 James Thompson, *Models of Value: Eighteenth-Century Political Economy and the Novel* (Durham, N.C.: Duke University Press, 1996).

165 Ibid., 7.

166 Walter Mignolo, "Signs and Their Transmission: The Question of the Book in the New World," in *Writing without Words: Alternative Literacies in Mesoamerica and the Andes,* ed. Elizabeth Hill Boone and Walter D. Mignolo (London: Duke University Press, 1994), 233.

167 Ibid., 234.

168 D. F. McKenzie, *Bibliography and the Sociology of Texts* (Cambridge: Cambridge University Press, 1999), 41.

169 David Jay Bolter, *Writing Space: The Computer, Hypertext, and the History of Writing* (Hillside, N.J.: Lawrence Erlbaum Associates, 1991), 4.

170 Ibid., 116.

171 Ibid., 117.

172 Ibid., 2.

173 Striphas, *Late Age of Print,* 2.

174 Ibid., 3. Hayles, *How We Think,* 2.

175 In August 2012, Amazon reported that e-book sales outstripped hardback and paperback books combined, at a ratio of 114 to 100. See http://www .guardian.co.uk/books/2012/aug/06/amazon-kindle-ebook-sales-overtake -print.

176 Kim Cascone, cited in Florian Cramer, afterword to *Post-Digital Print: The Mutation of Publishing since 1894,* by Alessandro Ludovico (Eindhoven, Netherlands: Onomatopee, 2012), 162. Cramer credits Cascone with coining the term *post-digital,* with regard to glitch aesthetics in electronic music.

177   Florian Cramer, "What Is Post-Digital?," *Post-Digital Research* 3, no. 1 (2014), http://www.aprja.net/?p=1318.

178   Florian Cramer, "Post-Digital Writing," *Electronic Book Review,* 2012, http://www.electronicbookreview.com/thread/electropoetics/postal.

179   Murphie, "Ghosted Publics," 105.

180   Nina Power, *A Pamphlet about a Book about a Blog* (London: Banner Repeater, 2012).

181   Simon Worthington, "Danger: Contains Books," in *I Read Where I Am: Exploring New Information Cultures,* ed. Mieke Gerritzen, Geert Lovink, and Minke Kampman (Amsterdam: Valiz, 2011), 174. In keeping with the critical sensibility of the post-digital, the purpose of Worthington's intervention here is to break with the distracting and disabling talk of the book's imminent demise and to tip instead into critical engagement with the more pertinent question of the political economy of corporate and small press publishing.

182   Jacques Derrida, *Paper Machine,* trans. Rachel Bowlby (Stanford, Calif.: Stanford University Press, 2005), 17.

183   Johanna Drucker, *SpecLab: Digital Aesthetics and Projects in Speculative Computing* (Chicago: University of Chicago Press, 2009), 166.

184   Jerome McGann, *Radiant Textuality: Literature after the World Wide Web* (New York: Palgrave, 2001), 184.

185   See, among other works, Johanna Drucker, "Diagrammatic Writing," *New Formations* 78 (2013): 83–101, and Drucker, *SpecLab.*

186   Gary Hall, "The Unbound Book: Academic Publishing in the Age of the Infinite Archive," *Journal of Visual Culture* 12, no. 3 (2013): 497. See also Joost Kircz and Adriaan van der Weel, eds., *The Unbound Book* (Amsterdam: Amsterdam University Press, 1994).

187   http://p-dpa.net.

188   Silvio Lorusso, Post-Digital Publishing Archive, https://ia600509.us .archive.org/15/items/p-dpa_booklet/p-dpa_booklet.pdf.

189   Cramer, "What Is Post-Digital?"

190   Cramer, "Post-Digital Writing."

191   These fairs and institutions have all been established since 2000, with the exception of the London Anarchist Bookfair, first held in 1983; Book Works, established in 1984; Franklin Furnace, established by Martha Wilson in 1976; and Printed Matter, founded by Lucy Lippard, Sol LeWitt, and others in 1976.

192   "AND About," http://www.andpublishing.org/events/coming-soon/.

193   Simon Reynolds, *Retromania: Pop Culture's Addiction to Its Own Past* (London: Faber and Faber, 2012). Jess Baines, "Radical Print Revolution? Objects under Capitalism," *STRIKE!* 8 (2014): 20–21.

194   Derrida, *Paper Machine,* 47.

195 Hayles, *Writing Machines*, 29–34.
196 Christina Kiaer, *Imagine No Possessions: The Socialist Objects of Russian Constructivism* (Cambridge, Mass.: MIT Press, 2005).
197 Deleuze, *Cinema 2*, 150. Gilles Deleuze, *Essays Critical and Clinical*, trans. Daniel W. Smith and Michael A. Greco (Minneapolis: University of Minnesota Press, 1997), 118.

2. COMMUNIST OBJECTS AND SMALL PRESS PAMPHLETS

1 Guy Debord to Ivan Chtcheglov, April 30, 1963, http://www.notbored.org/debord-30April1963.html. In a later text written at the time of the demise of the Situationist International, Debord's ambivalence about the journal form extends also to its role of "holding on to a base," where its periodicity is tied to conservative habits of consumption. Ending the journal has the merit, as he sees it, of "interrupt[ing] the conditioned reflex of a spectator crowd . . . who had awaited the next number of the review which it had picked up the habit of consuming, so as to bring to light its 'knowledge' and its dreamed of orthodoxy." "It seemed to us . . . better to cease the publication of a review which was beginning to enjoy a too routinish success. Other forms of situationist expression are more suitable to the new epoch." Unattributed [Guy Debord], "Notes to Serve towards the History of the S.I. from 1969–1971," in *The Veritable Split in the International*, by Situationist International (London: B. M. Chronos, 1985), 73, 74.
2 Jean-Luc Nancy, *The Inoperative Community*, trans. Peter Connor et al. (Minneapolis: University of Minnesota Press, 1991).
3 Jacques Rancière, *The Nights of Labor: The Workers' Dream in the Nineteenth Century*, trans. John Drury (Philadelphia: Temple University Press, 1989), 8.
4 Ibid.
5 Ibid.
6 Rancière, cited in Donald Reid, "Introduction," ibid., xxxi.
7 Ibid., xxxv.
8 Jacques Rancière, *Mute Speech: Literature, Critical Theory, and Politics* (New York: Columbia University Press, 2011), 58–59.
9 Ibid., 59.
10 Kiaer, *Imagine No Possessions*, 33.
11 Rodchenko, in ibid., 1. While the casual way that Rodchenko deploys slavery for metaphoric effect is objectionable, the relation he names contains the appalling truth that the social form of slavery reduced people to a-social and alienable units of property, precisely to the form of commodity object. Also problematic is his identification here of the racial trope of blackness with passivity (the sorry state of the "black and mournful"),

though blackness figures later in the letter in a more critical manner, as the "black work" of "reprisal against [the commodity's] oppressors." Aleksandr Rodchenko, *Experiments of the Future: Diaries, Essays, Letters, and Other Writings,* ed. Alexander N. Lavrentiev, trans. Jamey Gambrell (New York: MoMA, 2005), 169.

12 Kiaer, *Imagine No Possessions,* 7.

13 Boris Arvatov, "Everyday Life and the Culture of the Thing (toward the Formulation of the Question)," trans. Christina Kiaer, *October* 81 (1997): 120.

14 Ibid., 121, 126.

15 Ibid., 123.

16 Ibid., 123, 124.

17 Karl Marx, "Economic and Philosophical Manuscripts," in *Early Writings,* trans. trans. Rodney Livingstone and Gregor Benton, 279–400 (Harmondsworth, U.K.: Penguin, 1975), 352.

18 Arvatov, "Everyday Life and the Culture of the Thing," 122.

19 Karl Marx, *Capital: A Critique of Political Economy,* trans. Ben Fowkes (Harmondsworth, U.K.: Penguin, 1976), 1:165.

20 Ibid.

21 "Communisation and Value-Form Theory," *Endnotes* 2 (2010): 79.

22 Peter Stallybrass, "Marx's Coat," in *Border Fetishisms: Material Objects in Unstable Spaces,* ed. Patricia Spyer (New York: Routledge, 1998), 184. Whether Marx was fully aware of the joke he had made here or was using fetishism in a more conventional fashion to name a social illusion and, by way of analogy, undermine the pretensions to rationality of capitalist modernity is a moot point. For an exploration of the many dimensions of Marx's use of the anthropological concept of fetishism in currency at the time, see William Pietz, "Fetishism and Materialism: The Limits of Theory in Marx," in *Fetishism as Cultural Discourse,* ed. Emily Apter and William Pietz, 119–51 (Ithaca, N.Y.: Cornell University Press, 1993).

23 Arvatov, "Everyday Life and the Culture of the Thing," 121, 124.

24 Marx, "Economic and Philosophical Manuscripts," 352.

25 Ibid., 352, 390. As Peter Pels remarks, this passage does not at all exclude the possibility that "to be sensuous is 'to be subjected to the actions of another *thing*.'" Pels, "The Spirit of Matter: On Fetish, Rarity, Fact, and Fancy," in Spyer, *Border Fetishisms,* 101.

26 Arvatov, "Everyday Life and the Culture of the Thing," 126.

27 Boris Arvatov, "From *Art and Class* (1923)," in *The Tradition of Constructivism,* ed. Stephen Bann (London: Thames and Hudson, 1974), 45, 46.

28 Cited in Kiaer, *Imagine No Possessions,* 49.

29 Arvatov, "Everyday Life and the Culture of the Thing," 127. I should note that Arvatov's argument also contains a more conventional understanding of the conquest and mastery of nature.

30 Ibid., 128.

31 Ibid., 48, 47.

32 Lenin's proselytizing for Taylorism and labor discipline and Trotsky's championing of the "militarization of labor" are the overt expressions of this problem. See Thoburn, "Do Not Be Afraid."

33 Marx, "Economic and Philosophical Manuscripts," 351. Quotation of this passage from Marx can be found on two consecutive pages of the *Arcades Project*, one of which is the occasion for Benjamin to "deduce" the political import of the collector's critique of use. Walter Benjamin, *The Arcades Project*, trans. Howard Eiland and Kevin McLaughlin (Cambridge, Mass.: Harvard University Press, 2002), 209, 210.

34 Marx, "Economic and Philosophical Manuscripts," 352.

35 Ibid., 209, emphasis added. Theodor W. Adorno, "Exchange with Theodor W. Adorno on the Essay: 'Paris, the Capital of the Nineteenth Century,'" in Walter Benjamin, *Walter Benjamin: Selected Writings*. Vol. 3, *1935–1938*, ed. Michael W. Jennings, Howard Eiland, and Gary Smith (Cambridge, Mass.: Harvard University Press, 2002), 61.

36 Benjamin, *Arcades Project*, 9.

37 Ibid., 205, 206.

38 Esther Leslie, "Telescoping the Microscopic Object: Benjamin the Collector," in *The Optic of Walter Benjamin*, ed. Alex Coles (London: Black Dog, 2001), 80. Benjamin, *Arcades Project*, 206.

39 Benjamin, "Unpacking My Library," in *Illuminations*, ed. Hannah Arendt, trans. Harry Zohn (New York: Schocken Books, 2007), 60.

40 For Benjamin's critique of work, see Benjamin, "Theses on the Philosophy of History," in Benjamin, *Illuminations*, 259.

41 Benjamin, *Arcades Project*, 475, 204. Stephen Zepke has shown that a related formulation can be found in Mikhail Bakhtin's understanding of the work of art, which "emerges from a process that first of all 'isolates' something from its self-evidence in the world, giving it an 'active indetermination' within reality." Zepke, "From Aesthetic Autonomy to Autonomist Aesthetics: Art and Life in Guattari," in *The Guattari Effect*, ed. Éric Alliez and Andrew Goffey (New York: Continuum Books, 2011), 209.

42 Cesare Casarino, *Modernity at Sea: Melville, Marx, Conrad in Crisis* (Minneapolis: University of Minnesota Press, 2002), xxvii.

43 Ibid.

44 Benjamin, "Unpacking My Library," 60. N. A. Basbanes, *A Gentle Madness: Bibliophiles, Bibliomanes, and the Eternal Passion for Books* (New York: Henry Holt, 1999).

45 Benjamin, "Thesis on the Philosophy of History," 261, 262.

46 Benjamin, cited in Erdmut Wizisla, preface to *Walter Benjamin's Archive: Images, Texts, Signs,* ed. Ursula Marx, trans. Esther Leslie (London: Verso, 2007), 5.

47 Benjamin, "Unpacking My Library," 67.

48 Benjamin, cited in Ackbar Abbas, "Walter Benjamin's Collector: The Fate of Modern Experience," in *Modernity and the Text: Revisions of German Modernism,* ed. Andreas Huyssen and David Bathrick (New York: Columbia University Press 1989), 216.

49 Benjamin, "Unpacking My Library," 67. Douglas Crimp, *On the Museum's Ruins* (Cambridge, Mass.: MIT Press, 1993), 204.

50 Benjamin, *Charles Baudelaire: A Lyric Poet in the Era of High Capitalism,* trans. Harry Zohn (London: Verso, 1983), 181, 182.

51 André Breton, *Mad Love,* trans. Mary Ann Caws (Lincoln: University of Nebraska Press, 1988), 126.

52 Ibid., 28, 36.

53 Romy Golan, "Triangulating the Surrealist Fetish," *Visual Anthropology Review* 10, no. 1 (1994): 50–65.

54 Gilles Deleuze and Félix Guattari, "Balance-Sheet Program for Desiring Machines," in Félix Guattari, *Chaosophy,* ed. Sylvère Lotringer (New York: Semiotext(e), 1995), 135.

55 Denis Hollier, "The Use-Value of the Impossible," trans. Liesl Ollman, *October* 60 (1992): 20.

56 Georges Bataille, in ibid., 22.

57 Pels, "Spirit of Matter," 99.

58 William Pietz, "The Problem of the Fetish, I," *Res* 9 (1985): 5, 7.

59 Pels, "Spirit of Matter," 98.

60 Ibid.

61 Bakker's *Untitled Project: Commodity [Capital]* was exhibited at *The Irresistible Force* at London's Tate Modern in 2007 and was temporarily available for mail order at the same price as the Penguin edition.

62 Trish Travis, "Ideas and Commodities: The Image of the Book," http://web.mit.edu/comm-forum/papers/travis.html.

63 William Everson, "From the Poem as Icon—Reflections on Printing as a Fine Art," in *A Book of the Book: Some Work and Projections about the Book and Writing,* ed. Jerome Rothenberg and Steven Clay (New York: Granary Books, 2000), 50.

64 Benjamin, "Unpacking My Library," 66.
65 Walter Benjamin, "One-Way Street (Selection)," in *Reflections: Essays, Aphorisms, Autobiographical Writings,* trans. Edmund Jephcott (New York: Schocken Books, 1978), 61.
66 Agnes Blaha, "Tackling Tactility—What Is It That Makes Theorists Shy Away from the Haptic Domain?," in *NO-ISBN: On Self-Publishing,* ed. Bernhard Cella, Leo Findeisen, and Agnes Blaha, 277–84 (Cologne, Germany: Buchhandlung Walther König, 2015), 281.
67 Philip Dormer Stanhope, cited in Price, *How to Do Things with Books in Victorian Britain,* 3.
68 Benjamin, "Unpacking My Library," 62.
69 Theodor W. Adorno, "Bibliographical Musings," in *Notes to Literature* (New York: Columbia University Press, 1992), 2:21.
70 Ibid., 2:23.
71 Ibid., 2:20.
72 Ibid., 2:28.
73 Ibid., 2:21.
74 Theodor W. Adorno, *Minima Moralia: Reflections from Damaged Life,* trans. E. F. N. Jephcott (New York: Verso, 2005), 80, 101.
75 Adorno, "Bibliographical Musings," 2:25.
76 Ibid., 2:26
77 Ibid., 2:25.
78 Fredric Jameson, *Marxism and Form: Twentieth Century Dialectical Theories of Literature* (Princeton, N.J.: Princeton University Press, 1971), 7.
79 Adorno, "Bibliographic Musings," 2:30.
80 Ibid.
81 Ibid.
82 Ibid.
83 Ibid.
84 Ibid.
85 Ibid.
86 Ibid., 2:29.
87 Jameson, *Marxism and Form,* 8.
88 Adorno, "Bibliographical Musings," 2:31.
89 Ibid., 2:23.
90 I am not suggesting a historically continuous object over this period. As a mutable assemblage of changing technical skills, printing practices and conventions, materials, financial paradigms, reading habits, political constituencies, distribution circuits, and so on, the nature of the pamphlet has been a highly various object over time and place.

91   Drucker, *Century of Artists' Books,* 358, 8.

92   Price, *How to Do Things with Books,* 13.

93   Iain Sinclair, *Lights Out for the Territory: 9 Excursions in the Secret History of London* (London: Granta Books, 1997), 25.

94   Jason Skeet and Mark Pawson, *Counter Intelligence: Catalogue of Self-Published and Autonomous Print-Creations* (London, 1995).

95   See http://www.guest-room.net/.

96   Stéphane Mallarmé, "The Book: A Spiritual Instrument," trans. Bradford Cook, in *Critical Theory since Plato,* ed. Hazard Adams (New York: Harcourt Brace, 1971), 690, 691.

97   Gilles Deleuze, *The Fold: Leibniz and the Baroque,* trans. Tom Conley (Minneapolis: University of Minnesota Press, 1993), 31. Gilles Deleuze, *Proust and Signs,* trans. Richard Howard (New York: Braziller, 1972), 98, 103.

98   Deleuze, *The Fold,* 31.

99   Adorno, "Bibliographic Musings," 20.

100 Ibid., 27.

101 Deleuze, *Proust and Signs,* 100.

102 Ibid., 109, 101.

103 Deleuze, *The Fold,* 31.

104 Ibid., 86.

105 Beni Memorial Library, "The 'On Organization' Pamphlet—A Bibliographical Dissection," 1976, one A4 page.

106 Ibid.

107 Drucker, *Century of Artists' Books,* 358.

108 Henriette Heise and Jakob Jakobsen, "Info 2," http://infocentre.antipool .org/. The collaborative practice at Infopool included a number of people, most especially Anthony Davies, Emma Hedditch, and Howard Slater.

109 Infopool, "Operation Re-appropriation: Infopool @ Tate Modern, 9.2.2001," http://infopool.antipool.org/tate.htm.

110 Ibid.

111 Ibid.

112 Jakob Jakobsen, interview with the author, July 16, 2007.

113 Arvatov, cited in Kiaer, *Imagine No Possessions,* 68.

114 Infopool, "Operation Re-appropriation."

115 Derrida, *Paper Machine,* 42.

116 Joad Raymond, *Pamphlets and Pamphleteering in Early Modern Britain* (Cambridge: Cambridge University Press, 2003).

117 Ibid., 38, 39.

118 Ibid., 10.

119 Fabian Tompsett, interview with the author, September 8, 2013.

120 Drucker, *Century of Artists' Books,* 197.

121 Jakobsen, interview.

122 Jakob Jakobsen, "A New Table, Which Might Not Be Understood as Clean in Modern Terms," http://infopool.antipool.org/table.htm. This is one of two or three moments in *Anti-Book* that indicate possible contributions to an environmental politics of media. The ravaging effects of the energy-guzzling server farms, upgrade imperatives, precious metal mines, electronic waste, and so forth, that accompany the not-so-immaterial flow of digital information make a socioenvironmental politics of media materialities all too urgent. See Richard Maxwell and Toby Miller, *Greening the Media* (Oxford: Oxford University Press, 2012).

123 Benjamin, "Unpacking My Library," 68.

124 Adorno, *Minima Moralia,* 50. The words in the first quotation are by Joel Burges, from his "Adorno's Mimeograph: The Uses of Obsolescence in *Minima Moralia,*" *New German Critique* 40, no. 1 (2013): 72.

125 Adorno, *Minima Moralia,* 51.

126 It is worth underscoring how different Adorno's appreciation of the outmoded is to a fixation on the past: "The quest for an age past not only fails to indicate the way home but forfeits all consistency; the arbitrary conservation of the obsolete compromises what it wants to conserve, and with a bad conscience it obdurately opposes whatever is new." Adorno, *Philosophy of New Music,* cited in Burges, "Adorno's Mimeograph," 68.

127 See Burges, ibid. James Schmidt, "Language, Mythology, and Enlightenment: Historical Notes on Horkheimer and Adorno's *Dialectic of Enlightenment,*" *Social Research* 65, no. 4 (1998): 807–38.

128 Schmidt, "Language, Mythology, and Enlightenment," 811.

129 Ibid.

130 Cited in Raymond, *Pamphlets and Pamphleteering,* 5.

131 See http://www.56a.org.uk/archive.html.

132 Chris, interview with the author, July 12, 2007.

133 Ibid.

134 Ibid.

135 Ibid.

136 Adorno, "Bibliographic Musings," 24.

137 Ibid., 29.

138 Ibid.

139 Chris, interview.

140 Leslie, "Telescoping the Microscopic Object," 68.

141 Ibid.

142   Gilles Deleuze and Félix Guattari, *What Is Philosophy?*, trans. Graham Burchell and Hugh Tomlinson (London: Verso, 1994), 167–68, 176–77.

143   Hollier, "Use-Value of the Impossible," 23.

144   Ibid.

145   Andrew Feenberg and Jim Freedman, eds., *When Poetry Ruled the Streets: The French May Events of 1968* (New York: State University of New York, 2001).

146   Atelier Populaire, *Posters from the Revolution: Paris, May 1968* (London: Dobson Books, 1969), emphasis added.

147   This quotation from Judge Achille Gallucci's 1979 warrant is cited in the introduction to Antonio Negri, *Books for Burning: Between Civil War and Democracy in 1970s Italy,* ed. Timothy S. Murphy, trans. Arianna Bove et al. (New York: Verso, 2005), xiii.

148   Raymond, *Pamphlets and Pamphleteering,* 7.

149   For an introduction to the history and politics of U.K. cooperative print shops, see Jess Baines, "Free Radicals," *Afterall,* http://www.afterall.org /online/radical.printmaking/#.VbCwzYudLzI.

150   Ibid.

151   Ār. Im. Jūnz, *Tajrubīyāt-i Kumītah'hā-yi Kār'garī dar Inqilāb-i Rūsīyah,* trans. Kāvah (London: Unpopular Books, 1979). Jean Barrot [Gilles Dauvé], *What Is Communism* (London: Unpopular Books, 1983).

152   Fabian Tompsett, interview with the author, June 5, 2007.

153   Karl Marx to Wilhelm Blos, November 10, 1877, cited in Jacques Camatte and Gianni Collu, "About the Organisation," in Jacques Camatte, *Capital and Community: The Results of the Immediate Process of Production and the Economic Work of Marx,* trans. David Brown (London: Unpopular Books, 1988), https://www.marxists.org/archive/camatte/capcom/index.htm.

154   Unpopular Books, preface to *What Is Situationism: Critique of the Situationist International,* by Jean Barrot (London: Unpopular Books, 1987), 2.

155   Jørgen Nash, cited in Mikkel Bolt Rasmussen and Jakob Jakobsen, eds., *Expect Anything Fear Nothing: The Situationist Movement in Scandinavia and Elsewhere* (Copenhagen: Nebula, 2011), 223.

156   The text is taken from a photograph of a Popular Book Centre.

157   Asger Jorn, cited in Simon Crook, "Moving Mountains: 'Shamanic' Rock Art and the International of Experimental Artists," *Transgressions: A Journal of Urban Exploration* 4 (1998): 42. This split in the Situationist International, pertaining among other things to dispute concerning the revolutionary role of "art," is addressed in the first book published by Unpopular Books. See Stewart Home, *The Assault on Culture: Utopian Currents from Lettrisme to Class War* (London: Aporia Press/Unpopular Books, 1988).

158   "kArt Boo," unattributed, unpublished, and undated four-page typed manuscript by Fabian Tompsett, [1994].

159 Ibid., 2.

160 Ibid., 1.

161 Ibid.

162 Ibid. The title of kArt Boo seeks to foreground this, and Tompsett mentions, as an example, uneven exposure of text during platemaking and the insertion of ordinary typing into otherwise beautifully typeset pages, though my personal favorite is the typographic destabilization of the Poplar locale of Unpopular Books in the colophon to Daniel Lux, *The Camden Parasites* (London: Unpoplar Books, 1999).

163 Tompsett, interview, June 5, 2007.

164 I make this point hesitantly, because Tompsett has shown little sympathy for Marxist critiques that are weighted too heavily on the causality of the abstract, critiques that "sweep the real world—i.e. the sensuous world which we move around in—into the dustbin of history, so that we are met by simple abstract forces." It is only through concrete mediation that the abstract exists, and it is in such mediation where politics lies, not in a metaphysical struggle between abstract categories. F. T. [Fabian Tompsett], "Hegel on Acid: Response to 'Marxists and the So-Called Problem of Imperialism,'" [1988], http://libcom.org/library/hegel-on-acid-a-response-to-marxists-and-the-so-called-problem-of-imperialism.

165 "kArt Boo."

166 Asger Jorn, *Open Creation and Its Enemies,* trans. Fabian Tompsett (London: Unpopular Books, 1994), 47.

167 Raymond, *Pamphlets and Pamphleteering.*

168 McLuhan, *Gutenberg Galaxy,* 125.

169 Tompsett, interview, June 5, 2007. One cover places the pamphlet in relation to Jorn's wayfaring habits, with an image of a lithograph of Jorn astride a BSA motorcycle in front of the Eiffel Tower; the other indicates Jorn's interests in material form that I am pursuing here, with its image of the somewhat talismanic memorial stone he fabricated for his syndicalist friend Christian Christensen.

170 Tompsett, interview, June 5, 2007.

171 Walter Benjamin, *Charles Baudelaire: A Lyric Poet in the Era of High Capitalism,* trans. Harry Zohn (London: Verso, 1983), 55.

172 Stéphane Mallarmé, cited in Maurice Blanchot, *The Book to Come,* trans. Charlotte Mandell (Stanford, Calif.: Stanford University Press, 2002), 229.

173 Jorn, *Open Creation,* 32.

3. ROOT, FASCICLE, RHIZOME

1 Elizabeth L. Eisenstein, *The Printing Press as Agent of Change* (Cambridge: Cambridge University Press, 1980). Darnton, *Forbidden Best-Sellers*. Lucien Febvre and Henri-Jean Martin, *The Coming of the Book: The Impact of Printing 1450–1800*, trans. David Gerard (New York: Verso Books, 1997).

2 Jacques Derrida, *Of Grammatology*, trans. Gayatri Chakravorty Spivak (London: Johns Hopkins University Press, 1974), 18.

3 John Mowitt, *Text: The Geneaology of an Antidisciplinary Object* (Durham, N.C.: Duke University Press, 1992), 101.

4 For a materialist critique of Derrida's earlier formulations of the book, as well as one of the few engagements with Deleuze and Guattari's typology of the book, see Daniel Selcer's fascinating work *Philosophy and the Book* (London: Continuum, 2010), 6–10, 194–202.

5 Maurice Blanchot, "The Absence of the Book," in *The Infinite Conversation*, trans. Susan Hanson (Minneapolis: University of Minnesota Press, 1993), 424.

6 "We are writing this book as a rhizome. It is composed of plateaus.... To attain the multiple, one must have a method that effectively constructs it." Deleuze and Guattari, *A Thousand Plateaus*, 22.

7 At one point, they assess Artaud's spell for Hitler as a "BwO intensity map" of thresholds and waves, but only with regard to its textual content. Ibid., 164.

8 Gilles Deleuze and Félix Guattari, *Kafka: Towards a Minor Literature*, trans. Dana Polan (Minneapolis: University of Minnesota, 1986), 96.

9 Félix Guattari, *The Anti-Oedipus Papers*, ed. Stéphane Nadaud, trans. Kélina Gotman (Los Angeles, Calif.: Semiotext(e), 2006), 400.

10 Ibid., 343–44, 352, 371.

11 Deleuze, *Negotiations*, 144. Foucault, in Gilles Deleuze and Félix Guattari, *Anti-Oedipus: Capitalism and Schizophrenia Volume 1*, trans. Robert Hurley, Mark Seem, and Helen R. Lane (Minneapolis: University of Minnesota Press, 1983), xiii.

12 Selcer, *Philosophy and the Book*, 199.

13 Ernst Robert Curtius, *European Literature and the Latin Middle Ages*, trans. Willard R. Trask (Princeton, N.J.: Princeton University Press, 1953), 310.

14 Francis Bacon, *The Advancement of Learning* (Oxford: Clarendon Press, 1885).

15 Walter Mignolo, "From *Signs and Their Transmission: The Question of the Book in the New World*," in *A Book of the Book*, ed. Jerome Rothenberg and Steven Clay (New York: Granary Books, 2000), 351.

16 Jacques Verger, cited in Alain Boureau, "Franciscan Piety and Voracity: Uses and Strategems in the Hagiographic Pamphlet," in *The Culture of Print: Power and the Uses of Print in Early Modern Europe,* ed. Roger Chartier, trans. Lydia G. Cochrane (Cambridge: Polity Press, 1989), 17.

17 James Kearney, *The Incarnate Text: Imagining the Book in Reformation England* (Philadelphia: University of Pennsylvania Press, 2009), 17.

18 Martin Luther, cited in ibid., 24.

19 Kearney, *Incarnate Text,* 24.

20 Ibid., 38.

21 Deleuze and Guattari, *A Thousand Plateaus,* 127.

22 Ibid., 123.

23 Ibid., 124.

24 Ibid., 131.

25 For further discussion of the semiopolitics of monomania, see Nicholas Thoburn, "Weatherman, the Militant Diagram, and the Problem of Political Passion," *New Formations* 68 (2010): 125–42.

26 Deleuze and Guattari, *A Thousand Plateaus,* 122.

27 Ibid., 127.

28 Kearney, *Incarnate Text,* 10.

29 See ibid., 10–11.

30 Ibid., 11.

31 Pierre Bersuire, *Dictionarium seu reportorium morale,* [1355], cited in ibid., 14.

32 John Fisher, "Sermon . . . preached vpon a good Friday" [1531–34], cited in Kearney, *Incarnate Text,* 5.

33 Thomas Müntzer, cited in ibid., 23.

34 Deleuze and Guattari, *A Thousand Plateaus,* 127.

35 Mallarmé, "The Book: A Spiritual Instrument," 690.

36 For Marx and Engels, Max Stirner's *The Ego and Its Own* functions as "the perfect book, the Holy Book." It posits "the history of the kingdom of the unique [that] follows a wise plan fixed from eternity," a plan based on the egoists "delirious fantasy," in Stirner's words, of "the world as it is for me." Marx and Engels, *Collected Works,* 5:117, 126.

37 Daniel Leese, "A Single Spark: Origins and Spread of the Little Red Book," in *Mao's Little Red Book: A Global History,* ed. Alexander C. Cook (Cambridge: Cambridge University Press, 2014), 23. Roderick MacFarquhar and Michael Schoenhals, *Mao's Last Revolution* (Cambridge, Mass.: Harvard University Press, 2006), 240. The Bible is estimated at 5–6 billion copies published and the Qur'an at 800 million. Carl Wilkinson, *The Observer Book of Books* (Reading, U.K.: Observer Books, 2008), 29.

38 Mao himself remarked on the power of *Quotations,* writing in a 1966 letter to his wife, Jiang Qing, "I have never believed . . . that those little books of mine could have such fantastic magic, yet he [Lin Biao] blew them up, and the whole country followed." Mao, cited in Ross Terrill, *Mao: A Biography* (Stanford, Calif.: Stanford University Press, 1999), 370. Many thanks to Chung Yan Priscilla Kam for translating some of these and other posters from the Cultural Revolution.

39 Slavoj Žižek, "Mao Tse-Tung, the Marxist Lord of Misrule," in Mao Tse-Tung, *Slavoj Žižek Presents Mao on Practice and Contradiction* (London: Verso Books, 2007), 10.

40 Mao Tse-tung, "Analysis of the Classes in Chinese Society" (1926), in *Selected Works of Mao Tse-tung* (Peking: Foreign Languages Press, 1965), 1:22; Mao Tse-Tung, *Quotations from Chairman Mao Tse-tung* (Peking: Foreign Languages Press, 1966), 214.

41 Mao Zedong, "Talk on Questions of Philosophy" (1964), cited in Žižek, "Mao Tse-tung, the Marxist Lord of Misrule," 9.

42 Robert Jay Lifton, *Revolutionary Immortality: Mao Tse-tung and the Chinese Cultural Revolution* (Harmondsworth, U.K.: Penguin, 1970), 49.

43 Mao, *Quotations,* 260.

44 Mao in 1958, cited in Stuart Schram, *The Thought of Mao Tse-tung* (New York: Cambridge University Press, 1989), 128.

45 Cited in Lifton, *Revolutionary Immortality,* 72.

46 Mao, *Quotations,* 174.

47 Lifton, *Revolutionary Immortality,* 67.

48 Mao, *Quotations,* 201.

49 Ibid., 202.

50 Cited in Stuart Schram, *Mao Tse-Tung* (Harmondsworth, U.K.: Penguin, 1966), 295.

51 Lin Biao, cited in Alexander C. Cook, "Introduction: The Spiritual Atom Bomb and Its Global Fallout," in Cook, *Mao's Little Red Book,* 8.

52 Estimates of the death toll in eleven leading texts are tabulated in the Wikipedia entry for the Great Leap Forward, between 23 and 46 million people. The slogan quoted here is taken from Henry Yuhuai He, *Dictionary of the Political Thought of the People's Republic of China* (New York: East Gate Books, 2001), 413. For recent documentary analysis of the Great Leap Forward, see Yang Jisheng, *Tombstone: The Untold Story of Mao's Great Famine,* trans. Stacy Mosher and Guo Jian (London: Allen Lane, 2012).

53 Mao, cited Jung Chang and Jon Halliday, *Mao: The Unknown Story* (London: Jonathan Cape, 2007), 505.

54 Mao, *Slavoj Žižek Presents Mao on Practice and Contradiction,* 44. The source of the second quotation is not given, cited in Lifton, *Revolutionary Immortality,* 72. This is an opportunity to note that the subjective purity of Mao Zedong Thought is not the same thing as a commitment to principles; Mao, ever the politician, was perfectly capable of sacrificing his principles in the pursuit and maintenance of power, such that the corpus of his Thought in the *Selected Works* required careful editing and revision, and, unlike the other socialist demagogues, no "complete works" was published. Simon Leys, "Aspects of Mao Zedong," in *The Hall of Uselessness: Collected Essays,* 383–88 (New York: New York Review of Books, 2013).

55 For the more specific features of this metaphoric identification of Mao's Thought with nuclear fission, notably with regard to the energy derived from *splitting* in Mao's dialectical schema of "one divides into two," see Cook, "Introduction: The Spiritual Atom Bomb and Its Global Fallout."

56 Cited in Xing Lu, *Rhetoric of the Chinese Cultural Revolution* (Columbia: University of South Carolina Press, 2004), 65.

57 This structure of thematic selections arose not, as one might have assumed, from an effort to condense a larger book, at least not directly so, but from a *card file* system. The *Tianjin Daily* had found this means of thematically arranging famous passages from Mao's *Selected Works* to be an effective solution to the difficult task of sourcing suitable quotations of Mao's Thought to accompany each day's news stories. It is a neat reminder of the contingent and overdetermined nature of sociotechnical invention, as is the fact that the book's red plastic covers were not as inevitable a choice as they now appear, for two trial bindings of *Quotations* were made in light and dark blue, and, while the volumes used by PLA brigade teams were covered in red vinyl, in the first edition, high-ranking individual officers received copies in printed paper wrappers. The first trial editions were also of a slightly larger format; it was the need to have them fit neatly into the pockets of military uniforms that caused their unusually diminutive, and now so iconic, format. See Daniel Leese, *Mao Cult: Rhetoric and Ritual in the Cultural Revolution* (Cambridge: Cambridge University Press, 2011), 109–10, 112. Oliver Lei Han, "Sources and Early Printing History of Chairman Mao's *Quotations,* " 2004, 4, http://www.bibsocamer.org/BibSite/Han/index.html.

58 Leese, "A Single Spark," 31. Andrew F. Jones, "Quotation Songs," in Cook, *Mao's Little Red Book,* 46.

59 Cited in Jiaqi Yan and Gao Gao, *Turbulent Decade: A History of the Cultural Revolution,* trans. Daniel W. Y. Kwok (Honolulu: University of Hawaii Press, 1996), 179–80.

60 Deleuze and Guattari, *A Thousand Plateaus,* 127.

61 In Thomas W. Robinson, ed., *The Cultural Revolution in China* (Berkeley: University of California Press, 2001), 509.

62 Leese, "A Single Spark," 27–29.

63 Jones, "Quotation Songs," 46.

64 Rae Yang, cited in Melissa Schrift, *Biography of a Chairman Mao Badge* (New Brunswick, N.J.: Rutgers University Press, 2001), 79–80.

65 Terrill, *Mao,* 318. For photographs of *Quotations*-waving crowds in numerous settings, including Mao's sunrise audiences with the Red Guards, see Jiang Jiehong, *Red: China's Cultural Revolution* (London: Jonathan Cape, 2010).

66 The power of the word is accentuated in Chinese culture by the ideographic form of Chinese characters and the expressive art of calligraphy. The text itself reads, "Study Chairman Mao's writings, follow his teachings and act according to his instructions." On the rise and fall of Lin Biao, see Simon Leys, *The Burning Forest: Essays on Chinese Culture and Politics* (London: Paladin Books, 1988), 138–48.

67 Lu, *Rhetoric of the Chinese Cultural Revolution,* 132–33.

68 Ibid., 133–34.

69 Cited in MacFarquhar and Schoenhals, *Mao's Last Revolution,* 104, 126.

70 Central Committee of the Chinese Communist Party, "Decision Concerning the Great Proletarian Cultural Revolution," August 8, 1966, http:// www.rrojasdatabank.org/16points.htm.

71 Deleuze and Guattari, *A Thousand Plateaus,* 130.

72 Lifton, *Revolutionary Immortality,* 60–62.

73 Simon Leys, *The Chairman's New Clothes: Mao and the Cultural Revolution* (London: Allison and Busby, 1977). See also the incisive 1967 text by the SI, which was informed by the Situationist René Viénet's direct reports from China, Situationist International, "The Explosion Point of Ideology in China," in Knabb, *Situationist International Anthology,* 185–94. The publication of Leys's exposé of the Cultural Revolution, based on his close analysis of events while living in Hong Kong, was encouraged and arranged by Viénet, where it appeared in the latter's "Bibliothèque asiatique" series at Champ Libre. See Laurent Six, "China: How Pierre Ryckmans Became Simon Leys," http://www.notbored.org/leys.pdf.

74 Leys, *Chairman's New Clothes,* 13.

75 Simon Leys, *Chinese Shadows* (Harmondsworth, U.K.: Penguin, 1978), 207–8.

76 Ibid., 191.

77 *Chinois, encore un effort pour être révolutionnaires (a.k.a. Peking Duck Soup),* dir. René Viénet (1977).

78 Lowell Dittmer, "The Structural Evolution of 'Criticism and Self-Criticism,'" *The China Quarterly* 56 (1973): 724.

79 Leese, *Mao Cult,* 121.

80 Deleuze and Guattari, *A Thousand Plateaus,* 127.

81 Mao, *Quotations,* 61.

82 *The Words of the Chairman,* dir. Harun Farocki, http://www.harunfarocki .de/films/1960s/1967/the-words-of-the-chairman.html.

83 Terrill, *Mao,* 318.

84 Deleuze and Guattari, *A Thousand Plateaus,* 5.

85 Ibid., 11.

86 Ibid., 4.

87 Deleuze, *Negotiations,* 8–9.

88 Ibid., 5.

89 Ibid., 21.

90 Deleuze and Guattari, *A Thousand Plateaus,* 3.

91 Ibid., 9.

92 Ibid., 6.

93 Ibid. The choice of targets here is striking, for these three had great significance for Deleuze and Guattari. Guattari apparently had a lifelong obsession with Joyce, albeit that Beckett's sobriety with language has the upper hand in Deleuze and Guattari's work, against Joyce's overloading of text with illusion and metaphor. Borroughs's thought and method against "control" is a source of some considerable importance to their critique of "control society" and communication. And the impact of Nietzsche on Deleuze would of course be hard to exaggerate.

94 Ibid., 22.

95 Ibid.

96 Ibid., 22–23.

97 Ibid., 23–24.

98 Ibid., 520.

99 "Absolutment Nécessaire: The Politics of the Book: An Email Conversation between Jöelle de La Casinière and Andrew Bonacina," http:// dl.dropboxusercontent.com/u/32871722/Exhibitions/2011/Casiniere/Ca siniere%20Interview.pdf. See http://www.montfaucon.eu/ for images of a complete edition. I am grateful to Joëlle de La Casinière for sharing with me details of this book.

100 Deleuze and Guattari, *A Thousand Plateaus,* 4.

101 The most comprehensive account of the movement, one that should not be confused with Italian Futurism, is Vladimir Markov, *Russian Futurism: A History* (London: University of California Press, 1969). Images of complete

editions of a number of Russian Futurist books can be viewed at http://
www.getty.edu/research/. The first *zaum* poem, Aleksei Kruchenykh's
1920 "Kr dei macelli," can be heard on YouTube, https://www.youtube
.com/watch?v=pu-jrJVIcnk.

102 Deleuze and Guattari, *What Is Philosophy?*, 167.

103 Kruchenykh, cited in Markov, *Russian Futurism*, 347. Aleksei Kruchenykh,
"Declaration of Transrational Language," in *Russian Futurism through Its
Manifestoes, 1912–1928*, ed. Anna Lawton, trans. Anna Lawton and Herbert
Eagle (Ithaca, N.Y.: Cornell University Press, 1988), 182–83.

104 Deleuze and Guattari, *A Thousand Plateaus*, 117.

105 Aleksei Remizov, cited in Nina Gurianova, "A Game in Hell, Hard Work
in Heaven: Deconstructing the Cannon in Russian Futurist Books," in
The Russian Avant-Garde Book 1910–1934, ed. Margit Rowell and Deborah
Wye (New York: MoMA, 2002), 26.

106 Cited in Gerald Janecek, "Kruchenykh contra Gutenberg," in Rowell and
Wye, *Russian Avant-Garde Book*, 41.

107 Deleuze and Guattari, *A Thousand Plateaus*, 9.

108 Ibid., 386.

109 Johanna Drucker, "Pixel Dust: Illusions of Innovation in Scholarly Publishing," *Los Angeles Review of Books*, January 16, 2004, https://lareviewofbooks
.org/essay/pixel-dust-illusions-innovation-scholarly-publishing/#_edn
ref2. Peter Stallybrass, "Books and Scrolls: Navigating the Bible," in
Books and Readers in Early Modern England, ed. Jenny Anderson, 42–79
(Philadelphia: University of Pennsylvania Press, 2002).

110 Jared Ash, "Primitivism in Russian Futurist Book Design 1910–14," in
Rowell and Wye, *Russian Avant-Garde Book*.

111 Deleuze and Guattari, *A Thousand Plateaus*, 493.

112 Gurianova, "A Game in Hell." Deleuze and Guattari, *A Thousand Plateaus*, 402.

113 Gerald Janecek, *The Look of Russian Literature: Avant-Garde Visual Experiments, 1900–1930* (Princeton, N.J.: Princeton University Press, 1984), 117.

114 Aleksei Kruchenykh, "New Ways of the Word," in Lawton, *Russian Futurism through Its Manifestoes*, 76.

115 Deleuze and Guattari, *A Thousand Plateaus*, 499.

116 Ibid., 498.

117 Ibid., 494.

118 Ash, "Primitivism in Russian Futurist Book Design," 37.

119 Deleuze and Guattari, *A Thousand Plateaus*, 398, 386.

120 The first quotation here is Gurianova's characterization of the Futurist
understanding of the book; the second she takes from advertisements for
Futurist editions. Gurianova, "A Game in Hell," 25, 27.

121 Ibid.

122 Janecek, *Look of Russian Literature*, 112.

123 Kruchenykh, cited in Markov, *Russian Futurism*, 130.

124 Kruchenykh, "New Ways of the Word," 75.

125 Janecek, "Kruchenykh contra Gutenberg."

126 Janecek, *Look of Russian Literature*, 109.

127 Terentyev, in Lawton, *Russian Futurism through Its Manifestoes*, 179.

128 Deleuze and Guattari, *A Thousand Plateaus*, 4.

129 *Gris-gris,* the noun Artaud uses for these works, signifies charm, fetish, or amulet.

130 Six of Artaud's spells are reproduced in Margit Rowell, ed., *Antonin Artaud: Works on Paper* (New York: MoMA, 1996). As an example of the text, the spell to Roger Blin (Plates 5 and 6) reads in translation, "All those who banded together to prevent me from taking HEROIN, all those who touched Anne Manson because of that Sunday 21 May 1939, I'll have them pierced alive" (recto) "in a PARIS square and I'll have their marrows perforated and burned. I am in an Insane Asylum but this dream of a madman will become true and will be implemented by ME. *Antonin Artaud*" (149).

131 Antonin Artaud, "Letter to Henri Parisot, September 22 1945," cited in Gilles Deleuze, *The Logic of Sense,* ed. Constantin V. Boundas, trans. Mark Lester and Charles Stivale (New York: Columbia University Press, 1990), 84.

132 Deleuze, *Logic of Sense,* 87. Antonin Artaud, "From *The Nerve Meter* (1925)," in *Antonin Artaud: Selected Writings,* ed. Susan Sontag, trans. Helen Weaver (Berkeley: University of California Press, 1988), 87.

133 Deleuze, *Logic of Sense,* 86–87.

134 Artaud, cited in ibid., 84.

135 Ibid., 88.

136 Antonin Artaud, cited in Stephen Barber, *Antonin Artaud: Terminal Curses* (London: Solar Books, 2008), 67.

137 Ibid., 54.

138 Antonin Artaud, cited in Christopher Ho, "Antonin Artaud: From Centre to Periphery, Periphery to Centre," *Performing Arts Journal* 19, no. 2 (1997): 19. Artaud, in Rowell, *Antonin Artaud,* 42.

139 Antonin Artaud, cited in Paule Thévenin, "The Search for a Lost World," in Jacques Derrida and Paule Thévenin, *The Secret Art of Antonin Artaud,* trans. Mary Ann Caws (Cambridge, Mass.: MIT Press, 1998), 25.

140 Agnès de la Beaumelle, "Introduction," trans. Jeanine Herman, in Rowell, *Antonin Artaud,* 40.

141   Jean Dequeker, cited in Margit Rowell, "Images of Cruelty: The Drawings of Antonin Artaud," in Rowell, *Antonin Artaud,* 13.

142   Deleuze, *Logic of Sense,* 87.

143   Beaumelle, "Introduction," 39.

144   Thévenin, "Search for a Lost World," 15, 17.

145   Beaumelle, "Introduction," 40.

146   Antonin Artaud, "50 Dessins pour assassiner la magie," trans. Richard Sieburth, in Rowell, *Antonin Artaud,* 33.

147   Antonin Artaud, "Les figures sur la page inerte . . . ," trans. Richard Sieburth, in ibid., 42.

148   Guy Debord, "Attestations," trans. Reuben Keehan, http://www.cddc .vt.edu/sionline/postsi/attestations.html.

149   Karen Kurczynski, *The Art and Politics of Asger Jorn: The Avant-Garde Won't Give Up* (Burlington, Vt.: Ashgate, 2014), 165–66.

150   For the multitude of sources, see Ian Thompson's accompanying notes to his facsimile translation of *Mémoires,* http://isinenglish.com/2015/03 /20/memoires-footnotes-and-sources-of-detournements-edited-working -notes/.

151   The remarkable experiment of *Fin de Copenhague* includes covers comprising the disposable papier-mâché "flong" that molded stereographic plates for cylinder and rotary printing. A paradoxical conjunction of the unique and the mass produced, the flong used in this case, necessarily different for each copy of the book, was taken from conservative Danish dailies. See Thomas Hvid Kromann, "Montages Wrapped in Flong: A Material-Archaeological Investigation of Asger Jorn and Guy Debord's *Fin de Copen-hague,*" *Situationniste Blog,* January 2016, https://situationnisteblog.files .wordpress.com/2016/01/kromann_montages_english-summary-1.pdf.

152   Asger Jorn, "Dear Friends," letter to Permild and Rosengreen, February 15, 1958, *October* 141 (2012): 70–72. See Christian Nolle, "Books of Warfare: The Collaboration between Guy Debord and Asger Jorn from 1957–1959," *Vector,* http://virose.pt/vector/b_13/nolle.html. Jorn and Permild and Rosengreen were to have a long-standing publishing relation, and the publisher's handsome logo, still in use today, was designed by Jorn.

153   See especially Karen Kurczynski's book on Jorn, which garners much insight about *Mémoires* from a method that resists mapping too much of it back to the literal history of Debord's groups and that accords full weight to the role of Jorn's "supporting structures." Kurczynski, *Art and Politics of Asger Jorn.*

154   Francis Stracey, "Surviving History: A Situationist Archive," *Art History* 26, no. 1 (2003): 56–77.

155 Mustapha Khayati, "Captive Words: Preface to a Situationist Dictionary," in Knabb, *Situationist International Anthology*, 171. It is significant for my broader argument about communist forms of writing and publishing that the SI also level the critique of the "informationist" mode of language at the orthodox Left. In the same text, Khayati discusses the "Bolshevik order" of the "more or less magical, impersonal expressions," "inflexible" and "ritual formulas" that work in the image of the state to preserve its "purity" and "substance" in the face of obviously contradictory facts. Ibid., 173.

156 Situationist International, "All the King's Men," in Knabb, *Situationist International Anthology*, 114.

157 Deleuze, *Negotiations*, 175.

158 Gilles Deleuze, *Two Regimes of Madness*, ed. David Lapoujade, trans. Ames Hodges and Mike Taormina (New York: Semiotext(e), 2006), 322. Deleuze and Guattari, *What Is Philosophy?*, 99.

159 Guy Debord, cited in Patrick Greaney, *Quotational Practices: Repeating the Future in Contemporary Art* (Minneapolis: University of Minnesota Press, 2014), 33.

160 Anselm Jappe, *Guy Debord*, trans. Donald Nicholson-Smith (Berkeley: University of California Press, 1999), 96 .

161 Jorn, cited in Situationist International, "Détournement as Negation and Prelude," in Knabb, *Situationist International Anthology*, 55.

162 Khayati, "Captive Words," 175.

163 Situationist International, "Détournement as Negation and Prelude," 55.

164 Guy Debord and Gil J. Wolman, "A User's Guide to Détournement," in Knabb, *Situationist International Anthology*, 16.

165 Guy Debord, *Society of the Spectacle* (Detroit, Mich.: Black and Red, 1983), §160.

166 Ibid., §204. Guy Debord and Gil J. Wolman, "A User's Guide to Détournement," in Knabb, *Situationist International Anthology*, 11.

167 Tom McDonough, *"The Beautiful Language of My Century": Reinventing the Language of Contestation in Postwar France, 1945–1968* (Cambridge, Mass.: MIT Press, 2007), 8.

168 Even the degraded photographs of Debord's comrades and drinking companions are purloined from a photo-novel, Ed van der Elsken's *Love on the Left Bank,* which draws much from the scene at the Lettrist haunt Chez Moineau.

169 The translation is from Ian Thompson's expertly executed facsimile translation of *Mémoires,* available at https://www.academia.edu/11522988/Memoires_-_Guy_Debord_and_Asger_Jorn_English_Facsimile_.

170   Situationist International, "Détournement as Negation and Prelude," 56.
171   Kurczynski, *Art and Politics of Asger Jorn,* 170.
172   Jorn, *Open Creation and Its Enemies,* 31.
173   Jorn, "Dear Friends," 71.
174   For discussion of Jorn's homage and critique of Pollock, see Kurczynski, *Art and Politics of Asger Jorn,* 149–54.
175   Jorn, "Dear Friends," 71. It is clear that Jorn considered these to be considerable innovations, declaring in this letter, "I do not know if you realize how close we are coming to an entirely new understanding of the book."
176   David Banash, "Activist Desire, Cultural Criticism, and the Situationist International," *Reconstruction: Studies in Contemporary Culture* 1, no. 2 (2002), http://reconstruction.eserver.org/021/Activist.htm.
177   Regarding which, the SI defines the *dérive* thus: "A mode of experimental behavior linked to the conditions of urban society: a technique of transient passage through varied ambiances. Also used to designate a specific period of continuous dériving." Situationist International, "Definitions," in Knabb, *Situationist International Anthology,* 45.
178   This is not to say that the SI was unresponsive to the gender dimensions of French consumer culture at this time. For discussion of which, see Jen Kennedy, "Charming Monsters: The Spectacle of Femininity in Postwar France," *Grey Room* 39 (2012): 56–79.
179   Greaney, *Quotational Practices,* 35–37, quoting in translation a line from Debord, *Mémoires.*
180   Striphas, *Late Age of Print.*
181   McLuhan suggests that the vector of influence might also go in the opposite direction, whereby the printed book's nature as a manufactured mass commodity—an apparently autonomous entity, tending toward homogeneity across each copy—conferred a "subliminal faith" in the validity of the printed Bible as an independent source, bypassing the oral mediation and authority of the Church and of scholarship, "as if print, uniform and repeatable commodity that it was, had the power of creating a new hypnotic superstition of the book as independent of and uncontaminated by human agency." McLuhan, *Gutenberg Galaxy,* 144.
182   Travis, "Ideas and Commodities."
183   Anderson, *Imagined Communities.* Febvre and Martin, *Coming of the Book.* Striphas, *Late Age of Print.*
184   Kurczynski, *Art and Politics of Asger Jorn,* 162.
185   Jørgen Nash, from the Danish press release of *Mémoires,* trans. Jakob Jakobsen, cited in Jakob Jakobsen, "The Artistic Revolution: On the Situationists,

Gangsters and Falsifiers from Drakabygget," in Rasmussen and Jakobsen, *Expect Everything Fear Nothing,* 223.

186 Debord, "Attestations." The commercial republication of *Mémoires* raises questions I am unable to address here, but I take it as given that the reprints are very different entities to the 1959 work discussed in this chapter.

187 Guy Debord, "Potlatch (1954–57)," trans. NOT BORED!, http://www .notbored.org/potlatch.html.

188 Grail Marcus, *Lipstick Traces: A Secret History of the Twentieth Century* (London: Picador, 1997), 391.

189 Guy Debord, "The Role of Potlatch, Then and Now," from *Potlatch* 30 (July 15, 1959), cited in Jappe, *Guy Debord,* 148.

190 In a letter to the German Situationist Uwe Lausen, Debord proposes that Lausen sell copies of *Mémoires* to fund the publication of *Der Deutsche Gedanke,* noting that its "full price . . . is very high." Guy Debord, "Letter to Uwe Lausen, 9 September 1962," trans. NOT BORED!, http://www .notbored.org/debord-9September1962.html. On the contradictions involved in financing the SI, see SI, "Questionnaire," in Knabb, *Situationist International Anthology,* 142, 373–74. For discussion of the affective politics of the gift, see McDonough, *Beautiful Language of My Century,* 148–54.

191 Marcel Mauss, *The Gift: The Form and Reason for Exchange in Archaic Societies,* trans. W. D. Halls (London: Routledge, 1990).

192 McKenzie Wark, "The Secretary," in Guy Debord, *Correspondence: The Foundation of the Situationist International (June 1957–August 1960),* trans. Stewart Kendall and John McHale (Los Angeles, Calif.: Semiotext(e), 2009).

193 See Georges Bataille, "The Notion of Expenditure," in *Visions of Excess: Selected Writings, 1927–1939,* ed. Allan Stoekl, trans. Allan Stoekl with Carl R. Lovitt and Donald M. Leslie, 116–29 (Minneapolis: University of Minnesota Press, 1985).

194 Debord, "Attestations."

195 Banash, "Activist Desire."

196 Guy Debord, "Letter to Thomas Levin, 1 September 1989," trans. NOT BORED!, http://www.notbored.org/debord-1September1989.html.

197 Guy Debord, "The Hamburg Theses of September 1961 (Note to Serve in the History of the Situationist International)," letter to Thomas Levin, November 1989, trans. NOT BORED!, http://www.notbored.org/debord -November1989.html.

198 For the developing political orientations and tensions of the SI at this time, see the reports "The Fourth SI Conference in London" (held September 1960), http://www.cddc.vt.edu/sionline/si/goteborg.html, and "The Fifth

SI Conference in Göteborg" (held August 1961), http://www.bopsecrets .org/SI/5.conf4.htm. For documents relating to the split and the subsequent development of Scandinavian Situationist practice, see Mikkel Bolt Rasmussen and Jakob Jakobsen, eds., *Cosmonauts of the Future: Texts from the Situationist Movement in Scandinavia and Elsewhere* (Copenhagen: Nebula, 2015).

199 Debord, "Hamburg Theses."

200 Guy Debord, "Letter to Raoul Vaneigem," February 15, 1962, trans. NOT BORED!, http://www.notbored.org/debord-15February1962.html.

201 Ibid.

202 Jacques Camatte, in Camatte and Gianni Collu, "On Organization," trans. Edizioni International, in *This World We Must Leave and Other Essays,* ed. Alex Trotter (New York: Autonomedia, 1995), 20.

203 Attila Kotànyi, "The Next Step," from *Der Deutsche Gedanke* 1 (April 1963), trans. Reuben Keehan, http://www.cddc.vt.edu/sionline/si/nextstep.html.

204 Anthony Hayes, "Toward the Realisation of Philosophy: The *Situationist International* between 1957 and 1960," http://thesinisterquarter.wordpress .com/2014/01/06/toward-the-realisation-of-philosophy/.

205 Karl Marx, "A Contribution to Hegel's Philosophy of Right: Introduction," in *Early Writings,* 250.

206 In a more specific sense, this marks a separation from the historical workers' movement and the milieu of revolutionary groups that were nurturing its particular structures of antagonism and its conceptual field beyond their sociohistorical pertinence. The reference to Marx "signified that one must no longer give the least importance to the conceptions of any of the revolutionary groups that still existed as inheritors of the old social emancipation movement that was destroyed in the first half of our century." Debord, "Hamburg Theses."

207 Ibid., 256.

208 Karl Marx and Friedrich Engels, "The Holy Family, or, Critique of Critical Criticism," in *Collected Works,* 4:36.

209 Marx, "A Contribution to Hegel's Philosophy of Right," 256.

210 Howard Slater, "Divided We Stand: An Outline of Scandinavian Situationism," *Infopool,* no. 4 (London: Infopool, 2001).

211 Key SI texts about the practice of art after the split are René Viénet, "The Situationists and the New Forms of Action against Politics and Art," 1967, in Knabb, *Situationist International Anthology,* and Guy Debord, "The Situationists and the New Forms of Action in Politics or Art," 1963, in Elisabeth Sussman, *On the Passage of a Few People through a Rather Brief Moment in Time: The Situationist International 1957–1972* (Cambridge, Mass.: MIT Press, 1991).

212 Rumney's report was intended for the first issue of *Internationale situationniste,* its late arrival famously precipitating his expulsion from the SI. The filiform tract is described in Guy Debord, "To [Pinot] Gallizio," January 13, 1958, in Debord, *Correspondence,* 74. For details of the Censor scandal, see Gianfranco Sanguinetti, "The Doge: A Recollection," http://www.notbored.org/The-Doge.pdf.

213 For example, "What kind of *metallic cover* can we obtain in Holland? That is, continuing with the range of our covers, what can we find? / In France—the country is poor in this regard—we have just about exhausted everything with gold and silver. / Keeping in mind that it must have a *thickness* equal to n° 3, what *colors* can one find? (We would like *copper red* if possible.)" Guy Debord, "To Constant [Nieuwenhuys]," 26 January 1960, Debord, *Correspondence,* 324. Regarding the SI's taste in page aesthetics, see the amusing retort to left-wing critics of the journal's slick paper and price, those "detractors of typography" with their "mimeographed image . . . of the consciousness of a class in which they fervently seek their stereotype Joe Worker." Viénet, "The Situationists and the New Forms of Action against Politics and Art," 213.

214 McKenzie Wark, "No One Wants to Be Here: John Douglas Millar Interviews McKenzie Wark," *3:AM Magazine,* http://www.3ammagazine.com /3am/no-one-wants-to-be-here/. The anticopyright notice was brought from the back of the journal to the front in issue 3, when it was also worked up typographically to be a striking feature. The journal itself was not free. Number 12 was priced at 3 French franks, approximately $3.50 in 2015 prices, which, for comparison with other kinds of printed matter at the time, was less than one-fifth of the price of the first edition of *The Society of the Spectacle.*

215 Ruth Baumeister, *Asger Jorn in Images, Words, and Forms* (Chicago: University of Chicago Press, 2015).

216 See Karen Kurczynski, "Red Herrings: Eccentric Morphologies in the Situationist Times," in Rasmussen and Jakobsen, *Expect Nothing Fear Everything.*

217 Slater, "Divided We Stand," 20.

218 Jacqueline de Jong, "Critique of the Political Practice of Détournement," *The Situationist Times* 1 (May 1962).

219 Michèle Bernstein, "No Useless Indulgences," *Internationale situationniste,* no. 1 (June 1958), trans. NOT BORED!, http://www.notbored .org/no-useless-indulgences.html#_ednref8. I have included an image of de Jong's text to convey an impression of its material and emotional qualities, and thanks to Howard Slater's transcription, the content can

now be read with ease. See Jacqueline de Jong, "Critique of the Political Practice of Détournement," in Rasmussen and Jakobsen, *Cosmonauts of the Future,* 77–84.

220   It is well known that the SI contained other organizational tendencies, which included a strict adherence to internal group discipline as well as a certain aestheticization of organization and the practice of exclusion. For a compelling analysis of the organizational question in the SI and the Scandinavian Situationist groups, see Slater, "Divided We Stand."

221   Nancy, *Inoperative Community,* 31. The trope of "literary communism" appears in a number of places in the book and gives chapter 3 its title.

222   Debord, *Society of the Spectacle,* §220. For critique of the place of workers' councils in the SI's theory, see Jean Barrot, *What Is Situationism* (London: Unpopular Books, 1987).

223   Deleuze and Guattari, *A Thousand Plateaus,* 4.

224   Marx, "A Contribution to Hegel's Philosophy of Right," 253.

4. WHAT MATTER WHO'S SPEAKING?

1   I take this quotation from the translation of a 1973 *Invariance* text by Jacques Camatte, "Statements and Citations," in *This World We Must Leave and Other Essays,* ed. Alex Trotter, 172–80 (New York: Autonomedia, 1995). Camatte explains that its original source is not Bordiga's anonymously authored series, "Sul Filo del Tempo" (The thread of time), in the journal *Battaglia Comunista* (Communist struggle), but a journal with the same title that published a single issue in May 1953.

2   For critical analysis of anonymous and pseudonymous collective practice from feudal to contemporary scenes, see Marco Deseriis, "Improper Names: Collective Pseudonyms and Multiple-Use Names as Minor Processes of Subjectivation," *Subjectivity* 5 (2012): 140–60.

3   Maria Chehonadskih, "What Is Pussy Riot's 'Idea,'" *Radical Philosophy* 176 (2012): 1–7. Harry Halpin, "The Philosophy of Autonomous: Ontological Politics without Identity," *Radical Philosophy* 176 (2012): 19–28.

4   Michel Foucault, "What Is an Author?," in *Aesthetics, Method, and Epistemology,* ed. James D. Faubion, trans. Robert Hurley et al. (New York: New Press, 1998), 221.

5   Jeffrey T. Nealon, *Foucault beyond Foucault: Power and Its Intensifications since 1984* (Stanford, Calif.: Stanford University Press, 2008).

6   Foucault, "What Is an Author?," 205.

7   Ibid., 211–12.

8 Cited in Mark Rose, *Authors and Owners: The Invention of Copyright* (Cambridge, Mass.: Harvard University Press, 1993), 22.

9 Ibid., 15.

10 Foucault, "What Is an Author?," 212.

11 By a Rheinlander [Karl Marx], "Comments on the Latest Prussian Censorship Instruction," in Marx and Engels, *Collected Works*, 1:112.

12 By a Rheinlander [Karl Marx], "Debates on Freedom of the Press and Publication of the Proceedings of the Assembly of the Estates," supplement to *Rheinische Zeitung*, no. 139 (May 19, 1842), in Marx and Engels, *Collected Works*, 1:174. My discussion here is informed by the dialogue between Esther Leslie and Ben Watson, "'Write to Live; Live to Write': Trading Ideas in Academia and Journalism," http://www.militantesthetix .co.uk/critlit/livewrite.htm.

13 [Marx], "Debates on Freedom," 175.

14 John Locke, *Two Treatises of Government*, cited in Rose, *Authors and Owners*, 5. Roger Chartier writes that from the mid-eighteenth century, a "monetary appreciation of literary compositions, remunerated as labour and subject to the laws of the market, was founded on an ideology of creative and disinterested genius that guaranteed the originality of the work." Chartier, *The Order of Books: Readers, Authors, and Libraries in Europe between the 14th and 18th Centuries*, trans. Lydia G. Cochrane (Stanford, Calif.: Stanford University Press, 1992), 38.

15 Karl Marx, "The Class Struggles in France: 1848–1850," in *Surveys from Exile*, ed. David Fernbach (Harmondsworth, U.K.: Penguin 1973), 134. This feeling for the value of anonymity in journalism features in the earlier essays too. For instance, regarding efforts to deny freedom of the press to anonymous and pseudonymous writers, Marx jibes, "When Adam gave names to all the animals in paradise, he forgot to give names to the German newspaper correspondents, and they will remain *nameless in saecula saeculorum* [for ever and ever]." [Marx], "Debates on Freedom," 178.

16 Marx, "Class Struggles in France," 134.

17 Ibid., 178, 137.

18 Ibid., 135. The English translation here is actually "sinister anonymity," which diminishes the psychological dimension of *unheimlich*.

19 Margaret A. Rose, "The Holy Cloak of Criticism: Structuralism and Marx's *Eighteenth Brumaire*," *Thesis Eleven* 2 (1981): 83.

20 Karl Marx and Frederick Engels, *Manifesto of the Communist Party* (Beijing: Foreign Languages Press, 1973), 31.

21 Foucault, "What Is an Author?," 138.

22 Ibid., 207.

23 Ibid.

24 Michel Foucault, "The Masked Philosopher," trans. Alan Sheridan, in *Ethics: Subjectivity and Truth,* ed. Paul Rabinow (Harmondsworth, U.K.: Penguin, 1997), 321. Marx made a similar point in his justification for journalistic anonymity, that it ensures the reading public "sees not *who* is speaking, but *what* he is saying." Marx, "Justification of the Correspondent from Mosel," in Marx and Engels, *Collected Works* (London: Lawrence and Wishart, 1975), 1:334.

25 Foucault, "Masked Philosopher," 321.

26 Michel Foucault, "The Discourse of History," in *Foucault Live: Collected Interviews, 1961–1984,* ed. Sylvère Lotringer, trans. Lysa Hochroth and John Johnston (New York: Semiotext(e), 1996), 26.

27 Foucault, "Masked Philosopher," 28, 29.

28 Michel Foucault, *The Archaeology of Knowledge* (London: Tavistock, 1974), 17.

29 Nealon, *Foucault beyond Foucault,* 76.

30 In terms of Foucault's own work, the most significant instance of his anonymous writing was that undertaken as part of the Groupe d'information sur les prisons, where authorial anonymity played a role in constructing collective and situated political writing that was immanent to the "intolerable" conditions of the penal system. See Cecile Brich, "The Groupe d'information sur les prisons: The Voice of Prisoners? Or Foucault's?," *Foucault Studies* 5 (2008): 26–47. David Macey, *The Lives of Michel Foucault* (London: Random House, 1993), 257–89. Alberto Toscano, "The Intolerable-Inquiry: The Documents of the Groupe d'information sur les prisons," *Viewpoint Magazine* 3 (September 25, 2013), http://viewpointmag .com/2013/09/25/the-intolerable-inquiry-the-documents-of-the-groupe -dinformation-sur-les-prisons/.

31 Foucault, "Discourse of History," 28.

32 On this distinction with regard to Bourbaki, and the broader division between collective pseudonyms and multiple names, see Deseriis, "Improper Names."

33 Luther Blissett, "Richard Barbrook and Luther Blissett," http://www .lutherblissett.net/archive/322_en.html.

34 Karl Marx, "On the Jewish Question," in *Early Writings,* 230. For Luther Blissett's engagement with this text, see Luther Blissett, "Introduction to *Enemies of the State*: Criminals, 'Monsters,' and Special Legislation in the Society of Control," trans. Wuming Yi, http://www.lutherblissett .net/archive/078_en.html.

35 Marx, "On the Jewish Question," 230.

36 Ibid., 231.

37 Stathis Kouvélakis, "The Marxist Critique of Citizenship: For a Rereading of *On the Jewish Question*," *South Atlantic Quarterly* 104, no. 4 (2005): 707–21.

38 Luther Blissett, "Mondo Mitomane 1994–96," http://www.lutherblissett .net/archive/283_en.html.

39 Jean-Luc Nancy, *Being Singular Plural*, trans. Robert D. Richardson and Anne E. O'Byrne (Stanford, Calif.: Stanford University Press, 2000), 154.

40 Wu Ming 1, "Interview for *Contravenção,* 14.12.2003," http://www.wum ingfoundation.com/english/giap/Giapdigest24.html.

41 Wu Ming 1, "Stories Belong to Everyone: Tale-tellers, Multitudes, and the Refusal of Intellectual Property," http://www.wumingfoundation .com/english/giap/giapdigest11b.html.

42 Blissett, "Richard Barbrook and Luther Blissett." One could say that Marx himself was groping toward this conjunction of anonymity and general intellect in an 1843 text that includes justification of his choice of anonymity, albeit that his critical terrain was still liberal democratic: "*anonymity* is an essential feature of the newspaper press, since it *transforms* the newspaper from an assemblage of many individual opinions into the organ of *one mind.*" Marx, "Justification of the Correspondent from Mosel," 333–34.

43 Karl Marx, *Grundrisse: Foundations of the Critique of Political Economy (Rough Draft),* trans. M. Nicolaus (Harmondsworth, U.K.: Penguin, 1973), 706.

44 Ibid., 705, 694.

45 Paolo Virno, "Notes on the 'General Intellect,'" trans. Cesare Casarino, in *Marxism beyond Marxism,* ed. Saree Makdisi, Cesare Casarino, and Rebecca E. Karl, 265–72 (New York: Routledge, 1996).

46 Marx, *Capital,* vol. 1, chapter 25.

47 Uncertain Commons, *Speculate This!* (Durham, N.C.: Duke University Press, 2013), http://speculatethis.pressbooks.com/chapter/chapter-1/.

48 Sabrina Ovan, "*Q*'s General Intellect," *Cultural Studies Review* 11, no. 2 (2005): 69–76.

49 This comment about defeat was made by Wu Ming 1 in a radio interview with Aaron Bastani and James Butler on Resonance FM, June 4, 2013, http://novaramedia.com/2013/06/in-conversation-with-wu-ming/. The remark about allegory, which is presented as Benjamin's position, is by Wu Ming, cited in Marco Amici, "Urgency and Visions of the New Italian Epic," *Journal of Romance Studies* 10, no. 1 (2010): 10.

50 Luther Blissett, *Q,* trans. Shaun Whiteside (London: Harcourt, 2003), 743–44.

51 Ibid., 481. Sabrina Ovan, "Nameless History before and after *Las Meninas*: Luther Blissett's Archaeological Fiction," *Genre* 45, no. 3 (2012): 423–41.

52 Stewart Home, "The Return of Proletarian Post-Modernism Part II: Luther Blissett's Recent Best Seller," *Metamute*, June 10, 2003, http://www.metamute.org/editorial/articles/return-proletarian-post-modernism-part-ii-luther-blissettaposs-recent-best-seller-aposqapos.

53 Blissett, *Q*, 411.

54 Marx, *Grundrisse*, 278.

55 Blissett, *Q*, 403–4.

56 Ibid., 409.

57 Ibid., 743.

58 Wu Ming, radio interview.

59 Wu Ming, "Wu Ming: A Band of Militant Storytellers," interview by the Celluloid Liberation Front, *New Statesman*, May 29, 2013, http://www.newstatesman.com/world-affairs/2013/05/wu-ming-band-militant-storytellers.

60 Luther Blissett, "The Luther Blissett Manifesto," in *Mind Invaders: A Reader in Psychic Warfare, Cultural Sabotage, and Semiotic Terrorism*, ed. Stewart Home (London: Serpent's Tale, 1997), 43–44. This text is itself a performance of the multiple name: "Originally composed in Italian and placed on the Net in May 1995, this English language version bears little resemblance to the first provisional translation, which was accompanied by a request that it should be rewritten by everyone who found themselves in agreement with its theses." Ibid., 44.

61 Luther Blissett, "Missing Presumed Dead: How Luther Blissett Hoaxed the TV Cops," in Home, *Mind Invaders*, 4–9.

62 Luther Blissett, "Negative Heroes: Luther Blissett and the Refusal to Work," trans. John Foot, in "Luther Blissett, Football (Soccer) and the Refusal to Work," http://www.wumingfoundation.com/english/giap/giap digest33.htm.

63 Ibid.

64 See "Luther Blissett Fantasy Footballer," http://www.youtube.com/watch?v=3bRuTkmTIjg.

65 Foucault, "What Is an Author?," 119.

66 The essence of the hoax was that the (fabricated) English conceptual artist Harry Kipper had vanished on the Italo-Slovenian border while tracing the word "ART" across the continent, shortly after attending a conference in Bologna where he had proposed the collective adoption of the name Luther Blissett. Their attention piqued, interviews with Kipper's acquaintances drew the television crew of *Chi l'ha visto?* (Has

anybody seen them?) across Italy and as far as London's Isle of Dogs (or the "Isle of Leutha's Dogs," as it is in William Blake's "Jerusalem"), where Stewart Home and Richard Essex guided the TV crew to the wreck of Kipper's old residence. Unfortunately, the hoax was dashed, an overheard bar conversation resulting in the announced program being pulled shortly before broadcast, but not without the press getting wind of it and Luther Blissett being launched into the mediascape. See Blissett, "Missing Presumed Dead." Thanks to Fabian Tompsett for the Blake reference.

67 Luther Blissett, "Introduction to *Enemies of the State.*"

68 Henry Jenkins, "How *Slapshot* Inspired a Cultural Revolution: An Interview with the Wu Ming Foundation," 2006, http://www.henryjenkins .org/2006/10/how_slapshot_inspired_a_cultur_1.html.

69 Luther Blissett, "Why I Wrote a Fake Hakim Bey Book and How I Cheated the Conformists of Italian 'Counterculture,'" August 1996, http://www.evo lutionzone.com/kulturezone/bey/luther.blissett.fake.hakim.bey.

70 Gary Hall, *Digitize This Book! The Politics of New Media, or Why We Need Open Access Now* (Minneapolis: University of Minnesota Press, 2008). Gary Hall, "#Mysubjectivation," *New Formations* 79 (2013): 83–102.

71 Luther Blissett, "Seppuku 2000," in *Quaderni rossi di Luther Blissett,* accompanying booklet to Luther Blissett, *The Open Pop Star,* music and spoken word CD, Wot 4 Records.

72 Wu Ming 1, in Jenkins, "How *Slapshot* Inspired a Cultural Revolution."

73 Virginia Woolf, "Anon.," in "'Anon' and 'The Reader': Virginia Woolf's Last Essays," ed. Brenda R. Silver, *Twentieth Century Literature* 25, no. 3/4 (1979): 382.

74 Wu Ming, "Wu Ming: A Band of Militant Storytellers."

75 Blissett, *Q,* 89. 90.

76 Martin Luther, more generally, is deemed to have sold the hope of the Reformation back to the powerful, and to have "freed us from the Pope and the bishops, but . . . condemned us to expiate sin in solitude, in the solitude of internal anguish, putting a priest in our souls, a court in our consciences, judging every gesture, condemning the freedom of the spirit in favour of the ineradicable corruption of human nature." Ibid., 405.

77 Ibid., 406.

78 Ibid., 360.

79 Ibid., 472.

80 Ibid.

81 Ibid., 525.

82 Ibid., 535.

83 Gustav Metzger, "Manifesto Auto-Destructive Art," originally published 1960, http://radicalart.info/destruction/metzger.html.

84 Ibid., 454, 455, 456.

85 Ibid., 526.

86 Ibid., 483.

87 This point is developed in Bonnie Mak, *How the Page Matters* (Toronto: University of Toronto Press, 2012).

88 Marshall McLuhan, *Understanding Media: The Extensions of Man* (London: Routledge, 2001).

89 Kelsey, "Translator's Introduction," in Michèle Bernstein, *All the King's Horses,* trans. John Kelsey (Los Angeles, Calif.: Semiotext(e), 2008), 8.

90 Ibid. This doubling of *All the King's Horses* with *Reena Spaulings* picks up on a dynamic internal to Bernstein's novel, which is a self-conscious play on Pierre Choderlos de Laclo's 1782 novel of libertine manipulation, *Les liaisons dangereuses,* as well as Marcel Carnés's film *Les visiteurs du soir* (The devil's envoys), and forms a double with Bernstein's second novel, *La Nuit,* which feeds the same story through the scrambling techniques of the *nouveau roman.* In turn, the English translation of *La Nuit* was published with its own double, *After the Night* by Everyone Agrees, a reflexive engagement with Bernstein's text and the process of translation, as manifest also in the book's covers and design. See Michèle Bernstein, "Preface in the Guise of an Autobiography (or Vice Versa)," in *The Night,* trans. Clodagh Kinsella, ed. Everyone Agrees (London: Book Works, 2013), 9–10. Everyone Agrees, *After the Night: The Meeting of Failures: Act II* (London: Book Works, 2013).

91 Bernstein, *All the King's Horses,* 33.

92 Kelly Baum, "All the King's Horses (Review)," *TDR: The Drama Review* 56, no. 1 (2012): 161.

93 Michèle Bernstein, "Preface in the Guise of an Autobiography," 9–10.

94 Kelsey, "Translator's Introduction," 9–12.

95 This was not the only form of paid labor that Bernstein contributed to the SI. In an interview with Greil Marcus, as he reports it, she listed the following: "a racetrack prognosticator ('I made it all up'), a horoscopist ('That too'), a publisher's assistant, and finally a successful advertising director ('To us, you understand, it was *all* spectacle; advertising was not worse than anything else. We took our money where we could find it')." Marcus, *Lipstick Traces,* 377–78.

96 Kelsey, "Translator's Introduction," 13.

97 Ibid., 14.

98   Ibid.

99   Ibid., 9.

100   Bernadette Corporation, *Reena Spaulings* (New York: Semiotext(e), 2004), 2.

101   Ibid., 1.

102   Ibid.

103   Ibid., 2.

104   Henri Bergson, *Matter and Memory*, trans. Nancy Margaret Paul and W. Scott Palmer (New York: Zone Books, 1991), 9.

105   Ibid., 25, 149.

106   Ibid., 21.

107   Ibid., 95, 32.

108   Bernadette Corporation, *Reena Spaulings*, 1.

109   Ibid., 13.

110   Ibid., 13.

111   Ibid., 17, 14.

112   Ibid.

113   Ibid., 16.

114   Ibid., 3, 7.

115   Ibid., 63.

116   Ibid., 134.

117   Famously, Marx and Engels describe the conditions of "communist society" in *The German Ideology* as allowing "for me to do one thing today and another tomorrow, to hunt in the morning, fish in the afternoon, rear cattle in the evening, criticise after dinner, just as I have a mind, without ever becoming hunter, fisherman, herdsman or critic." Marx and Engels, *Collected Works*, 5:47

118   Bernadette Corporation, *Reena Spaulings*, 85.

119   "Monsieur Roubignoles presents *The Kelsey Collection Artforum 2004–2012*," http://www.johnkelseycollection.com.

120   Zac Dempster, Eric-John Russell, Veronika Russell, and Nicolas Vargelis, "Who, or What, Is John Kelsey? A Postscript," http://www.metamute.org/community/your-posts/who-or-what-john-kelsey-postscript#.

121   See http://tarnac9.wordpress.com/.

122   For more detail on the reception of Tiqqun and incisive assessments of its theses, see Joost de Bloois, "*Tiqqun, The Coming Insurrection* and the Idiosyncracies of an Epoch," *Historical Materialism* 22, no. 1 (2014): 129–47. Frére Dupont, "Release to Us the Field!," *Mute,* June 30, 2010, http://www.metamute.org/editorial/articles/release-to-us-field. *Endnotes,* "What Are We to Do?," in Noys, *Communization and Its Discontents,* 35. For an excellent analysis of the broader range of anonymous practice today,

including, significantly, its role amid the politics of undocumented migration, see John Cunningham, "Clandestinity and Appearance," *Mute,* http://
www.metamute.org/editorial/articles/clandestinity-and-appearance.

123 Invisible Committee, *The Coming Insurrection* (Los Angeles, Calif.:
Semiotext(e), 2009), 29.

124 Ibid., 204, 206.

125 Alexander R. Galloway and Jason E. Smith, "A Note on the Translation,"
in Tiqqun, *Introduction to Civil War,* trans. Alexander R. Galloway and
Jason E. Smith (Los Angeles: Semiotext(e), 2001), 7.

126 Invisible Committee, *Coming Insurrection,* 28.

127 It was two years after publication that its authors' identities were revealed
for the first time in print, in George Julian Harney's introduction to the
English translation by Helen Macfarlane.

128 Marx and Engels, *Manifesto of the Communist Party,* 31–32.

129 The title was thus shortened for the first time in the 1872 German edition.
See Eric Hobsbawm, "The Communist Manifesto in Perspective," http://
www.transform-network.net/journal/issue-112012/news/detail/Journal
/the-communist-manifesto-in-perspective.html.

130 Karl Marx, "Marx to Ferdinand Freiligrath," February 29, 1860, in Marx
and Engels, *Collected Works,* 41:82, 81, 87.

131 Amadeo Bordiga, "Considerations on the Party's Organic Activity when
the General Situation Is Historically Unfavourable," 1965, https://www
.marxists.org/archive/bordiga/works/1965/consider.htm.

132 Marx, "Marx to Ferdinand Freiligrath," 82.

133 Ibid.

134 Marx and Engels, *Manifesto of the Communist Party,* 49.

135 Alain Badiou, "Politics Unbound," in *Metapolitics,* trans. Jason Barker
(London: Verso, 2005), 74, 75.

136 Jacques Rancière, *The Philosopher and His Poor,* trans. John Drury, Corinne
Oster, and Andrew Parker (London: Duke University Press, 2003), 86.

137 "Spontaneity, Mediation, Rupture," *Endnotes* 3 (2013): 240.

138 For development of this point, see Thoburn, "Weatherman."

139 Puchner, *Poetry of the Revolution,* 52.

140 Helen Macfarlane, *Red Republican: Essays, Articles, and Her Translation
of the Communist Manifesto,* ed. David Black (London: Unkant, 2014).
Puchner, *Poetry of the Revolution.*

141 *Comité,* "[Communism without Heirs]," 92.

142 *Comité,* "On the Movement," in Blanchot, *Political Writings,* 106, 108.

143 *Comité,* "[Communism without Heirs]," 93.

144 Ibid.

145 See Blanchot, *Political Writings*, 189–90. The use of square brackets in many of the *Comité* essay titles in *Political Writings* is said to be because the journal did not in most cases use titles, but inspection of *Comité* reveals that the titles are not missing but embedded (and uppercase) in the opening paragraphs.

146 *Comité*, "[The Possible Characteristics]," in Blanchot, *Political Writings*, 85. It would have been a striking opening text to *Comité*, as *Political Writings* implies, but "[The Possible Characterisitics]" is part of the body of paratexts associated with the fashioning of the journal. Many thanks to Zaki Paul for answering my questions about Blanchot's publishing practices.

147 Jacques Camatte, 1972 preface to Camatte and Collu, "On Organization," 20.

148 *Comité*, "[The Possible Characteristics]," 85.

149 Kevin Hart, "Foreword: The Friendship of the No," in Blanchot, *Political Writings*, xxiv. *Comité*, "[The Possible Characteristics]," 85.

150 Karl Marx, "Letter to Arnold Ruge," September 1843, in Marx and Engels, *Collected Works*, 3:142.

151 Jasper Bernes, "Logistics, Counterlogistics and the Communist Prospect," *Endnotes* 3 (2013): 173.

152 Marx, "Letter to Arnold Ruge," 145.

153 "Crisis in the Class Relation," *Endnotes* 2 (2010): 12. "What Are We to Do?," 35.

154 "Editorial," *Endnotes* 3 (2013): 10.

155 "About *Endnotes*," http://endnotes.org.uk/about. "Editorial," 1.

156 "About *Endnotes*."

157 Ibid.

158 Ibid.

159 Camatte and Collu, "On Organization," 33.

160 "Editorial," 1.

161 Ibid.

162 *Comité*, ["The Possible Characteristics"], 86. This remained just intent, because only one issue was published.

163 *Insipidities*, "Have a Care: Endnotes 3 and the Resplendent Quetzal," http://insipidities.blogspot.co.uk/2013/11/have-care-will-endnotes-3-ever -become.html.

164 Ibid.

165 "The Holding Pattern," *Endnotes* 3 (2013): 12–54.

166 *Sonogram of a Potentiality*, in *Tiqqun #2*, trans. Tiqqunista, ed. D. E. Machina (Brooklyn: Pétroleuse Press, 2011), 8. I read this in the form of a PDF scan of a water-stained pamphlet, downloaded from the text-sharing resource AAAAARG.org. Such scanned printed works present rich post-digital

materialities, as Sean Dockray has so eloquently described. A scan is an "ambivalent image," it "oscillates back and forth: between a physical page and a digital file, between one reader and another, between an economy of objects and an economy of data." But much else is encoded in the image: "An incomplete inventory of modifications to the book through reading and other typical events in the life of the thing: folded pages, underlines, marginal notes, erasures, personal symbolic systems, coffee spills, signatures, stamps, tears, etc. Intimacy between reader and text marking the pages, suggesting some distant future palimpsest in which the original text has finally given way to a mass of negligible marks." Dockray, "The Scan and the Export," *Fillip* 12 (2010), http://fillip.ca /content/the-scan-and-the-export.

167 Junius Frey, "Letter to the Editor," in Tiqqun, *Theory of Bloom,* http:// libcom.org/files/blooms.pdf.

168 Ibid.

169 *Comité,* "[Tracts, Posters, Bulletins]," in Blanchot, *Political Writings,* 95.

170 *Comité,* "[Reading Marx]," in Blanchot, *Political Writings,* 105.

171 Ibid.

172 Frey, "Letter to the Editor."

173 Tiqqun, *Introduction to Civil War,* 177, 179.

174 Ibid., 174.

5. PROUD TO BE FLESH

1 This chapter draws on an interview I conducted with the founders and directors of *Mute,* Pauline van Mourik Broekman and Simon Worthington, and the editor, Josephine Berry Slater, in London on September 7, 2010.

2 Mute, "About Us," http://www.metamute.org/about-us.

3 "Ceci n'est pas un magazine," *Mute* 19 (2001): 24–25.

4 "The Magazine That Mistook Its Reader for a Hat!," *Mute* 25 (2002): 8–9.

5 Regarding his militancy in Operaismo, Negri describes the magazine form as pivotal to the break with the Italian Communist Party: "Until the mid-'60s our movement was a magazine movement, then we used leaflets as well, which were distributed in factories." Antonio Negri, interviewed with Verina Gfader, "The Real Radical?," in *EP Vol. 1, The Italian Avant-Garde: 1968–1976* (Berlin: Sternberg Press, 2013), 202.

6 Antonio Negri, "Postface to the Complete Text of the Journal *Futur Antérieur* (1989–98)," multitudes.samizdat.net/Postface-to-the-Complete -Text-of.

7 Deleuze and Guattari, *A Thousand Plateaus,* 9.

8 Ibid., 25.

9 Josephine Berry Slater, "Disgruntled Addicts—*Mute* Magazine and Its History," in *Proud to Be Flesh: A* Mute *Magazine Anthology of Cultural Politics after the Net,* ed. Josephine Berry Slater and Pauline van Mourik Broekman (London: Mute Publishing, 2009): 15.

10 Ibid., 25.

11 Pauline van Mourik Broekman, post on *Empyre* LISTSERV, June 15, 2010, http://www.mail-archive.com/empyre@lists.cofa.unsw.edu.au/msg02124.html.

12 Anthony Davies and Simon Ford, "Culture Clubs," *Mute* 18 (2000): 29–33, 30, 35. For Davies's analysis of the situation *after* the dotcom crash, 9/11, and the Enron bankruptcy, as capitalist culture reverted to its conservative instincts, see his "Basic Instinct: Trauma and Retrenchment 2000–4," *Mute* 29 (2005): 67–77.

13 Angela Mitropoulos, "Precari-Us?," *Mute* 29 (2005): 90.

14 Siegfried Zielinski, *[. . . After the Media] News from the Slow-Fading Twentieth Century,* trans. Gloria Custance (Minneapolis: Univocal, 2013), 1.

15 Van Mourik Broekman, post on *Empyre.*

16 The forty thousand print run of each issue thus cost a mere £800. See Pauline van Mourik Broekman, Simon Worthington, and Damian Jaques, *Mute Magazine Graphic Design* (London: Eight Books, 2008).

17 Ibid., 12.

18 Berry Slater, "Disgruntled Addicts," 16; Pauline van Mourik Broekman, "Mute," transcript of a presentation at Publications on (Not Only) Art: Cultural, Social, and Political Uses, Seville, June 15–18, 2011, http://ayp.unia.es/dmdocuments/public_doc06b.pdf.

19 To locate this point more historically, if the *Daily Courant* was the first newspaper to be published in London's Fleet Street, the *Financial Times* was by this stage paradigmatic of the industry after Rupert Murdoch relocated the News International presses to Wapping and the decimation this visited on the print profession and its unions. Dramatizing the new situation, the corridors of the Docklands site were apparently lined with portraits of printers past, a now familiar practice of the representation of labor as depoliticized heritage in sites where it no longer has physical presence and conflictual force. Van Mourik Broekman et al., *Mute Magazine Graphic Design,* 18.

20 Rosalind E. Krauss, *"A Voyage on the North Sea": Art in the Age of the Post-Medium Condition* (London: Thames and Hudson, 1999). Rosalind E. Krauss, *Under Blue Cup* (Cambridge, Mass.: MIT Press, 2011).

21 Krauss, *A Voyage on the North Sea,* 7.

22 Deleuze and Guattari, *A Thousand Plateaus,* 67, 502–3. In keeping to the usual meanings of "content" and "form," I have had to take some liberties with Deleuze and Guattari's terminology, because for them "content" refers to something closer to what I hear mean by "form" (with "expression" taking the role played here by "content"). There are further dimensions to Deleuze and Guattari's content–expression dyad that I do not pursue here.

23 Hayles, *Writing Machines,* 25.

24 Guattari, *Schizoanalytic Cartographies,* 253, 255.

25 Pauline van Mourik Broekman, in Jodi Dean, Sean Dockray, Alessandro Ludovico, Pauline van Mourik Broekman, Nicholas Thoburn, and Dmitry Vilensky, "Materialities of Independent Publishing: A Conversation with AAAAARG, Chto Delat?, I Cite, Mute and Neural," *New Formations* 78 (2013): 178.

26 Deleuze, *Foucault,* 38. Gilles Deleuze, "What Is a *Dispositif?*," in *Two Regimes of Madness: Texts and Interviews 1975–1995,* ed. David Lapoujade, trans. Ames Hodges and Mike Taormina (Los Angeles, Calif.: Semiotext(e), 2006), 338.

27 Deleuze, *Foucault,* 38.

28 Ibid.

29 "Magazine That Mistook Its Reader for a Hat!," 8.

30 Ibid.

31 See Puchner, *Poetry of the Revolution.* This volitional aim is apparent in van Mourik Broekman's description of the minifesto as a "promise, or commitment, . . . a token of faith to an imagined reader." Van Mourik Broekman, "Mute."

32 Van Mourik Broekman, interview.

33 Pauline van Mourik Broekman, "On Being 'Independent' in a Network," *Free Bitflows exStream, Collaborative Media* (2004): 5. Van Mourik Broekman, interview. Toni Prug, "Introducing OpenMute," *Mute* 25 (2002): 8–9.

34 Gilles Châtelet, *Figuring Space: Philosophy, Mathematics, and Physics,* trans. Robert Shore and Muriel Zagha (Dordrecht, Netherlands: Kluwer Academic, 2000), 8, 7, 3. I owe this reference to John Cussans, with thanks, and to discussions at the Diagram Research Use and Generation Group.

35 Ibid., 10.

36 Ibid., 9.

37 Ibid.

38 Ibid., 20.

39 Ibid.
40 "Magazine That Mistook Its Reader for a Hat!," 8.
41 Dictionary.com, s.v. "hybrid."
42 See http://www.metamute.org/editorial/video/video-forever-blowing
    -bubbles-walking-tour-peter-linebaugh-and-fabian-tompsett-2008.
43 Deleuze, *Foucault*, 38. While for Deleuze the diagram is not a visual entity,
    in contrast to Châtelet, as a virtual "non-place," it is illusive and needs
    touchstones, often visual ones, to grasp it. This point is well made in Jakub
    Zdebik, *Deleuze and the Diagram: Aesthetic Threads in Visual Organization*
    (New York: Continuum Books, 2012).
44 Deleuze, *Foucault*, 34. This fortuitous characterization of the diagram as
    "mute" adds a diagrammatic valence to the connotations of *Mute*'s name,
    a name chosen in part as "a comment on the liberatory rhetoric of . . . new
    technologies," connoting that "new technologies didn't automatically grant
    a voice; that, in fact, this was to do with operations of power at a social
    level." Van Mourik Broekman, "Mute."
45 Deleuze, *Foucault*, 38.
46 Châtelet, *Figuring Space*, 54.
47 Van Mourik Broekman et al., *Mute Magazine Graphic Design*, 131.
48 Van Mourik Broekman, interview.
49 "Ceci n'est pas un magazine," 24. "Magazine That Mistook Its Reader
    for a Hat!," 6.
50 J. J. Charlesworth, "Crisis at the ICA: Ekow Eshun's Experiment in Dein-
    stitutionalisation," *Mute* 2, no. 15 (2010): 20–31. The extended comments
    on Charlesworth's article, which included a response from the ICA, were
    lost to view in one of *Mute*'s later platform changes.
51 Prug, "Introducing OpenMute," 9.
52 See the *Mute* issue "Web 2.0: Man's Best Friendster?," 2, no. 4 (2007),
    especially Dmytri Kleiner and Brian Wyrick, "Info-Enclosure 2.0," and
    Angela Mitropoulos, "The Social Softwar."
53 "Magazine That Mistook Its Reader for a Hat!," 6.
54 Van Mourik Broekman, post on *Empyre*.
55 Laura Oldfield Ford, in Josephine Berry Slater and Anthony Iles, eds., *No
    Room to Move: Art and the Regenerate City* (London: Mute Books, 2010), 106.
56 Nancy, *Inoperative Community*, 74.
57 Van Mourik Broekman, in Dean et al., "Materialities of Independent
    Publishing," 165.
58 Ibid.
59 J. J. King, "The Packet Gang: Openness and Its Discontents," *Mute* 27
    (2004): 80–87. See also Howard Slater, "Prepostoral Ouragonisations,"

Mute 28 (2004): 88–90, and Jo Freeman, "The Tyranny of Structureless-ness," http://libcom.org/library/tyranny-structurelessness-jo-freeman.

60 Prug, "Introducing OpenMute," 8–9. Van Mourik Broekman et al., *Mute Magazine Graphic Design.*

61 Van Mourik Broekman et al., *Mute Magazine Graphic Design,* 102.

62 "CrCollaborativeReviewLibraryContract," http://uo.twenteenthcentury.com/index.php?title=CrCollaborativeReviewLibraryContract.

63 Worthington, "Danger: Contains Books," 174.

64 See http://www.metamute.org/services/r-d/progressive-publishing-system.

65 See Simon Worthington, *Dynamic Publishing: New Platforms, New Readers!,* 2013, http://www.consortium.io/research-plan.

66 Van Mourik Broekman et al., *Mute Magazine Graphic Design,* 130. Alessandro Ludovico, *Post-Digital Print: The Mutation of Publishing since 1894* (Eindhoven: Onomatopee, 2012).

67 Berry Slater, in Berry Slater and van Mourik Broekman, *Proud to Be Flesh,* 20.

68 Van Mourik Broekman and Berry Slater, interview. Berry Slater, in Berry Slater and van Mourik Broekman, *Proud to Be Flesh,* 20.

69 Van Mourik Broekman et al., *Mute Magazine Graphic Design,* 106–7.

70 Ibid., 102.

71 Van Mourik Broekman, interview.

72 Pauline van Mourik Broekman and Josephine Berry Slater, in Max Jorge Hinderer, "Proud to Be Flesh: An Interview with Pauline van Mourik Broekman and Josephine Berry Slater," *Springerin,* 2009, http://www.springerin.at/dyn/heft_text.php?textid=2263&lang=en.

73 Critical engagement with POD has since become more widespread, though see the note of caution from Temporary Services regarding its excessive cost for larger print runs relative to offset and Risograph printing. Temporary Services, *Publishing in the Realm of Plant Fibers and Electrons* (Chicago: Temporary Services, 2014), 26.

74 Berry Slater addresses this generic magazine strategy with regard to 1990s lifestyle magazines such as *The Face* and *I-D*: "The (beautiful) face becomes the magnified signifier of (exceptional) identity, sold to us as something which stands out and resists homogenization whilst, at the same time of course, providing the ultimate lure for consumption and conformity." Berry Slater, "Editorial," *Mute* 2, no. 15 (2010): 6.

75 Van Mourik Broekman et al., *Mute Magazine Graphic Design,* 133.

76 http://www.metamute.org/editorial/articles/we-are-bad.

77 Howard Slater, "Guttural Cultural," *Mute* 2, no. 5 (2007): 72, 67.

78 Berry Slater, interview.

79 Van Mourik Broekman and Berry Slater, interview.

80 "Up to now the communist press has differentiated itself from the capital-
    ist press only in terms of content, through the propagation of communist
    principles. In its organization, structure, and numerous specific aspects it
    remains under the determining influence of the capitalist press." Adalbert
    Fogarasi, "The Tasks of the Communist Press," in *Communication and
    Class Struggle: 2, Liberation and Socialism,* ed. Seth Siegelaub and Armand
    Mattelart (New York: International General, 1983), 151.

81 Ibid., 152.

82 Ibid., 150–51.

83 Lenin, *What Is to Be Done?,* 200, 197, 207, 201.

84 Van Mourik Broekman, post on *Empyre.*

85 Van Mourik Broekman and Berry Slater, in Hinderer, "Proud to Be Flesh."

86 Maurice Blanchot, "[The Gravity of the Project]," in *Political Writings,*
    57. Blanchot's words here come from his preparatory texts for *Revue inter-
    national,* a journal that became a victim before it started of its attempted
    reach and experimental form. See Zakir Paul's discussion in Blanchot,
    Political Writings, xliv–xlvii.

87 Berry Slater, interview.

88 Deleuze, *Cinema 2,* 148.

89 Ibid., 150; Gilles Deleuze, *Essays Critical and Clinical,* trans. Daniel W.
    Smith and Michael A. Greco (Minneapolis: University of Minnesota
    Press, 1997), 118.

90 Gary Genosko, *Félix Guattari: A Critical Introduction* (Cambridge: Pluto
    Press, 2009), 44–45. For more on Guattari's relationship to the practical
    politics of publishing, see Gary Genosko, "Busted: Félix Guattari and
    the *Grande Encyclopédie des Homosexualités,*" *Rhizomes* 11–12 (2005–6),
    http:// www.rhizomes.net/ issue11/genosko.html, and François Dosse,
    Gilles Deleuze and Félix Guattari: Intersecting Lives, trans. D. Glassman
    (New York: Columbia University Press, 2010).

91 Genosko, *Félix Guattari,* 41.

92 Anderson, *Imagined Communities,* 33.

93 Pauline van Mourik Broekman, "Editorial: Just a Few of Our Many Prod-
    ucts," *Mute* 25 (2002): 5.

94 Worthington, interview.

95 Berry Slater, interview.

96 Bergson, *Matter and Memory,* 95, 32.

97 Josephine Berry Slater, "Editorial," *Mute* 2, no. 15 (2010): 6. Typical
    of *Mute*'s empirically routed approach to these more abstract themes,
    her point here is made in reference to Ekow Eshun's formulation of the

ICA's vision, where his statement "All that matters is now" serves as an innovation-sounding apology for accommodation with neoliberal cultural and economic norms.

98 Bergson, *Mater and Memory*, 33.

99 Van Mourik Broekman, interview.

100 Pauline Van Mourik Broekman and Simon Worthington, foreword to Berry Slater and van Mourik Broekman, *Proud to Be Flesh*, 11.

101 Deleuze and Guattari, *Anti-Oedipus*, 8. The quotation actually refers to "desiring-machines," the precursor concept to "assemblage."

102 Van Mourik Broekman et al., *Mute Magazine Graphic Design*, 130.

103 The first minifesto was inspired by Quim Gil, who suggested to the board that readers would be keen to hear about the magazine's processes of transformation.

104 Van Mourik Broekman, "Mute."

105 "CrCollaborativeReviewLibraryContract."

106 "Fallout, 1999/2000," http://www.metamute.org/fallout_1999_2000.

107 Comedia, "The Alternative Press: The Development of Underdevelopment," *Media, Culture, and Society* 6 (1984): 95–102. Charles Landry, Dave Morley, Russell Southwood, and Patrick Wright, *What a Way to Run a Railroad: An Analysis of Radical Failure* (London: Comedia Publishing, 1985).

108 Ibid., front matter.

109 Van Mourik Broekman and Worthington, foreword, 12.

110 Van Mourik Broekman, "On Being 'Independent' in a Network," 4.

111 Ibid., 5; van Mourik Broekman and Berry Slater, in Hinderer, "Proud to Be Flesh."

112 Comedia, "Alternative Press," 97. Van Mourik Broekman et al., *Mute Magazine Graphic Design*, 130. For critique of the Lockean model of the proprietorial laboring subject that is implicit in some discussion of "free labor," see Mitropoulos, "Social Softwar," though the point here concerns simply the difficulty of earning a living.

113 Gholam Khiabany, "*Red Pepper*: A New Model of the Alternative Press?," *Media, Culture, and Society* 22, no. 4 (2000): 447–63.

114 Deleuze, *Cinema 2*, 77.

115 Ibid.

116 Ibid.

117 Van Mourik Broekman, "Mute."

118 Van Mourik Broekman, "*Mute*'s 100% Cut by ACE—A Personal Consideration of *Mute*'s Defunding," *Mute* 3, no. 1 (2011): 18.

119 Josephine Berry Slater, "Editorial," *Mute* 3, no. 1 (2011): 21.

120 Van Mourik Broekman et al., *Mute Magazine Graphic Design*, 130.

121 Pauline van Mourik Broekman, "New Model Mute," http://www.meta
mute.org/editorial/articles/new-model-mute.

6. UNIDENTIFIED NARRATIVE OBJECTS

1 Zhisui Li, *The Private Life of Chairman Mao,* trans. Tai Hung-chao (London: Arrow Books, 1996), 115–16.

2 Nikita S. Khrushchev, *The Crimes of the Stalin Era: Special Report to the 20th Congress of the Communist Party of the Soviet Union* (New York: The New Leader, 1962), 7.

3 Alain Badiou, "The Cultural Revolution: The Last Revolution?," in *The Communist Hypothesis,* trans. David Macey and Steve Corcoran (New York: Verso, 2010), 151.

4 Mao Tse-tung, *Mao Tse-tung Talks to the People,* ed. Stuart Schram (New York: Macmillan, 1975), 99–100.

5 Ibid., 38.

6 Marx, as cited in Khrushchev, *Crimes of the Stalin Era,* 8.

7 Marx's letter to Blos is usually seen as the origin of the concept of the personality cult, though its first signs can be traced back earlier, to Marx's reaction to such patterns of association attendant on Ferdinand Lassalle, as apparent in an 1865 letter where he objects to Lassalle's "bombastic self-adulation" and *Der Social-Demokrat*'s "lick-spittling cult of Lassalle." Karl Marx, "Letter to Ludwig Kugelmann, 23 February 1865," in Marx and Engels, *Complete Works,* 42:101.

8 Yves Cohen, "The Cult of Number One in an Age of Leaders," trans. Steven E. Harris, *Kritika: Explorations in Russian and Eurasian History* 8, no. 3 (2007): 601.

9 Ibid., 599. Cohen shows that this disavowal was intrinsic to the Bolshevik personality cult, fashioning its formal aspects in particular ways.

10 Louis Althusser, "Note on 'The Critique of the Personality Cult,'" in *Essays in Self-Criticism,* trans. Grahame Lock (London: New Left Books, 1976), 80.

11 Badiou, "Cultural Revolution," 150, 151.

12 *The Economist,* May 24–30, 2014. Amy Kazmin, "Modi Personality Cult Dominates India Election," *Financial Times,* April 8, 2014, http://www.ft.com/cms/s/0/96b8ca94-bed0-11e3-a1bf-00144feabdc0.html#axzz35FkEXAiA. For a damning critique of Modi's culpability in the 2002 genocide in Gujarat and the fascist underpinnings of his Hindutva ideology, see Gautam Appa and Anish Vanaik, eds., *Narendra Modi Exposed: Challenging the Myths Surrounding the BJP's Prime Ministerial Candidate*

(London: Awaaz Network and the Monitoring Group, 2014). Thanks to Chetan Bhatt for this reference.

13 Wu Ming, "Grillismo: Yet Another Right Wing Cult Coming from Italy," March 8, 2013, http://www.wumingfoundation.com/english/wuming blog/?p=1950.

14 Alain Badiou, "The Idea of Communism," in *Communist Hypothesis,* 151.

15 Ibid., 253.

16 Ibid., 250, 252.

17 Ibid., 251.

18 Ibid., 251–52.

19 Amadeo Bordiga, "The Guignol in History," 1953, https://libcom.org /library/guignol-history-amadeo-bordiga.

20 Jacques Camatte, *This World We Must Leave and Other Essays,* ed. Alex Trotter (New York: Autonomedia, 1995), 176.

21 For details of the many domains and dimensions of the personality cult, a truly "multimedial" and "intermedial" production, see Cohen, "Cult of Number One."

22 Debray, "Socialism: A Life-Cycle," 14, 18, 15.

23 Deleuze, *Cinema 2,* 266.

24 Berlin was not alone; each of the thirty-four university cities debased itself with its own book burnings.

25 Hitler's relationship to the author-function also included its property form. In a letter recommending early release, his prison governor noted of *Mein Kampf,* "[Hitler] hopes the book will run into many editions, thus enabling him to fulfill his financial obligations and to defray the expenses incurred at the time of his trial." Oberregierungsrat Leybold, "Oberregierungsrat Leybold's Statement about Adolf Hitler in Prison," September 1924, http://www.hitler.org/writings/prison/. Nazism was of course funded by industrial capital, not by individual book sales, but the latter did no harm to Hitler's personal finances. By 1933 he had apparently made about 1.2 million Reichsmarks from the income of his book, some 250 times more than the annual income of a teacher. http://en.wikipedia .org/wiki/Mein_Kampf.

26 My focus here on the *textual* production of myth is in no sense intended to obscure its other modalities. For a captivating mythopoesis across the mediums of performance, installations, and comics, see David Burrows and Simon O'Sullivan's project *Plastique Fantastique,* http://www.plas tiquefantastique.org/.

27 Wu Ming and Vitaliano Ravagli, *Asce di guerra* (Milan, Italy: Tropea, 2000). Wu Ming, *54,* trans. Shaun Whiteside (London: William Heinemann,

2005). Wu Ming, *Manituana,* trans. Shaun Whiteside (London: Verso 2009). Wu Ming, *Altai,* trans. Shaun Whiteside (London: Verso, 2013). Wu Ming, *L'armata dei sonnambuli* [The army of sleepwalkers] (Turin, Italy: Einaudi, 2014). Wu Ming has also published a novella, *Previsioni dei tempo* [Weather forecasts] (Milan, Italy: Ambiente, 2008), and a sizeable body of short stories, as well as numerous books under their individual monikers of Wu Ming 1, Wu Ming 2, and so on (where the numerals are derived from the alphabetical order of their surnames). This chapter is not a close reading of Wu Ming's novels but a critical treatment of their work available in English translation and toward my specific concern with mythopoesis.

28 Wu Ming 1, in Robert Baird, "Stories Are Not All Equal: An Interview with Wu Ming," *Chicago Review* 52, nos. 2–4 (2006): 250.

29 Wu Ming, "Spectres of Müntzer at Sunrise/Greeting the 21st Century," in *Wu Ming Presents Thomas Müntzer,* trans. Michael G. Baylor (London: Verso, 2010), xxxvii.

30 Jenkins, "How *Slapshot* Inspired a Cultural Revolution."

31 Wu Ming, "Spectres of Müntzer at Sunrise," xxxvii–xxxviii.

32 Ibid., xxxix.

33 Wu Ming 1, "Interview for *Contravenção,* 14.12.2003," *Giap Digest 24,* http://www.wumingfoundation.com/english/giap/Giapdigest24.html.

34 Georges Sorel, cited in Wu Ming 1, "Tute Bianche: The Practical Side of Myth Making (in Catastrophic Times)," 2001, http://www.wumingfoun dation.com/english/giap/giapdigest11.html.

35 Wu Ming, "From the Multitudes of Europe Rising Up against the Empire and Marching on Genoa (19–20 July 2001)," 2001, http://www.wuming foundation.com/english/giap/Giap_multitudes.html.

36 Wu Ming, "Spectres of Müntzer at Sunrise," xxxvi.

37 Ibid., xxxvi–xxxvii.

38 Ibid., xxxvi.

39 Gilles Deleuze, "Bartleby; or, the Formula," in *Essays Critical and Clinical,* 86. Deleuze, *Cinema 2,* 219. I have explored the political ramifications of this thesis, and its intimate relationship to Marx's formulation of the proletariat, in Nicholas Thoburn, *Deleuze, Marx, and Politics* (New York: Routledge, 2003).

40 Deleuze, *Cinema 2,* 223. Gilles Deleuze and Félix Guattari, *Kafka: Toward a Minor Literature,* trans. Dana Polan (Minneapolis: University of Minnesota Press, 1986), 17.

41 Deleuze, *Cinema 2,* 171.

42 Deleuze, *Negotiations,* 176.

43 Marco Amici, "Urgency and Visions of the New Italian Epic," *Journal of Romance Studies* 10, no. 1 (2010): 14.

44 Wu Ming 1, "New Italian Epic: We're Going to Have to Be the Parents," http://www.wumingfoundation.com/english/outtakes/NIE_have_to_be _the_parents.htm. Wu Ming, *New Italian Epic: letteratura, sguardo oblique, ritorno al futuro* (Turin, Italy: Einaudi, 2009), cited in Amici, "Urgency and Visions of the New Italian Epic," 7.

45 Walter Benjamin, "Theses on the Philosophy of History," in *Illuminations,* ed. Hannah Arendt, trans. Harry Zohn (New York: Schocken Books, 2007), 258.

46 Wu Ming, "1954, a Pop-Autonomist Novel: A Re:inter:view with Wu Ming," 2002, http://www.wumingfoundation.com/english/giap/giapdi gest16.html. Wu Ming, "The Best Interview Since . . . ," 2000, http://www .wumingfoundation.com/english/giap/Giapdigest3.htm.

47 Deleuze, *Cinema 2,* 131, emphasis added.

48 Ibid., 46, xii.

49 Timothy S. Murphy, *Wising Up the Marks: The Amodern William Burroughs* (Berkeley: University of California Press, 1997), 44.

50 Dimitri Chimenti, "Unidentified Narrative Objects: Notes for a Rhetorical Typology," *Journal of Romance Studies* 10, no. 1 (2010): 40.

51 Wu Ming 1, "New Italian Epic." The subject of a considerable volume of debate and argument in Italy, the New Italian Epic (NIE) named a loose constellation of themes, literary techniques, and political investments along the lines that I am exploring here, but it was not intended to establish a new genre and was deemed to have soon passed. As Wu Ming 1 reflected in 2009, "the time element is important, because it prevents the NIE from transforming into a current, or worse, a school. The NIE, as a nebula of works published between 1993 and 2008, is already finished. On the other hand, the common features identified in those works definitely will return in new novels, but the challenge is to go beyond the 'already seen' and 'already cataloged.'" Jadel Andreetto, "Intervista con Wu Ming sul New Italian Epic," *Panorama,* http://archivio.panorama.it/cultura/libri/Intervista-con-Wu -Ming-sul-New-Italian-Epic, my loose translation with Google Translate.

52 Pier Paolo Pasolini, cited in Emanuela Patti, "*Petrolio,* a Model of UNO in Giuseppe Genna's *Italia De Profundis,*" *Journal of Romance Studies* 10, no. 1 (2010): 92.

53 Deleuze, *Cinema 2,* 269.

54 Valerio Evangelisti, "Literary Opera," http://www.carmillaonline.com /2008/05/06/literary-opera-evangelisti-e-lucarelli-sul-new-italian-epic/, translated on the Wu Ming "New Italian Epic" entry in Wikipedia.

55 Chimenti, "Unidentified Narrative Objects," 42.

56 Wu Ming, cited in Patti, "*Petrolio,* a Model of UNO," 86.

57 Wu Ming, "1954, a Pop-Autonomist Novel."

58 Wu Ming, "The Perfect Storm, or Rather, the Monster Interview," trans. Jason Di Rosso, 2007, http://www.manituana.com/documenti/0/8246/EN.

59 As Simone Brioni has recently explored in an interview with Wu Ming 1, *Manituana* here exemplifies a concern with postcolonial questions—of empire and nation, racialization, migration, and liminal territory—that features in much of Wu Ming's writing, most especially in the more recent works produced under their individual monikers, often in collaboration with writers outside the collective. Simone Brioni and Wu Ming 1, "Postcolonialismo, Subalternità e New Italian Epic," http://www.wumingfoundation.com/giap/?p=20012.

60 Emanuela Piga, "Metahistory, Microhistories, and Mythopoeia in Wu Ming," *Journal of Romance Studies* 10, no. 1 (2010): 56.

61 Deleuze, *Cinema 2,* 219.

62 Ibid.

63 Wu Ming, in Loredana Lipperini, "Manituana, the Clash of Civilizations and George Bush's Ancestors," http://www.manituana.com/notizie/20/8188.

64 Wu Ming, *Manituana,* 160–61.

65 Ibid., 6.

66 Piga, "Metahistory," 58.

67 Deleuze, *Cinema 2,* 141.

68 Ibid., 220. Deleuze mentions as an example the work of Charles Burnett, Robert Gardner, Haile Gerima, and Charles Lane, though he detects related experimental procedures also in the Arab cinema of Youssef Chahine and in Pierre Perrault's cinema of Quebec, among a number of other "third world" or "minority" cinemas, which form a groping movement toward a "modern political cinema" that unfurls the condition that "*the people are missing.*" Ibid., 216.

69 Wu Ming, *54,* 1.

70 Wu Ming 5, in Baird, "Stories Are Not All Equal," 253.

71 Wu Ming, "A Class Apart, That Is: A Hundred Years of Cary Grant," trans. Bianca Colantoni, http://www.wumingfoundation.com/english/outtakes/100yearsofcarygrant.htm.

72 Ibid. The embedded quote is from Italo Calvino's *Lezioni Americane.*

73 Wu Ming, *54,* 50.

74 Ibid., 49.

75 Ibid., 42.

76 Wu Ming 1, "Cary Grant: Style as a Martial Art: A Conversation with Wu Ming 1," 2005, http://www.wumingfoundation.com/english/giap/giapdigest32_3.htm#style.

77 Ibid.

78 Chris Petit, "The Concept of Cary," *The Guardian,* May 21, 2005, http://www.theguardian.com/books/2005/may/21/highereducation.fiction.

79 Deleuze, *Cinema 2,* 222.

80 Ibid., 148. Deleuze draws selectively on Mikhail Bakhtin and Pasolini in developing his concept of free indirect discourse, a term that is more usually associated with the bourgeois aesthetic form of the novel, as I noted in chapter 1.

81 Wu Ming 1, "New Italian Epic."

82 Ibid.

83 Rachel Donadio, "Underworld," http://www.nytimes.com/2007/11/25/books/review/Donadio-t.html?_r=0.

84 Deleuze, *Cinema 2,* 150. Gilles Deleuze, "The Shame and the Glory: T. E. Lawrence," in *Essays Critical and Clinical,* 118.

85 Blissett, "Mondo Mitomane."

86 Wu Ming 1, "New Italian Epic."

87 Wu Ming, *Manituana,* 33.

88 L. M. Findlay, "Print Culture and Decolonizing the University: Indigenizing the Page: Part 2," in *The Future of the Page,* ed. Peter Stoicheff and Andrew Taylor (Toronto: University of Toronto Press, 2004), 131.

89 Ibid., 129.

90 Angelo Petrella, cited in Roslba Biasini, "Reconsidering Epic: Wu Ming's *54* and Fenoglio," *Journal of Romance Studies* 10, no. 1 (2010): 72.

91 Wu Ming 1, "The First Time I Saw Malcolm," 2005, http://www.wumingfoundation.com/english/outtakes/malcolm.htm.

92 Wu Ming 1, "Malcolm's 'X' and Memory," 2005, http://www.wumingfoundation.com/english/outtakes/malcolm.htm.

93 Ibid.

94 Wu Ming 1, "First Time I Saw Malcolm."

95 Wu Ming 1, "Interview for *Contravenção.*"

96 Gilles Deleuze, "Nietzsche's Burst of Laughter," in *Desert Islands and Other Texts, 1953–1974,* ed. David Lapoujade, trans. Michael Taormina (New York: Semiotext(e), 2004), 130.

97 Ibid.

98 Wu Ming 1, "The First Time I Saw Malcolm"; Wu Ming 5, "From Malcolm to Hip Hop through Ghost Dog," 2005, http://www.wumingfoundation.com/english/outtakes/malcolm.htm.

99   Angela Y. Davis, "Afro Images: Politics, Fashion, and Nostalgia," *Critical Inquiry* 21, no. 1 (1994): 37–45.

100   Ibid., 43.

101   Wu Ming, "Perfect Storm."

102   Ibid.

103   There is an engaging consonance here with Deleuze's comments on the desubjectifying "sonorous particles" of the voice: "Some of us can be moved by certain voices in the cinema. Bogart's voice . . . it's a metallic thread that unwinds, with a minimum of intonation; it's not at all the subjective voice." Gilles Deleuze, "Cours Vincennes: On Music 03/05/1977," http://www.webdeleuze.com/php/texte.php?cle=5&groupe=Anti%20 Oedipe%20et%20Mille%20Plateaux&langue=2.

104   Wu Ming 1, in Enrico Manera, Giuliano Santoro, and Wu Ming 1, "Il più odiato dai fascisti. Conversazione su Furio Jesi, il mito, la destra e la sinistra," *Giap,* January 15, 2013, http://www.wumingfoundation.com /giap/?p=10807.

105   Wu Ming, "1999–2009. Hey, You Bastards, We're Still Here! Experiment #1," 2009, http://www.wumingfoundation.com/english/wuming blog/?p=310. Wu Ming's "portrait" was created before the 2011 Egyptian revolution and the subsequent restoration of authoritarian state power, events that lend it significant further associations.

Index

Aboriginal Australians, 48
abstract labor, 42–43, 67–68, 105, 155, 254
"ACE Digital Uncut" forum, 269
Adorno, Theodor W., 57, 61, 72, 81–87, 96–99; commodity book, 81–82; critique of universal communicability, 82; mimetic relation between content and form, 82–85; *Philosophical Fragments,* 97; revolutionary leaflets, 99. *See also* "barbaric asceticism"
Alberro, Alexander, 11
Albert, Saul, 263
Allen, Gwen, 12–13, 224
All the King's Horses (novel), 197–99, 342n90
Althusser, Louis, 273, 275
Amazon (company), ix–x, 45
Amazon Noir, x, xii
Amici, Marco, 283
Anabaptists, 184, 193
Anderson, Benedict, 42, 259
AND publishing, 55
anonymous authorship, 58–59, 168–77, 191–92, 197, 205–7, 210, 212–14, 216–19, 337n15, 338n30, 339n42
"Anonymous" (hacker) movement, 169

anti-book, 1–3, 11–16, 25–26, 48–49, 110–11, 149–50, 154–57, 275; definition of, 1–2
Apple (company), 38
Arab Spring, 35, 38
Ark of the Covenant, 118
Artaud, Antonin, 111–12, 145–49, 164, 166
artists' book, 3, 9–13, 53, 105, 303n23, 304n39. *See also* bookwork
Art-Language (journal), 11
Arts Council England (ACE), 251, 265–69
Arvatov, Boris, 66–74, 92, 95
"assemblage" concept, 139, 225, 233–34, 240–41, 262, 269–70
Assembling (serial publication), 13–15
Atelier Populaire, 100–101
author-function, 58, 170–76, 210
authors: and the division of labor, 43–44, 337n14; punishment of, 171
Autonomia movement, 101

Babbage, Charles, 43
Bacon, Francis, 115, 121
Badiou, Alain, 27–28, 39, 59, 209, 272–76, 283
Baines, Jess, 55
Bakker, Conrad, 78
Balestrini, Nanni, 101

Banash, David, 157–58

Banner Repeater, 13, 51, 55

"barbaric asceticism," 96–97

Barber, Stephen, 147

Barrot, Jean, 102. *See also* Dauvé, Gilles

Basbanes, N. A., 73

Bataille, Georges, 75–76, 157

Baudelaire, Charles, 84, 95, 149

Baum, Kelly, 198

Baumeister, Ruth, 162

Beaumelle, Agnès de la, 147–48

Beck, Glenn, 204

Beckett, Samuel, 96, 175

Benefit of Christ Crucified, The, (fictionalized book in *Q*), 192, 194–96

Beni Memorial Library, 88–89

Benjamin, Walter, 57, 64, 71–76, 79–81, 91, 96, 99, 107, 276, 284; critique of "use value," 71– 3; "fringe areas" of libraries, 79; theory of collecting, 71–74, 79–80, 84, 95, 97, 99

Bergson, Henri, 200–202, 259–60

Bernadette Corporation (collective pseudonym), 58–59, 169, 197–200, 203

Bernes, Jasper, 215

Bernstein, Michèle, 58–59, 163, 197–202, 342n95

Berry Slater, Josephine, 228–29, 252, 257–60, 268

Bey, Hakim, 190

Bezos, Jeff, 45

Bible, the, 82, 116, 121–22, 182

black cinema (U.S., 1970s), 88, 357n68

#BlackLivesMatter, 38

Blaha, Agnes, 80

Blake, William, xi–xii, 303n19

Blanchot, Maurice, 24, 59, 110–11, 212–14, 256

Blissett, Luther (footballer), 187–89. *See also Luther Blissett* (collective pseudonym)

Bodley, Thomas, 98

Bolter, Jay David, 48–49, 52

book industry, 41–45, 155. *See also* books: as commodities

books: authority of, 47, 51, 114–18, 121; burning of, 193, 195, 276; in Christianity, 114–20; and class, x, 18–19, 33, 41, 43, 45–47, 80; codex form of, 4, 6, 47–48, 52–53, 112, 114, 118, 120, 142, 192, 196, 231; collections of, 79–80; and colonialism, 47–48, 116, 293; as commodities, ix–x, xii, 41–48, 80–83, 97, 107, 155, 190; figures of, 52; and gender, x, 18, 33, 46, 80, 220; materiality of, 109–11, 138–40, 150; and mimesis, 82–85; properties and characteristics of, 78–80, 86–88, 95, 110–11; and race, 47, 80; and regimes of signs, 178

bookwork, 3, 9–16. *See also* artists' book

Bordiga, Amadeo, 168–70, 208, 210, 275

bourgeois class and culture, 43–46, 161–62

Breton, André, 75

British Library, 54

Burroughs, William, 138, 284–85

business practices in radical publishing, 264–66

Camatte, Jacques, 88, 103, 159, 210, 213, 217, 275
capitalism, 22–26, 66–68, 229
Carrión, Ulises, 10
Carroll, Lewis, 146
Casarini, Luca, 279–80
Casarino, Cesare, 73
Cascone, Kim, 50
Casinière, Joëlle de la, 139
Castro, Fidel, 296
Catholicism, 116, 120–21, 194, 276
Ceauşescu, Nicolae, 276
censorship, 172, 174
Centre for Disruptive Media, 38, 53
Century City exhibition (Tate Modern, 2001), 92
Charlesworth, J. J., 244
Chartier, Roger, 6, 337n14
Chartists, 211
Châtelet, Gilles, 224, 236, 241
Chesterfield, Earl of, 80
Children's Crusades, 139
Chimenti, Dimitri, 285
Chto Delat? group and newspaper, 54–55
cinema, 72, 111, 266, 276, 283–84, 288, 290
Clarke, Ami, 13
cognitive capacity and digital media, 46
collections of objects, 72–74, 91; public and private, 74. *See also* Benjamin, Walter: theory of collecting
Collu, Gianni, 88, 103, 217
colonialism, 47–48, 116, 293
Comedia group, 264–67
Coming Insurrection, The, 204, 206

Comité (journal), 59, 170, 212–13, 217–21
Comité d'Action Etudiants-Ecrivains, 170, 212
commodification of artworks and artists, 11
commodity fetishism, 67–71, 76–77, 155
"communal being," 178–81, 191, 200
communism, 21–27, 39, 57–60, 69–70, 112, 150–51, 164, 168–69, 200, 202, 205, 212–13, 274; and bookwork, 16; of textual matter, ix–xi, xiii, 1
Communist League, 207–8
Communist Manifesto, The, 26, 34, 206–11; authorship of, 206–8; translation of, 207, 211
"communist object" concept, 64–65, 71, 75–78, 85, 101–2, 108
communist party, theory of, 168, 170, 205–18, 222
communist writing and publishing, 3, 13–18, 35, 58, 214–16, 220–21, 254
communization theory, 21–25
conceptual art, 11
Constructivism, 66, 70, 72
Cooper, Gary, 289–90
Copenhagen Free University, 90
copyright, 32, 34, 44, 170, 173, 190; anticopyright, 162, 190, 267, 335n214
corporate practices in arts funding, 268–69
Cramer, Florian, 50, 54
credit facilities for consumers, 45
Crimp, Douglas, 74

"criticism–self-criticism," 125, 133
Cubo-Futurists, 140–41
Cultural Revolution, 112, 122, 126–36, 272
culture, value accorded to, 41
Curtius, Ernst Robert, 114, 121

Daily Courant, The, 231
Dauvé, Gilles, 18
Davies, Anthony, 229–30
Davis, Angela, 296–97
Dawson, Richard, 251
Dean, Jodi, 36–40
Debord, Guy, 14, 16, 28, 59, 61, 103–4, 111, 149–66, 197–99; *Mémoires,* 16, 58, 103–4, 111, 149–58, 163–66, 198, 333n190
Debray, Régis, 14–23, 61–62, 256, 276
Deem, Melissa D., 29
de Gaulle, Charles, 149
de Jong, Jacqueline, 162
Deleuze, Fanny, 112–13
Deleuze, Gilles, xii, 36, 47, 58, 60, 75, 87–88, 100, 109–22, 128, 134–46, 151, 155, 165–66, 225, 227, 233, 240–41, 253, 257, 262, 266, 269, 272, 276, 282–92, 295–96; compulsion to communicate, 36; myth, 272, 282–83, 286–87, 290–92, 295–96; writing machine, 112–13. *See also* "assemblage" concept; diagrams, theory of; "falsifying narration"; "fascicular root-book" concept; free indirect discourse; "rhizome-book" concept; "root-book" concept
dérive, 154
Derrida, Jacques, 48–49, 52, 56, 92–93, 110

Descartes, René, 121
détournement, 133, 149, 151–54, 162, 198–99
Deutsch-Französische Jahrbücher (journal), 215
"diagrammatic publishing," 59, 225, 232, 235, 237–44, 253, 255, 262, 267–71
"diagrammatic writing" (Drucker), 53
diagrams, theory of, 224–25, 232, 234, 236–37, 240–43, 262
digital rights management, x, 45, 50–51
Disobedienti group, 279–80
distributed authorship, 253–54
Dittmer, Lowell, 133–34
Documents (journal), 75, 100
Donadio, Rachel, 291
Donaldson v. Becket, 44
Drucker, Johanna, 9, 52–53, 86, 90, 142
Duras, Marguerite, 212
Dzerzhinsky, Felix, 273

e-books, 45, 52
Economist, The, 274
Eisenstein, Elizabeth L., 7–8
Elijah Muhammad, 295
Endnotes (journal), 68, 170, 215–19
Engels, Friedrich, 26–27, 103, 122, 207, 272–73
English language, 293
engraving: in the emergence of abstract labor, 43
Enlightenment, the, 19, 116
ephemerality of print media, 30–31, 37, 85, 94, 97–101, 120, 149
Essex, Richard, 106, 341n66. *See*

also Tompsett, Fabian

Evangelisti, Valerio, 285

Facebook, 37–40, 56, 246
Fahs, Beanne, 30
"Fallout" art project, 263–64
"falsifying narration," 283–90
Farocki, Harun, 134–35
Farrachi, Armand, 139
"fascicular root-book" concept, 138–39
Febvre, Lucien, 42
Fellini, Federico, 266
Feltes, N. N., 44–45
feminism, 12, 27–29, 34, 98
fetishism, 76–77. *See also* commodity fetishism
54 (novel), 288–90
56a Archive, 98, 101
financial crisis (2007–8), 250
Financial Times, The, 231–32, 347n19
Fin de Copenhague, 150, 330n151
Findlay, L. M., 293–94
Fisher, John, 120–21
Five Star Movement, 274
Flusser, Vilém, 17–18
Fogarasi, Adalbert, 254–55
Ford, Laura Oldfield, 246
Ford, Simon, 229–30
Fordism, 21
Foucault, Michel, 58, 109, 113, 169–72, 175–77, 189–90, 295, 338n30
"found object" *(objet trouvé),* 74–75
fragment, theory of, 88, 221
free indirect discourse, 257–58, 291–92
Freeman, Jo, 247
Freiligrath, Ferdinand, 208

Freud, Sigmund, 121
Fuller, Buckminster, 251
Futur Anterieur (journal), 226, 260, 269
Futurist books, 111, 140–44, 149

Galileo, 121
Gehl, Robert W., 37
"general intellect," 189–90
Genet, Jean, 48–49
Genoa: anti-G8 events in, 279–81
Genosko, Gary, 257–58
Giacometti, Alberto, 75
Giap, Vo Nguyen, 296
Gilmartin, Kevin, 18
Girodias, Maurice, 30
Gitelman, Lisa, 3
Giuliani, Carlo, 280–81
Goebbels, Joseph, 276
Goethe, Johann Wolfgang von, 121
Golan, Romy, 75
Goldsmith, Kenneth, 4
Gomorrah, 291
Goncharova, Natalia, 144–45
Google (company), 38, 246
Gornick, Vivian, 30
Gough, Maria, 70
Grant, Cary, 288–92, 299
Greaney, Patrick, 154
Great Leap Forward, 127, 120, 132
Greenberg, Clement, 9–10
Grillo, Beppe, 274
Grin without a Cat, A (film), 296
Gruppe SPUR, 159
Guattari, Félix, xii, 11, 47, 58, 75, 100, 109–22, 128, 134–46, 155, 165–66, 225, 227, 233–34, 240–41, 253, 257, 262, 269, 282; institutional psychotherapy and

journal publishing, 257–58; on writing *Anti-Oedipus,* 113–14. *See also* "assemblage" concept; diagrams, theory of; "fascicular root-book" concept; "rhizome-book" concept; "root-book" concept
Guestroom press, 87
Gurianova, Nina, 144
Gutenberg letterpress, xii, 2, 42–44, 106, 142, 144, 153

Hall, Gary, 53, 191
Hamburg Theses, 158–63
Hampton, Michael, 13
haptic aesthetics, 143–44
Haraway, Donna, 28, 34
Hardt, Michael, 34–36
Harron, Mary, 31
Hart, Kevin, 213
Hayes, Anthony, 160
Hayles, N. Katherine, 4–6, 10, 50, 57, 234
Hayward Gallery, 54
Hedditch, Emma, 90
Hegel, G. W. F., 48–49
Heine, Henriette, 90
Heller, Dana, 31
heretical texts, 44
"hieroglyphs of the anti-commodity" (Rancière), 62–64
Hitchcock, Alfred, 289
Hitler, Adolf, 145, 276, 354n25
Hoffman, Abbie, x
Hollier, Denis, 76, 100
Home, Stewart, 90, 184, 341n66
Horkheimer, Max, 97
Hume, David, 121
hybrid publishing, 51, 53, 224–25, 228, 235, 240, 242, 251–52, 269
hypertext, 48–49, 52–53

illuminated books, xi–xii, 121
Info Centre, 90
Infopool project, 90–95
Ingold, Tim, 43
"inline metadata," 4
Insipidities (blog), 218
Institute for Social Research, 97
Institute of Contemporary Arts, 244
Internationale situationniste (journal), 61, 162, 313n1, 335n213, 335n214
International Standard Book Number (ISBN) system, 45, 106
Invariance (journal), 88–89
Israeli state, 35

Jack the Ripper, 154
Jakobsen, Jakob, 64, 90–91, 95–97
Jameson, Fredric, 83–84
Janecek, Gerald, 143
Jesi, Furio, 279
Jesus Christ, 117, 120–21
Johns, Adrian, 7–9
Jones, Andrew F., 128–29
Jones, Rod, 102
Jorn, Asger, 14, 16, 103–8, 111, 149–55, 159, 162, 166, 199; *Mémoires,* 16, 58, 103–4, 111, 149–58, 163–66, 198; *Open Creation and Its Enemies,* 106–8
journalism, 254–55
journals, 61–62, 85–86, 102–3
Joyce, James, 121, 138

Kafka, Franz, 84, 99, 112
Kandinsky, Wassily, 153

Kant, Immanuel, 84
Karen Elliot (collective pseudonym), 187
kArt Boo, 105–6
Kearney, James, 114–15, 120
Keller, George, 159
Kelsey, John, 197, 199, 203
Khlebnikov, Velimir, 144
Khrushchev, Nikita, 127, 272–75
Kiaer, Christina, 57, 65–66
King, J. J., 247
Korn, Henry James, 13
Kostelanetz, Richard, 11, 13, 15
Kotànyi, Attila, 158–60
Kouvélakis, Stathis, 178
Krauss, Rosalind, 1, 9, 11, 224, 232, 234
Kruchenykh, Aleksei, 141–45
Kurczynski, Karen, 149, 153

Lacan, Jacques, 113
Larionov, Mikhail, 144
"late age of print, the" 49–50
Latham, John, 195
Leadbeater, Charles, 230–31
Leese, Daniel, 128–29
Leibniz, Gottfried, 73, 88
Leigh, Mike, 80
Lenin, V. I. (and the Leninist model of publishing), 17, 19, 255–58, 272–73
Leroux, Pierre, 17
Leslie, Esther, 72, 99
Letters (journal), 54
Lettrist International, 152–53, 156
Leys, Simon, 132–33
libraries and librarianship, 79, 98
LIES (journal), 54
Lifton, Robert Jay, 125–26, 131

Lin Biao, 127–30, 134
Linebaugh, Peter, 240
Lippard, Lucy, 11–12
Lissitzky, El, 1
Little Red Book. *See* Mao Zedong: *Quotations from Chairman Mao Tsetung*
Locke, John, 173
London Psychogeographical Association (LPA), 86, 104, 107–8
Lorusso, Silvio, 53–54
Ludovico, Alessandro, 50
Luther, Martin, 44, 116, 121, 276, 310n154, 341n76
Luther Blissett (collective pseudonym), 44, 58, 169, 177–81, 187–95, 200, 278, 292; portrait, 188
Lyon, Janet, 28–29, 34

Macfarlane, Helen, 211
MacPherson, C. B., 178
Mad Love, 75
Makdisi, Saree, xi–xii
Malcolm X, 292–98
Mallarmé, Stéphane, 87–88, 108, 121–22, 138
manifesto, xiii, 1, 26–36, 81, 113, 145, 164, 189, 207, 235–36; avant-garde, 27–28; feminist, 28–34
Manituana (novel), 286–87, 293
Maoism, 112, 122, 125–26, 135, 299
Mao Zedong, 58–59, 111, 122–34, 141, 144, 165, 272, 292, 298–99, 325n54; *Quotations from Chairman Mao Tsetung,* 122–31, 134–35, 140–44, 165, 324n38, 325n57
Marcus, Grail, 156
Marker, Chris, 296

Martin, Henri-Jean, 42
Marx, Karl, 19–23, 26–27, 43, 58–60, 62, 65–78, 82–84, 103, 107, 121–22, 149–50, 160, 167, 169–80, 202, 206–10, 214–15, 221, 272–75; anonymous authorship, 173–75, 207–8, 337n15, 338n24, 339n42; author-function, 172–75; bourgeois rights and individuality, 178–79; against dogma, 214–15; estrangement and emancipation of the senses, 67, 69; against personality cult, 272–73, 275, 353n7; sales of *Capital,* 19. *See also* commodity fetishism; "communal being"; *Communist Manifesto*; communist party, theory of; "general intellect"; proletariat
Marxism, 23, 65–66, 71, 122, 158, 272
Mascolo, Dionys, 212–13
Masson, André and Lili, 75
"material text," 3–9, 57
Mauss, Marcel, 157
McCalman, Iain, 19
McCann, Graham, 288–89
McDonough, Tom, 152
McGann, Jerome, 53
McKenzie, D. F., 43, 48
McLuhan, Marshall, 142, 196, 332n181
"media ecology" (Debray), 16, 18, 20, 61, 256
"media specific analysis" (Hayles), 57
Meins, Holger, 134–35
Melville, Herman, 182
Metzger, Gustav, 182, 195
Mignolo, Walter, 47–48, 52, 115

militant books, 113–14
Miller, Laura J., 41–42, 45
mimeographs, 30–31, 61, 89, 94, 97, 156, 335n213
"minifestos," 235–37, 241–45, 253, 261, 263
Mitropoulos, Angela, 230
Moby-Dick, 182
Modi, Narendra, 274
Mohawk language, 293
"Monsieur Roubignoles presents *The Kelsey Collection Artforum 2004-2012,*" 203
Montaigne, Michel de, 121
"monument" concept, 100
Moore, Samuel, 211
More, Thomas, 121
Moretti, Franco, ix
Moses, 118–19
Mowitt, John, 110
Moylan, Michele, 4–5
"multiple single" concept, 179–80, 183–91. *See also* anonymous authorship
Müntzer, Thomas, 121, 194, 278–81
Murphie, Andrew, 3, 51
Murphy, Timothy, 284–85
musical notation, 83
Mute (magazine), 59, 224–71; "Ceci n'est pas un magazine," 224, 228, 263; commissioning practices, 252–55; editorial voice, 255–58; financial model, 264–71; and magazine immanence, 226–31, 241–43, 252–54, 262, 269–70; "The Magazine that Mistook Its Readers for a Hat!," 225, 235–43; *Metamute* archive and website, 235, 240, 243–45, 259–63, 268;

OpenMute, 244, 247–48; POD quarterly, 244, 249–51, 259, 268; temporal dimension to, 258–60. *See also* "diagrammatic publishing"
myth and mythopoesis, 59, 78–98

Nancy, Jean-Luc, 62, 164, 179, 246
Nasser, Gamal Abdel, 296, 299
Native Americans, 286, 294
Nazism, 276
Nealon, Jeffrey, 170, 176–77
Nedd Ludd (collective pseudonym), 169, 187
Negri, Antonio, 34–36, 101, 225–27, 231, 233, 241, 260, 269, 346n5
neoliberalism, 23, 59, 180, 191, 203, 229–30, 244, 251, 259, 268–70
Nesic, Karl, 18
New Economic Policy, 66
New Italian Epic, 285, 356n51
News International, 105–6
New Space book shop, 89
New York City, 200–203, 208
Nicolas Bourbaki (pseudonymous collective mathematician), 177, 347n19
Nietzsche, Friedrich, 138
nomadic art, 142–44
"noncommunication" (Deleuze), 151
novels, 3, 46–47, 197–200

Occupy movement, 35, 38, 204
Oken, Lorenz, 80
Olympia Press, 30–31
Olympic Games (London, 2012), 252
open access publishing, 191

open source business models, 55
Osbaldeston, David, 250
Oury, Jean, 257
Ovan, Sabrina, 181–82, 184

Palestine, 35
pamphlets, 57, 62, 64, 78–80, 85–97, 101–3, 106–8, 193; ephemerality of, 30–31, 85, 94, 97–101; etymology of, 101–2; as monad, 73, 87–90; and self-institution, 91–92, 95; vulnerability of, 91
paper stock, 92–94, 249
Pasolini, Pier Paolo, 285
Pawson, Mark, 86–87
PDF files, 50–51, 345–46n166
Peking Duck Soup (film), 133
Pels, Peter, 76–77
Permild, Verner, 150, 330n152
personality cults, 59–60, 103, 168, 272–79, 283, 298–99, 353n7
Petrella, Angelo, 294
Phillpot, Clive, 9–12, 303n23
Picasso, Pablo, 75
Pietz, William, 76
Piga, Emanuela, 286
Piper, Adrian, 90
piracy, 8
Pollock, Jackson, 153
Popular Book Centre, 104
post-digital publishing, 3, 48–56
Post-Digital Publishing Archive, 53
post-Fordism, 50, 181, 248
Postone, Moishe, 22
Potlatch bulletin, 156
potlatch exchange, 155–57
Power, Nina, 51
press freedom, 172–74
Price, Leah, xii–xiii, 80, 86

printed matter, 78–81, 85–86, 90
printing process 6–8, 42–44, 105
print on demand (POD), 55, 248–51, 350n73
"programmatism," 21, 26
proletariat, the, 21–24, 63, 133, 160, 164–66, 184–85, 209, 213–14, 282
"prosumers," 256
Protestantism, 7, 44, 115–16, 120–21, 276
Proust, Marcel, 83–84
pseudonymous authorship, 58, 177–79, 197
publishing industry, 19–20, 41, 43, 45, 54–56, 105
Puchner, Martin, 26, 211
Pussy Riot group, 169

Q (novel), 181–86, 189–96, 278, 294
quotation: as a literary genre, 129; resistance to, 82–83. See also Mao Zedong: Quotations from Chairman Mao Tsetung
Qur'an, 182

racism, 35, 189
Rancière, Jacques, 62–64, 80–81, 107, 209
rationalism, 19
Raymond, Joad, 93–94
reader, role of, 5–6, 8, 12, 14–15, 19, 32, 44–45, 81–84, 86–87, 108, 130–31, 154, 176, 198, 220–22, 244–45, 254, 256, 302n12
Real Report on the Last Chance to Save Capitalism in Italy, The, 161
Red Army Faction, 134–35
Red Guards, 130–35
Red Republican, 211

Reena Spaulings (novel), 197, 200–203
Reformation, the, 115, 120
Renaissance, the, 47
Return of the Durutti Column, The, 198
"rhizome-book" concept, 58, 109–14, 136–41, 145, 149, 164–66
Rich, Kate, 263
Rising Free (bookshop and press), 102
Rodchenko, Aleksandr, 57, 61, 65, 145, 313–14n11
Rogovin, Nikolai, 144
"root-book" concept, 58, 109–11, 114–16, 121, 126–28, 134–45, 150, 155–57, 165–66, 221
Rose, Margaret, 174
Rose, Mark, 171
Rousseau, Jean Jacques, 121
Ruge, Arnold, 170, 214–15

Sacks, Oliver, 235
Saviano, Roberto, 291
Schiller, Friedrich, 84
scrolls, 6, 52, 114, 120, 142
SCUM Manifesto, 28–32, 307n98
Selcer, Daniel, 114
"self-differing medium" (Krauss), 9–10, 232–33, 303n26
self-disclosure, 37
self-publishing, 56–57, 86–87, 90, 94, 98
semiotic systems, 116–17
Seveso disaster (1976), 90–91
Shah of Iran, 134
Shakespeare, William, 149
Sinclair, Iain, 86
Situationist, 61, 90, 102, 104, 149,

151, 154, 158, 161–62, 198–99, 202
Situationist International (SI), 104, 132, 150–63, 197–99, 326n73, 331n155, 336n220
Situationist Times, The (journal), 162–63
Skeet, Jason, 86–87
Skeggs, Beverley, 37
Slater, Howard, 90, 161–62, 252
slavery, 46, 65, 120, 178, 286, 295, 313n11
socialism and print, 16–21, 280
social media, 20, 35–40, 49, 255
Solanas, Valerie, 28–33
Sorel, Georges, 280
Soviet Union, 22
Speculate This!, 181
spells (Artaud), 145–49, 166
Squires, Claire, 45
Stalin, Josef, 190, 272–80
Stallybrass, Peter, 68–69, 76, 142
Statute of Anne (1709), 44
Steiner, George, 45–46
Stevenson, Robert Louis, 149
Stiles, Lane, 4–5
Stracey, Francis, 151
STRIKE! Magazine, 54
Striphas, Ted, 41, 45, 49–50
student movement (UK, 2010–11), 253
Surrealism, 61, 74–76

Tao te Ching, 278
Tarnac 9, 204
Tatlin, Vladimir, 70, 144
Taylorism, 21
Tazartès, Ghédalia, 252
"technotext" (Hayles), 5–6, 10, 234

television, 20
Théorie Communiste (journal), 21–23
Theory of Bloom, The, 220–22
Thévenin, Paule, 148
Thompson, James, 46
Tiempo Muerto (newspaper), 54
Tiqqun (journal), 203–6, 220–22
Tito, Marshal, 289
Tompsett, Fabian, 64, 86, 94, 102–8, 220–22, 240
transgressive writing, 171
transreason and "zaum," 140–41
Travis, Trish, 41, 79
Trotsky, Leon, 66
Twitter, 4, 18, 51, 56

"unbound publishing," 53
unidentified narrative objects (UNOs), 283, 290–94
Unpopular Books (publisher), 64, 86, 88, 102–7, 321n162
user-generated content, 237, 244–45, 255–56
"use value," 71–72, 77

Vaneigem, Raoul, 102, 158
van Mourik Broekman, Pauline, 228–31, 234, 236, 246, 256, 260–61, 263–68
Venegas, Alejo, 115–16, 128
Vernon, James, 18–19
Victoria and Albert Museum, 54
Viénet, René, 133, 326n73
Voltaire, 121, 287

Wagner, Richard, 121
Warhol, Andy, 30–33
Wark, McKenzie, 162
Warner, Sara, 30–31

Washington, George, 295
waste material, 95–96
Watts, Mary Jo, 30
We Are Bad group, 252
Weeks, Kathi, 28, 34
White Overalls movement, 280
Willats, Steven, 263–64
Wired magazine, 94
Wittenborn and Company, 157
Wolman, Gil, 152
Woolf, Virginia, 168, 191–92, 202
Words of the Chairman, The (film),
    134–35
workers' movement, 14–17, 20–26,
    46, 63, 161, 256, 284, 334n206

working-class identity, 21–23
Worthington, Pam, 250
Worthington, Simon, 51–52, 228,
    247–48, 259, 261, 264–65
Wu Ming (collective pseudonym),
    59–60, 190, 272, 274, 278–98;
    self-portrait, 299

Xing Lu, 130

Yuill, Simon, 37

Zielinski, Siegfried, 230
zines, 54, 98
Žižek, Slavoj, 39, 125

Nicholas Thoburn is senior lecturer in sociology at the University of Manchester. He is author of *Deleuze, Marx, and Politics* and coeditor of *Deleuze and Politics* and *Objects and Materials*. He has published on political theory, media aesthetics, and social movements and is on the editorial board of the journal *New Formations*.